GOD IN THE DETAILS

GOD IN THE DETAILS

AMERICAN RELIGION IN POPULAR CULTURE

Edited by
ERIC MICHAEL MAZUR
AND KATE MCCARTHY

Routledge
New York and London

Published in 2001 by
Routledge
29 West 35th Street
New York, NY 10001

Published in Great Britain by
Routledge
11 New Fetter Lane
London EC4P 4EE

Printed in the United States of America on acid-free paper.
Design: Jack Donner

10 9 8 7 6 5 4 3 2 1

Library of Congress Cataloging-in-Publication Data

God in the Details : American religion in popular culture / edited by Eric Michael Mazur, Kate McCarthy.
     p.   cm.
  Includes bibliographical references.
   ISBN 0–415–92563–0 — ISBN 0–415–92564–9 (pbk.)
   1. United States—Religion—1960– 2. Popular culture—United States.
 I. Mazur, Eric Michael. II. McCarthy, Kate, 1962–
BL2525.G625 2000
306'.0973—dc21   00–035309

To Scott Baradell and William Mandel,
who taught me just about everything I know about popular culture,
and Jody Mazur, Amy Mazur, and Leslie Needham,
who taught me the rest.
—E.M.M.

To Duncan, my dearest boy,
who made it nearly impossible and understands none of it.
—K.M.

CONTENTS

ACKNOWLEDGMENTS

Our biggest and most heartfelt thanks go to the contributors—some of whom have been involved in the project for what probably seems an eternity—for making this a diverse, thought-provoking, and fun assortment of ideas and insights that we have enjoyed from the very beginning. Though the idea of the collection was ours, the product is theirs, and we are grateful for their participation and support.

Several of the chapters were presented at meetings of various professional organizations, including the American Academy of Religion, the Popular Culture Association, and the Society for the Scientific Study of Religion. We appreciate the members of those organizations who responded thoughtfully to the papers and helped us sharpen the materials presented herein.

Some of these chapters were also used in classes at the California State University, Chico; Hartwick College; Millsaps College; and Bucknell University. The comments and reactions of students in these classes—whose pop culture insight was often sharper than our own—have been helpful, and we appreciate their willingness to be guinea pigs and to help us clarify various points in this collection.

Finally, we would like to acknowledge our colleagues in the religious studies department at the California State University, Chico, and the religion department at Bucknell University for their assistance, patience, and encouragement for this project. Though conversations sometimes wandered from the sublime to the ridiculous, all of the comments have helped in some way or another. You can stop feigning interest now!

Financial resources were also provided by the College of Arts and Sciences at Bucknell University and the Stephen Golden Faculty Enrichment Fund of the Gallatin School of Individualized Study at New York University. We are grateful for their assistance.

Introduction

Finding Religion in American Popular Culture

> If our thinking is not to be pseudo-thinking, we must think about life; for such a thinking is a thinking about God. And if we are to think about life, we must penetrate its hidden corners, and steadily refuse to treat anything—however trivial or disgusting it may seem to be—as irrelevant.
>
> —Karl Barth, *The Epistle to the Romans*

> What if God was one of us?
>
> —Joan Osborne

In a now-clichéd article in *American Anthropologist*, Horace Miner introduces his readers to the strange rituals of a tribe he identifies only as the Nacirema (Miner 1956). He focuses most of his attention on their bodily rituals, particularly their preoccupation with rituals of cleanliness and the body, and describes these people with a sense of wonderment, like the true "outsider" anthropologist, exposing a fascinating system of practices that seems both exotic and yet strangely familiar. Of course, the mystery of the identity of these people lasts only as long as the reader is unable to recognize words written backward, and, like many exercises designed to make a point, Miner's piece has proved to be a "one-gag bit"—once you know the Nacirema are in fact Americans, the anthropological point is made, and Miner ends his article quickly and mercifully.

But even after forty years, Miner's short article continues to have a value to the study of American[1] culture. On one level, it is a reminder that Americans do participate in rituals like other cultures do, but that we rarely examine ourselves. By maintaining this apparent inability to find ritualized patterns in our own behavior we all too often assume that rituals are activities only of non-industrialized, unenlightened "others." And yet, while Miner's lesson was probably a healthy corrective for some early anthropologists, by now the literature examining our own culture is so voluminous as to be overwhelming. Anthropological studies of American culture have taken seriously Miner's jest and have provided us with ample discussions of our own ritualized behavior.

But there is another point in Miner's small piece that is still of value for analyses of contemporary American culture. If the evidence of ritualization in our own lives is not the lasting point of his article, maybe it is the ability—and even the need—to find meaning in the familiar, even if we exoticize it. We have been shown a method (albeit one that is firmly tongue-in-cheek) of finding meaning where we may not otherwise have looked. In the visit to the dentist, the bathroom, or the hospital, we find meaning—and greater understanding of culture—that would have been missed if we had simply overlooked these areas to concentrate on those events traditionally plowed for "deeper" meaning, such as life-cycle and rite of passage events, annual rituals of religious and quasi-religious communities, and so on. For both the observer and the observed, religious meaning can be found in activities that are often considered meaningless. That premise is the point of departure for the essays that follow.

LIFE IN THE BORDERLAND

From once dismissing it with disdain, academia currently appears to be in the throes of a full-scale infatuation with popular culture. One can read analyses of Hollywood movies, rap music, and comic books in the most high-brow academic journals, and humanities and social science programs now widely offer courses, if not majors, in the critical study of everything from graffiti to sitcoms. Both the field of popular culture studies and the material it examines, though, seem to be growing at a pace that outstrips the available analytical categories and methods. It is useful, therefore, to clarify what we mean when we use key words in this expanding conversation. What constitutes "culture" (popular or otherwise) and "religion," and where do they meet in everyday experience?

In today's American culture, it seems that religion is everywhere. "What Would Jesus Do?" bracelets can be purchased at huge discount department stores. Pastors of suburban megachurches speak of their "target markets" and "product positioning." There are churches of Elvis and prime-time television dramas about angels. The lines between religion and culture blur in contemporary America in ways that leave scholars dizzy. Though this melding of religion and culture has been going on in the form of popular religion for ages, in the contemporary American world of high technology and late capitalism, the boundaries have blurred more than ever before.

The conventional distinction between popular religion and popular culture is worth noting. Popular religion, whether it be defined by its extrainstitutional status, its non-elite practitioners, its immediacy and informality, or the sheer numbers of people it draws, still refers to behavior and ideas recognized by both participant and observer as *religious*, even if the practices are not condoned by the religious elites. Included here are such phenomena as religious folk art, domestic altars, and practices of interreligious syncretism. Investigation of this field is enjoying a burst of activity today, enriching and complicating our understanding of American religious identity past and present.[2] Popular culture, by contrast, includes a much wider range of products and practices that, while they may take on religious connotations, remain ostensibly secular sites of experience that neither the participant nor the casual observer would identify, at least at first glance, as religious. American popular culture studies have examined the deeper significance of everything from soap operas to baseball trading cards, adding new material and methods to countless other fields of inquiry, from history and literature to class and gender studies. Of course, such a contrast between that which is religious and that which is cultural is only intelligible in a society like that of the United States, which, for many at least, has made of religion a special category of experience and not the stuff of daily life that it is and has been in other places and times.

A major task is to draw attention back to this intersection of religion and culture in the ordinary experience of Americans. It is this strange terrain that these essays visit, the borderland where traditional religious language, for instance, may not be spoken but where its accent is clearly heard. Sometimes the authors included in this collection stand closer to the territory of popular religion, as in Jennifer Rycenga's report from the Precious Moments chapel, but the gaze from those positions is always outward toward the larger and more confusing world of popular culture. More often, they stand in the territory of popular culture itself, listening for the tastes, accents, and rhythms of the religious world across the border. These are not studies of popular Catholicism, for instance, but, as in the case of Suzanne Holland's contribution, of the *possible* Catholicism of such things as confessional radio and television talk shows.

As it turns out, the borderland where religion and culture meet in popular expression is also a borderland of another sort. As the following chapters show, these quasi-religious popular culture sites serve as points of intersection—sometimes harmonious, often conflictual—for people of very diverse and disparate identities. The Burning Man festival finds wealthy urban art lovers sharing tent space with disaffected college students and twenty-something Silicon Valley employees. On the animated television series *The Simpsons*, Hindu, Jew, and evangelical Christian are brought into a kind of dialogue that would leave many ecumenists reeling. Bruce Springsteen concerts bring together working-class conservatives and liberal intellectuals.

What is noteworthy is that these are not the casual meetings diverse people make every day in supermarkets and traffic jams; rather, these essays show that they are encounters in which questions of ultimate meaning and identity are being struggled over, if not entirely worked out. They are places where members of a society that has tended to privatize religion and demarcate solid denominational lines come (or are thrown) together to explore some very interesting religious questions.

Why should popular culture (rather than the church, the town hall, or the classroom, for instance) be the venue for such encounters? It is often noted that religion has been edged out of the public square in American culture (Neuhaus 1984; Carter 1993). What this observation misses, though, is that while institutional religion may indeed have been denied entry into such official public sectors as government and education, the unofficial public square of television, shopping mall, and stadium parking lot have expanded to accommodate the overflow. Media are especially important in this new religious landscape. As Catherine Albanese notes, "The media are mass language brokers and, so, mass culture brokers" (1996, 740). In the same way that religion in the West changed dramatically with the introduction of the printing press, so has religion changed drastically with the invention of radio, television, and, most recently, the computer. The ubiquitous quality of these popular culture venues (especially by virtue of technologies of mass distribution) make them accessible; that many are entertainment products makes them attractive; and their distance from "official" religious sites makes them flexible and open to many types and levels of interpretation. Church is church, but rock concerts, for instance, seem to be nearly whatever their followers want them to be, often including experiences of intense spiritual transformation. For these and other reasons, popular culture appears well situated as a contemporary religious venue.

WEBS OF SIGNIFICANCE

One way of talking about what people are doing when they are engaged in a religious activity—whether they are singing a hymn, sitting in a sweat lodge, writing theology, lighting a candle, or teaching a child right from wrong—is to say that they are making the world meaningful (or discovering it to be so). When we look at the world around us with this eye toward behavior that carries significant personal and collective meanings, a wide range of apparently nonreligious phenomena become religiously significant. The essays in this volume represent some of those places where religion conventionally understood is not readily—or at least unambiguously—present, but where at least one observer has glimpsed its workings.

To those familiar with various theories of religion, it will not be surprising to find that many of our contributors draw on the work of anthropologist Clifford Geertz. Though other theorists (like sociologist Emile Durkheim, history of religions scholar Mircea Eliade, psychologist Sigmund Freud, anthropologist Victor Turner, and cultural theorist Michel Foucault, among others) appear throughout the collection, a majority of the authors have relied on the approach articulated by Geertz because of their attention to the "doing" aspect of religion; his functionalist—rather than essentialist—framework permits them to explore what religion does for its adherents rather than what religion is. According to Geertz, religion and culture are not really things in and of themselves; they are the systems of meaning that humans give to things, to the stuff of everyday life. They are the "webs of significance" (1973, 5) that connect human thought and behavior, and not so much things that can be calibrated, measured, replicated, or easily diagrammed. They are real enough—or rather, their perception is clothed with "an aura of factuality"—and they are based on things out there (somewhere), but their significance lies in the meanings given to those things by the people who use them in whatever fashion. Using this view here, we are relieved of the burden of finding religious *things*, and can look more widely for the religious meanings attached, explicitly or not, to such activities as eating, dancing, and calling in to a radio talk show.

Important to our collective investigation is Geertz's observation that cultural meanings are necessarily conversational, that is, social and dynamic. In assembling those webs of significance, he argues, we are creating ourselves as social beings. Individual humans don't create culture as a hobby or a byproduct, but need the system of thought created and transmitted collectively in order to survive. Sociologist Peter Berger makes a similar observation when he argues that society is the collective effort to construct meaning that is conferred through processes both external (observed) and internal (intellectual) to the individual. Thus humans are incomplete without the information and meaning encoded in, delivered by, and internalized from the social institutions that they all create without recognizing that participation (Berger 1969). As Geertz concludes, since culture is the process by which collective symbolic meaning is negotiated among individuals, "Culture is public because meaning is" (1973, 12).

If culture and meaning are public, it is the task of the observer to learn to read signs and symbols in order to interpret them. In our case, it means scholars need to learn the "language" of particular popular constituencies, language that is communicated often without words, but certainly in a different idiom than that commonly used in the academic world. The observer must get to know not only what the participant knows, but how the participant knows it, and must learn to see what the participant sees but may not question, since it is automatically understood by the participant. In the same way a non-native must learn the mechanics of grammar as well as the basics of vocabulary in mastering a foreign language, so must the observer, often using terminology and logic unfamiliar to the participant, learn the mechanics as well as the language that the participant has simply "picked up" through the environment.

THE DIFFICULTIES OF DEFINING RELIGION

But if culture is the collection of all of the webs of significance, the problem remains of deciding what it is that counts as religious—how one draws the boundaries (if there are any) between religious systems of meaning and other cultural systems. It is hard enough to say exactly what is religious about a sacred text or a worship service; to try to do so for a television cartoon or a football game is to invite failure. Two principles seemed to serve the contributors to this volume in this effort, though no consensus on such things was sought.

First, obviously, the conception of religion used here is necessarily very broad. If the essays assume any common definition of religion, it is probably that put forth by Geertz (1973) in his well-known essay "Religion as a Cultural System." Religion, he writes, is "a system of symbols which acts to establish powerful, pervasive, and long-lasting moods and motivations in men by formulating conceptions of a general order of existence and clothing these conceptions with such an aura of factuality that the moods and motivations seem uniquely realistic" (90). But we are content to let it remain fuzzier than that. The identification of such phenomena as Jimmy Buffett concerts, comic strips, and the Super Bowl as "religious" hangs not so much on a definition of religion as on a set of markers that are suggestive of religious meaning. These include the formation of communities of shared meanings and values, the presence of ritualized behaviors, the use of language of ultimacy and transcendence, the marking of special, set-aside "sacred" times and spaces, and the manipulation of traditional religious symbols and narratives. Where one or more of these markers are present, we collectively argue, we have entered terrain worthy of religious analysis. Of course, it is up to each individual author to make the case for the religious significance of the particular phenomenon he or she describes.

Second, aware of how complex, varied, and subjective such phenomena are, the authors of these short studies have strived to stay very close to the experience of those being studied. This is good practice for any well-trained ethnographer; it is vital when you are presuming to attach religious meanings to activities participants do not recognize as such. Here we think of one of Wilfred Cantwell Smith's criteria for the "humane" study of those of a different religious tradition. While we would not go so far as to accept as valid, as he did, only those statements about our subjects that they themselves would accept (1981, 97), we do firmly believe that the participant should at least be able to recognize him- or herself in the scholar's descriptions. We see it as a strength of these pieces, then, that many of the scholars are themselves participants in the communities of meaning they describe.

Objectivity in religious studies, as elsewhere, is a problematic goal. Instead, we more commonly aim for clarity in the relationship between ourselves as observers and the people and things we observe. Anthropologist Ruth Behar speaks of the "vulnerable observer," who "is able to draw deeper connections between one's personal experience and the subject under study," developing "a keen understanding of what aspects of the self are the most important filters through which one perceives the world and, more particularly, the topic being studied" (1996, 13). In more or less explicit ways, this is the approach taken by these essays. The contributors are unabashed in their affection for the aspects of popular culture they analyze: Roof is a Southern meat eater, Dalton and his colleagues are dedicated *Simpsons* viewers, Ingersoll is a self-proclaimed Parrothead. The challenge, then, lies not in overcoming the "otherness" of our subjects of study, but in choreographing the dance that allows us to come into intimate closeness with these subjects and then step back to do critical analysis, then to move in and out again.

A PROFILE OF THE POPULAR

A few comments about our sense of the "popular" in popular culture are also in order. Typically, it is taken to refer to the wide diffusion of the product, usually via mass media;[3] its acceptance by the majority of a given population; or its source in non-elite segments of the society. No one of these seems adequate in and of itself, but neither can they all be used as criteria for defining the popular, since they are not necessarily compatible descriptors of a given cultural product.

What's more, attempts at defining the "popular" in popular culture have themselves become politically charged acts. The very term "popular culture" implies for some a particular ideological position, a "facile populism that uncritically equates popular cultural forms with the voice of the 'people' and disregards questions of ideology and social control altogether" (Fluck 1987, 3). Aware of the naïveté of venerating popular culture as the source of an authentic, spontaneous expression of the mind and will of the common folk, we nonetheless maintain the connection between the "popular" in popular culture and its Latin root *popularis* ("of the people").[4] Certainly as many theorists exploring the production of popular culture have noted, much of the mode of communicating popular culture is controlled by the dominant culture—or more specifically, those with the wherewithal to control the expensive technology so important for its dissemination—often making much of popular culture very one-sided.

But the popular culture industry, however exploitative, is successful only to the degree to which it responds to its audience's needs and desires, and therefore its products can tell us something authentic about that audience.[5] In other words, the relationship between the products of popular culture, their producers, and their consumers is complex; each is significantly shaped by the other two. We would expect then that the expressions of popular culture can accurately serve as mirrors of that culture, even while they are also reflective of the commercial interests that function as so powerful a part of culture. Thus one descriptor of the "popular" in culture is its authentic connection, however mediated and admittedly manipulated, with broad segments of the population. What's more, modes of communication are democratizing the dissemination of popular culture, and many once subcultural products—such as rap/hip-hop and Tejano music—are gaining wider audiences, making mainstream popular culture somewhat more representative of the diversity of the American population.

A second feature of popular culture that these essays highlight is its "everyday" quality. If culture is a web of meaning, it is important to note the ordinary source of most of the materials used in that web's construction. What we watch and listen to for entertainment, the clothes we wear, magazines we read, even the foods we eat are the context of our meaning making. These mundane products are themselves often the basis for much of the construction and maintenance of meaning that is so important in the fabric of culture, playing a larger role, often, than the "official" purveyors of meaning associated with religious and educational institutions.

Another aspect of the popular that bears especially strongly on these discussions of the American situation is what Catherine Albanese, in the introduction to an issue of the *Journal of the American Academy of Religion* devoted to the study of religion and popular culture, calls its "creole" character. Popular culture, she writes, "always pieces and patches together its universe of meaning, appropriating terms, inflections, and structurations from numerous overlapping contexts and using them as so many ad hoc tools to order and express, to connect inner with outer, and to return to inner again" (1996, 740). There is thus a messy element in the study of popular culture. Just as each piece of popular culture is itself a pastiche of inherited bits and pieces, so each of us works with a wide range of cultural phenomena in making meaning for ourselves. People do not derive their worldview, for instance, solely from a comic strip. The challenge is to try to see, as Jean Graybeal does in her essay, how readers of the *Cathy* strip might integrate that one minute per day of entertainment with other messages about and personal experience with body image and dieting so as to make positive, personally empowering meaning.

But it is important to emphasize that these popular cultural products do not provide meaning unambiguously. Rather, they often represent those points in the culture where inherited values and actual experience conflict, as several essays show quite forcefully. A final dimension of our sense of the popular, then, is this ambiguous quality. Popular culture venues are contested sites where multitudes come together and negotiate the conflicts with which individuals, and groups of individuals, must reckon in the course of social participation. In some of the following essays this tension is the focus of analysis; all of them operate from the assumption that popular culture products are interesting and revelatory precisely because they do not simply mirror or dictate cultural norms, but are ambiguous expressions of conflict and change in social groups.

TOWARD A THEORY OF RELIGION IN TURN-OF-THE-MILLENNIUM AMERICA

It is entirely possible that those who are studied here will read these pieces and find the religious analyses completely superfluous, if not wrongheaded. As one of our students commented on an early draft of McCarthy's chapter, "Come on. It's just Bruce." Or, one might say of Roof's chapter, sometimes a sparerib is really just a sparerib. Perhaps. But there is a larger purpose to these essays that we believe warrants the risk of such responses.

Numerous scholars note that American religion in the second half of the twentieth century was considerably different from what it was in the first half. Sociologists including Phillip Hammond (1992), James Davison Hunter (1991), Robert Wuthnow (1988), and Robert Bellah (1986) have all commented independently that in the years following World War II, the structure of religion in the United States changed to reflect the changes in American culture. Some of those changes include a wider mainstream acceptance of non-Christian, or even non-Western, religious traditions, as well as the increasing frequency of a lack of religious affiliation. As historian Robert Handy has noted, religion in the United States, legislatively freed from government control with the ratification of the First Amendment to the Constitution, was by the end of the nineteenth century also ostensibly freed from its Protestant monopoly. By the end of the twentieth century religious affiliation was loosened significantly from all social institutions generally (Hammond 1992). More and more people have pursued religious commitments based on their personal preferences, and have either abandoned, reinterpreted, or supplemented the religious tradition into which they were born (Roof 1993). The public monopoly once enjoyed by a segment of Protestant Christianity is now a veritable smorgasbord of religious groups, each relatively free to "advertise" to anyone willing to listen.

However, the increased religious freedom has not stopped simply with the expanded ability of non-Protestant religious communities to participate more fully in American society. Individuals can now choose among competitors in the marketplace of meaning construction and meaning maintenance, even among options that traditionally might have seemed nonreligious. As religious institutions have lost their monopoly on the construction and maintenance of meaning, religiosity has found expression in a wide variety of human activities. It is not that religion was slowly disappearing with modernity, as many scholarly observers have predicted throughout this century, but that society was changing the manner in which it expressed itself religiously (Yamane 1997). Notes Hammond:

> In any era, therefore, when religion, at least as commonly understood, is receding, vitality of the sacred may thus come as a surprise. The present era would seem to fit such a description, and we find ourselves unable to comprehend the sacred. The past accretions that transformed the sacred into religion—accretions which in many instances have been corroded by secularization—keep us from the refocusing necessary if we are to study the sacred in a secular age ... unless we can revise our thinking about secularization. (1985, 5)

Eric Mazur and Tara Koda make this their central foundation when they argue in their essay that Disney (in all of its various and extensive trappings) provides for some a possible replacement for religion. Careful not to suggest that Disney is in fact a religion, Mazur and Koda suggest that in the creation of a sacred space and sense of sacred time in its parks, and through the inculcation of signs, symbols, and lessons in its various media enterprises, Disney provides for its fans (young and old alike) much that would ordinarily have been provided by religions, traditionally understood.

Does all this mean that every activity in which one can engage is religious? Well, yes and no. It could be that the essays collected here will provide readers with a better understanding of the limitations of an expansive definition of the religious just as they might see the limitations of a more restricted definition. The most important check on this possibility is the scholar's ongoing relationship with the popular culture (and its participants) that he or she hopes to illuminate. The academic study of culture and the role of religion in that culture is an endeavor that requires a close examination of the public, and a realization that academic solutions are only as successful as their ability to resonate among those whose activities we are interpreting.

In the end, our sympathies lie with the position taken by David Chidester in a recent issue of the *Journal of the American Academy of Religion*: "If we only relied upon the standard academic definitions of religion, those definitions that have tried to identify the essence of religion, we would certainly be informed by the wisdom of classic scholarship, but we would also still be lost" (1996, 760). Like others before him (J. Z. Smith 1982, for example), Chidester suggests that by providing a definition for religion, the scholar limits what is and is not included in the study. Though working from a definition of religion is perhaps a necessary exercise, it is one that is often not problematized, and scholars fail to ask themselves why some things *shouldn't* be considered religious. "In the end," Chidester continues, "we will need to answer that question. By saying 'we,' however, I refer in this case to all of us who are in one way or another engaged in the professionalized and institutionalized academic study of religion. Participants in American popular culture have advanced their own answers."

Indeed. Part of the motivation behind this collection is to provide comparisons between the seemingly "secular" segments of peoples' lives and the "religious" framework often used only sparingly by scholars of religion. As Geertz (and others) have argued, the search for meaning is at the heart of the question of religion, and, though not everything is to be considered religious, everything connected with that search can certainly be compared to those elements usually reserved for institutional religion.

In addition, this collection problematizes the very definition of religion for the readers of these chapters. We want to encourage readers to think about what they mean when they say "religion," particularly in contemporary America, and what others might mean when they deny its presence. We think that the fact that people engaged in the activities portrayed in the collection might deny the "religiosity" of their activities is itself evidence of the significance of the problem of defining religion in our culture. Theorists for decades have noted an increasing suspicion of religious institutions among Americans. Tom Beaudoin, author of *Virtual Faith: The Irreverent Spiritual Quest of Generation X* (1998), identifies this characteristic as central, for instance, to the spirituality of that generation. For many Americans, it seems, "religion" is identified with institutional religion, and it is precisely their resistance to those institutions that makes such things as music, food, sports, and film attractive alternative sites for meaning making. It is therefore no surprise that so many would reject any reference to religion as a descriptor for their activities. But we strongly believe that this does not mean that the observer ought to be barred from applying religious analyses. This is a difficult issue, and one that many of the contributors address directly in their pieces. It is also one of the most important and interesting issues raised in the project, critical for those who want to explore the meanings of contemporary culture to consider.

FOUR ORGANIZING CATEGORIES

It would be tempting to sort the following chapters according to genre — music, television, radio and film, mass public events, and the like. Such a structure would make it easy for those interested in a particular cultural area to move from one case study to the next and would likely prompt interesting comparisons and conclusions. But genre, it has become clear, does not necessarily closely correlate with the kinds of religious meaning being found and made in these events. In some cases authors studying very different kinds of phenomena reached strikingly similar kinds of conclusions about their religious significance. In this case, it seems, the medium is not the message.

In order to bring these religious dimensions to the foreground in the most provocative way, then, we have organized the popular culture expressions examined here into four categories widely used in the study of religion: myth and legend, ritual, spirituality and morality, and institution ("churches"). These are hardly exhaustive headings for the analysis of religious phenomena; contemporary studies of religion also often employ doctrinal or theological, philosophical, and historical categories, among others. When looking specifically at the quasi-religious aspects of popular culture, though, these four broad categories seem especially useful because of their inherent elasticity. "Myth," for instance, in both its specific references to the sacred narratives of religious traditions and its broader evocation of powerful, culture-defining symbols and stories, proves to be a fascinating lens for looking at such things as the posthumous popular reverence for slain Tejano singer Selena and the end-time visions of Hollywood films. Juxtaposing the Super Bowl and the Burning Man festival under the heading of "ritual" likewise raises very interesting questions about the meaning, and indeed the possibility, of shared symbolic activity in a multicultural, multireligious society. Turning to radio's Dr. Laura and the *Cathy* comic strip, for instance, as venues for popular "spirituality and morality" challenges us to take seriously the extent to which such popular forms function for their audiences as spiritual directors and maps of a moral world, complementing if not replacing those offered by traditional religious communities. As alternative "churches," such phenomena as hip-hop culture and the Disney empire are treated in the last section of the book, provoking perhaps the most radical interpretive possibility, that in these popular culture activities we are seeing not only elements once reserved for religious institutions, but fully wrought alternatives to traditional religion.

Overlaying these four religious categories on these (mostly) apparently non-religious activities does at least two things. It offers a way of demonstrating that what is going on in these activities, because it fits the traditional definitions of myth, ritual, spirituality and morality, and institution, may be comparable to religion as it is traditionally understood. At the same time, it stretches those categories and therefore our understanding of religion itself to better accommodate the strange new world of religion in contemporary America. At the beginning of each of these four sections, we offer a short introductory essay highlighting the major themes and possible implications of the chapters that follow, though we hope each reader will be drawn into the interpretive act and will come to see how it is that many Americans are finding God in the details of their lives.

NOTES

1. By *American* (here and throughout the text), we mean to refer to citizens and residents of the United States.
2. For a few examples of the excellent work being done in this area, see Hall 1997, McDannell 1995, Moore 1994, Williams 1989, and Orsi 1985. For an annotated bibliography, see Lippy 1996.
3. According to Catherine Albanese, this is the defining feature of popular culture

for the contributors to the issue of the *Journal of the American Academy of Religion* for which she wrote the introduction (Albanese 1996, 737).

4. The American Heritage Dictionary defines "popular" as:

> Widely liked or appreciated . . . Of, representing, or carried on by the common people or the people at large . . . Fit for or reflecting the taste and intelligence of the people at large . . . Accepted by or prevalent among the people in general . . . Suited to or within the means of ordinary people . . . Originating among the people.

See *The American Heritage Dictionary*, 2d college edition (Boston: Houghton Mifflin, 1991). The second definition, referring specifically to a person as the object of popularity, has been omitted.

5. In this vein, Camille Paglia has written, "Academic commentary on popular culture is either ghettoized as lackluster 'communications' tarted up with semiotics, or loaded down with grim, quasi-Marxist, Frankfurt School censoriousness: the pitifully witless masses are always being brainwashed by money-grubbing capitalist pigs. But mass media is completely, even servilely commercial. It is a mirror of the popular mind. All the P.R. in the world cannot make a hit movie or sitcom. The people vote with ratings and dollars. Academic Marxists, with their elitest sense of superiority to popular taste, are the biggest snobs in America" (1992, ix).

REFERENCES

Albanese, Catherine L. 1996. "Religion and Popular Culture: An Introductory Essay." *Journal of the American Academy of Religion* 59, 4 (fall): 733–42.

Barth, Karl. [1933] 1968. *The Epistle to the Romans*, 6th ed. Translated by Edwyn C. Hoskyns. New York:Oxford University Press.

Beaudoin, Tom. 1998. *Virtual Faith: The Irreverent Spiritual Quest of Generation X*. San Francisco: Jossey-Bass.

Behar, Ruth. 1996. *The Vulnerable Observer: Anthropology That Breaks Your Heart*. Boston: Beacon Press.

Bellah, Robert N., Richard Madsen, William M. Sullivan, Ann Swidler, and Steven M. Tipton. 1986. *Habits of the Heart: Individualism and Commitment in American Life*. Berkeley: University of California Press.

Berger, Peter L. 1969. *The Sacred Canopy: Elements of a Sociological Theory of Religion*. Garden City, N.Y.: Doubleday.

Carter, Stephen L. 1993. *The Culture of Disbelief: How American Law and Politics Trivialize Religious Devotion*. New York: Basic Books.

Chidester, David. 1996. "The Church of Baseball, the Fetish of Coca-Cola, and the Potlatch of Rock 'n' Roll: Theoretical Models for the Study of Religion in American Popular Culture." *Journal of the American Academy of Religion* 59, 4 (fall): 743–65.

Fluck, Winfried. 1987. "Popular Culture as a Mode of Socialization: A Theory about the Social Functions of Popular Cultural Forms." *Journal of Popular Culture* 21, 3 (winter): 31–46.

Geertz, Clifford. 1973. *The Interpretation of Cultures: Selected Essays by Clifford Geertz*. New York: Basic Books.

Hall, David, ed. 1997. *Lived Religion in America: Toward a History of Practice.* Princeton, N.J.: Princeton University Press.

Hammond, Phillip E. 1992. *Religion and Personal Autonomy: The Third Disestablishment in America.* Columbia: University of South Carolina Press.

———, ed. 1985. *The Sacred in a Secular Age.* Berkeley: University of California Press.

Handy, Robert T. 1984. *A Christian America: Protestant Hopes and Historical Realities,* 2d ed. New York: Oxford University Press.

———. 1991. *Undermined Establishment: Church-State Relations in America, 1880–1920.* Princeton, N.J.: Princeton University Press.

Hunter, James Davison. 1991. *Culture Wars: The Struggle to Define America.* New York: Basic Books.

Lippy, Charles H. 1996. *Modern American Popular Religion: A Critical Assessment and Annotated Bibliography.* Westport, Conn.: Greenwood Press.

McDannell, Colleen. 1995. *Material Christianity: Religion and Popular Culture in America.* New Haven: Yale University Press.

Miner, Horace. 1956. "Body Ritual among the Nacirema." *American Anthropologist* 58, 3 (June): 503–507.

Moore, R. Laurence. 1994. *Selling God: American Religion in the Marketplace of Culture.* New York: Oxford University Press.

Neuhaus, Richard John. 1984. *The Naked Public Square: Religion and Democracy in America.* Grand Rapids, Mich.: William B. Eerdmans.

Orsi, Robert. 1985. *The Madonna of 115th Street: Faith and Community in Italian Harlem, 1880–1950.* New Haven: Yale University Press.

Paglia, Camille. 1992. *Sex, Art, and American Culture.* New York: Vintage Books.

Roof, Wade Clark. 1993. *A Generation of Seekers: The Spiritual Journeys of the Baby Boom Generation.* San Francisco: HarperCollins.

Smith, Jonathan Z. 1982. *Imagining Religion: From Babylon to Jonestown.* Chicago: The University of Chicago Press.

Smith, Wilfred Cantwell. 1981. *Towards a World Theology.* Philadelphia: Westminster Press.

Williams, Peter W. 1989. *Popular Religion in America: Symbolic Change and the Modernization Process in Historical Perspective.* Urbana: University of Illinois Press.

Wuthnow, Robert. 1988. *The Restructuring of American Religion: Society and Faith Since World War II.* Princeton, N.J.: Princeton University Press.

Yamane, David. 1997. "Secularization on Trial: In Defense of a Neosecularization Paradigm." *Journal for the Scientific Study of Religion* 36, 1 (March): 109–22.

part 1: popular myth and legend

At a recent conference on using popular culture in the university classroom, an English professor made the case that the popular sitcom *Friends* is a clever repackaging of Shakespeare's *Much Ado about Nothing*, that *Star Wars* retells Book One of *The Faerie Queene*, and that *The Simpsons* is really a contemporary take on Goldsmith's *She Stoops to Conquer*. A given culture, such parallels would suggest, has a finite number of good stories to tell. But good stories are capable of infinite retelling.

Some of the best stories are to be found in the religious traditions that have had such a profound effect in shaping culture. Virgin births, hero journeys, stories of death and resurrection, battles between good and evil, revelatory encounters with supernatural beings—these are what enliven the sacred scriptures of the world's religions. In a monocultural society, common knowledge and public retelling of such myths reinforce the religious and social identities of community members. In a culturally diverse and officially secular society like the United States, there is no central fire around which a singular set of stories gets told by an authoritative narrator. Instead, as the following chapters explore, the myths and legends of various religious traditions resurface—by themselves, in fragments, and in strange combinations—in what look like wholly secular spaces, in a process that both keeps the stories alive and radically reframes their meaning.

Many of the narratives that inform traditional religious institutions are alive and well in American popular culture, though those "reading" them in song lyrics, movies, and television talk shows may be completely unaware of their sacred roots. In some cases the stories are preserved with their basic narrative structure and cultural function largely intact. Kate McCarthy, for instance, traces the language and imagery of the biblical Exodus account through two decades of Bruce Springsteen's music, where it serves, as it has for countless Jewish and Christian generations, as a powerful symbol of personal and collective promise, as well as "an indictment of America's failure to make real its transcendent promise." McCarthy sees this myth and all its troubling ambiguities being retold not only in Springsteen's song lyrics but also in concert parking lots, Internet chat rooms, and in the persona of Springsteen himself. While listeners may or may not catch the biblical references, McCarthy argues, Springsteen's use of the story of deliverance from bondage into a promised land of opportunity and grace makes the ideological stakes higher here than they are in most rock music.

A mythic genre from the other end of the Bible, apocalypses akin to the Revelation of John, also survives in secular popular culture, according to Jon Stone's analysis of popular film. Stone defines the genre carefully, reminding us that not all accounts of a cataclysmic end of the world are apocalyptic. Rather, apocalypses involve a consistent set of markers, including otherworldly revelation and warning and heroic intervention. Stone goes on to examine three types of apocalyptic films that reveal how compelling and flexible the genre has been in allowing several generations of Americans to reckon with the fear of perceived threats to our world—whether they be nuclear, environmental, or technological—just as it helped first-century Christians cope with Roman persecution. The difference is that those who absorbed these and other mythic stories through Scripture as interpreted by traditional religious communities understood the texts as divinely revealed, while contemporary fans of Springsteen and the *Terminator* movies are conscious of the wholly human origin—in the mind of the filmmaker and musician—of these cultural products. An interesting question raised by these discussions is what difference this difference makes: Is confidence in an otherworldly source requisite for cultural narratives to have life-shaping impact, or has the human imagination now taken over that role?

The stories of exodus and apocalypse, though they are radically resituated, largely maintain their original shape in the popular manifestations McCarthy and Stone consider. Other religious narratives arrive in popular culture in fragments, their powerful component symbols resurfacing alone or in interesting combination with other secular and religious elements. Leonard Primiano observes this process in his analysis of the discussions of the supernatural on American television talk shows. Here the angels and demons of Christian mythology mingle—sometimes in the narratives of a single guest—with UFOs, ghosts, and pagan goddesses in what Primiano identifies as a centuries-old American eclecticism regarding the supernatural.

This eclecticism makes for a highly ambiguous relationship between the narrative symbols and their religious sources. On the one hand, as Primiano notes, American fascination with the supernatural means that ABC found it profitable to film and broadcast a Roman Catholic ritual of exorcism, apparently increasing and potentially enhancing the cultural presence of this religion. On the other hand, the treatment of this sensational event in isolation from broader Catholic theological and ritual tradition—in which exorcism has a very small place—means the perpetuation of a distorted and potentially derogatory image of Catholicism. One might question whether Catholicism was really the subject of the program at all.

Similar questions arise out of Karen Anijar's treatment of the posthumous veneration of slain Tejano singing star Selena in the Mexican-American community. Anijar reports on the overflow of mythic symbols attached to Selena by grieving fans—both the traditional Christian symbols of angel, saint, healer, savior, virgin, ghost, and Madonna and the specifically Mexican-American symbols of the Virgin of Guadalupe and the Dark Virgin (La Virgin Morena). In one sense the reinterpretation of this woman's life through these symbols represents conventional Mexican-American Catholic piety. At the same time, these symbols also represent the eclectic assemblage of a mythic narrative that is capable of sustaining "populist, anarchical and anti-clerical" resistance.

One of the most exciting things going on in the popular retelling of sacred stories and reworking of sacred symbols is the emergence of countless new voices in the storytelling process itself. Who tells the story, and who has the authority to interpret it, are critical factors in determining the meaning or meanings of a given myth or legend. Primiano argues that television talk shows have taken over the role of the traditional storyteller in American culture and that the multivocal quality of these programs diffuses the power of religious storytelling over a broad population. Telling stories of encounters with the supernatural on national television, he claims, is not only a continuation of the American narrative traditions of religious testimonials and "memorate" recitation, but also a kind of performance in which participants have opportunities for creative shaping of religious identity. Primiano believes that this is particularly significant for an understanding of women's spirituality, which has never been embraced and rarely even been acknowledged by mainstream religious institutions. In the talk show medium, he argues, women have "narrated the creation of their own religious roles as mystics, healers, visionaries, mediums, objects of possession, and devotees of sacred figures," roles that, by extension, are validated for the women who make up the majority of the talk show audience.

The mythmaking by Selena fans is similarly empowering, according to Anijar's analysis. Selena is more alive in her death than she was in life, Anijar argues, thanks to the power of her fans' storytelling. The images of Selena generated by devotees following her murder in 1995, in testimonials, spontaneous shrines, Internet chat rooms, and other popular expressions, have constructed a "hyperreal" Selena that "informs and sustains a sense of agency among particular class fragments in the Tejano–Chicano–Mexican–American community." This agency involves cultural pride, resistance to dominant Anglo culture, aspiration for better futures, and a reimagining of female identity and possibility. In the process, she notes, the facts of Selena's life have been dramatically rewritten (not the least of which is the Catholicization of this woman whose family members were Jehovah's Witnesses). Anijar's essay reminds us that the power of myths lies less in their historical accuracy than in their potency for engaging a community's imagination.

But these myth-making sites, though populist and empowering, are also, these authors show, commodified and conflict ridden. The democratic impact of television talk shows is bounded by the commercial interests of networks and advertisers; the power of the Selena image to promote subversive Chicano pride is compromised by the very marketing forces that keep the image in broad circulation. Because popular culture sites are very often commercial sites, their role in religious meaning making is always ambiguous. We are not so naïve as to suggest that the "products" of traditional religious organizations have not always been commodified in various ways, but the central (and legitimated) place of commercial interests in the television, music, and film industries that are the vehicles of these popular myths and legends add an additional layer to the retelling of these classic stories. While such sites can be venues for the self-expression and redefinition of marginalized groups, they can also, and simultaneously, represent back that marginal status when to do otherwise threatens the profitability of their stories as products.

Because they are so multivocal, popular myths make visible a truth of all mythology that is not always evident within religious structures: the abundance of their interpretive possibilities. A story whose meaning is fixed and universally agreed upon is not, by definition, a myth; the potency and longevity of myths lie in their ability to mean different things to different people in different historical settings. Paradoxically, while myths unite groups of people in common appreciation of the story, they also serve as venues for intragroup conflict. As historian of religion Wendy Doniger puts it, "[a] myth is like a gun for hire, like a mercenary soldier: it can be made to fight for anyone" (*Myth and Method*, 1996, 119). This conflictual element is prominent in McCarthy's treatment of Springsteen, where she highlights the odd ways his music brings together those with very different ideological identities, from liberal intellectuals to disenfranchised Vietnam veterans to working-class conservatives. These groups share an appreciation of Springsteen, but perhaps little else. The music becomes a venue for conversation that might not otherwise have occurred across these lines. As she notes, in "debating the significance of his draft status on an Internet chat group, meeting and sharing beers in a stadium parking lot with strangers whose bumper stickers they find repugnant, Springsteen fans are engaged in a cultural conversation about some of the most meaningful issues in American, or any other, society."

The power of myths, these pieces show, is this power to connect, amiably or conflictually, those with otherwise very disparate lives and views. In a multi- or nonreligious society, the power of myth is somewhat obscured but no less real. The stories become divorced from their institutional and doctrinal contexts, get fragmented and remixed, and reappear in sometimes startling ways in popular culture. From campfire, pulpit, and family dinner table, the telling of the myths shifts to, among other places, concert hall, chat group, and CD liner notes. We learn from the popular materializations of these stories some things that might not otherwise be clear. Television talk shows reveal that Americans are still deeply interested in questions of the supernatural; the veneration of Selena tells us that cultural resistance and traditional piety can coexist; the popularity of Bruce Springsteen indicates that Americans are still profoundly idealistic (and therefore in conflict) about what if means to be an American; apocalyptic films expose our deep and persistent fear of the military, industrial, and technological powers we so celebrate. While they lose the specificity of their transcendent referents, sacred stories as employed in popular culture continue to help us reckon with questions of meaning and identity and promote real cultural encounters in a society for which that is increasingly difficult.

Deliver Me from Nowhere

Bruce Springsteen and the Myth of the American Promised Land

KATE MCCARTHY

> We got one last chance to make it real
> To trade in these wings on some wheels
> Climb in back, heaven's waiting on down the tracks
> Oh come take my hand
> We're riding out tonight to case the promised land
> —Bruce Springsteen, "Thunder Road"

> The importance of bar bands all across America is that they nourish and inspire that community. So there are the very real communities of people and characters, whether it's in Asbury Park or a million different towns across the land. And then there is the community that it was enabling you to imagine, but that you haven't seen yet. You don't even know it exists, but you feel that, because of what you heard or experienced, it could exist.
> —Bruce Springsteen, 1998

I grew up in an assortment of East Coast suburban towns where devotion to Bruce Springsteen was like a local dialect. I remember lying on the living room floor with my sisters, studying album covers and fantasizing ourselves as Mary, the archetypal girlfriend in "Thunder Road," dancing out the screen door to meet Bruce, who would drive us away to meet our destinies. Years later, I would return to those same songs with feminist rage. Still, I was moved and challenged by the later Springsteen's tender portraits of struggling factory workers, illegal immigrants, and single mothers, for whom the American Dream had slipped out of sight, even while I bristled at the fact that those songs were written in the comfort of a multimillion-dollar southern California mansion. And I would still point to Springsteen concerts as some of the most transcendent experiences of holy community I have ever had.

Apparently, I am not alone in my highly charged response to this musician. In 1997, thirteen years since he produced a top ten single, Springsteen was the subject of two major books, Fred Goodman's *The Mansion on the Hill* and Jim Cullen's *Born in the USA*. Each boasting hundreds of notes and exploring such themes as "inherited imagination," "the collision of rock and commerce," and "republican character," these are no glossy fan panegyrics but scholarly analyses of the life and music of a rock 'n' roll artist. What is important to both writers is not the music or even Springsteen himself, but his appropriation (or misappropriation) of major themes in American cultural identity. The similarity between the two works ends there. Goodman is disdainful of Springsteen, a "mainstream, commercial performer" whose "mildly liberal politics" are "safe as milk" (1997, 346), while Cullen lauds Springsteen by placing him in the tradition of Whitman, Steinbeck, James, Dewey, Twain, and King.

Few of those with whom I've waited for tickets or pressed against to get closer to the stage have read books by authors like these. But the seriousness of their analyses would not strike many Springsteen fans as misplaced. All fans are devoted to their favorite musicians, but with Springsteen (as with Bob Dylan, the Grateful Dead, Madonna, and a few others), musician, fans, and the wider society have acted jointly (though not necessarily in agreement) to make out of an American rock musician a cultural icon, a symbol of the aspirations, anxieties, and tensions of a particular moment. So while fans, music critics, cultural analysts, and politicians who have invoked his music may read different meanings into, say, "Born in the USA," they are oddly united in the assumption that in this music there is something going on that is more significant than the stuff of most Top 40 hits.

Such momentous assessments of Springsteen are conceivable and often compelling because Springsteen is linked with a myth much larger than himself, a myth that reaches back not only to the formation of American identity but to the Bible. Specifically, Springsteen's work and person invite analysis in terms of the biblical themes of exodus and promised land, themes widely invoked in his lyrics but also applicable to the phenomenon of Springsteen's performances, social commentaries, and status as cultural icon. By virtue of that mythic connection, Springsteen's music and persona become contested sites for ongoing negotiation over what is good and true—and ugly and shameful—about America.

My own interpretation of Springsteen is that of a middle-class white woman, politically progressive, marginally Catholic, irremediably cerebral. Certainly the mythic lens I employ is only one among several possible interpretive tools for this music; much of it is better read as standard-issue rock and roll celebrations of freedom, sex, and rebellion. And I do not impute intentionality to musician or fan in the religious meanings I read in their words and behavior (though often these meanings are explicit). But I am convinced by the pervasiveness of this imagery that analysis of the symbols of exodus and promised land provide one useful route into one place in the culture where real conversation about the spiritual meanings of being an American is occurring.

PROMISED LAND AS MYTH

One of the most potent narratives of the Jewish and Christian traditions is the story of the Hebrew people's escape from slavery in Egypt and journey to a land promised them by God, as told in the books of Exodus, Numbers, Leviticus, and Deuteronomy. The power of this story is attested by its place in an ostensibly secularized America. Though many Americans know the story more from Cecil B. DeMille than from the Bible, this religious text has become a foundational narrative in American (usually Christian) self-understanding. It is cited by politicians and social activists, exploited by advertising agencies, and emerges frequently in the long history of American popular music, from African-American spirituals to Hootie and the Blowfish.

It is important to note that this is a cultural (as opposed to a cosmological) myth; its focus is on a particular group, and the impact of the story depends on appropriating that group's perspective. If we were to read it from the perspective of the Egyptians, or the Canaanites already inhabiting the "promised land," for instance, its meaning would be radically altered. If we assume the Hebrews' perspective, though, the story presents the following elements for ongoing cultural appropriation.

First, it offers an account of human suffering. The book of Exodus opens with a description of the oppression of the Hebrew slaves wrought by their Egyptian taskmasters who "made their lives bitter with hard service in mortar and brick and in every kind of field labor" (Ex 1:14). Identification with the Hebrews' misery provides one important entry into this story. Generations to follow have found in these words resonance of their own suffering under conditions of (perceived) injustice, and thereby made sacred meaning of that suffering.

Second, the story tells us that God is on the side of these victims of oppression, and shares empathically in their grief. "I have observed the misery of my people who are in Egypt," God says; "I have heard their cry on account of their taskmasters, indeed, I know their sufferings" (Ex 3:7). This is a God who will actually intervene on behalf of the Hebrews, who promises to deliver them from their suffering and lead them to "a good and broad land, a land flowing with milk and honey" (Ex 3:8). The myth thus presents a God who is engaged in history and takes sides in conflicts. The biblical theme of chosenness, whereby God elects one particular person or group for a sacred destiny, is a strong element in this narrative.

A third theme of this text that is relevant to its resurfacing in popular American culture is that of the sacred journey. God does not liberate the Hebrews immediately; rather, they are forged into a holy nation through a forty-year period of God-led but often conflictual migration. This motif of a transformative journey, through which a person or group gains freedom, new identity, and transcendent wisdom, is common in myth; this particular version resurfaces in a wide range of American expression, from the Joads' drive across the dusty plains in Steinbeck's *Grapes of Wrath* to *The Wizard of Oz*.

Finally, the concept of the promised land itself is packed with interpretive possibility. It is significant that the Hebrews do not inherit the land they have been working for generations but are led by God to a new place, one already occupied by others but whose conquest God mandates. It is no wonder, then, that this myth should figure so prominently in American rhetoric. The conviction of divine right to a particular piece of geography is a powerful current in American political and cultural history.

To claim that Bruce Springsteen's music is mythic, then, is on one level simply to point to the frequency of allusion to these elements in his lyrics. But more important, it is to see in this music the ongoing function of myth to crystallize complex cultural issues. When Springsteen invokes this myth, he is engaging in a dialogue not only with the Bible and the Jewish and Christian religious traditions but also with long traditions of American history and self-understanding.

CITY ON A HILL: THE AMERICAN PROMISED LAND TRADITION

American history is deeply infused with the conviction that this particular land has a unique place in God's plan. That conviction emerges in evocations of the exodus narrative for a variety of purposes, from national self-congratulation to radical cultural criticism. The Puritans of the Massachusetts Bay Colony were convinced that their communal experiment was one of divine significance comparable to that of the ancient Israelites. John Winthrop's sermon "A Model of Christian Charity" (1630), in which the New England plantation is identified as the "City upon a Hill" on which all eyes were focused (cited in Cherry 1971, 43), established a permanent theme in American religious reflection. It is heard in Jonathan Edwards's revivalist confidence that "the latter-day glory is probably to begin in America" (Cherry 1971, 55), served the Mormon self-definition as a persecuted people led by God to a western Zion, and was put to extraordinary use in a speech by Senator Albert Beveridge in 1900 defending U.S. imperialism in the Pacific. Such expansion, he argued, was America's "high and holy destiny" (Cherry 1971, 153).

Images of exodus and promised land have also worked as vehicles of radical self-criticism in America. Henry Ward Beecher used these images to sustain the abolitionist cause in the face of "the Red Sea of war" (Cherry 1971, 165), seeing in the biblical parallel more of a terrible challenge than a guaranteed mandate. Martin Luther King, Jr., claimed the exodus narrative for African Americans who had borne the brunt of society's claims to a holy destiny. His last speech made clear that the promised land is conceivable, but does not exist, cannot exist in racist America. More recently, Mario Cuomo chided Ronald Reagan's 1984 invocation of the Puritan city on the hill motif, reminding us that America is a shining city "only for those relative few who are lucky enough to live in its good neighborhoods" ("Two Cities," excerpted in Bellah et al. 1987, 413). Evocation of the promised land has been a powerful way to express competing constructions of American destiny and multiple deconstructions of the hypocrisy underlying such conceptions and their mockery of the real experience of millions of Americans.

A comparable range of meanings can be discerned in popular music's treatment of these images. Evocations of exodus and promised land have figured centrally in the music of African Americans. The connection between their situation and the Hebrews' is explicit in the spirituals, but even in the blues, these biblical themes are evident. In their uncompromising reckoning with the painful realities of black existence in racist America and their expression of confidence in the possibility of *another* reality, access to which is symbolized by journeys— by foot, on buses, and on trains—blues artists continued to express a communal will to be, an exertion of "somebodiness" in a world bent on denying it,[1] and continued to invoke biblical imagery in the process.

Inheritor of these traditions, rock music has kept alive this theological tradition with deep American roots; we hear refrains from Exodus in a wide range of rock songs, from Chuck Berry's "Bye Bye Johnny" to Creedence Clearwater Revival's "Up Around the Bend" to Sheryl Crow's "Leaving Las Vegas." The post–World War II generations of white Americans who have been the main producers and consumers of rock have tended to repudiate both the institutions of American Christianity and its historic confidence in this society's holy destiny. But there remains in their musical expressions a profound sense of the transcendent possibilities of this place; while the music rejects the dominant culture and its institutions, it does so in a way that re-establishes the legitimacy of language of ultimacy—mythic language—to describe America. This is nowhere clearer than in the songs of Bruce Springsteen, who emerged from and claims to speak for the white, lower-middle- and working-class Americans who are the inheritors of this myth and its increasingly problematic meanings.

CASING THE PROMISED LAND: THE SONGS

The complex interplay between myth and music(ian) is most simply approached through lyric analysis. In Springsteen's case, such an analysis reveals a consistent use of biblical imagery to evoke the transcendent dimensions of experience, whether of family conflict ("Adam Raised a Cain"), sexuality ("Fire"), or a factory worker's despair ("Youngstown"). Springsteen's frequent use of the promised land theme is highly ambiguous and often ironic, serving the same cultural-critical function it has had for centuries of American artists and rhetoricians. His songs celebrate the American road and its joyous possibilities (in industrial New Jersey of all places), but beneath these celebrations is an indictment of America's failure to make real its transcendent promise. Springsteen's critique of the "runaway American dream" is a rock 'n' roll take on the working-class laments of John Steinbeck and Woody Guthrie, laying bare the exploitation and alienation that have built the city on the hill. From the image of his father "walking through them factory gates in the rain" in *Darkness on the Edge of Town* (1978) through his depictions on *The Ghost of Tom Joad* (1995) of the plight of Mexican immigrants, ex-cons, and unemployed workers, Springsteen's music has turned a light on the limits of America's promise. For all their grimness, Springsteen's songs also project hope in a real American promised land. These songs are full of defiant movements out of conditions of limitation and toward, if not into, worlds of possibility.

The Early Lyrics: Exodus as (Sexual) Escape

In his earlier songs these limits are usually personal—dead-end jobs and relationships, oppressive small towns, and restrictive familial obligations. Exodus accounts on these early records (*Greetings from Asbury Park, New Jersey* [1973], *The Wild, the Innocent and the E Street Shuffle* [1973], and *Born to Run* [1975]) are simple escapes, usually temporary, often sexual, almost always in cars. His 1975 anthem "Born to Run" stands as an archetype of this 1970s version of exodus as escape, where "tramps like us" can "ride through mansions of glory on suicide machines."

The overwhelming impact of this song with its huge guitar sound is one of surging masculine power. While the protagonist identifies with the chrome-wheeled, fuel-injected machine sprung free on Highway 9, Wendy is invited only to hold on, to "wrap your legs round these velvet rims and strap your hands 'cross my engines." It is this kind of exodus via sex and machine on American highways, where men have agency and women have flowing hair, that one also hears in Steppenwolf's "Born to Be Wild" and any number of '70s and '80s heavy metal songs.

Another similar expression comes through in "Thunder Road" (1975), which gets at the fuller spiritual import of automotive exodus. It opens with Mary, the mythic Girl who figures in so much of Springsteen's music, dancing across her porch to Roy Orbison's "Only the Lonely." "Thunder Road" becomes a plea for Mary to get in the singer's car and come away with him, and in the process creates a vivid description of both the bondage of their lives and the alternative world waiting out on the highway.

The religious references are explicit. Mary has been "praying in vain for a savior to rise from these streets," one who would release her from the suffocation of getting older and going nowhere in a "town full of losers." He makes clear that he is not that kind of savior, but he does tell Mary that "heaven's waiting on down the tracks," which they can reach if they are willing to "trade in these wings on some wheels." Reflecting the Christianized reading of the promised land myth that dominates American culture, Springsteen explicitly identifies it with heaven: "we're riding out tonight to case the promised land." The conflation of these two symbols—this-worldly promised land and other-worldly heaven—points to a major and long-standing tension in American spirituality: Is our religious destiny to be fulfilled here in the real world, or is that world only prelude to our true destiny of personal spiritual fulfillment after death? In this song Springsteen offers one rough attempt at an answer, one that apparently resonated with a sizable portion of baby boomers in the early 1970s.

The car becomes a metaphor for the rejection of otherworldly religious promises and the affirmation of the possibility of an alternative, this-worldly redemption. He and Mary can stay where they are, in a kind of death-in-life suggested by images of burned-out Chevrolets and ghosts haunting dusty beach roads, or they can *move*, pull out and leave it all behind for a more real life in which ordinary—especially sexual—experience itself is the source of meaning and connection. Heaven/the promised land can be reached by car, "Thunder Road" suggests, but only by those who are willing to give up prayer but show faith in the night, give up crosses but also sacrifice dreams.

There are, of course, problems with the automotive exodus experience for those of us who view it through Mary's eyes. Throughout rock music the traps from which male artists depict liberating flight are typically those of the family or meaningless labor. Symbolic flights of this kind are often identified as the hallmark of youth and subcultural expression. But, as Angela McRobbie argues, there are often overlooked gender implications to this pattern. She reminds us that "it is monstrously more difficult for women to escape (even temporarily)" and that "these symbolic flights have often been at the expense of women (especially mothers) and girls" (1980, 69). Recalling Springsteen's invitation to Wendy in "Born to Run," she notes, "in the literary sensibility of urban romanticism that resonates across most youth cultural discourses, girls are allowed little more than the back seat on a drafty motorbike" (69).[2]

In these early songs, Springsteen's women are silent accessories to male fantasy. Later they will become more complex, and honored for their greater ability to manage life's complexity, as in 1987's "Spare Parts," in which the young man is too afraid to deal with the responsibilities of unexpected parenthood, while the young woman pulls herself together and gets on with it. Such changes are part of the larger evolution of Springsteen's songwriting toward a vision of a promised land that is real, complicated, and inclusive of the domestic world from which these early heroes seek escape.

The Middle Lyrics: Exodus as Personal Redemption

Another layer of meaning is added by songs from *Darkness on the Edge of Town* (1978), *The River* (1980), and *Nebraska* (1982). *Darkness*'s "The Promised Land" summarizes the album's recurring themes: alienating work, intergeneration conflict, relationships that become traps—all made more painful by the awareness, however vague, that another kind of life is possible. Despite "feel[ing] so weak I just want to explode," the protagonist still ends each refrain with the insistence that "Mister, I ain't a boy, no I'm a man /And I believe in a promised land." Here the promised land has no more specific content than its contrast with conventional life. Importantly, it is evoked through violent imagery: explosions, knife fights, twisters. It is as if these acts of destruction are the only way the speaker can convince himself of his own existence. Consciously or not, Springsteen here taps into an old blues tradition, the assertion of manhood, of "somebodiness," through acts of violence against a world whose more subtle violence the protagonist can no longer bear.

This sense of exodus as escape out of anonymity into an authentic sense of self is still connected with the automotive experience, as indicated by "Open All Night" (*Nebraska*), a tight, tense song about a worker finishing a long shift, on "an all-night run to get back to where my baby lives." A drive through North Jersey becomes its own exodus, through the power of the car and its radio. The sound is at once lonesome and exhilarated, moving at a deliberate, urgent pace that threatens to but never quite bursts its restraints. The opening lines, "I had the carburetor cleaned and checked/With her line blown out she's hummin' like a turbojet," are reminiscent of the macho world of "Born to Run," but there's something else going on here. The singer is uneasy, and brings us in on that uneasiness: "This turnpike sure is spooky at night when you're all alone." He's low on gas, late for arrival, and can't find a gas station or a pay phone. The mood is heightened by the mounting pressure of the lyric structure; there is not a repeated line in the song.

Finally, it is the music on the radio that offers release. Fighting through frequencies "jammed up with gospel stations," he prays, "Hey Mr. Deejay, won'tcha hear my last prayer/Hey ho, rock and roll, deliver me from nowhere." In this prayer, Springsteen offers a précis of this stream of his rock 'n' roll theology: It rejects the Christian faith the culture offers, identifying it with an irrelevant, and often oppressive, otherworldly spirituality, but at the same time reaches for its own "long-distance salvation" through rock 'n' roll radio. This music claims the power to reorient experience so dramatically that only the language of religion is adequate to expressing it. It "saves" and "delivers" its listeners by connecting them not only with this music, but also, through the shared radio experience, with each other. Here Springsteen takes part in a long-standing tradition of rock 'n' roll radio as both source and medium of holy community, in which the radio transports the listener into a virtual, temporary promised land.

This communitarian element is central to Springsteen's vision of an ideal America. Even in those lyrics that depict cars and highways as a celebratory escape from the cares of the long workweek, there is an element of collective salvation. Jim Cullen points to the importance of the shift to the first-person plural in the last verse of *Darkness*'s "Racing in the Street." The song is evocative of Martha and the Vandellas' "Dancin' in the Streets" (1964), a pop dance hit whose widely known subtext was an ebullient announcement of the urban riots of the '60s. Springsteen's much quieter song seems to lack any of the larger social meaning, until the last verse. The refrain lines about blowing away all comers in drag races on the strip have been heard twice by this point. Then just before the final refrain comes this verse:

For all the shut-down strangers and hot-rod angels
Rumbling through this promised land
Tonight my baby and me we're gonna ride to the sea
And wash these sins off our hands

The collective redemptive power of the singer's own purificatory drive is then reflected in the song's last lines:

> Tonight, tonight, the highway's bright
> Out of our way mister you best keep
> 'Cause summer's here and the time is right
> For racin' in the street . . .

The plural pronoun suggests that Springsteen's use of promised land imagery is developing a more complex theological meaning; escape from the world of those who "start dying little by little, piece by piece" can't be had alone. The compassion of the last verse indicates a sense of the collective quality of human suffering and the necessarily collective nature of liberation, even when it takes the form of a drag race. "Play becomes communitarian, something one does not only to save oneself, but also something one does for (or at least in honor of) others" (Cullen 1997, 121). This shift marks the beginning of Springsteen's development of a fully wrought vision of an American promised land built on the premise of mutual responsibility.

The Later Lyrics: Exodus as Political Plea

Beginning with *The River* (1980), and more explicitly with *Nebraska* (1982), *Born in the USA* (1984), and *The Ghost of Tom Joad* (1995), Springsteen's use of promised land and exodus imagery is put to increasingly political use. The limits to authentic life in America are increasingly seen as collective; his lyrics tell us that America cannot be the promised land until it is made hospitable to Vietnam vets, downsized steelworkers, farmers, single mothers, and illegal immigrants. Springsteen expresses a personal sense of culpability for this national failure, a sense that he urges upon us all. As he said at a Vietnam veterans benefit concert in Los Angeles, preparing to sing Woody Guthrie's "This Land Is Your Land," "There's a lot in [United States history] . . . that you're proud of, and then there's a lot of things in it that you're ashamed of. And that burden, that burden of shame, falls down. Falls down on everybody" (quoted in Gilmore 1990, 295). For Springsteen the space between rock 'n' roll performance and political activism has become thin; he hopes that the images that drive his songs will also drive concert goers and CD buyers into their communities as spokespeople for the voiceless.

The grimness of his most recent album has led some critics to argue that Springsteen has abandoned hope in America's transcendent possibility.[3] But the songs on *The Ghost of Tom Joad* can be read differently. The title song sets a scene very close to despair, with a "shelter line stretchin' 'round the corner/Welcome to the new world order." In this America, the road is a metaphor of failure, not promise. "The highway is alive tonight," Springsteen sings, echoing dozens of earlier lyrics, "but nobody's kiddin' nobody about where it goes." This is a road that ends in homeless shelters, jail, or death. In one of the bleakest of his allusions to the promised land, he resurrects Steinbeck's Preacher, who is

Waitin' for when the last shall be first and the first shall be last
In a cardboard box 'neath the underpass
Got a one-way ticket to the promised land
You got a hole in your belly and a gun in your hand

Here the promised land images seem to serve nothing but irony; the wait for that day and the ticket to the promised land seem equally hopeless. A similar effect is achieved in the songs about Mexican immigrants. "Across the Border" evokes the outsider's hopes for America as promised land, but set beside "Sinaloa Cowboys," "The Line," and "Balboa Park," these images become something like a cruel joke. In these songs, the immigrants who make it across the border are reduced to hustling, drug dealing, smuggling, and a variety of ignominious deaths, as other people's cars "rush by so fast."

But the last verse of "The Ghost of Tom Joad" offers the barest hint that redemption is still possible in this hard land. The luckless narrator who sits with "no home, no job, no peace, no rest" invokes Steinbeck's Everyman and recounts his parting words to his mother:

Now Tom said, "Mom, wherever there's a cop beatin' a guy
Wherever a hungry newborn baby cries
Where there's a fight 'gainst the blood and hatred in the air
Look for me, Mom, I'll be there
Wherever there's somebody fightin' for a place to stand
Or a decent job or a helpin' hand
Wherever somebody's strugglin' to be free
Look in their eyes, Mom, you'll see me."

By raising Tom Joad's ghost this way, Springsteen situates his dark vision of America within a rich populist tradition. The stories of the album's tragic characters are enlarged and dignified by this association, and their portrayals become a plea for the more humane and inclusive America that we have at least collectively imagined. For Springsteen, America is still worth singing about, still a source of mythic tales, and in this sense still a holy landscape.

What I have presented thus far is an unambiguous reading of the meaning of these ancient symbols in one site of American popular culture. Were we to stop here, we could enjoy a neat picture of Springsteen as a contemporary Moses, putting transcendent truths in understandable words, pointing to a better reality, a holier destiny, chiding us when we fail to live up to the promises we have made ourselves and each other. But the reality is far more ambiguous, because the lyrics discussed above do not exist simply on the page, but (1) as performed, in both recorded and live contexts; (2) as interpreted through the experiences of those who encounter those performances; and (3) as refracted by the public personae of Springsteen not only as musician but also as home town hero, adulterer, businessman, family man, activist, and multimillionaire. These concentric interpretive contexts add complexity to the music's reports of the American promised land and point to the truly mythic—because multivalent—meaning of popular culture.

"DO YOU HAVE ENOUGH BEERS IN YOUR CAR?"
PARKING LOT PROMISED LAND

Springsteen's fans are a devoted lot. The adoring "Bruuuuuce" that greets him when he appears on stage is something akin to what the pope receives on visits to Latin America. In parts of New Jersey a negative comment about him is cause for violence. It is not unusual to hear his significance put in religious terms, as the editor of a long-running fanzine does, recalling his first show: "Springsteen ended up playing a guitar solo standing atop my table, and as he dripped sweat on me that hot summer night, I imagine I was baptized in some alien way. I came out of the theater a changed sixteen-year-old" (Cross 1989).

For many, the impetus for such adulation goes far beyond musical appreciation. Fans adore Springsteen because he offers a vision of themselves and their society as inhabitants of a promised land that is truer, more authentic than their daily experiences. The word "real" shows up with striking frequency in discussions of Springsteen's music, in concert and album reviews, and in fan reports of what the music means to them. But just what does "real" mean in this context? Intersecting, overlapping, and conflicting understandings of the promise held out by Springsteen's music show the complexity of apparently shared cultural symbols like the promised land.

On the one hand, what is real about Springsteen are the people his songs depict. These are unglamorous working-class folks who drive real cars on real New Jersey highways, are too tired to play with their children, and see themselves facing the same destinies for which they cursed their parents. But Springsteen grants a dignity and a hopefulness to these characters that make their plight seem meaningful. The "real" world of screen doors, backstreets, factory gates, and neighborhood bars is presented in the lyrics as a world of sublime possibility, where transcendent moments—windows rolled down, hair blown back, radio up loud—shine a transformative light on everything else.[4]

For fans, Springsteen concerts often become such moments. At a Springsteen concert at the New Jersey Meadowlands in 1984, I was stuck in one of two very slow-moving lines of cars making their way into the huge parking lot. The summer evening was still hot, the air damp and sticky in our un-air-conditioned car. Windows were open all down the lines and conversations struck up over bootlegged tapes. Noticing our California plates, a young woman in the crowded car next to us leaned out and called, "You came all the way from California? Do you have enough beers in your car?" One assumes this is not an offer she would have made stopped at a traffic light just outside the stadium. I have had similar encounters in suburban Los Angeles and outside Boston Garden, where I saw panic move down a line of college-age ticket-buyers when it was learned that the box office would not accept checks. I watched as those who had extra cash took (probably rubber) checks from those who didn't, the only apparent concern being to maximize the number of us who would get to see Bruce. These are moments of what Victor Turner would call spontaneous *communitas*,[5] here made possible by common connection to a particular vision of America, one in which time moves slowly, neighbors are trusted, and the good life can be had over a shared beer. The performance context thus suggests that in addition to *depicting* a kind of promised land, the music also conjures it, makes it temporarily real for those participating.

Like all ritual, Springsteen performances and their peripheral events are able to sustain the intense communitas experience by virtue of their removal from "real" space and time. In this case, people share beer, money, and affection with others who, outside the performance context, they would be unlikely to share a conversation with. Lines of class, politics, and geography (though not, notably, race), seem to dissolve within the "sacred" space and time of the concert experience. And while rock concerts of many varieties can and have been identified as sources of this kind of experience, in this case the sense of intimate, uncomplicated, unstructured connectedness is powerfully aided by the *mythic* quality of the images in the music. Were Springsteen to explicitly lay out a sociopolitical analysis of American ideals and failures, such a vision (in addition to being very bad rock 'n' roll) would appeal to only a small portion of the audience. As it is, his reports of "badlands," out of which one can drive on "streets of fire" past "the mansion on the hill" to "the river" to "wash these sins off our hands" invite liberal intellectuals and conservative blue-collar workers alike to read themselves into the narrative. In these songs the story of enslavement ("the working, the working, just the working life") and the promise of deliverance ("I believe in a promised land") are made relevant to contemporary American experience, but at the same time are sufficiently removed from the actuality of that experience to remain available for appropriation by diverse if not competing constituencies.

This was hilariously illustrated in the controversy that erupted in 1984 over the Reagan campaign's effort to appropriate Springsteen's "Born in the USA" as a conservative anthem. Columnist George Will offered a review of a Springsteen show that cast Springsteen as Republican cheerleader: "He is no whiner, and the recitation of closed factories and other problems always seems punctuated by a grand, cheerful, affirmation: 'Born in the U.S.A.!'" (quoted in Cullen 1997, 3). Reagan himself invoked Springsteen a few days later at a campaign stop in New Jersey, where he aligned himself with Springsteen's "message of hope" (Gilmore 1990, 298). Along with many other Springsteen devotees, Dave Marsh, Springsteen's biographer and most reverent critic, erupted in outrage, later writing that Will's statement "was such a perversion of what Springsteen was trying to communicate that it constituted an obscenity" (quoted in Cullen 1997, 5). Springsteen distanced himself from the president's embrace in comments at subsequent shows, and later said, "I think people got a need to feel good about the country they live in. But what's happening, I think, is that that need—which is a good thing—is getting manipulated and exploited. And you see the Reagan reelection ads on TV—you know 'It's morning in America.' And you say, well, it's not morning in Pittsburgh. It's not morning above 125th Street in New York. It's midnight, and, like, there's a bad moon risin'. And that's why when Reagan mentioned my name in New Jersey, I felt it was another manipulation, and I had to disassociate myself from the president's kind words" (Springsteen 1984, 154). Springsteen, who has described Reagan as a mythic character riding on nostalgia for a mythical America (155), seems to recognize that his own effective use of mythic symbols for the purposes of American cultural critique depend on their not being tied too closely to any particular American agenda.

MOSES IN THE HOLLYWOOD HILLS:
SPRINGSTEEN AS AMBIGUOUS CULTURE HERO

The "realness" celebrated by Springsteen fans also refers to the musician himself. Coming to national celebrity in an era of synthetic disco sounds and performers defined as much by costume and makeup as music, an era in which rock had become unabashedly big business, Springsteen was celebrated as the real thing, a return to rock's purer, simpler roots, when the music was what mattered. Jon Landau's famous designation of Springsteen as the future of rock 'n' roll was part of a larger statement in which he expresses this widespread image of Springsteen:

> In my own moments of greatest need, I never gave up the search for sounds that can answer every impulse, consume all emotion, cleanse and purify—all things that we have no right to expect from even the greatest works of art but which we can occasionally derive from them. Tonight, there is someone I can write of the way I used to write, without reservation of any kind. Last Thursday, at the Harvard Square theatre, I saw my rock 'n' roll past flash before my eyes. And I saw something else: I saw rock 'n' roll future and its name is Bruce Springsteen. And on a night when I needed to feel young, he made me feel like I was hearing music for the very first time. (quoted in Goodman 1997, 226–27)

The hyperbole of Landau's assessment of Springsteen points to the religious quality of this popular image of Springsteen and his music as somehow more authentic than the rest. Landau here invests rock 'n' roll with a salvific function and identifies Springsteen's music as the genuine article, the sound that can, at last, fulfill that holy promise. There is a baptismal quality to what Landau celebrates in these lines; the Harvard Square show has left him cleansed, purified, feeling reborn.

But to hear others tell it, behind all this reality and authenticity is in fact a carefully orchestrated presentation by record producers, promoters, critics, and, at least since the release of *The River*, Springsteen himself, that masks the wide cracks that have developed between the New Jersey working-class guitar hero and the savvy Los Angeles multimillionaire. The most obvious of these gaps, of course, is money. The son of Freehold, New Jersey, now lives in a $14 million Hollywood Hills mansion and faces none of the hard realities against which his songs' characters struggle so nobly. "Money changes everything," Cyndi Lauper realized. So did Springsteen, according to Fred Goodman, who argues that as his popularity increased, the naïve young rocker gradually came to accept and even embrace the music industry's profit-driven logic. That Goodman should devote the better part of a four-hundred-page book to documenting this transformation in Springsteen is itself evidence that with this artist the stakes are very high. It is significant that *Springsteen* should have sold out to this version of the American dream precisely because of his iconic representation of a holier America, one defined by the dignity of labor, the loyalty of family, the integrity of community, the transcendent power of sexual love. As the local boy who made good, Springsteen has been represented as one who did not just write and sing about but also embodied this American promised land, re-presenting its values back to those from whom the vision might have begun to recede.

Exposing the tycoon beneath the leather jacket as Goodman seeks to do, then, is bookworthy because it problematizes important aspects of American self-understanding. Mainstream American culture, if such a thing can still be talked about, is perhaps unique in seeing itself as simultaneously elect and common; one reason the exodus narrative remains so relevant to this culture is because of its fusion of divine chosenness with social and political powerlessness. The breakdown of Springsteen's identification with the disempowered masses he represents throws into question the possibility of our own arrival in the promised land, or at least of arriving with souls intact and of finding there something other than a theme park version of what was promised.

This breakdown is even more evident in the increasing ideological gap between Springsteen and his listeners. Springsteen's audiences, almost exclusively white, have always been an interesting mix of working-class locals and liberal intellectuals in from the suburbs. The small size of the latter class, however, has always made the former the core Springsteen constituency. As his music and especially his performances have become more explicitly politicized, the distance between Springsteen and his fans has grown. The illegal Mexican immigrants he sings about on *The Ghost of Tom Joad* are unlikely to show up at a concert or buy a CD, and Springsteen's championing of their rights is falling on increasingly hostile ears among blue-collar concertgoers. At a large New Jersey show shortly after the 1992 election of Bill Clinton, Springsteen's plea that we all "give the guy a chance" was met with boos from a crowd that moments before had risen to its feet in adoration.

Springsteen's 4-F Vietnam draft status has also served to alienate some fans who are Vietnam vets, ironically only after he began singing about the war and bringing the plight of vets to the attention of his audiences. One fan writes in an Internet chat group, "I liked the early Springsteen up until the time he started singing & talking about the Vietnam War, and I found out he had never even been in the military.... There's a big difference between someone speaking against injustice and a wannabe seeking notoriety by trying to make it sound like they were there" (Utne Chat "Music.30: Bruce Springsteen: the Man and His Music," May 3, 1996).

This strange alienation between the musician and his fans became clearest to me at a small concert at the opening of the *Tom Joad* tour in 1996. It was a hometown crowd at the intimate State Theater of New Jersey in New Brunswick. When Springsteen appeared on stage, solo, with just a stool and an acoustic guitar, and began to play, the crowd cheered and got ready to begin the participatory rituals of singing and clapping along, doing its part in the call-and-response, and chanting its affection, but was surprised by Springsteen's first words. "These songs took a lot of quiet to write, and they need to be heard that way. Please don't clap or, for God's sake, sing along." It was said with a smile, but the audience was clearly chastened, and remained wary for the rest of the subdued show.

This album reveals the ambiguities of Springsteen's efforts to inspire a holier America as clearly as anywhere; as the landscape shifts from song to song, various listeners will find themselves drawn in and then edged out. The struggling American-born laborer, for instance, will likely be moved by the story of the second-generation blast furnace worker in "Youngstown," who once saw holiness in the industry ("Taconite, coke and limestone/Fed my children and made my pay/Them smokestacks reachin' like the arms of God/Into a beautiful sky of soot and clay") but now sees "just scrap and rubble" and laments to his invisible higher-ups, "Once I made you rich enough/Rich enough to forget my name." But for that same worker, who might have seen his job shipped south, the illegal Mexican immigrants depicted in other songs on *The Ghost of Tom Joad* are not likely objects of sympathy. What's more, he might find the power of these defenses of the poor and working-classes undercut by Springsteen's own socioeconomic distance.

Springsteen himself appears to be well aware of these gaps, and of the inherent ambiguity of enormous wealth and celebrity built on a "regular guy" image.

The very personal songs on 1992's *Lucky Town* and *Human Touch* acknowledge how good he now has it, but insist that a satisfying life is as elusive for those of privilege as it is for the poor. His wealth and fame have made a myth of Springsteen himself, he has said, one from which he has had to struggle to free himself:

> It's like you're a figment of a lot of other people's imaginations. And that always takes some sorting out. But it's even worse when you see yourself as a figment of your own imagination. . . . [Y]ou can get enslaved by your own myth or your own image, for lack of a better word. And it's bad enough having other people see you that way, but seeing yourself that way is really bad. It's pathetic. (Springsteen 1992, 322)

To get past this myth, Springsteen seems to have turned to the work of interpersonal intimacy.

He has acknowledged that much of his earlier music's obsession with cars, highways, and movement had to do with his own restlessness and inability to establish for himself the kind of connectedness his characters so hungrily chased (323). More stationary images fill *Tunnel of Love* (1987), *Human Touch*, and *Lucky Town*, the dark, scary intimacy of the tunnel of love replacing wide-open highways. He has said that buying the big house in Los Angeles, where he now lives with second wife, Patti Scialfa, and their children, symbolized his willingness to take on the hard work of settling down, giving up the metaphor of the road for the reality of family, the most basic locus of social responsibility (Springsteen 1992, 322–28). From looking for a heaven that waited "down on the tracks," he now sees "living proof" of God's mercy in the form of his sleeping son.

Home now becomes the metaphor for the holy landscape in this version of the sacred journey, as the last lines of "Better Days" reveal: "Every fool's got a reason for feelin' sorry for himself/And turning his heart to stone/Tonight this fool's halfway to heaven and just a mile outta hell/And I feel like I'm comin' home." The proximity of heaven and hell, bondage and freedom seem to be part of the realization of the aging American idealism represented here. And just as being excluded from the American dream cannot be justification for hardheartedness, neither, he tells us here, can the angst of fame and fortune.

As *Tom Joad* makes clear, Springsteen's work continues to depict and decry the huge American wealth gap, but does so now from knowledge of life on the other side of that chasm. While it will not be persuasive to all, his ruminations about how hard it is to get comfortable in the mansion on the hill at least indicate an awareness of the complexity of the relationship between wealth and happiness. One of the most dangerous versions of the American promised land myth is the one that identifies the promise with the trappings, he tells us.

> I understood that it's the music that keeps me alive, and my relationships with my friends, and my attachment to the people and the places I've known. That's my lifeblood. And to give that up for, like, the TV, the cars, the houses—that's not the American dream. . . . Those are the booby prizes. And if you fall for them—if, when you achieve them, you believe that this is the end in and of itself—then you've been suckered in. Because those are the consolation prizes, if you're not careful, for selling yourself out, or lettin' the best of yourself slip away. So you gotta be vigilant. You gotta carry the idea you began with further. And you gotta hope that you're headed for higher ground. (Springsteen 1984, 164–65)

His own reckoning with the gap between myth and reality seems to add another layer to the meaning of an American promised land for Springsteen, suggesting that it must be an interior as well as exterior landscape.

Springsteen's "authenticity" is thus a common flashpoint in debates about his music. As his work becomes increasingly explicit in its identification with liberal political causes, his credibility with critics seems to improve, while it ironically erodes his working-class fan base. Now firmly established as a cultural icon, Springsteen has not had a major hit in years, and while increasingly the subject of articles like this one, his songs are rarely heard on the radio. His music, by invoking the biblical language of a promised land to cast American ideals and realities in mythic terms, has thus become a contested site, prompting a series of hard questions for its listeners: What makes America a promised land? To whom was the promise made? How far, and at whose expense, can its offer be extended? Whose responsibility is its massive failure to deliver on the promise? How much does our individual and collective arrival in that land depend on internal, spiritual dispositions, and how much on outward social and political struggle?

THE MYTH OF THE PROMISED LAND AND AMERICAN POPULAR CULTURE

The biblical myth of exodus and promised land has been good to Bruce Springsteen, allowing him to evoke powerful responses in a wide range of American listeners. Viewed collectively, these evocations offer insight into the evolving spirituality of an ostensibly secularized segment of the American population, by sketching changing understandings of what it is that constitutes human bondage, what redemption from that captivity might feel like, and what vehicles might take one there.

From the adolescent sexual frustration of "Rosalita" (1973), to the alienation of meaningless anonymous labor in "Factory" (1978), to the abandonment by their country of Vietnam vets in "Born in the USA" (1984), to the dead-end route of illegal Mexican immigrants in "Sinaloa Cowboys" (1995), Springsteen's songs depict experiences of bondage that are given weight by religious language and allusion. Similarly, journeys—on motorcycles, cars, and amusement park rides, and across towns, rivers, and state and national borders—become by means of these references symbols of personal and collective salvation. In their superimposing of biblical with American landscapes, these songs evoke (positively or negatively) profoundly idealistic visions of American possibility. But these are not just patriotic songs. The weight of biblical references also points to the burden of being a chosen people, the challenges of establishing and defending the borders of a promised land and the invisible, interior struggles the journey there requires.

As his own and the national life have shifted, so has Springsteen's use of these images, but they consistently explore the tension that Robert Bellah and his colleagues have identified as a defining feature of the contemporary American character: the drive for individual freedom of all kinds, but especially from institutional determination, and the simultaneous quest for a meaningful sense of community (Bellah et al. 1985, 144). *Born to Run* uses the exodus theme to express the raw power of the former; *Tom Joad* uses it to press the moral imperative of the latter. This tension is inherent in Exodus itself. The biblical story of the escape from Egypt and the journey to the promised land of Canaan is a complex study in social inclusion and exclusion; the Hebrews are the excluded outsiders trapped inside Egypt but become, in their journey, the included of God, led to a place where they claim the divine right to exclude the native inhabitants. And of course within their own community are degrees of inclusiveness; the promise made to Moses apparently did not extend equally, for instance, to the Hebrew women (Plaskow 1990, 25–28). The push to freedom, the story implies, is always accompanied by the challenge of new opportunities to include and exclude.

The applicability to the American experience is obvious. In Springsteen's music, the tension between these two perspectives, those of the trapped insider wanting out and the excluded outsider wanting in is a defining theme. In this sense, Springsteen's work is conservative in an important way. His characters do not want to tear down but to find a meaningful place *within* the system: "My characters aren't really antiheroes. Maybe that makes them old-fashioned in some way. They're interested in being included, and they're trying to figure out what's in their way" (Springsteen 1998, 38).

What's in their way has changed from album to album, involving increasingly complex issues of class, race, and interpersonal and ultimately personal soul-searching. The intersection of these issues reminds Springsteen's listeners that getting to the promised land is not a matter of simple escape from one place to another. It must be imagined, negotiated, pieced together out of the scarce resources at hand in the places we already live. At its best, Springsteen knows, his music fosters that kind of imagination.

But as indicated above, audience experiences of Springsteen and his music are not univocal. It is the complexity of these responses that points to the truly mythic quality of this work. In religious settings, myths are the central stories in light of which individual and collective lives are made meaningful in some ultimate sense. They do not require that all members of the myth-sharing group derive the same meanings, only that all remain in some way tied to the story. In fact, the contested text is the real locus of encounter; without it, the differing constituencies have neither the impetus nor the resources for real conversation. So it is with the secularized myth of the promised land in the music of Bruce Springsteen. In booing his sympathy for Clinton, attending the *Tom Joad* concert but resenting the instruction to be quiet, debating the significance of his draft status on an Internet chat group, and meeting and sharing beers in a stadium parking lot with strangers whose bumper stickers they find repugnant, Springsteen fans are engaged in a cultural conversation about some of the most meaningful issues in American, or any other, society.

NOTES

The second epigraph is taken from an interview published in the spring 1998 issue of *Double Take*, pp. 36–43.

1. This idea is developed fully in James Cone's *The Spirituals and the Blues* (Cone 1972). Jon Michael Spencer argues for a similar function of contemporary rap music: "Rap, as a resentment listening music, collectively comprises the power of emancipated knowledges, the determination to change established society, and the anticipation of liberation" (Spencer 1992, 448).
2. For an analysis of the construction of masculinity in Springsteen's music, see Palmer 1997.
3. See, for instance, Gerics 1996, 20.

4. It is for this revelation of the transcendence of the ordinary that Catholic sociologist Andrew Greeley praises Springsteen and other popular culture artists who display a "Catholic imagination." See Greeley 1988.

5. According to Turner, *communitas* refers to the antistructural component of ritual life, characteristic of the relationships of those jointly undergoing ritual transformation. Communitas relationships are "undifferentiated, equalitarian, direct, extant, non-rational, I-Thou (in Feuerbach's and Buber's sense). . . . Communitas is spontaneous, immediate, concrete—it is not shaped by norms, it is not institutionalized, it is not abstract" (1974, 274).

REFERENCES

Bellah, Robert N., Richard Madsen, William M. Sullivan, Ann Swidler, and Steven M. Tipton. 1985. *Habits of the Heart: Individualism and Commitment in American Life*. Berkeley: University of California Press.

——, eds. 1987. *Individualism and Commitment in American Life: Readings on the Themes of Habits of the Heart*. New York: Harper and Row.

Cafe Utne: "Music.30: Bruce Springsteen: The Man and His Music" (www.utne.com/cafe/index.html), May 3, 1996.

Cherry, Conrad, ed. 1971. *God's New Israel: Religious Interpretations of American Destiny*. Englewood Cliffs, N.J.: Prentice Hall.

Cone, James. 1972. *The Spirituals and the Blues*. Maryknoll, N.Y.: Orbis Books.

Cullen, Jim. 1997. *Born in the USA: Bruce Springsteen and the American Tradition*. New York: HarperCollins.

Cross, Charles R., and the editors of *Backstreets* magazine. 1989. *Backstreets: Bruce Springsteen: The Man and His Music*. New York: Harmony Books.

Gerics, Joseph. 1996. "A Melancholy Boss: Springsteen's New Sound." *Commonweal*, February 9, 20–21.

Gilmore, Mikal. 1990. "Bruce Springsteen: What Does It Mean, Springsteen Asked, to Be an American?" Reprinted in *Bruce Springsteen: The Rolling Stone Files*, ed. editors of *Rolling Stone* (New York: Hyperion, 1996), 291–302.

Goodman, Fred. 1997. *The Mansion on the Hill: Dylan, Young, Geffen, Springsteen and the Head-On Collision of Rock and Commerce*. New York: Random House.

Greeley, Andrew. 1988. *God in Popular Culture*. Chicago: Thomas More Press.

McRobbie, Angela. 1980. "Settling Accounts with Subcultures: A Feminist Critique." Reprinted in *On Record: Rock, Pop, & the Written Word*, ed. Simon Frith and Andrew Goodwin. New York: Pantheon Books, 1990.

Palmer, Gareth. 1997. "Bruce Springsteen and Masculinity." In *Sexing the Groove: Popular Music and Gender*, ed. Sheila Whiteley. New York: Routledge.

Plaskow, Judith. 1990. *Standing Again at Sinai: Judaism from a Feminist Perspective*. New York: HarperCollins.

Spencer, Jon Michael. 1992. "Rhapsody in Black: Utopian Aspirations." *Theology Today* 48 (January): 444–51.

Springsteen, Bruce. 1998. "Rock and Read: Will Percy Interviews Bruce Springsteen." *DoubleTake* 12 (spring 1998): 36–43.

——. 1992. "The *Rolling Stone* Interview: Bruce Springsteen." By James Henke.

Reprinted in *Bruce Springsteen: The Rolling Stone Files*, ed. editors of *Rolling Stone* (New York: Hyperion, 1996), 318–33.

———. 1984. "The *Rolling Stone* Interview: Bruce Springsteen." By Kurt Loder. Reprinted in *Bruce Springsteen: The Rolling Stone Files*, ed. editors of *Rolling Stone* (New York: Hyperion, 1996), 151–65.

Turner, Victor. 1974. *Dramas, Fields and Metaphors: Symbolic Action in Human Society*. Ithaca, N.Y.: Cornell University Press.

Oprah, Phil, Geraldo, Barbara, and Things That Go Bump in the Night

Negotiating the Supernatural on American Television

LEONARD NORMAN PRIMIANO

No study of "God" in the details of everyday life in America would be complete without an account of the voluminous representations of religion/spirituality found on television. A major venue for such expressions is found in the personal religious narratives that are a staple of the television talk show.[1] Discussions on heaven and hell, pilgrimages to the Marian apparition site of Medjugorje in Catholic Croatia, hauntings, UFO abductions, near-death experiences, and angel visitations have been frequently found as a part of the talk show "genre" since its ascent in the 1980s. This chapter explores how these programs reflected the spirituality of North Americans at the end of the millennium and what they tell us about the process of vernacular religion—religion as it is lived in everyday life.

Talk shows, especially those with studio audiences and telephone callers, make constant use of the content and performance of what folklorists would technically call the "personal experience narrative," especially the "memorate," a first-person account of a supernatural experience.[2] Such stories serve numerous functions in the medium of television: they entertain; they act as cautionary and morality tales, illustrating the outcomes of certain actions; they exemplify the character and personal values of guests; they present traditional spiritual beliefs (see Dolby 1996, 557; Stahl 1989). Media producers use such stories to allure, keep, and focus an audience providing content that poses, but never completely examines or answers, significant existential questions for viewers.

One day Oprah Winfrey, popular American daytime talk show host, recounted on her broadcast an extraordinary story from her own life. It was not a narrative about her childhood, her trials with weight loss and gain, or her experiences with men. She was telling a ghost story, a memorate. The theme of this very entertaining 1991 episode of *Oprah* was haunted houses. The genesis of the program was a book on ghost/poltergeist experiences in homes that have been recently built over cemeteries, a theme also explored in the popular 1982 film *Poltergeist*. Residents of a suburban development built over grave sites stated that they were frightened to live in these homes. Ethereal figures appeared in the homes, and objects moved by themselves, the residents said. At about midpoint in a broadcast filled with statements of belief, disbelief, rationalization, and skepticism from the panel of "haunted" home owners, learned scholarly experts, and audience members, Ms. Winfrey unexpectedly complemented the ghostly sightings of her guests with a narrative of her own:

> Listen, I don't want to read about this in the tabloids, but . . . I live very high up . . . next to some buildings with lights. So [one night] I got up . . . [and] . . . I saw this thing, I don't know if it was a ghost or what, in a shadowlike white form, almost transparent, gliding across the floor. So I think, am I crazy, am I asleep? No, I get up, I go to the window, I look outside the window to make sure no lights, no planes, no helicopters are flickering. I saw the thing, so the next day . . . a friend of mine [who] was staying at my house . . . my guest bedroom, she said, "Oh I had such a terrible evening. There was a spirit in my room, and I was fighting it. I was fighting the spirit. . . ." This was just like her . . . yeh [I said], you fought it—into my room!. . . So I think that maybe certain people maybe attract this type of phenomenon.

In her brief account of a ghostly experience, and her own explanation of how spirits may be attracted to certain individuals, Oprah Winfrey continued the tradition of people telling folktales, legends, and personal-experience stories about revenants. Such ghost lore has circulated widely in oral tradition, in print, and in the mass media, especially television. In the case of memorates, television acts as both a conduit and a constraint on the transmission of such experiential narratives. Television conditions the message by the very nature of the electronic medium, because sustained, lengthy recitation of narrative experiences is not possible. Television offers brief, intense forms of communication. Fears that viewer interest will fade if visual stimulation lags, together with the necessities of packaging content and analysis into short segments because of the preeminence of advertising time, make short accounts of everyday life the preferred form of editorial style.

In her brief account, Winfrey confirms for many of her viewers beliefs in the supernatural they may have learned in childhood or developed as adults.[3] Such broadcasts not only provide a contemporary tableau of belief and disbelief in the supernatural and spiritual, but these occasions also allow viewers to observe in a public forum lively negotiations of belief and disbelief that are commonly a part of their own lives. These shows exemplify, even in their limited and controlled presentation, the vernacular religion of the American people:

a religiosity brimming with interpretation and negotiation of ultimate questions of the supernatural, of alternative belief systems, and of creative expressions of belief and practice (see Primiano 1995). Television, especially in its talk shows, highlights the religious negotiations of believers; guests justify what and why they believe and respond to alternative views by "expert" witnesses and average citizens like themselves. The vernacular religion of the laity as well as the clergy is represented by the comments of guest priests and ministers who reflect their own negotiations of normative religious traditions.

Though supernatural themes have been frequent topics on American television talk shows for twenty years, the history of such themes on prime-time comedy and drama dates to the early years of television. Situation comedies on the supernatural were inhabited by friendly ghosts such as *Topper* (1953–56 CBS, NBC, ABC) and *The Ghost and Mrs. Muir* (1968–70 NBC, ABC), both inspired by cinematic treatments; episodic dramas of empathetic angels interacting with humans, like Michael Landon's *Highway to Heaven* (1984–89 NBC) and *Touched by an Angel* (1994– CBS), have also been successful network series. The emotional impact, moralistic tone, and sense of moral accountability of such shows reflect the American need for hope and faith in the second half of the twentieth century (see Primiano 1998).[4]

American television has especially dramatized the supernatural through the presentation of occult/horror/suspense/fantasy/science fiction anthologies: *One Step Beyond* (syndicated title for *Alcoa Presents,* 1959–61 ABC); Rod Serling's *The Twilight Zone* (1959–64 CBS) and *Night Gallery* (1970–73 NBC); *The Outer Limits* (1963–65 ABC); *Journey to the Unknown* (1968–69 ABC); *Ghost Story* (1972–73 NBC); *Alfred Hitchcock Presents* (1955–65, 1985–86 CBS, NBC); *Thriller* (1960–62 NBC); *Tales of the Unexpected* (1977 NBC); *Tales from the Darkside* (1984–88 Syndicated); *Amazing Stories* (1985–87 NBC); *Friday the Thirteenth: The Series* (1987–90 Syndicated); and more recently the Fox Network's *Tales from the Crypt* (1994–FOX), *The X Files* (1993– FOX) and *Millennium* (1996–99 FOX). These fictionalized dramas emphasizing suspense often draw on an immense resource of supernatural and anomalous legendry: ghosts, vampires, werewolves, devils, aliens, and various mysterious killers. Supernatural evil and its destructiveness are the central themes of these programs. They portray everyday living in the modern world as morally ambiguous, frightening, ugly, and out of control. As a reflection on the moral climate of post–World War II America, these programs promote a sense of real disillusionment in institutions and the state of the world and teach their viewers that innocence is no protection in the face of such overpowering evil.

One should not be surprised by either the number of times supernatural programs have been presented on television or their appeal and absorption by the public. Since the early era of colonization, European residents of North America have been fascinated with the occult, such as Kabbalah, Free Masonry, Tarot, and astrology, as well as mixing supernatural ideas with their own institutionally learned Christianity to create their own brand of what Jon Butler has called "occult Christianity." He argues, "Magic and Christianity in colonial America were not generally different entities but were subsets of the same phenomenon—religion. They posited a resort to superhuman powers and they offered techniques for invoking those powers to control human events" (1979, 319). Butler has traced the roots of America's fascination with magical and occult arts, including astrology, divination, and witchcraft, showing them to be a potent force before 1720 and persisting, though in increasingly hidden forms, into the nineteenth century (Butler 1979, 1990; Albanese 1990). That trend, of course, is not limited to pre-modern America, but has continued into twentieth- and twenty-first century America, witnessed by the popular devotional literature on occultism, magic, witchcraft, and paganism (see Eller 1995; Harvey and Hardman 1996; Lewis 1996; Adler 1997; Starhawk 1999).

This trend has been exemplified by the success of cable access channels, non-network syndicated specials, and the syndicated talk show format pioneered by Phil Donahue, dedicated to frequent presentations of the supernatural using a "reality-based" approach, one that uses ordinary people telling their own stories.[5] From national network, syndicated, and cable talk/service programs (moderated by such hosts as Phil Donahue, Oprah Winfrey, Geraldo Rivera, Sally Jessy Raphaël, and Larry King), to news/talk magazines (with commentators such as Barbara Walters, Jane Pauley, and Ted Koppel) to local interview shows in every time slot, reality-based programs consistently used supernatural topics to boost ratings and stimulate imaginations.[6] Geraldo Rivera, the host of a daytime talk show which frequently tapped into supernatural topics as a resource for provocative subject matter, referred to his style of programming in a *New York Times* article as "nonfiction TV" (December 16, 1988, A39). Some critics have designated it "nonintelligent TV," "tabloid TV," or mere "sensationalism" because they see such media as presenting viewers with impressionistic and superficial analyses (see Jones 1989).

Sensationalized reports of supernatural events with a media personality presenting the facts of a case to an enthralled public are not restricted to television. Print media has a long history of popularizing and commercializing the supernatural. One of the most notorious cases centered on the "Cottingley fairies," tiny winged supernatural creatures which two young cousins reported to have photographed in the summer of 1917 in a Yorkshire village. None other than Sir Arthur Conan Doyle wrote an article about the incident in the quickly sold Christmas issue of *The Strand Magazine*. The article and two photographs supposedly capturing the image of fairies appeared under a banner headline "Fairies Photographed: An Epoch-Making Event Described by A. Conan Doyle" (Smith 1991, 388).[7]

The two standard bearers that all other talk shows attempted to imitate have been those hosted by Phil Donahue and Oprah Winfrey. These hourlong shows had a wide array of supernatural topics and guests. Phil Donahue, considered to be the "father" of the contemporary television talk show format, was the first host who actually interacted not only with guests, but also with studio audience members and noncelebrity telephone callers. His broadcast often presented information-oriented programs about both organized religion and popular spirituality. He, for example, devoted an entire hour to a discussion on the existence of heaven (October 31, 1988). Three Christian believers, two differing fundamentalists and a liberal Catholic priest, argued over issues of predestination, free will, universal salvation, biblical literacy, and interpretation. Also on the show were two former Christians, one currently a Wiccan priestess, the other a professed atheist, who talked about their religious perspectives. The show presented a magnificent exposition of traditional Christian belief positions about the afterlife and challenges to those perspectives, such as belief in reincarnation, with interaction from both the studio audience and home viewers.

The *Donahue Show* also programmed discussions of little known, mysterious, and maligned religious traditions such as contemporary witchcraft, neo-paganism, and Vodou, whose magical and supernatural practices were evoked through ritual occasions enacted for the television viewers. The program on the African-based religion Vodou (March 9, 1988) was precipitated by the release of the sensationalized motion picture of ethno-botanist Wade Davis's book *The Serpent and the Rainbow* (1986). Guests included a professor of religious studies, an actor from the film, an African-American "voodoo priestess," and a young, white, female journalist who was questioned about her own participation in a New York Vodou community. Though a movie may have precipitated this presentation, the discussion itself reflected the growth of African-based religions in urban America and balanced the more frequent stereotypical and sensational portrayals of Vodou.

Oprah Winfrey presented more experience-oriented shows, with children's near-death experiences, alien abductions, demonic possession, and supernatural erotica, such as the gray-haired, pie-baking woman on sexually inhibiting cardiac medication who reported having "an intense sexual experience" with a ghost (October 31, 1988). Winfrey used her own knowledge of Christianity and of the Christian Bible to interact with these guests, as she had in an earlier episode featuring a formerly possessed young woman and two "experts" on demonic possession (a Lutheran pastor and a former Jesuit, May 11, 1987). Winfrey questioned their beliefs on the power of demonic possession by appealing to a Biblical verse: "Well, the Bible says no weapon formed against me shall prosper, and if you believe that, and put on the whole armor of God, how is it that the devil can enter you?" This episode richly illustrated the negotiated beliefs of a Lutheran exorcist whose acceptance of possession and the ritual response of exorcism is unusual, as well as of the possessed woman herself, who claimed that she had never seen films like *The Exorcist* and that the idea of personal demonic possession was "contrary to my beliefs."

Oprah's affirmation of Christian belief through her own experience was unusual for American network television outside of televangelistic programming. She also seemed guided by her knowledge of Christianity when interacting with several brands of Satanists, especially Colonel Michael Aquino of the Temple of Set and his wife, Lilith (February 17, 1988). During the 1980s and into the 1990s, many television talk shows presented Satanism theme shows with Satanists as guests, as well as individuals who said they were possessed by the Christian devil. Satanists in these broadcasts were often juxtaposed with various anti-Satanists or purported vicitims of satanic abuse.

Live studio audiences are a significant component of all television talk shows. Populated by individuals who support or oppose the subject, they provide heated discussions and energize such a topic as contemporary Satanism. Audience members also become important to the viewing experience when the cameras pan the studio audience to register their reactions. Clearly one of the intended purposes of the program is to highlight audience reaction over and above the content of what a guest is actually saying. These audiences are intended not simply to react to what guests are saying, but also to participate more dynamically in the broadcast itself. The influence of producers is evident in this as they select audience members with opinions distinct from scheduled guests in the hopes of creating an atmosphere of provocation.

Both Phil Donahue and Sally Jessy Raphaël presented discussions on how toys can be used as teachers of Satanism in regard to devotional iconography of world religions. Hinduism and Buddhism, for example, were inappropriately described by Christian panelists as proponents of satanic ideas because of their use of devotional images of deities, as well as representations of the demonic (ghosts, demons, evil spirits, that is, spiritual beings of ambivalent or negative moral character). Because of a fear of spreading ideas about Satanism to impressionable children and teenagers who listened to such programs after returning home from school, and pressure from parents, educators, and civic authorities, American talk shows limited their presentation of satanic themes in the 1990s.

The four American television networks dominant in this period (American Broadcasting Company, Columbia Broadcasting System, National Broadcasting Corporation, and FOX Broadcasting) also presented discussions of supernatural phenomena on prime-time "specials" and theme segments of prime-time television magazines. Two prominent examples are the NBC television documentary by Geraldo Rivera, "Devil Worship: Exposing Satan's Underground," and the presentation of a filmed Roman Catholic exorcism on ABC's newsmagazine, *20/20*.

The "Devil Worship" special, shown on October 25, 1988, thrived on negativity, controversy, and misinformation. On this occasion, Geraldo Rivera presented an "investigative report" composed of filmed segments, satellite hookups, and studio interviews with clergy, police officials, former members of satanic cults, Satanist organizations, concerned parents, teenagers, heavy metal performers, social workers, and other mental health professionals. These guests represented a tapestry of traditional Christian fears of the devil and satanic worship. Such fears include belief in the existence of ritual abuse, ritual sacrifice, possession and exorcism, and the satanic influence on the young through popular music and entertainment media. The program's major point also expressed a traditional Christian anxiety concerning diabolical activity combined with a traditional American anxiety concerning the conspiracy of covert organizations, whether sociopolitical or religious. It presented and affirmed belief that North America harbors a network of satanic groups who covertly practice ritual sexual abuse and torture, as well as animal and human sacrifice. The program made no attempt to distinguish between demonic possession and exorcism in Roman Catholicism, constitutionally safeguarded Satan worshipers, teenage heavy metal/punk dabblers, and mentally unbalanced individuals who "murder for Satan." It also did not distinguish acknowledged Afro-Caribbean religions, such as Vodou and Santeria, which practice animal sacrifice, from Satanism.

The primary message of this Geraldo special was that an underground of Satan-worshiping groups has infiltrated every public and private sphere, engaging in covert and malicious activities. There is, however, no supportable testimony or evidence of human sacrifice by Satanists. Those who have come forward as "survivors" of satanic groups and claim to have borne children in captivity for ritual sacrifices have been shown to be frauds, in one case by an evangelical Christian magazine called the *Cornerstone* (see Passantino et al. 1989), which tracked down ambiguities and inconsistencies in one survivor's account. Thus, although the Geraldo special purported to represent an enormous diversity of opinion, testimony, and factual evidence, the substance of this program simply nurtured the growing cultural hysteria concerning Satanism in America, which some scholars have labeled the "Satanic Panic" (see Richardson et al. 1991; Victor 1993). Its body of evidence has been challenged by vigilant and rigorous scholarly examination and analysis, as well as by investigations by law enforcement officials, showing that these beliefs in satanic conspiracy are unfounded.[8]

Notable from a folkloristic perspective is how this program spread these fearful attitudes. In fact, paranoia has been encouraged by television reporters and talk show hosts who themselves had been convinced of the reality of satanic activity by a cycle of contemporary legends.[9] For the public, the media functioned in this case as the electronic equivalent of a tradition bearer, spreading beliefs, images, interpretations, and even the associated vocabulary of any number of contemporary legends concerning Satanism, satanic crimes, and abuses (see Richardson et al. 1991; Victor 1993). Geraldo, like many of the tabloid programmers, has made an art of reporting on legends as if they were "factual" news. To quote folklorists Linda Dégh and Andrew Vazsonyi: "It is not enough to acknowledge that mass media has a 'role' in modern legend-transmission. It is closer to the truth to state that the mass media are *part* of folklore—maybe the greater part. The legend makes a part of its way—presumably the lesser—on foot and continues on the longer trail through the speedy modern vehicle" (1973, 37; see also Dégh 1994, 25). In Geraldo's program it is possible to see how people negotiate a legend into a fact, and for that matter a belief or experience into a legend which can eventually be reported in print and electronic media (see Oring 1990).

Perhaps the most extraordinary reportage of the supernatural on television was a *20/20* hosted by Hugh Downs and Barbara Walters, broadcast on April 5, 1991, in which reporter Tom Jarriel interviewed all of the participants in a Roman Catholic ritual of exorcism both before and after the ceremony was filmed in a Florida convent. This included the priest who was to perform the exorcism, the Florida teenager who was thought to be possessed, the child's psychiatrist, and the various clerical and health professionals who assisted. What was particularly amazing about this program was, first, that exorcisms were still being performed under Catholic auspices in the 1990s, and, second, that the Catholic Church and the girl's family would allow it to be videotaped and televised. Traditionally, the identity of possessed individuals and their families is kept private. In this case, however, the identity of the exorcist was, as has been the traditional practice, kept secret to preserve him from the spiritual danger of attracting the attention of demonic forces in the world, but the girl in question was named and filmed with the full consent of her mother and the Church.

Although exorcism has a long history in the Catholic Church, after the changes and reforms of the Second Vatican Council, many such ritual practices fell into disfavor and disuse. It is not clear whether the Church's interest in publicizing such rites when it appeared to have deemphasized them in the contemporary Western world is a result of the Church's perception of the rise of the demonic in the world or an increase in human susceptibility to such forces.[10] One of the priests involved with the exorcism did indicate that the Roman Catholic hierarchy agreed to this broadcast because the general secularized population seems to disbelieve that personified evil exists in the world, and in this case one presumes he means specific supernatural causes of evil behavior.[11] At the same time, a priest who was also a psychiatrist spoke openly that as a trained medical practitioner he would be troubled with any diagnosis declaring someone demonically possessed. His comments highlighted his own negotiations of the Church's beliefs and practices regarding possession and exorcism with his beliefs and training as a scientist. Although far removed from the Rivera special in treatment, tone, and content, the 20/20 program also conformed to the frequent television portrayal of the supernatural as fearful and threatening.

Writing about framing conflict on the daytime talk show, folklorist Dylan Eret has argued that it is common to see "the polarization of viewpoints on the show, especially if the show's topic centers around some controversial issue. Because of these prefabricated constraints, participants on the talk show are usually forced to firmly hold onto their own beliefs or viewpoints and are less accepting of others. Agreement becomes devalued and argumentation becomes the primary mode of communication" (Eret 1997). An additional problem with this polarization of perspectives is that it does not allow for an appreciation of the nuanced and negotiated beliefs held by members of organized religions. In the defense of a particular stand, institutionalized "religion," therefore, is represented as one-dimensional, insular, unchanging.

When guests do not fit into these stereotypes, such as the appearance of a progressive Roman Catholic priest on Phil Donahue's program on the existence of heaven, viewers can become confused because they expect a traditionally conservative representation of the clergy.

As a balance to such religious representations of the spirituality, television has also offered more neutral representations. From the group-oriented experience of pagan spirituality at the 1990 summer solstice on a local Philadelphia morning show to the personal ecstasy of the near-death experience recounted by a woman on Oprah Winfrey's program in October 1990, affirmations of personal and group engagement with the supernatural were evident.

The interview with the woman who had a near-death experience was broadcast in the months following the success of the movie *Ghost* (1990). Typical of television talk shows, the memorate of Caryl Roberts, a highly articulate woman, was interrupted and hurried along by the host during her interview. The integrity of her first-person narrative of the supernatural, however, remained intact, sustained by her creative association of it with her Christian religious beliefs, her rational assessment of evidence as to the reality of this supernatural incident, and her enthusiastic retelling of this narrative. When asked by Oprah about the validity of her out-of-body experience, she said with great power: "I was there. I was more there than I am here right now." For her part, Oprah treated her guest's experience positively, affirming it through her receptive approach to the information and her respect for the integrity of her guest.

These televised discussions also offered invaluable occasions for the observation of the vernacular religious process among women. Daytime talk shows are said to have been produced specifically with a female audience in mind, and they reflect both the intimacy of women's communication and the artfulness of women's spiritual belief and practice.[12] Women's exclusion or marginalization from power within institutional Christianity in America has stimulated them to express their independent voices through vernacular religion while their traditional role within the institutional Church has promoted their acceptance of patriarchal boundaries limiting women. The existence and influence of the vernacular religion of women have been expressed in a multitude of active and passive ways, frequently presented on television talk shows. Women have told stories of their strong attraction and commitment to particular religions and have narrated the evolution of their own religious roles as mystics, healers, visionaries, mediums, vessels of possession, and devotees of sacred figures.

For some viewers, a given broadcast may have been where they first learned about a particular spiritual experience. For others, it reinforced or supplemented a belief tradition they already accepted. While television has been regarded as a destabilizing and secularizing influence on the public's relationship to organized religion, it has acted as a fertile transmitter of traditional beliefs, personal spiritualities, mystical experiences, and supernatural phenomena. The nature of television is that it expresses individuals' views while simultaneously influencing them. Television media treatment may often trivialize and sensationalize personal experiences of the supernatural, but it can also inspire and inform. Producers of talk shows, news magazines, or episodic dramas perceptively pick up interests within the American population and produce cultural products that continue discussions that viewers are already having with each other. Additionally, programs representing the supernatural appeal to the broadest range of American audiences because they do not relate to a particular denominational perspective within America's religious pluralism; rather, they complement the more general interest in all things spiritual. In their presentation of a plurality of perspectives, television talk shows and newsmagazines in the 1980s and 1990s became forums for the views of institutional religious representatives and a variety of belief systems described as contemporary spiritualities.[13] "Religion" presented on such programs can be perceived as organized, established forms of religious belief and practice: that is, religious traditions that have taken institutional form. "Spirituality," however, can be understood as more multilayered belief and practice, representing the core truths of one or several religious traditions, contributing to the creation and nurturing of private (and sometimes communal) belief systems.

Scholarship on post-1950s American religion (Wuthnow 1998; Roof 1993, 1999) has stressed that Americans have shifted from a "spirituality of dwelling" within organized religious denominations to a "spirituality of seeking" the meaning of the sacred within one's life.[14] Robert Wuthnow sees America's social complexities causing a sense of "spiritual homelessness" because of social fragmentation, increasing social mobility, and a movement away from denominational affiliation. A "dwelling-oriented" spirituality, therefore, is difficult to maintain. An important element within seeking-oriented spirituality for Wuthnow is the negotiation by individuals of sacred beliefs and practices. Such negotiations free one "to maneuver among the uncertainties of contemporary life and capitalizes on the availability of a wide variety of sources piecing together idiosyncratic conceptions of spirituality"

(1998, 168). This spirituality of seeking is characterized by a deeply personal but transient religiosity with roots in traditional religious beliefs and practices; an interest in noninstitutionalized religious contexts; and an eclectic, idiosyncratic, and at times isolated spirituality fascinated with the supernatural. Talk show episodes on the supernatural in the 1980s and 1990s reflect the sense of negotiation within religious lives related to this "seeking-oriented spirituality" (Wuthnow 1998, 114–41).

Television programs devoted to spirituality have allowed viewers to experience two important traditions of religious narrative in contemporary America: religious testimonial and memorate recitation. Along with the content within these electronic forms of religious folklore, viewers are able to witness an informant utilizing verbal art and breaking through into performance, even if prompted by the host/interviewer. Such performances are an art form worthy of consideration.[15] Whether it is the first or one hundredth time these religious narratives have been told, there remains a process of creativity involved in their performance. Powerful contemporary narrative traditions of the supernatural can, thus, be discerned even within their compartmentalized and sensationalized presentation on television. Such occasions build an appreciation of a living and vital narrative belief tradition integral to everyday life both formed by and yet transcending the borders of the media context. Beyond the sentimentality or artificiality of the television context, the quality of religious negotiation inherent in these oral performances remains. This spirituality of negotiation and choice, however, is not merely a contemporary phase of American religious life, but an expression of a continuum of religious negotiation intrinsic to the reality of being a vernacularly religious person. This vernacular media process bridges historic and contemporary religion. There is an ocean of spiritual beliefs being negotiated in these contemporary media "texts" hosted by Oprah, Phil, Geraldo, and Barbara which will continue to stimulate and inform America's viewing public and stand as a witness to our experience of God in the details of everyday life.

NOTES

1. I include in this genre "news/talk magazines" and "talk/service programs" found in network, syndicated, and local daytime and prime-time evening broadcasts.
2. See von Sydow (1948), Honko (1989), Sweterlitsch (1996), Pentikainen (1997).
3. Sparks, Hansen, and Shah (1994) and Sparks, Nelson, and Campbell (1997) conducted communications research into the possible relationship of exposure

by viewers to television programs with "paranormal" content and their belief in such phenomena. I use the term "supernatural" rather than paranormal in this article because I believe it to be a more inclusive and appropriate term for religious studies. In the West, the term has been used commonly to encompass the human experience of the sacred, holy, and the ultimate within various spiritual traditions. "Paranormal" is a pseudo-scientific term for experiences that can be explained as purely mental processes, as well as the social motivations that condition such processes, whereas the "supernatural" is only meaningful within a religious belief system (see Despland 1987).

4. While affiliation with organized religious institutions has dropped in the United States in the last thirty years, the public interest and belief in things spiritual has remained vigorous (see Gallup and Newport 1991; Gallup 1996). Gray and Sparks (1996) found in a preliminary study that "over half of prime time programs contain at least one mention or depiction" of "paranormal phenomena." Research from a 1997 edition of *TV Guide* considering the theme "God and Television" reported that 68 percent of American poll respondents "were particularly eager to see more prime time spirituality." The magazine defined spirituality as "a belief in a higher being, but not necessarily an affiliation with a particular organized religion" (Kaufman 1997, 34). For a late 1990s perspective on "TV's new openness to spirituality," see also Rosenberg (1999).

5. The issue-oriented daytime talk show is what most Americans think of when they consider pre-1994 talk shows. In the 1980s, the four highest rated talk shows according to the A. C. Nielsen ratings, were *Geraldo* (1986– Syndicated), *The Oprah Winfrey Show* (1986–Syndicated), *The Phil Donahue Show* (1969–96 Syndicated), and *Sally Jessy Raphael* (1984–Syndicated). Shattuc comments that it was in 1994 that the talk show form started to change direction (1997, 3). The 1990s saw a shift in such shows, especially with the development of "confrontational" panel shows, such as *The Jerry Springer Show* (1991–). For a discussion of the future of TV talk shows, see Abt and Mustazza (1997).

6. I could also cite documentary series (such as *Unsolved Mysteries* (1988– NBC) and tabloid television newsmagazines such as *A Current Affair* (1986–96 Syndicated), *American Journal* (1993–98 Syndicated), and *Hard Copy* (1989– Syndicated).

7. This incident continues to be memorialized, with these "fairies" having made the technological progression from photograph to film in the recent movie directed by Charles Sturbridge, *Fairy Tale: A True Story* (1997).

8. For a critical review of this special in the popular press, see Nathan (1988). It must also be noted that local law enforcement has often played a significant role in perpetuating the negative public opinion of satanic activities and influence.

9. See Mechling (1996) for a brief introductory discussion on mass media and folklore. See also Bird (1976), Klintberg (1981), Oring (1990), Smith (1997). In this context, the concept of "legend" refers to narratives generated by people's beliefs and not specific historical or actual events, so they are believed to be true, but not actually true.

10. In 1999, the Roman Catholic Church issued a new Revised Rite of Exorcisms in

an eighty-four page Latin text which replaced the 1614 version. See Tagliabue (1999).

11. See Turque (1991) for a report on reaction to the broadcast.

12. Shattuc sees talk shows in the years 1980–95 (specifically *Geraldo, The Oprah Winfrey Show, The Phil Donahue Show,* and *Sally Jessy Raphael*) as important venues for average stay-at-home Americans, especially lower- and middle-class women, "to debate social issues that affected their everyday lives" (1997, 197–98). These daytime talk shows functioned to assist individual needs of viewers, but they also worked to gather together the collective consciousness of their female audience. "Their claim to personal fulfillment through commercial consumption is counterbalanced by their veiled feminism and a consciousness of the inequalities of power. Their principal social aim has been to build up women's self-esteem, confidence, and identity.... The shows are venues where women of different races and classes attempt to claim power" (1997, 121–22). Significant changes in the themes and guests of the programs hosted by Rivera, Winfrey, Donahue, and Raphael started in 1994–95 especially because of conservative political pressures. "The coherence of this group became clearer with the rise of the 'youth' talk shows of the 1990s [e.g. *Jenny Jones* (1991– Syndicated); *The Ricki Lake Show* (1993– Syndicated)], which shifted the genre away from identity politics toward a more apolitical and ironic treatment of social issues" (1997, 9).

13. In the 1980s and 1990s, according to Roof, spirituality reemerged "as a grassroots movement.... The diversity of spirituality reflects, of course, a consumer culture, but also a rich and empowering melding of traditions and existential concerns" (Roof 1993, 243–44; see also Wuthnow 1998, 72–74).

14. This spirituality of seeking has been especially associated with the American "baby boomer" generation, who were born over the span of years from 1946 to 1964 and represent a population of 76 million men and women (Roof 1993, 1).

15. Even if the believer is a "paid" guest or is retelling the story for attention, these conditions do not devalue the artfulness of the telling, and they provide valuable lessons to those studying "religious folklore" in context. For further explanations of religious folklore, see Primiano (1997) and Danielson (1986).

REFERENCES

Abt, Vicki, and Leonard Mustazza. 1997. *Coming After Oprah: Cultural Fallout in the Age of the TV Talk Show.* Bowling Green, Ohio: Bowling Green State University Popular Press.

Adler, Margot. 1997. *Drawing Down the Moon: Witches, Druids, Goddess Worshippers and Other Pagans in America Today.* New York: Viking.

Albanese, Catherine L. 1990. *Nature Religion in America: From the Algonkian Indians to the New Age.* Chicago: University of Chicago Press.

Bird, Donald Allport. 1976. "A Theory for Folklore in Mass Media: Traditional Patterns in Mass Media." *Southern Folklore Quarterly* 40: 285–305.

Butler, Jon. 1979. "Magic, Astrology, and the Early American Religious Heritage, 1600–1760." *American Historical Review* 84 (2): 317–46.

———. 1990. *Awash in a Sea of Faith: Christianizing the American People.* Cambridge, Mass.: Harvard University Press.

Danielson, Larry. 1986. "Religious Folklore." In *Folk Groups and Folklore Genres: An Introduction,* ed. Elliott Oring, 45–69. Logan: Utah State University Press.

Davis, Wade. 1986. *The Serpent and the Rainbow.* New York: Simon and Schuster.

Dégh, Linda. 1994. *American Folklore and the Mass Media.* Bloomington: Indiana University Press.

Dégh, Linda, and Andrew Vazsonyi. 1973. "The Dialectics of the Legend." *Folklore Preprint Series* 1: 6.

Despland, Michel. 1987. "The Supernatural." In *The Encyclopedia of Religion,* ed. Mircea Eliade, 14: 159–63. New York: Macmillan.

Dolby, Sandra K. 1996. "Personal-Experience Story." In *American Folklore: An Encyclopedia,* ed. Jan Harold Brunvand, 556–58. New York: Garland.

Eller, Cynthia. 1995. *Living in the Lap of the Goddess: The Feminist Spirituality Movement in America.* Boston: Beacon Press.

Eret, Dylan. 1997. "Arguing About Belief: The Public Presentation of Belief on the Donahue Show 'Is There a Hell?'" Unpublished paper.

Gallup, George H., Jr. 1996. *Religion in America: 1996 Report.* Princeton, N.J.: Princeton Religion Research Center.

Gallup, George H., Jr., and Frank Newport. 1991. "Belief in Paranormal Phenomena Among Adult Americans." *Skeptical Inquirer* 15: 137–146.

Gray, K., and G. G. Sparks, 1996. "A Content Analysis of Paranormal Events on Prime-Time Television." Unpublished data.

Hadden, Jeffrey K. 1993. "The Rise and Fall of American Televangelism." *The Annals of the American Academy of Political and Social Science* 527: 113–30.

Hadden, Jeffrey K., and Charles E. Swann. 1981. *Prime Time Preachers: The Rising Power of Televangelism.* Reading, Mass.: Addison-Wesley.

Harvey, Graham, and Charlotte Hardman eds. 1996. *Paganism Today.* London: Thorsons.

Honko, Lauri. 1989. "Memorates and the Study of Folk Belief." In *Nordic Folklore: Recent Studies,* ed. Reimund Kvideland and Henning K. Sehmsdorf, 100–9. Bloomington: Indiana University Press. Reprint of 1964 *Journal of the Folklore Institute.*

Jones, Alex S. 1989. "'Trash TV' Debated at Editors' Convention." *New York Times,* April 13, C36.

Kaufman, Joanne. 1997. "Tuning in to God." *TV Guide,* March 29–April 4, 33–35.

Klintberg, Bengt. 1981. "Modern Migratory Legends in Oral Tradition and Daily Papers." *ARV: The Scandinavian Yearbook of Folklore* 37: 153–60.

Lewis, James R., ed. 1996. *Magical Religion and Modern Witchcraft.* Albany: State University of New York Press.

Mechling, Jay. 1996. "Mass Media and Folklore." In *American Folklore: An Encyclopedia,* ed. Jan Harold Brunvand, 462–63. New York: Garland.

Nathan, Debbie. 1988. "Devil Worship: Exposing Geraldo's Special." *The Village Voice*, November 8: 57–58.

Oring, Elliott. 1990. "Legend, Truth and News." *Southern Folklore* 47: 163–77.

Passantino, Gretchen, and Bob Passantino with Jon Trott. 1989. "Satan's Sideshow." *Cornerstone* 18 (90): 23–28.

Pentikainen, Juha. 1997. "Memorate." In *Folklore: An Encyclopedia of Beliefs, Customs, Tales, Music, and Art*, ed. Thomas A. Green, 553–55. Santa Barbara, Calif.: ABC-CLIO.

Primiano, Leonard Norman. 1995. "Vernacular Religion and the Search for Method in Religious Folklife." *Western Folklore* 54: 37–56.

———. 1997. "Folk Religion." In *Folklore: An Encyclopedia of Beliefs, Customs, Tales, Music, and Art*, ed. Thomas A. Green, 710–17. Santa Barbara, Calif.: ABC-CLIO.

———. 1998. "On Angels and Americans." *America* 179 (10 October): 15–17.

Richardson, James T., Joel Best, and David Bromley, eds. 1991. *The Satanism Scare*. New York: Aldine de Gruyter.

Roof, Wade Clark. 1993. *A Generation of Seekers: The Spiritual Journeys of the Baby Boom Generation*. San Francisco: Harper San Francisco.

———. 1999. *Spiritual Marketplace; Baby Boomers & the Remaking of American Religion*. Princeton, N.J.: Princeton University Press.

Rosenberg, Howard. 1999. "TV's New Openness to Spirituality Shows in Unexpected Places." *Philadelphia Inquirer*, June 17, E6.

Shattuc, Jane M. 1997. *The Talking Cure: TV Talk Shows and Women*. New York: Routledge.

Smith, Paul. 1997. "Contemporary Legend." In *Folklore: An Encyclopedia of Beliefs, Customs, Tales, Music, and Art*, ed. Thomas A. Green, 493–95. Santa Barbara, Calif.: ABC-CLIO.

———. 1991. "The Cottingley Fairies: The End of a Legend." In *The Good People: New Fairylore Essays*, ed. Peter Narváez, 371–405. New York: Garland.

Sparks, Glenn G., Tricia Hansen, and Rani Shah. 1994. "Do Televised Depictions of Paranormal Events Influence Viewers' Paranormal Beliefs?" *Skeptical Inquirer* 18: 386–95.

Sparks, Glenn G., C. Leigh Nelson, and Rose G. Campbell. 1997. "The Relationship between Exposure to Televised Messages About Paranormal Phenomena and Paranormal Beliefs." *Journal of Broadcasting & Electronic Media* 41: 345–59.

Stahl, Sandra K. Dolby. 1989. *Literary Folkloristics and the Personal Narrative*. Bloomington: Indiana University Press.

Starhawk. 1999. *The Spiral Dance: A Rebirth of the Ancient Religion of the Great Goddess—Rituals/Invocations/Exercises/Magic*. San Francisco: HarperCollins.

Sweterlitsch, Richard. 1996. "Memorate." In *American Folklore: An Encyclopedia*, ed. Jan Harold Brunvand, 472–73. New York: Garland.

Tagliabue, John. 1999. "The Pope's Visit: The Doctrine; Vatican's Revised Exorcism Rite Affirms Existence of Devil." *New York Times*, January 27, A16.

Turque, Bill. 1991. "The Exorcism of Gina." *Newsweek*, April 15, 62.

Victor, Jeffrey S. 1993. *Satanic Panic: The Creation of a Contemporary Legend.* Chicago: Open Court.

von Sydow, Carl Wilhelm. 1948. *Selected Papers on Folklore: Published on the Occasion of His 70th Birthday.* Copenhagen: Rosenkilde and Bagger.

Wuthnow, Robert. 1998. *After Heaven: Spirituality in America since the 1950s.* Berkeley: University of California Press.

A Fire in the Sky

"Apocalyptic" Themes on the Silver Screen

JON R. STONE

The wildly evocative image at the conclusion of Stanley Kubrick's 1964 movie *Dr. Strangelove*, of Slim Pickens riding the "Bomb" downward through the sky, as if he were trying to tame a raging bull, points out, in perhaps the most perverse way, the irony of a society living in fear of the very weapon it sees as its salvation from fear. As we know from the film, an insanely paranoid Air Force general (Sterling Hayden) has sent a flight of bombers on a preemptive nuclear airstrike against the Soviet Union. By the final scene of the movie, with the threat of Soviet retaliation looming over them, the U.S. authorities have succeeded in their frantic attempts to recall or have the bombers shot down. All of the planes and their crews have been neutralized except one: *Leper Colony*, the renegade B-52 piloted by Pickens. Over the drop site its bomb-bay doors jam. To free the bomb, Pickens throws himself atop its steely back. With a bump and a yelp, Pickens releases the "bull" from its pen. Both rider and beast plummet earthward: mission accomplished.

The message of *Dr. Strangelove*'s comically dark conclusion seems clear enough: a society can no more safely hold the destructive power contained in a nuclear warhead than it can control the unbridled spirit of a wild and willful beast. In fact, this "beast" has a way of controlling those who think themselves its master. Tragically, modern society's predicament becomes an inescapable dilemma: our future is as much in our hands as it is out of our hands. Once it is unleashed by human science, the destructive power of nuclear weapons is no longer ours to control. The bomb becomes as much a demon as it is a god. In the end, the only logical response to this Damoclesian dilemma, as the subtitle of this film wryly puts it, is to learn "to stop worrying and love the bomb."

The twisted humor of the closing scene—the Soviets' swift and devastating nuclear retaliation that destroys the world, with the final burlesque of A-bomb explosions mushrooming high into the earth's atmosphere—is not meant to frighten the moviegoer as much as it is to accustom the viewer to the sight, the sound, and the grand drama and pageantry of the end of humankind. There is, as it were, an exaggerated vaudevillean quality that takes away the sting even as it stings: actors and audience laugh at the absurdity of each other and at the senseless circumstance into which they have together fallen. That is, actors and audience see themselves and their situation in the reflection of the other. Both are doomed. The unfortunate fact about the bomb that stays with the audience even after the house lights have gone up is the realization that the images on the screen and the circumstances of modern life are really no laughing matter.

POSTWAR AMERICAN ANGST

Living in the shadow of the mushroom cloud was an inescapable fact of life for Americans who came of age soon after World War II ended. Ironically, though a remarkably resourceful and resilient generation of Americans had defeated one fascist regime after another, it could not evade the truth that, in doing so, it had resorted to military technologies possessing a destructive force that could not be imagined or described except in biblical—that is, "apocalyptic"—terms. Now, for the first time in human history, human beings had the power to anni- hilate whole civilizations, the power to incinerate their own planet, the power, indeed, to destroy themselves and even the memory of themselves. The atomic exclamation point that ended the Second World War became a looming ques- tion mark over the future of world civilization. For the immediate postwar gen- eration, then, who saw the newsreel footage of the war's thunderous conclusion, the destructive power that it had unleashed to save the free world from the nightmare of fascist totalitarianism became an even greater power to fear.

Notwithstanding its menacing presence, the atomic bomb represented but one of a number of inescapable existential facts with which Americans living during the postwar period and into the present have had to grapple. Threats to the natural environment, as predicted by Rachel Carson in her 1962 exposé, *Silent Spring*, about the consequences of the unchecked use of pesticides, were likewise couched in "apocalyptic," end-of-the-world, language. As a result of the unprecedented growth of industrial civilization in the nineteenth and twen- tieth centuries, human society had created the conditions under which, by the latter half of the twentieth century, ecological "meltdown" became not only possible but almost inevitable. While humankind had made significant advances in science and technology—advances that lengthened and improved the lives of people throughout the world—those same humans were contaminating their environment through the unregulated dumping of toxic waste and other pol- lutants into the sky, the land, and the sea. Even as humanity was attempting to escape the nightmare of a nuclear holocaust through diplomacy and détente, it was poisoning itself through careless management of the environment. An environmental holocaust was in the making, one in which humankind would slowly choke itself by its own polluted hands.

The blame, many believed, lay entirely at the feet of the twin gods of science and technology. Science and technology, heralded as the champions of modern civilization, had proved instead to be its betrayers. The promise that human science and technology held out for a greater tomorrow did not come without serious problems. Their supposed benefits had unpredictable, and sometimes deadly, consequences for human society. In fact, as some would claim, the very advances that science and technology offered as solutions to one urgent problem oftentimes gave rise to a series of new problems which, in turn, demanded even more urgent solutions. For instance, while the automation of factory assembly lines sped production of and provided less expensive products for middle-class homes, it inadvertently led to factory layoffs of large populations of unskilled laborers as well as the downsizing of many skilled laborers. At the same time, technology, especially in the computer field, advanced beyond the capacity of a work force it was intended to aid, making many "virtual" slaves of the machines that had been created to serve them. The recent Y2K computer scare illustrates yet another instance of human subservience to technology.

So, as with the atomic bomb and with industrial pollution, by the latter half of the twentieth century, technology itself, the idea of human progress through the application of scientific discovery, had likewise threatened to destroy humanity even as it sought to save it. It is not surprising, then, that such fears found expression in the film and print media of the postwar period, especially in science fiction, a genre well suited to "apocalyptic" themes. It is upon this genre of film that this essay focuses.

"APOCALYPSE" AND "APOCALYPTIC"

It has become commonplace to speak of any cataclysmic event as an "apocalypse" or as "apocalyptic." Such colloquial misuse of these potent terms, though widespread, stems from a conceptual and definitional misunderstanding. By definition, apocalypses are revelatory texts whose sources of knowledge are otherworldly or divine. As such, an apocalypse reveals a reality not previously known to the apocalypt, the recipient of the revelation, or to its intended audience. As a literary genre, an apocalypse has two common elements: its revelatory narrative framework and its eschatological orientation, an orientation that anticipates final judgment and punishment of the wicked. Apocalypses sometimes include other elements, such as belief in the supernatural control or divine predetermination of human history, in the inevitable triumph of good over evil, in divine judgment of all persons living and dead, and in the renewal of the cosmos or in the eventual restoration of a golden age. To be sure, while what is usually revealed to the apocalypt is sometimes pandemic in its scope and often cataclysmic in its effect, one should not confuse the *source* of the apocalypse with its eschatological (end of the world) *content*, especially if one seeks to draw analytical distinctions among genre of literature or, in this case, film.[1] To do so would empty literary terms of their analytical usefulness. Put differently, while a common motif of an apocalypse is the "destruction of the wicked," the mere triumph of good over evil does not an apocalypse make. The prediction of imminent and utter destruction may very well be part of an apocalypse, but such content does not define this genre as a whole. It has a far deeper and more intentioned meaning that goes far beyond fire and brimstone.[2]

Interestingly, as a worldview or as a way of making sense of human events, the elements that typify apocalyptic literature are found in other cultural media, media that likewise make claims of "otherworldly" sources. In fact, one can discern the apocalyptic or revelatory worldview in a variety of cultural artifacts of modern American society, from popular fiction to popular films. This revelatory element is especially evident within films broadly classed as science fiction.

"APOCALYPTIC FICTION"

Movies function both as a reflection and as a critique of society. Most, however, while pointing to perilous flaws in modern life, do not point to otherworldly sources as the source of their critique of culture. But, over the past several decades, a more specialized genre of science fiction film has developed that presents a vision of what the future may hold for the modern scientific age. We might call this revelatory genre of film "apocalyptic fiction," not because its subject is cataclysmic per se but because its generic form is similar to that of an apocalypse and its underlying function is that of a warning of imminent danger and of a way to avert impending doom.[3]

Indeed, the medium through which apocalyptic fiction conveys its revelatory material — the motion picture — is well suited as a channel of divine or otherworldly warning in that, like ancient apocalypses, its dramatic message is also broadcast through the immediacy of words and a parade of vivid images. The pictures cast upon the movie screen not only project images that are intended to shock and awaken the audience, but these images also reflect back to society something of its own fears and concerns. As a mediator between the revealed message and its intended audience, the "silver screen" fulfils two purposes: it is at once a *medium* that presents images of interest and concern to the audience and at the same time a *mirror* that reflects back upon its viewers. In the latter instance, much like a mirror that reveals what stands before it as it really appears, the movie screen becomes a device that shows us ourselves—warts and all.[4] As before, it is this revelatory aspect of the movie screen that interests us in this essay, for it is in this genre, "apocalyptic fiction," that the latent uneasiness of postwar American society dramatically reveals itself.[5]

If an apocalypse is a revelation of esoteric or previously inaccessible knowledge, then it is fair to ask what specific kind of knowledge apocalyptic fiction reveals. In essence, the revelation is of a reality not previously known to the apocalypt, such as the revelation of a heavenly realm, of coming destruction, or of cosmic regeneration. For instance, while in the case of the film *Blade Runner* (1982), the revelation is of a bleaker tomorrow, the revelation may also be of a brighter tomorrow; such is the case with the onetime popular futuristic movie *Logan's Run* (1976).[6] In addition to the revelation of either a pessimistic or optimistic future for humankind, we might add that apocalyptic fiction also contains a number of elements that may or may not be present in other types of popular science fiction films. These include: (1) the tyranny of science and technology; (2) human helplessness in the face of an evil system or corrupt world order; (3) heightened Cold War antagonisms, usually resulting in a nuclear holocaust; (4) a messianic component in which an anointed person will rescue humanity; (5) the inescapable fact that the protagonist must embrace his or her destiny or calling; (6) the expectation of the eventual destruction of the world through some humanly engineered disaster; and (7) the need for outside or otherworldly intervention to remedy hopeless circumstances.

Additionally, there seem to be two key differences between literary apocalypses and what I am calling American "apocalyptic fiction," one having to do with the *message* and the other with the *messenger*. The first difference is that in every case it is assumed that the predicted cataclysmic event can be averted by human action. The second difference is that, in most cases, the messenger of the apocalypse or the one to whom the message is given becomes the agent of salvation, that is, the savior of humanity. In American apocalyptic fiction—and perhaps in American films more generally—there appears to be an underlying optimism that defies the bleak outlook these films initially portray. There is, in short, an underlying belief that circumstances need not be as they are and that acquiescence in the face of doom is not the proper heroic response.[7]

At the same time, the narrative *pattern* we find in most apocalyptic fiction films differs somewhat from the standard science fiction tales that typically feature a male hero who ventures forth to seek his fortune, or to rescue a captive maiden, or to discover his true identity and fulfill his cosmic destiny (see, for instance, Gordon 1995, whose analysis centers on the movie *Star Wars* [1977]). By contrast, the most pervasive thematic structure in apocalyptic fiction, which frames its plot, is that of revelation and rescue: society will be saved, and this despite its disbelief in or disregard for the message of warning that the hero or heroine brings. In this instance, the hero or heroine plays a dual role, serving as both messenger and savior. This "apocalyptic pattern," then, is threefold: first, the hero or heroine receives a special message or revelation, usually from outside the present circumstances; second, the civil authorities (or so-called "experts" of society) reject the warning or refuse to act to avert catastrophe (instead, their energies are absorbed harassing the hero); third, the hero or heroine, along with a ragtag collection of compatriots, rescues society from near disaster, destroys the menacing force, and makes the world safe once more.[8]

In the sections to follow, this essay will examine apocalyptic fiction in terms of the three conditions of postwar American society that seemed to point toward inevitable doom. What is revealed to postwar society through the steady production of apocalyptic fiction films is a culture on the brink of nuclear, environmental, and technological destruction. In addition, the films within this genre tend to follow the same narrative pattern discussed above, that of revelation of coming disaster, of resistance from society and its authorities, and of eventual rescue by the heroic efforts of the recipient of the revelation. I will return briefly to the discussion of this recurring pattern in the conclusion of this essay. But first, let's consider these three main types of apocalyptic fiction.

NUCLEAR APOCALYPTIC FICTION

Since the very first atomic bombs were detonated over Japan at the end of the Second World War, the potential of another nuclear conflagration and its frightening aftermath of sickness and suffering have remained fearfully fresh in the mind of postwar American society. With the heightening of Cold War tensions during the late '40s and early '50s , punctuated by news that the Soviet Union and then Red China had the bomb, it is not surprising to find the silhouette of mushroom clouds rising above the fictional cityscapes in numerous science fiction films of the period. The escalation of hostilities between East and West that led to the Korean crisis and armed conflict between China and the United States gave rise to fears that a nuclear exchange between the superpowers was inevitable.

During this period, some science fiction films also took a turn toward the apocalyptic, not in their portrayal of the coming nuclear nightmare but in their collective message that such a war could not be won and therefore must not be fought. One such film, still considered a cult classic among science fiction devotees, is the 1951 full-length feature *The Day the Earth Stood Still*, directed by Robert Wise. Released during the "hot" period of the Korean War, this mysteriously gripping film used aliens from a near distant planet as its messengers. These aliens, led by Klaatu (Michael Rennie), traveled to Earth with a special mission of warning: human aggression and nuclear terror must not expand into the solar system. "Man," they explained, was not only a threat to his own kind, but he and his growing nuclear arsenals were a threat to all intelligent life. Resistance to the alien mission by the U.S. military only confirmed their message: humans were hell-bent on destroying themselves and thus were in need of extraterrestrial mediation.

More recent examples of nuclear apocalyptic elements in popular films include the Mad Max series, particularly *Beyond Thunderdome* (1985), and the youth-oriented nuclear suspense thriller, *WarGames* (1983). While both movies concern the use of nuclear warheads, the first, starring Mel Gibson, reveals a postnuclear holocaust world that thrives, and for the most part survives, on the production of methane gas from pig excrement. Though "civilization" has sunk to a crude subsistence level called "Bartertown," run by a bosomy no-nonsense matriarch, Aunty Entity (Tina Turner), the story actually concerns a troupe of children who were in flight during the bombings and thus escaped annihilation. In hiding among the desert caves beyond the reach of Bartertown, the children anxiously wait for the coming of a prophesied savior, whom they come to believe is the unassuming but handsome hero, Gibson. In the movie's climactic battle scene, Gibson unwittingly fulfils his destiny by first destroying the evildoers and then by freeing the society from its *lex taliones* structure, a structure in which every offense is punished either by a duel to the death or banishment to the outer desert.

The latter film, *WarGames*, starring Matthew Broderick as a computer whiz kid who accidentally hacks his way into the U.S. nuclear defense system, focuses instead on contemporary American society whose serenity is about to be disrupted through a chain of events that, it seems, will inevitably lead toward thermonuclear world war. As a result of Broderick's hacking, "Joshua" (Hebrew for Jesus, meaning "savior"), the gigantic mainframe computer that controls the U.S. nuclear arsenal, has decided to launch a preemptive strike on the Soviet Union. All safeguard measures fail; a computer-initiated nuclear war is inescapable. Interestingly, while in the *Mad Max* saga the main character is hailed by the children he rescues as the messiah — a mantle Gibson's character reluctantly accepts — Broderick's fresh-face character employs his computer expertise to save the planet. Seconds before the destructive launch, Broderick's character breaks the security code and convinces the renegade mainframe computer, who thinks Broderick is its long-lost creator, not to initiate its planned nuclear attack.

While *Beyond Thunderdome* seems aimed at quelling Reagan era arms race bravado through its grim portrayal of a postnuclear holocaust world, the message *WarGames* communicates is the futility of waging nuclear war in the first place. Since all parties involved would be utterly destroyed, there can be no winner in such a contest. Or, as the computer Joshua announces at the end of the movie, the only real way to win the nuclear "war game" is not to play it.

What is common to these two examples of nuclear apocalyptic fiction is that they reveal a humanity pitted against itself through mistrust and fear, tragically unable to accept its cultural and political differences. What is likewise revealed in these films is that civilized life is really no more than a thin veneer covering savageness and incivility. The response to the threat of nuclear destruction does not arise from humanity's collective unconscious fear of death but from its unspoken fear of returning to its cave-dwelling barbarous past. As we are reminded, whether it results in the deaths of millions or in the death of civilized life, nuclear terror is an inescapable fact of modern life, a radioactive cloud that will continue to cast a large shadow of uncertainty over the future of humanity. Apocalyptic fiction is meant to convey the message that it does not have to be this way. Human civilization need not live in fear of such weapons of mass destruction but should work instead to avert this deadly "manmade" threat.

ENVIRONMENTAL APOCALYPTIC FICTION

During the postwar period, active concern in environmental issues by interest groups and government agencies heightened. As scientists and citizens began to warn of imminent environmental disaster, the authorities responded with legislation and think tank proposals aimed at reversing the effects of decades of environmental negligence. In 1956, for instance, the Water Pollution Control Act, which mandated wastewater treatment, was passed. Soon after, other environmentally sensitive measures were put into place that sought (1) to ban above-ground testing of nuclear weapons (the 1963 Nuclear Test Ban Treaty), (2) to address the problems of acid rain and airborne pollutants (the 1970 Clean Air Act), and (3) to phase out the use of harmful pesticides, such as DDT (passed in 1972). In 1970, the year the United States held the world's first Earth Day observance, the government established the Environmental Protection Agency. The country seemed to be right on track toward putting its environmental house back into order.

But all this public awareness and all these governmental initiatives did not prevent environmental disasters from happening. Oil spills off the California coast in the early 1970s left once pristine beaches and shorelines forever marred. But this only spelled the beginning of a series of environmental mishaps that marked the years to follow. In 1978, Love Canal, New York, was evacuated after it was discovered that it had been the site of a major chemical dump, creating concerns over the health of its residents and their children. The very next year, in March 1979, a near reactor-core "meltdown" occurred on Three Mile Island, Pennsylvania, when its nuclear power plants malfunctioned. And in 1986, a reactor meltdown and explosion at the nuclear power plant in Chernobyl, Ukraine, killed workers and some residents and caused widespread contamination of the air and soil throughout the old Soviet Union and much of Northern Europe. About that same time, a release of highly lethal chemical gases in Bhopal, India, killed thousands of people and raised questions about the effectiveness of existing industrial safeguards in preventing such deadly disasters. With each environmental mishap, the peoples of the earth were repeatedly reminded of the fragility of the natural world and of their own negligent stewardship.

Environmental concerns such as these did not escape the notice of film makers, who began producing a host of movies depicting the consequences of human mismanagement of the natural world.[9] Among a number of environmentally oriented sci-fi films produced during this period, two stand out as examples of this genre. The first, *Logan's Run* (1976), reveals a hopeful future for humankind and its relation to the natural world, while the second, *Soylent Green* (1973) presents a very bleak picture of human existence in the near future.

The resilience of nature, despite the poisoning of its rivers and oceans, the contamination of its soil, and the decimation of its bird and fish populations by human nuclear and industrial waste, is at the heart of *Logan's Run*'s futuristic (and hedonistic) Edenic setting. Human society lives underground, presumably having been forced centuries earlier to seek safety from mounting environmental disasters. Generations have passed and the memory of life above ground has faded into legend. Since this new Eden can be sustained only through rigorous control of human population, all persons are compelled to die at age thirty. The passing of time is marked by a luminous flower-shaped disk implanted in the palm of each person's right hand. When one's time has expired, the disk begins flashing. Death takes place daily through an elaborate communal ritual, ironically named "Renewal." As the crowds of people chant "renew," the participants are drawn up into the sky by a magnetic force and then electrocuted by a flash of artificial lightning. All die. No one is ever renewed. Indeed, those who try to escape the ritual—called "runners"—are hunted down by a special security force (the "sandmen") and summarily eliminated.

The revelatory element of *Logan's Run*, comes when the state decides to investigate and root out rumors of a "sanctuary" where runners are said to be hiding. The main character, Logan, a "hunter" played by Michael York, though sent to infiltrate this sanctuary, discovers instead that the world above has "renewed" itself and can once more sustain human life. Through his heroic efforts, Logan breaks the hold of the central authority—appropriately, a computer—and leads the people out of their underground prison and into a true Edenic paradise.

In the movie *Soylent Green*, the audience is presented with the bleak image of a future world irreparably polluted by chemical and industrial waste, a world with scarce resources, little fresh food, and far too many people for its polluted surface and meager resources to sustain. Human society has become a police state in which panic and near chaos are the order of the day and the misery of human life is exacerbated by totalitarian controls on population growth and life-sustaining resources. The human diet has been reduced to the eating of protein-enriched soy and lentil crackers of differing colors called "soylent." Even this bland diet is not enough to promote or sustain healthy life, as attested to by the piles of dead and dying bodies that line the streets—presumably overcome by the combined effects of malnutrition and air and water pollution—only to be scooped up and hauled away like garbage by the city's sanitation trucks.

The main character in *Soylent Green*, Officer Thorn (Charlton Heston), is a twenty-first-century metropolitan New York cop investigating a high-profile murder. His attention is diverted after a deathbed conversation with an elderly friend, a police researcher played by Edward G. Robinson (in his last screen role), who tells him what human life was like before the world was overrun by people and pollution. Though the plot sometimes verges on camp—the movie is clearly a child of the '70s—the depressing backdrop of the film sets the stage for the hero's great discovery, which, in horrifying disbelief, he proclaims to the aimless hoards of human cattle in the movie's dramatic final scene: "Soylent green ... is people!" Having destroyed its environment, humanity, he learns, is reduced to feeding off its dead.

TECHNOLOGICAL APOCALYPTIC FICTION

Dehumanization and the loss of personal autonomy and self-worth that has resulted from society's overreliance on technology have become inescapable facts of modern life. Machines not only rule people's lives but also make much human labor virtually unnecessary. What is more, human thought and ingenuity are slowly being replaced by artificial intelligence. In fact, some critics of modern technology fear that machines designed to think for humans will slowly become machines that act independently of them, eventually coming to control their lives.

The revelatory element of "techno" apocalyptic fiction is one in which humans are seen as inadequate before machines and are therefore insignificant to the workings of the modern world. Three themes characterize these films. First, we find the recurring message that technology can be cruel and dehumanizing. People who live in technologically controlled societies live cold and emotionally detached lives, devoid of existential meaning or purpose. Second, while technology is meant to provide greater freedom for humanity, in truth, it has enslaved humankind—individually as well as collectively—and controls its future. Humans have become subservient to thier own machines. Third, in "techno" apocalyptic fiction, science and technology are clearly the villains, with humanity pitted against machines in a life-or-death struggle. In many cases, the techno-villain is himself a personification of technology: cold, calculating, brutal, the very face of mechanized evil.

With perhaps the exception of the bad-to-the-bone Darth Vader in the *Star Wars* trilogy (which, incidentally, is *not* an apocalypse in form or content),[10] there is probably no better example of this personification of technological evil than in the film *Terminator* (1984) and its highly popular sequel, *Terminator 2: Day of Judgment* (1991), both directed by James Cameron of *Titanic* (1997) fame.

In the first *Terminator*, we learn from Kyle Reese (Michael Biehn), a visitor from the future, that by the year 2029, the world will be under the ruthless domination of machines, which have turned on their human creators and subdued them by computer-initiated warfare. No match for the technological and military superiority of the machines, humans have become a hunted breed. There exists, however, a small but strong underground resistance movement led by John Connor, a resourceful and charismatic leader. In order to root out the resistance, the machines concoct a plan to kill Connor's mother, Sarah (Linda Hamilton), before he is born. To carry out this deed, the machines send back in time a Terminator unit (Arnold Schwarzenegger), a relentless and virtually unstoppable killing machine. Having learned of the plan, Connor sends Reese, his most loyal lieutenant, back in time to warn and protect his not-yet-pregnant mother. (In a strange, mind-bending twist, we learn that Reese, who does not survive the movie, is in fact Connor's father, in essence both siring a son and then dying a decade or two before he himself is born.)

Programmed to kill, the Terminator does not deviate from its pursuit of Sarah Connor. As it moves through the streets of suburban Los Angeles, it literally kills or maims everyone in its way. In the end, human ingenuity—and a lot of luck—triumphs over this symbol of runaway scientific technology. Though the now-pregnant Hamilton is safe—at least for the time being—the future of humankind remains in doubt. Before the credits roll, Hamilton drives south into the Mexican desert to hide out until her son is born, matures, and takes his place in the fight against technology.

In the sequel, *Terminator 2: Day of Judgment* (or simply *T2*), the preteen John Connor (Edward Furlong) is living in a foster home, his mother having been committed to a mental institution because of her obsession over the future rebellion of the machines. In *T2*, Sarah Connor is more wild-eyed doomsday prophetess and anti-technology militant than the helpless and harried mother-to-be in *T1*. Interestingly, while she is haunted by the grim vision of a future high-tech world, her son, who is of the generation not frightened by rapid technological advances, becomes a mediator—a messiah of sorts—between present and future worlds.

The premise of *T2* is simple: the machines that rule the future world send a more advanced T-1000 Terminator unit (Robert Patrick) back to the present, this time to assassinate the young Connor. Learning of this mission, the Connor of the future world sends a rival but weaker T-800 Terminator, played once more by Arnold Schwarzenegger, to protect his present-day self. To his mother's initial discomfort, her old nemesis is now one of the good guys. While the boy and his Terminator are running from the marvelously protean T-1000, the mother is bent on finding and killing Miles Dyson (Joe Martin), the scientist responsible for designing the computer chip that sets the entire endtime scenario into motion. (Partway through the film, in a chilling dreamlike playground scene, Sarah envisions the fiery nuclear destruction of civilization. Rather than continue to brood over the fate of humanity, she decides to join the others in their efforts to change the course of the future.) At the climax of the movie, both Terminators and the special chip are destroyed in a vat of molten steel and the Connors—mother and son—save human civilization. (Dyson dies earlier in an explosive hail of fire and bullets.)

Aside from the conceptual difficulties and implausible premises of the *Terminator* films, we learn a number of things about the ambivalence of modern society in the face of technological advance (ironically, the films themselves are technological marvels). While in one breath we praise the boundless genius of the human mind to create, at the same time we are struck dumb by the realization that humans are often unable to see beyond what appear to be the immediate benefits of their creative ideas. Humans, we learn, rarely consider the unforeseen and unintended consequences of their ideas or their actions. But, additionally, we learn that the fruits of human ingenuity need not be destructive. The warning that the American apocalypt issues has an underlying message of hopefulness: Men and machines can work together for the benefit and advance of humankind.

CONCLUDING COMMENTS

The main point of the foregoing discussion of apocalyptic fiction is that in an analysis of contemporary films, it is not enough to say that movies that depict the end of the world or scenes of cataclysmic destruction of human civilization are "apocalyptic." As a genre of film, apocalyptic fiction possesses several common elements that distinguish it as "apocalyptic," the most telling of which is its revelatory framework. This is not to say that apocalypses differ from other film genres because they "reveal" something. All films have a mimemsic or reflective quality. That is, all films naturally reflect the times and the cultures in which they are produced. But in the case of what I am calling "apocalyptic fiction," the revelatory characteristic refers to a message whose *source* comes from elsewhere—that is, outside the present conditions or circumstances—and is mediated through an agent who stands between these worlds. Whether the agent or the receptor of the message becomes the "hero" is irrelevant to classifying a film as apocalyptic fiction. The otherworldly source of the message, its mediated character, and its inherent call to change destiny are what differentiate apocalyptic from other genres of film.

At the same time, what we have discovered in the above discussion is that the source of the revelation need not come from another world *per se*. While in one of the examples of nuclear apocalyptic fiction—*The Day the Earth Stood Still*—the apocalypt did come from outer space, in other examples the apocalypt came from the world of the future or was connected to the world of the past. In other words, the apocalypt is someone (or something) not altogether belonging to the society in danger, that is, someone (or something) from the outside.

What is more, not only is the source of the revelation otherworldly but the message that the apocalypt brings contains a warning, usually of impending doom or of cataclysmic destruction of the world *in toto*. It is this unforeseen threat that inspires the apocalypt and this same threat that frames the content of his or her message.

But the apocalypt is not, in all cases, simply an appointed messenger. In some cases, he or she becomes the savior as well. In these instances, not only does the apocalypt deliver a message of warning but he or she also delivers society from imminent danger, either by providing the necessary information to save society or, in many cases, the necessary firepower. Indeed, this apocalypt-*cum*-redeemer plot device in apocalyptic fiction tends to follow a similar pattern in which the messenger or the person to whom the message is directed must likewise act on the revelation him- or herself. The pattern, again, is threefold: (1) after receiving the revelation, (2) the hero(ine) warns society of its precarious circumstances. After being rejected by the civil authorities, (3) the hero(ine) determines to save society through his or her own actions. While most action and suspense movies tend to follow a similar plotline, what makes this apocalyptic is the revelatory framework of the film, that is, the "otherworldly" source of its revelation.

We see an example of this apocalypt-*cum*-redeemer in *Logan's Run*. After he discovers that the renewed world above is a greater paradise than the world below, to save his fellow humans from death at age thirty, Logan must fight against and defeat the system. We see another example of this in *Terminator 2* in that the T-800 Terminator is the messenger and, for the most part, an armed savior. This apocalypt-*cum*-redeemer device is also evident, but to a lesser extent, in some of the other films highlighted in this essay, such as *Mad Max: Beyond Thunderdome* and *WarGames*. One can also see evidence of this plot device in films not touched on above, such as *Waterworld* (1995) and perhaps

Contact (1997).

A final observation that one can make from the foregoing discussion is that while apocalyptic fiction films tend to "demonize" technology as destructive and dehumanizing it is interesting to note that they also hold out the hope that these same technologies, if properly applied, can be salutary. In one's struggle against the ill effects of modernity, one need not overthrow modern science. The defining difference is in the ways these technologies are used and in the intentions of those who use them. One cannot separate action from the actor or from that actor's intent either to empower or to overpower others.

But, as these films also reveal, the faith that people have in science, technology, medicine, and the like may very well be a misplaced faith that, like faith in politics or religion, leaves them vulnerable to visionary promises of utopia. In a touch of irony, apocalyptic fiction points out that our faith in these technologies, and the beguiling promise they hold out of heaven on earth, may very well damn us to a hell of our own making. In the end, they may condemn humanity to living in a cold and inhospitable future world, one defined—in truly biblical proportions—by warfare, disease, starvation, totalitarian governments, savage barbarism, and death.

NOTES

1. An apocalypse (or "revelation") is a genre of visionary literature that emerged during the Hellenistic period of Western antiquity (c. 200 BCE–200 CE) and is characterized by the revelation of heavenly knowledge through means of a heavenly journey or through the visitation of a heavenly messenger. The use of "apocalypse" and "apocalyptic" as metaphorical synonyms for "cataclysmic end of the world" is derived from the *Apocalypse of John*, the Greek title of *The Revelation to St. John the Divine*, the final book of the Christian Bible. The Revelation (always singular) recounts the heavenly vision the Apostle John received concerning God's destructive judgment upon a sinful unbelieving world. While the book, traditionally dated about 96 CE, is more than likely a veiled critique of the Roman Empire's anti-Christian policies, its revelatory content has inspired countless predictions of "imminent destruction" and "kingdom come" by overly zealous biblical interpreters—both learned and unlearned—throughout the past nineteen centuries (for specific examples, see Cohn 1970, Barkun 1986, Weber 1987, Boyer 1992, Stone 1993, Robbins and Palmer 1997, and Stone 2000).

2. There are five identifying features common to all apocalypses. First, apocalypses typically feature a supernatural source from which a secret knowledge comes. These sources of special knowledge often come through visions, dreams, angelic visitations, heavenly journeys, and the opening of a heavenly book or sealed scroll. A second identifying feature of apocalypses is their interest in

otherworldly forces, usually angelic and demonic. In this case, the angels and the demons have material or quasi-material form—usually human—as well as cosmic names or titles. These titles include such descriptive words as Lightbearer, Destroyer, Morning Star, Accuser, and the like. A third characteristic feature of apocalypses is the firm belief in divine intervention in human history, usually culminating in the end of an evil person or power, or sometimes the end of time itself. Also characteristic of apocalyptic literature is the restoration of paradise on Earth. The scenario of this fourth feature includes the termination of the old world and its transformation into a new world order. A final feature of an apocalypse is the dispensing of rewards and punishments to men and women in the afterlife. The reward or punishment is determined by the degree of faithfulness to God that a person showed in this life, especially in the face of trial and persecution (see Collins 1984, 1–32, and 1997, 1–8; see selected essays in Hellholm 1983). Apocalyptic literature differs from eschatological literature in that the knowledge provided by means of the heavenly journey or by the heavenly messenger does not always speak of the future in end-of-the-world imagery. An apocalypse may or may not be grounded in millennial expectation and may or may not speak of the dawning of the millennium, the golden age of peace. Also, though the message of the apocalypt may anticipate the coming of a messianic figure who emerges to rescue those in distress, messianic intervention is likewise not a defining feature of an apocalypse. With this in mind, it is therefore no surprise that the *metaphorical* use of "apocalypse" and "apocalyptic" have led to flawed and confusing analyses, even by scholars who claim a measure of expertise regarding things apocalyptic (for a few recent examples, see Ostwalt 1995, Miles 1996, and selected essays in Robbins and Palmer 1997, especially those by Lamy and Lee).

3. While films such as *Dr. Strangelove* certainly communicate to their audiences the sense of impending doom that awaits human society if it does not act to avert disaster, these are not apocalyptic in form. There is no otherworldly source, *per se*, that reveals impending doom or that recommends a course of action that will avert disaster. By definition, then, what we are calling "apocalyptic fiction" does not include films about nuclear buildup, Cold War tensions, or the aftermath of nuclear holocaust, such as *Fail-Safe* (1964), *On the Beach* (1959), or the shocking TV movie *The Day After* (1983). It also does not include pseudo-religious films about the coming of an anti-Christ or a prophesied end of the world, such as *The Omen* theater trilogy (1976–81), *The Seventh Sign* (1988), *The Rapture* (1991), or *End of Days* (1999). This essay, then, is not merely a survey of movie titles lumped haphazardly under a catchall metaphorical category called "apocalypse," such as one finds in Ostwalt (1995), or of pseudo-religious films about the Second Advent of Christ, such as those discussed in Miles (1996).

4. With Nietzsche, who wrote in *Beyond Good and Evil* that "when you gaze long into an abyss the abyss also gazes into you," we might likewise say that if we as a society gaze long at the silver screen, it soon begins to look into us. The screen shows us ourselves in objectified form and, in so doing, reveals to us something of the terror of living in the modern technological age. It also shows us the urgent need for salvation from our predicament, either coming from within our-

selves or from someone or some force standing outside our precarious circumstances. Of course, Nietzsche, through the mouth of his prophet Zarathustra, strenuously argued for the former.

5. A criticism of this scheme might come in the fact that all movies "reveal" something to the viewer, that is, they all have a point their writers and directors are trying to make. This critical point is understood. However, in keeping with the proper meaning of the word "apocalyptic" as "revelatory," the distinction this essay seeks to make is between movies that are apocalyptic in form, not simply revelatory in content or in intention. Otherwise, it would make little sense to speak of apocalypse as a distinct genre of literature or film.

6. David Harvey provides an interesting postmodernist "reading" of the film *Blade Runner* in his well-known study, *The Condition of Postmodernity* (1990).

7. We might add that the apparent inevitability of disaster is not acceptable to the hero or heroine who seeks instead to subvert the fixed order of things. Even as the hero(ine) follows his or her destiny, that same destiny, at least in terms of what it holds for society, can and will be thwarted by the hero.

8. This comment is not meant to suggest that only apocalyptic fiction films follow this heroic pattern but that this is a pattern that films of this genre tend to follow.

9. It should be noted that while many of the films of this period point out the destructive consequences of such negligence—to the extent that in some cases nature begins to fight back—not all environmentally interested sci-fi films are apocalyptic. For instance, films that depict large-scale epidemics and their terrifying consequences, such as *The Andromeda Strain* (1971), *The Omega Man* (1971), *Outbreak* (1995), and *Twelve Monkeys* (1995), do not appropriately fall within the genre of film I am identifying as "apocalyptic"; period pieces, such as *Silent Running* (1971), that strive for environmental awareness, likewise fall outside this generic type.

10. Incidentally, though it may appear to have apocalyptic (revelatory) features, the *Star Wars* trilogy (1977–83) and its prequel, *The Phantom Menace* (1999), do not properly fit the apocalypt-*cum*-redeemer pattern. This series resembles the so-called American monomyth (Jewett and Lawrence 1977; Gordon 1995).

REFERENCES

Barkun, Michael. 1986. *Crucible of the Millenium*. Syracuse, N.Y.: Syracuse University Press.

Boyer, Paul. 1992. *When Time Shall Be No More*. Cambridge: Belknap/Harvard.

Cohn, Norman. 1970. *The Pursuit of the Millennium*. New York: Oxford University Press.

Collins, John J. 1984. *The Apocalyptic Imagination*. New York: Crossroad.

———. 1997. *Apocalypticism in the Dead Sea Scrolls*. London and New York: Routledge.

Gordon, Andrew. 1995. "*Star Wars*: A Myth for Our Time." In *Screening the Sacred*, ed. Joel W. Martin and Conrad E. Ostwalt, Jr. Boulder, Colo.: Westview Press, 73–82.

Harvey, David. 1990. *The Condition of Postmodernity*. Oxford: Basil Blackwell.

Hellholm, David, ed. 1983. *Apocalypticism in the Mediterranean World and the Near East*. Tübingen: J. C. B. Mohr.

Jewett, Robert, and John Shelton Lawrence. 1977. *The American Monomyth*. Garden City, N.Y.: Doubleday.

Lamy, Philip. 1997. "Secularizing the Millennium: Survivalists, Militias, and the New World Order." In *Millennium, Messiahs, and Mayhem*, ed. Thomas Robbins and Susan J. Palmer, 93–117. New York: Routledge.

Lee, Martha F. 1997. "Environmental Apocalypse: The Millennial Ideology of 'Earth First!'" In *Millennium, Messiahs, and Mayhem*, ed. Thomas Robbins and Susan J. Palmer, 119–37. New York: Routledge.

Miles, Margaret R. 1996. *Seeing and Believing: Religion and Values in the Movies*. Boston: Beacon Press.

Ostwalt, Conrad E., Jr. 1995. "Hollywood and Armageddon: Apocalyptic Themes in Recent Cinematic Presentation." In *Screening the Sacred*, ed. Joel W. Martin and Conrad E. Ostwalt, Jr., 55–63. Boulder, Colo.: Westview Press.

Robbins, Thomas, and Susan J. Palmer, eds. 1997. *Millennium, Messiahs, and Mayhem: Contemporary Apocalyptic Movements*. London and New York: Routledge.

Stone, Jon R. 1993. *A Guide to the End of the World: Popular Eschatology in America*. New York: Garland.

——, ed. 2000. *Expecting Armageddon: Essential Readings in Failed Prophecy*. London and New York: Routledge.

Weber, Timothy P. 1987. *Living in the Shadow of the Second Coming: American Premillennialism, 1875–1982*. Chicago: University of Chicago Press.

Selena—Prophet, Profit, Princess

Canonizing the Commodity

KAREN ANIJAR

I write the myths in me, the myths I am, the myths I want to become.
—Gloria Anzaldúa

Selena was like a shooting star, flying in the night, one glimpse and you remember it for the rest of your life.
—Selena fan

On March 31, 1995, paramedics arrived at the scene of a homicide in a motel in Corpus Christi, Texas. A twenty-three-year-old woman lay dying from gunshot wounds. The setting was hauntingly reminiscent of black-and-white detective movies complete with the comely heroine-victim naming her killer with her dying breath. Richard Fredrickson, one of the paramedics who frantically but futilely tried to save the young woman's life, noticed that her right fist was clenched around something. "When I opened it," Fredrickson stated, "a ring fell out, a fourteen-karat gold and diamond ring covered with blood" ("Dying Selena" 1995, A4). The ring was a gift from the young woman's killer.

During the trial, which was filled with gripping, often gruesome testimony, the victim's family fought back tears as motel employees recounted each gory detail of the murder scene. The crime was so heinous that spectators in the courtroom renamed the accused "a witch," "*una maranna*" (a sow), and "a hag," and shouted "Put her to death," "Kill her," "Let her hang," and "Let her rot!" *Perry Mason, Matlock,* or any other television courtroom drama pales by comparison. The victim was described as a talented, charismatic, beautiful, and innocent child-woman, filled with love and life. The accused was identified over and over as a spurned lesbian lover, an embezzler, and a maniac. "It was more than a tragedy," said Edilberto Campos, "it was an assassination" (Turner and Reinert 1995). While one woman kissed a photo of the victim, a group of women held up posters and chanted, "Guilty! Guilty! Guilty!" Prayers were offered with the hope that the jury would find the accused guilty. One newspaper editorialist noted, "For many Mexican Americans this was the trial of the century" (Russell 1995). When the verdict was read, the National Public Radio broadcast on *All Things Considered* noted that a mass of people had gathered in the streets near the court, and described the scene as "almost like a Cinco de Mayo parade." "I wanted to jump up and down and yell," said Ofelia Bradshaw, who was at the trial. "Happy? Yes, I'm happy." Other spectators at the trial were overjoyed, too. "Let her rot in prison! Thirty years in prison. She'll be an old hag when she gets out," shouted Denise Martinez, another courtroom spectator. Others could be heard yelling *"cien anos"* (a hundred years), and "the death penalty."

Meanwhile, in Corpus Christi, hundreds of jubilant people also "honked car horns," "flashed victory signs," and "held up posters" as the guilty verdict was announced (Pinkerton 1995). Chanting *"'culpable,'* Spanish for guilty, people came from across Texas. The throng of spectators awaiting the verdict mixed with the downtown rush hour traffic to create a frenzied ... celebratory reaction" (Zuniga and Dyer 1995, A39). On what would have been Selena's twenty-fourth birthday, three thousand people celebrated an Easter Mass "in memory of the gran muchacha del barrio Molina." "Is it a coincidence that we celebrate [her] birthday on the same day we celebrate the victory of Jesus over death?" Monsignor Michael Heras of Our Lady of Perpetual Health Catholic Church asked in his sermon. "I don't think so. Death was defied forever. That's what this day is about. Forever!" At the conclusion of the Mass, children released twenty-four doves—each representing a year of Selena's life (Mitchell 1995). The day she was shot was popularly renamed "Black Friday."

SELENA WHO?

Elvis, John Lennon, Kurt Cobain and Jerry Garcia . . . roll over: Selena is here to grant voice to the silenced and oppressed.
—Ilan Stavans

Media and popular accounts corroborate that Selena Quintanilla Perez was Tejano music's brightest hope for the future. Had she lived she might well have been the first international superstar to come out of the Tejano market. The first biography of the singer, a brief account that could be read in English or Spanish (by flipping the book upside down), rose to the top of the *New York Times* best-seller list immediately following her death, where it stayed for a month. The New York–centered publishing world was undoubtedly surprised. Who—outside of Chicano/Latino communities—had ever heard of Selena, or Tejano music more generally? "Here comes a brown woman," said film maker (and fan) Lourdes Portillo, who described Selena as "very beautiful and very talented, taking up a space that had never been filled by someone else. She represented people that traditionally had not had a presence. I think that's her real importance" (Liner 1999).

Publisher, editor, and author Catherine Vasquez Revilla saw Selena's death as having a cultural significance far beyond the loss of a young entertainer. As he said, "The death of Selena Quintanilla Perez, while a great loss to the community, also brings recognition to Mexican Americans, and unity to Hispanics" (Liner 1999). Poet Sandra Cisneros—who says she was never a Selena fan—has a Selena keychain "because it was the first time I saw a Chicana on a keychain that wasn't Our Lady of Guadalupe" (Liner 1999).

Selena was a wife, a daughter, a singer, a fashion designer, and a business woman. She was a conglomerate in sequins and leather. She personified both sexuality and innocence. She was a contradiction in life, a conundrum in death. Framed as a Spanish language crossover singer to English, Selena was actually forced by her father to learn Spanish—even though her first language was English—because he thought "she could more easily find a following singing in Spanish" (Stavans 1995, 24). In death, however, she has become much more than a singer, her appeal going much deeper than the music. Her murder gave birth to a legend that, according to Virgilio Elizondo, transformed Selena into an instant cultural myth. "It is the people saying what she meant to us.... In their testimonies, she is becoming more alive than she ever was in life" (Vara 1995).

But, as John Fiske reminds us, "people" is an abstraction: it "is not a stable ... category; it cannot be identified and subjected to empirical study, for it does not exist in objective reality" (1989, 24). "The people," writes John Street, "are colored by whichever artist paints them" (1997, 152). The concepts of "the popular" and "the people" must be understood through "vibrant symbolic life and symbolic creativity of everyday activity and expression" (Willis 1990, 1), out of which "collective and individual identities" are forged (6). "It implies living within the signs ... engaging in the contradictory pleasures of fashion, style" (Street 1997, 161). As Dick Hebdige argues, we must identify the "messages inscribed in code on the glossy surfaces of style, to trace them out as maps of meaning" (1979, 18), trying to re-present and comprehend the complicated way messages and meanings are constructed in the popular. Thus, Cisneros's Our Lady of Guadalupe statement is not far off the mark, especially given what transpired after Selena's death.

What magical qualities did this twenty-three-year-old have that could justify shrines, buildings, altars, parks, bronze statues, baby names, Catholic masses, and an official holiday (April 19) sanctioned by the governor of Texas in her honor, as well as the attribution of such divinely inspired qualities as the ability to heal the sick, keep young people off drugs, and encourage young people to stay in school?

SELENA THE ICON

According to Robert Karimi, it was raining in San Antonio the day Selena was shot. It was raining the day of the funeral as well.

> At noon, hundreds packed the Cathedral. Many were wearing pink ribbons in her memory. A line formed afterwards, people formed the sign of the cross and kissed a poster at the front of the cathedral. . . . By Tuesday, Selena Etc., Selena's boutique on the 3700 block of Broadway Ave. had become a shrine to the Tejana star. Balloons. Flowers. Poems. Pictures. Art. All created their own mural on the walls of the boutique. Strangers, friends, and families came together. (Karimi 1995)

Narratives like this one and others from Selena fans help explain the transformation of Selena Quintanilla from singer to sacred object. Similar to explorations of the images of other cultural icons (such as Elvis Presley, Jim Morrison, Princess Diana, and Che Guevara), these narratives give us insight into the way in which public memory is transformed through representations, and how those representations possess the uncanny ability to construct and reconstruct realities. But are these images liberating, transformative, or do they recapitulate a rather static social and religious order? What messages does Selena send? How are they marketed and mediated? How is Selena consumed as an object of veneration as well as exploitation? "We are in the process of mythifying Selena, getting away from the facts of her life and refining her image to the truth that people believe about her," said one fan. "She has become part of the pantheon of secular saints" (McLemore 1997, A1).

Selena's transformation from singer to Marian image (which was particularly ironic because she was a Jehovah's Witness) was far more than mere material transformation. It was perhaps a greater crossover hit than was anticipated for her in life. The news that followed her death reveals an insurgent educational process. The creation of Selena-Madonna has been an active and creative process conceived and constructed at the juncture between media culture, commodity culture, and the organizing and mobilizing principles emerging from '90s populist pronouncements.

Far too often, studies concerning news, entertainment, and lived experiences are reduced to cause-effect approaches or essentialized definitions of culture. It is difficult for observers grounded in modernist experience to comprehend the form-shaping but nonetheless undetermined ideology that is generated by electronic information and images. The media are never socialized monolithically, even in what is labeled a postmodern historical period. History does transform, but we are all not transformed in the same ways. The reading and writing of what constitutes reality is a terrain of struggle and negotiation. We live in a media culture "in which images, sounds and spectacles help produce the fabric of everyday life, dominating leisure time, shaping political views, and social behavior and providing the materials out of which people forge their identities" (Kellner 1995, 1). Everything that comes in contact with our incurably mediated eyes has differing meanings, interpretations, and degrees of significance in the discourses of the particular social groups that talk about what they see and hear. Different social groups use very distinctive languages for evaluating what goes on in politics, in education, in media, in religion, and in all other aspects of life.

The commercial canonization of Selena provides us with an example of a critical public pedagogy, an educational mechanism, that occurs outside of both school and church and explains issues of tremendous social and political significance. Selena, read as a curricular religious text and a pedagogical forum, is "not just an individual exercise but a process that always takes place within a social context" (Grumet 1991, 76). "The problem after all is not with the voices that speak, but with the ears that cannot hear" (Casey 1995, 223), or with the eyes that privilege renders blind. So while Selena has become *una leyenda del pueblo* (a legend of the people), she is rarely discussed among members of the dominant American cutlure, even though a popular movie, several documentaries, and many books have been made about her life, murder, and the trial that ensued.

How Mexican Americans who canonize Selena understand her (as opposed to how they once understood her), how they create and re-create the trinity of the real body, the electronic mediated body of the dead rock star, and the object-commodity body, is an active reading of the text that gives voice to social and political positions through religious expression. Joe Nick Patoski has noted the saint-like status Selena achieved, with street murals honoring her and hundreds of Texas babies being named for her. He suggests that, for many of the crying fans at the courthouse when Selena's murderer was found guilty, "Selena had already evolved from a pop star into an icon of grief" (1995, 102)—an icon that has taken on supernatural, spiritual dimensions. As sociologist Robert Wuthnow observed, "Religion is deeply embedded in the broader social environment" (1989, 15). This suggests that religious symbols can be found outside the strictly "sacred" realm in a variety of social settings.

Selena's mortal body is dead. But transformed into an object of veneration her body informs and sustains a sense of agency among particular class fragments in the Tejano-Chicano-Mexican-American community.

> During a recent trip to South Texas, I talked to a respectable old man who told me Selena had died because heaven was desperate for another cherub. Selena was "a celestial beauty," he sighed, "whose time on earth was spent helping the poor and unattended." In San Antonio, a mother of four has constructed an altar at home, with the dead singer's photograph surrounded by candles and flowers, just below the image of the Virgen de Guadalupe, Selena's holy predecessor among Mex-Americans. Amalia Gonzalez, a Spanish-language radio host, told a journalist that Selena had visited us "to unite all creeds and races." And a young lady from Corpus Christi, one of Selena's passionate fans, who spends a good portion of her days singing "selenatas," swears she has repeatedly seen Selena's ghost at night on her TV screen—once her set has been turned off. (Stavans 1995, 24)

The phantasmagorical Selena is not part of what was; Selena is not fossilized into memory. She takes on new life as part of a process in which her phantom presence is constantly becoming (provided she continues to sell). Selena's spirit walks the earth negotiating and inhabiting new spaces and places. Constantly resignified and rewritten, Selena becomes symbolic spiritual material that presents us with a critical language through which we can examine ideological and political impulses that are forged in the popular and represented in religious language.

This phenomenon in which a person becomes more powerful as a representation reminds us that we live in a world where signs, symbols, and images bombard our sensibilities at breakneck speed. The never-ending proliferation of messages and advertisements creates a situation (known as hyperreality) where the images become more real than reality itself. It is a world where images gather up into themselves the complexities and ambiguities of an event, where everything is a representation, and where the distinction between fact and fiction becomes irrelevant. The copy merges with the original, the image merges with that to which it refers, until there is no longer a distinction of any significance. It is at this point, suggests Jean Baudrillard, that culture becomes a "kind of deathly surplus in which we witness the death of imagination, the death of meaning, the death of aesthetics" (Elliot 1999, 165). With nothing new to consider, we recycle, pillage, and ransack the past to create something of interest.

What gives Selena particular purchase-value in media-saturated hyperreality is that she connects with a variety of other images and reference points cutting across time, space, and history. She becomes a postmodern political configuration, transformed from child into woman, woman into child, real body into ghostly body, real flesh into perfected illusion. She becomes a Mexican Madonna. Selena's spectral presence cuts deeply to the core of the heart of Texas, reproducing while also undermining the existing static social order. Selena's transformation into religious object uncovers populist, anarchical, and even anticlerical elements in the "underground stream nourishing Marian apparitions and pilgrimages" (Doyle 1997, 171). Or, as one fan put it, "Selena gives us hope."

RESIGNIFYING THE VIRGIN

Go anywhere on either side of the Mexico–United States border and you will find the Virgin of Guadalupe. She is on video store walls, in supermarkets, and even on the stark face of an electrical generating station. According to the United States Department of Commerce, there are 12.6 million people of Mexican descent in the United States. "Everywhere," note Jeanette Rodriguez and Virgilio Elizondo, "Our Lady of Guadalupe is known to them: a brown skinned woman surrounded by the sun cloaked in a blue mantle covered with stars, standing on a crescent moon held by an angel. She looks down, and the expression on her face is one of kindness, compassion and strength" (1994, xxv).

In the borderlands where the Virgin is constantly resignified, she is above all an ethnic sign. Indeed, as Alicia Gaspar de Alba points out, the Virgin of Guadalupe, known as the "empress of Mexico," has come to represent "the biological source of Chicano brotherhood (i.e., the Mexican motherland) and also constituted a symbol of indigenist resistance to spiritual colonization, transmuted by the goals of la Causa into a symbol of Chicano/a resistance to assimilation and territorial conquest" (1998, 47). Images of Madonna gather significance from the communities that she nourishes.

Selena as Tejana Madonna, marketed by corporations large and small, enters into a space where popular hunger for religious images of personal meaning, particularly in a time of crisis, is essential for any sense of personal and political agency. Jo Ann Zuniga describes how, on *Dia de los Muertos* (Day of the Dead), one fan decorated an altar with "framed photos of Selena Quintanilla Perez hugging family members," heart-shaped candles in Selena's favorite color (purple), and "Selena's flower of choice," white roses. She added marigolds—an Aztec symbol of death—and a sign that read *"Con Tu Adios Te Llevas Mi Corazon"* (your goodbye takes my heart). "This was the only way I could let go of the sadness I was feeling," the fan said (Zuniga 1995, A39).

WAS SHE REAL OR MEMOREX?

For Mexican Americans, Selena's success became their success. She inspired confidence and ethnic pride. The stage lights that shone on her also reached across to include Mexican Americans by highlighting their language, music, and culture. Her greatest gift was that her talent, beauty, and success empowered all Hispanics.

—Catherine Revilla-Vasquez

Selena's transfiguration into Marian phantasm is as complex and contradictory as Selena herself. Fans called her *"una mujer del pueblo"* (a woman of the people). She emerged out of a white suburban middle-class English-speaking environment (reconstructed as working class), and rose into the consciousness of Tejana-Latina culture. Her murder contributed to her being recast as a timeless cultural symbol. As Elisabeth Bronfen wrote:

[T]he death of a beautiful woman emerges as a requirement for a preservation of existing cultural norms and values.... Over her dead body, cultural norms are reconfigured or secured, whether because the sacrifice of the virtuous, innocent woman serves a social critique and transformation or because a sacrifice of the dangerous woman reestablishes an order that was momentarily suspended due to her presence. (1992, 181)

Selena thus was transformed from the body human into the original, "the quintessential tragic lover, beautiful princess, angel of mercy, and doting mother." Diana Taylor argues that Selena's "sudden uniqueness, her tragic magnitude, allowed us to forget for a moment that she was also very much the product of a long history of collective imaginings that have normalized heterosexuality, glorified maternity, fetishized youth and femininity, glamorized whiteness, eroticized imperialism, and promoted a discourse of volunteerism" (1999, 59). At the same time, her image fostered a creative, positive spiritual space reconstituting the Virgin and connecting her to a community of mothers, comrades, and sisters in a way that resisted its original naming and framing.

The struggle to control and to write metaphorically upon Selena's body remains a struggle among particular power formations at the intersection of globalizing imperialist powers and local forces, a struggle that is waged in the hyperreal. Selena's body is rescripted in such a way that it negotiates a terrain where age, social class, gender, and ethnicity interanimate highlighting points of control, where political and cultural power are both applied and contested.

SITUATING SELENA

People want to touch something of her, to have an object that, in some way, makes her alive to them.

—David McLemore

Stephen Kline (1995, 11) argues that we find "meaning, comfort and solace" in our relationship with goods that are marketed and shaped by media representation and that take on importance and meaning beyond the original purchase-value of the object itself. Objects in a consumer culture are vested with symbolic significance. We define who we are by the objects we possess. This process, often called objectification, starts at a very young age. Ellen Seiter observes, "Consumer culture provides children with a shared repository of images, characters, plots, and themes: it provides the basis for small talk and play, and it does this on a national, even global scale." She concludes, "Mass-market commodities are woven into the social fabric of children's lives: they are seen on sleepovers, at show-and-tell in school, on the block or in the apartment building, on the T-shirt" (1999, 297). In other words, if I am wearing Nike shoes, they are no longer just sneakers. They mean something, they symbolize something. If they did not, young people would not kill or be killed over them. The object becomes part of a narrative that is invented and reinvented, articulated and rearticulated, contingent on the speaker. As David McLemore writes, "Adoration makes for strong incentives for entrepreneurs to fill that need. Where there is demand, there will soon be supply" (1997, A1).

What is the difference between a Jesus shirt and a Selena shirt, or between *God: A Biography* and the various biographies about Selena? Jesus sells because he's really "big," and Selena sells for a similar reason. If none of these objects sold, if they were no longer "hot" or "big," they would no longer be marketed. Media scholar Stewart Hoover argues that, "For religion to exist in contemporary life, it has to exist in the media and public spheres." To successfully spread the gospel, "marketing and PR principles rule the day" (Apodaca 1998, A1). To make sure that Selena is kept alive within the community, she too must be marketed and packaged in a particular fashion.

IMAGE CONTROL

Hours after the singer was shot by her assistant, Yolanda Saldívar, last March, the first signs of commercialism over Selena's death emerged, with hastily designed T-shirts hitting the market. Even Saldívar's query to police as to the whereabouts of her lawyer—"Where's Larry?"—during negotiations for her surrender, was emblazoned on shirts during her criminal trial.

—Toni Cantu

Who controls and markets the image is of consequence. Those who control the rights also control how the image is marketed, what they want the public to see, and what the public wants to see. The Catholic Church controls the pope's image, Graceland controls Elvis's image, and in Selena's case the family employs two law firms to monitor for unauthorized merchandise. "We spend a tremendous amount of time and money to block the exploiters," said Burt Quintanilla, a cousin who heads the marketing efforts for Q Productions, the family's production company. Since the murder, the volume of black-market trade in Selena-related material has exploded. "The exploitation of Selena strikes a raw nerve with us," Quintanilla continued. "She was family, and she was special to millions of people who saw her as a role model, someone who touched them. We don't want to see Selena reduced to a key chain" (McLemore 1997, A1). Unless, that is, the key chain is sold at Selena Etc., Selena's boutique. The shop launched her line of clothes and sells mementos of various sorts—including "perfume, dolls, commemorative magazines, posters, and T-shirts"—that range in price from $6 to $350. "People seem to want anything that relates to Selena," said manager (and cousin) Debra Ramirez (McLemore 1997, A1).

MONEY CAN BUY ME LOVE

"Selena was very special to me," said Betty Sanchez, 30, as she bought a couple of Selena T-shirts and coffee mugs amid the aroma of nail polish and hairspray. "I took it very hard when Selena passed away."

—Quoted in Doreen Bowens

In the contemporary world, human beings are objectified, and Selena becomes an image on a T-shirt, an objet d'art, a shrine, and a statue. But it is not just

Selena. Everybody, everything, and every impulse—including religious impulses—are thrown into the increasingly intensified (all encompassing) marketplace of products. Reduced to combinations of objectifiable, commodifiable characteristics, people have particular symbolic (purchase) value. Each of these visible characteristics has value whose currency is determined by the most economically powerful. Mexicans, like any other group, are thereby signified as having a particular value in a capitalist marketplace. One fan gave voice in a personal interview to this phenomenon in this way:

> Selena makes me proud. Proud not only of who I am and where I come from, but proud that such a beautiful and talented woman made all her dreams come true despite any barriers.... There was a scene in the movie when Selena came to California for the Grammys and she wanted to buy her friend a dress. They picked out a dress they liked, and asked the store employee if they could try it on. The store employee (who was an Anglo woman) replied she did not think Selena would be interested in it. And when Selena asked why, she replied "because it costs $800." Later when the movie had finished and the audience was gathered outside of the theater, I overheard a group of Anglo people talking about that scene. They didn't feel it was a relevant scene in the movie and that it was overdramatized. What they don't and could not understand is that this happens all the time. I've experienced it and I have friends who have experienced it—our community has long been ignored.

How Mexicans, Mexican-Americans, Chicanos, Latinos, and "Hispanics" are named, defined, and objectified is of tremendous consequence to the Selena story. Lauraine Miller describes one fan, "Veronica," who said that Selena had opened her eyes: "I was acting more American, and she made us realize our heritage was important." On the other hand, another fan responded that she didn't know "where Veronica lives, but, in the United States nobody ever lets you forget you are a Mexican-American" (1996, A1).

> For those mourning her, she was a brave, astonishingly courageous Chicana, ambivalent about but never ashamed of her background. Selena drove her Porsche to the Wal-Mart. "You'd see her shopping at the mall," people in South Texas told me. "And you'd see her working at home. A real sweetheart." They like to recall how accessible she was—una de nosotros.... Had Selena been visited by the angel of death only a few years later, a very different story would have been told. She

would have been an American Star, and her misfortune would not be useful today to highlight the reticence with which la frontera in particular, and Latino culture in general, is taken in by the rest of the country. (Stavans 1995, 24)

Selena symbolizes Mexican-American pride in a community under siege, particularly in California and the Southwest. There is a sense of community, breaking through layers of anomie in a mass-marketed religious celebration of iconography and identity. As one fan wrote to the *Minneapolis Star Tribune*, "She inspired me to return to my roots.... I have never been prouder to be a Mexican-American" (Burr 1996).

ILLEGAL ALIEN

Now Selena is a pantheistic deity in la frontera—everywhere you look, there she is: on TV screens and CDs, on book covers and calendars, on velvet slippers, T-shirts, lithographs, baseball hats, stickers, plastic bracelets, shampoos. . . . "Thanks to her, tejanos are being heard," a disc jockey from Houston told me. "She put us in the news—and on the front page of the *New York Times*." Meanwhile, many people north and south of the Rio Grande have been engaging in active prayer to Vergen Selena, their own Madonna, so that heaven above might send some miracles to la frontera: more dolares descending once the media craze is over, for instance; or a less condescending attitude toward its idols while they are alive. Otherwise Mex-American youngsters might get the wrong message, thinking they will only be heard by Anglo ears after they are dead and buried.

—Ilan Stavans

With the recent passage in California of legislation considered to be hostile to immigrants, the value of Mexicanness both in the symbolic and real political economy of the United States becomes quite clear. Certainly the sense of pride and solidarity that Selena has generated as a sign and as an object is of tremendous consequence given the frenetic anti-Mexican backlash in the United States. Ramón Gutiérrez argues that "caricatures, stereotypes and images, born of ignorance, fed by fantasy, shaped and distorted by the media and explained by folk aphorisms, are the currency of popular discourse. Whatever the genesis of these perceptions, distorted as they are, they shape the way middle-class Americans refract reflections of themselves onto the 'illegal aliens.' Those nonhuman creatures from another world called Mexico, who constantly threaten to invade sovereign United States space and destroy the essence of American life" (1996, 254).

In this environment, Selena's resignification as an object, as a source of pride in a community that continues to endure blatant racialized hatred in the United States, must be contextualized as a form of resistance to laws that some people see as frighteningly reminiscent of the laws of Nazi Germany. Holly Sklar, after recounting a series of horrendous anti-immigrant events, notes that "it is not far fetched to see the seeds of ethnic cleansing—the widely adopted euphemism for genocide in the former Yugoslavia—in the widespread support [for the California legislation]." She ponders "How easy it's been to roll back civil liberties with the excuse of fighting the racially based 'War on Drugs.' How easy it's become to spend more money on prisons and less on education. How easy it's been to re-label millions of children as illegitimate" (1995, 133).

In many ways, as awful as it may sound, Selena might have died just in time. For some, the image of the Virgen Selena is powerful, potent, political, transformative, and often transcending. Selena sustains a sense of *mestizaje* goodness, kindness, worthiness, and beauty. As one fifteen-year-old Mexican-American fan noted, "Selena touched me in a way I can never explain fully in words. She was and is an inspiration to me to keep fighting and keep reaching for my dreams." Another female fan, as if addressing Selena in the afterlife, said that the singer had given her "hope that we could fulfill those promises you fought for, and the hope you gave us, helps us carry on." Finally, another fan asked, "Why did God create an angel who was so full of life then take her back so quickly?" She had found inspiration, she said, in Selena's words about never giving up on one's own dreams. "When I had heard that she had died I lost a little part of me as well. She was my inspiration, and mentor that I will never forget," she said. "Though her body died, her spirit and dreams keep on living, in all of us, in all Latinos."

History is not so much a product of the past, but a process constructed in the present by people for particular purposes. The selections, silences, gaps, and embellishments are always arbitrary. There are never uninterpreted experiences. History is not connected to the experiential, but reconstructed memory is. History is also a commodity. After her death, television airwaves were filled with images of shrines built to honor Selena, fans visiting her grave to be healed, and descriptions of Selena sightings in which the spirit offered encouragement and hope for the poor (Blosser 1995, 24–25). What became most venerated about Selena's life was her strong tie to the Tejano community and to her family, her innocence, her spirituality, and her life after death, not her skimpy costumes, her sensuality, or the scandals that surrounded her family life. In this process, public memory as transforming created a version of Selena whose life as lived became inconsequential. In many ways it is ironic, for Selena is better

known today than she was at the peak of her career. Among those who acco-
modate the needs that Selena's new popularity has created is Jose Behar, the
president of EMI Records Latin Division, the company that groomed Selena
for stardom. "It is our responsibility," he said "to continue her legacy and to
really bring to the forefront the beautiful gift she left us.... We can't change
the tragedy. I wish we could but we can't. So we now have a responsibility to
share her music with the world, which is what she wanted most" (Burr 1997, 9F).

Events have taken on new meaning to construct the present. Selena's life
was appropriated for very important political exigencies within particular fragments of the Tejano community. Secularly sainted Selena shows a face that may
not have existed in real life, but it puts the community's best foot forward. As
one fan stated, "She embodies everything a Hispanic woman should be" (Diaz
1999, A47). The events that began with the murder and continued through the
trial, her burial, and the rescriptings of Selena's life and death are reconstruc-
tions that help secure particular identities, creating an ideal that enables her
fans to negotiate and resist the present order of things. Selena represents an oppo-
sitional narrative that challenges dominant cultural histories and opinions, and
in the process Selena's image is transformed for strategic purposes. In such a
way, her life begins to make sense because of her death. Her death begins to
make sense because of how her life has been constructed. In other words, the
significance does not rest with the facts, but with the way the relationship
between events and facts are created and re-created—strung like a pearl
necklace—to create a whole image, a whole reality.

MARIAN IMAGES

She was a beautiful young lady and a person who loved everyone,
especially children. Selena is singing with the angels now.
                                                            —Selena fan

La Virgen de Guadalupe is venerated as the mother and the nurturer; she has
endured pain and she is willing to serve (Nieto 1974, 37). Nevertheless, images
of suffering are also appropriated and commodified in a hyperreal, intensified,
capitalist world. Suffering is framed to appeal at visceral, emotional, and moral
levels. As we have already noted, these images have values; however, their value
is different across communities. Alba Garcia suggests that "for many Chicanos ...
these same values have been a source of solace and strength to fight racism and
resist oppression by the dominant group. The dedication that many women have

for their families—and many men's commitment to uphold their side of the bargain by hard work in the agricultural fields, brutal work in factories, and low-paid, unskilled labor—has made it difficult for Chicana feminists to question these values.... Some Chicanas have not seen the advantages of challenging patriarchy, and others have been afraid to betray their communities by joining any feminist cause" (1989, 225).

Against this backdrop, Selena is framed in a particular fashion—both eso-teric and prosaic—that parallels the Lady of Guadalupe. Her image is used to build community solidarity around something that transcends everything else, combining, reflecting, and manipulating the body human and the Marian body while bringing together differing dimensions of material and political posi-tions. Forms of individual collective narratives surrounding the use of Marian imagery in connection with Selena's body are not disconnected from real polit-ical, economic, religious, or cultural life. This narrative genre of life histories, oral histories, and histories of community extends the scope of what constitutes legitimate knowledge to include those who have been politically, culturally, and economically excluded from the dominant culture, displacing the urge to cat-egorize that is the gatekeeper of knowledge, and thus of interpretation "for any-one who has ever felt shunted aside" suggest Neal and Janice Gregory, "by someone who thought they were of a better class" (1997, 234). We could also include race or ethnicity. Selena, much like Elvis Presley, is an incredibly pow-erful symbol, and the imagery of the silent woman who embodies the suffer-ing of the Mexican people provides a powerful counterpoint to Anglo domination and exploitation.

SELENA-ELVIS

Mark Gottdiener notes that the founders of the world's major religions are known principally by what they said. "Their words are enshrined in text," he notes. "Most American Christians are, perhaps, unaware that there are people who came to know Jesus not through the text or the discourse but through bod-ily actions" (1997, 190). As should be clear by now, many seem to have come to Selena in the same way. People seek to feel what it was she was feeling, they seek to re-create her feelings through themselves. In Gottdiener's words, "They seek to possess the abundance of material objects sacralized by [her] aura through commodification, and to be [her] through impersonation, or to embody the characteristics ascribed to her through what educators call modeling. Modeling what is understood as Selena's best characteristics is another form of veneration." Little girls cling to their Selena dolls and dream of being just like her when they grow up. Twelve thousand young women flood the audition for the Selena movie in the hope that they will be chosen as she was. Drag queens mimic Selena in shows all along the border, while Selena-designed clothes are sold at official Selena stores, Selena websites, and J.C. Penney's so schoolgirls can mimic Selena too.

The dead Elvis may be our other Jesus, since we "unabashedly and actively celebrate his commodification in a million material manifestations" (Gottdiener 1997, 191). Selena, however, is another Mary, a material girl, a different sort of Madonna, whose followers experience personal self-expression and liberation. Gottdiener maintains that Elvis as Jesus is a form of liberating religious expression experienced in a manner that Jesus cannot be: materially. This particular aspect, he argues, "is the powerful force behind the Dead Elvis phenomenon. Attaching oneself to the dead Elvis is an act of liberation from the constraints of most religions because it enables you to celebrate popular culture, secular ideas, commodity fetishism, eroticism, black white integration and most specifically Southern culture" (1997, 192). Selena liberates her followers in a similar way. She celebrates her people, she celebrates a secular form of Catholicism and a postmodern form of Chicanismo through the popular. Selena becomes an act of empowerment through a form of religious expression. She is a form of resistance challenging an increasingly hostile Anglo environment. Selena becomes an activity, an action, not just a substitute for action.

However, just because members of a marginalized group have adopted a distinct style or icon does not—cannot—mean that they "now articulate a coherent critical response to their own oppression" (Street 1997, 163). Once something is vested into the popular it may become not only an expression of defiance and resistance, but also a form of politicized management. The conditions, reasons, and pleasures of consumption are not equal for everyone. Culture and religion are never simply sources of meaning. They are processes that are invariably interactive. In other words, we produce culture, but we are also produced by it. Religious impulses in the popular work through affect that is "organized according to maps which direct people's investment in it and the world," thus involving "the generation of energy and passion, the construction of possibility" (Grossberg 1992, 79–80, 85). Selena becomes a way of experiencing feelings and passions, she provides solace and sustenance, and she reaches out to the other—in this case the Anglo other—in peace. Selena-worship is a way of maintaining a modicum of optimism and possibility. Selena someday may be able to instill in her followers a sense of agency to resist increasingly oppressive forces, or she may be relegated to the dustbin of what might have been. But in either case, her significance will rest less in who she was, and more in what she was to the people who knew her.

REFERENCES

Anzaldúa, Gloria. 1987. *Borderlands/La Frontera: The New Mestiza*. San Francisco: Spinsters/Aunt Lute.

Apodaca, Patrice. 1998. "Southland: Television's Bible Belt." *Los Angeles Times*, January 12, A1.

Blosser, John. 1995. "Selena Reaches Out from the Grave." *National Enquirer*, August 22, 24–25.

Bowens, Doreen C. 1999. "Visitors Mark Anniversary of Selena's Death." *Corpus Christi Caller-Times*, April 1.

Bronfen, Elisabeth. 1992. *Over Her Dead Body: Death, Femininity and the Aesthetic*. New York: Routledge.

Burr, Ramiro. 1996. "Selena's Impact Still Felt." *Minneapolis Star Tribune*, March 31, 9F.

Cantu, Toni. 1996. "Cashing in on Selena." *Hispanic* 9, 6 (June): 18–23.

Casey, Kathleen. 1995. "New Narrative Research in Education." *Review of Research in Education* 21: 211–53.

Diaz, Madeline Baro. 1999. "Fans Flooding Selena Museum to See Singer's Clothes, Personal Belongings." *Dallas Morning News*, June 27, A47.

Doyle, Jacqueline. 1997. "Assumptions of the Virgin and Recent Chicana Writing." *Women's Studies* 26, 2: 171–202.

"Dying Selena Held Bloody Ring." 1995. *Newsday*, October 14, A4.

Elliot, Anthony. 1999. *The Mourning of John Lennon*. Berkeley: University of California Press.

Fiske, John. 1989. *Understanding Popular Culture*. Boston: Unwin Hyman.

Garcia, Alba. 1989. "The Development of Chicana Feminist Discourse, 1970–1980." *Gender and Society* 3, 2: 217–38.

Gaspar de Alba, Alicia. 1998. *Chicano Art Inside/Outside the Master's House: Cultural Politics and the CARA Exhibit*. Austin: University of Texas Press.

Gottdiener, Mark. 1997. "Dead Elvis as Other Jesus." In *In Search of Elvis: Music, Race, Art, Religion*, ed. Vernon Chadwick, 189–200. Boulder, Colo.: Westview Press.

Gregory, Neal, and Janice Gregory. 1997. "When Elvis Died: Enshrining a Legend." In *In Search of Elvis: Music, Race, Art, Religion*, ed. Vernon Chadwick, 225–43. Boulder, Colo.: Westview Press.

Grossberg, Lawrence. 1992. *We Gotta Get out of This Place: Popular Conservatism and Postmodern Culture*. New York: Routledge.

Grumet, Madeleine R. 1991. "The Politics of Personal Knowledge." In *Stories Lives Tell: Narrative and Dialogue in Education*, ed. Carol Witherell and Ned Noddings, 67–77. New York: Teachers College Press.

Gutiérrez, Ramón. 1996. "The Erotic Zone: Sexual Transgression on the U.S.-Mexican Border." In *Mapping Multiculturalism*, ed. Avery F. Gordon and Christopher Newfield, 253–62. Minneapolis: University of Minnesota Press.

Hebdige, Dick. 1979. *Subculture, the Meaning of Style*. London: Methuen.

Karimi, Robert. 1995. "San Antonio Remembers Selena." *La Prensa de San Antonio*, April 7.

Kellner, Douglas. 1995. *Media Culture: Cultural Studies, Identity, and Politics between the Modern and the Postmodern*. New York: Routledge.

Kline, Stephen. 1995. *Out of the Garden: Toys, TV, and Children's Culture in the Age of Marketing*. London: Verso.

Liner, Elaine. 1999. "Independent Film on Selena's Impact Airs on PBS." *Corpus Christi Caller-Times*, July 13.

Maguire, Brendan, and Georgie Ann Weatherby. 1998. "The Secularization of Religion and Television Commercials." *Sociology of Religion* 59, 2 (summer): 171–78.

McLemore, David. 1997. "Secular Sainthood: Movie Premiere Heightens Fans' Fascination with Anything Tied to Slain Singer Selena." *Dallas Morning News*, March 15, A1.

Miller, Lauraine. 1996. "Pilgrims Remember Their Star: First Anniversary of Selena's Slaying." *Houston Chronicle*, April, A1.

Mitchell, Rick. 1995. "In Life, She Was the Queen of Tejano Music. In Death, the 23-Year-Old Singer Is Becoming a Legend." *Houston Chronicle*, May 21, 6 (Texas Magazine).

Nieto, Consuelo. 1974. "The Chicana and the Women's Rights Movement: A Perspective." *Civil Rights Digest* 6, 3: 36–42.

Patoski, Joe Nick. 1995. "The Sweet Song of Justice." *Texas Monthly*, December, 102.

Pinkerton, James. 1995. "Singing Selena's Praises." *Houston Chronicle*, October 24, A11.

Revilla-Vasquez, Catherine. 1995. "Thank You Selena." *Hispanic* 8, 4 (May): 96.

Rodriguez, Jeanette, and Virgilio P. Elizondo. 1994. *Our Lady of Guadalupe: Faith and Empowerment among Mexican-American Women*. Austin: University of Texas Press.

Russell, Jeanne. 1995. "'Selena Trial' Stirs Hispanics' Passions." *Newsday*, October 16: A8.

Seiter, Ellen. 1999. "Children's Desires/Mothers' Dilemmas: The Social Contexts of Consumption." In *Children's Culture*, ed. H. Jenkins, 297–317. New York: New York University Press.

Sklar, Holly. 1995. "The Dying American Dream: And the Snake Oil of Scapegoating." In *Eyes Right!: Challenging the Right Wing Backlash*, ed. Chip Bertlet, 113–34. Boston: South End Press.

Stavans, Ilan. 1995. "Dreaming of You (Tejano Singer Selena)." *New Republic*, November 20, 24–26.

Street, John. 1997. *Politics and Popular Culture*. Philadelphia: Temple University Press.

Taylor, Diana. 1999. "Dancing with Diana: A Study in Hauntology." *TDR* 43, 1 (spring): 59–82.

Turner, Allan, and Patty Reinert. 1995. "Devoted Fans of Selena Arrive before Trial Starts." *Houston Chronicle*, October 9, A1.

Vara, Richard. 1995. "Cultural Myth of Selena." *Houston Chronicle*, May 21, 1 (Texas Magazine).

Willis, Paul E. 1990. *Common Culture: Symbolic Work at Play in the Everyday Cultures of the Young*. New York: Milton Keynes, Open University Press.

Wuthnow, Robert. 1989. *The Struggle for America's Soul: Evangelicals, Liberals, and Secularism*. Grand Rapids, Mich.: W. B. Eerdmans Publishing.

Zuniga, Jo Ann. 1995. "Selena Remembered in Day of Dead Altars." *Houston Chronicle* October 20, A39.

———, and R. A. Dyer. 1995. "Frenzied Fans Hail Verdict with Tears, Cheers." *Houston Chronicle*, October 24, A1.

part 2: popular ritual

When does eating become a ritual? Certainly when it occurs in a religious context, like a Passover seder, and also, most would probably agree, when it is part of secular family and cultural celebrations, like Thanksgiving. We might even see ritual in the intensely personal and carefully choreographed food manipulation of the anorexic. In his contribution to this section, Wade Clark Roof suggests that we might also find ritual, with all its powerful religious undertones, in the preparation, consumption, and celebration of pork barbecue in the "pig-loving" American South. If this is so, if the most (apparently) mundane visit to the neighborhood barbecue joint can be said to bear transcendent meaning, it would seem that nothing is safe from the ritual theorist's gaze.

And this is perhaps as it should be. For while many Americans have loosened their ties to organized religious institutions, they do not seem have lost their need for ritualized meaning-making activity; rather, they've just relocated it to places like athletic fields and art festivals. While the contributors to this section might not agree on what exactly constitutes ritual behavior, religious or otherwise, they uncover several themes in their explorations of the ritual dimension of popular culture that collectively point to both the permanent power of ritual and its unique place in contemporary America.

The first of these themes is the power of ritual to define a space and/or time set apart from daily experience, a kind of sacred setting where issues of ultimate concern come into focus. Churches and temples are such places, as are Native American sweat lodges, the holy sites of Mecca, and the river Ganges. So too, one could argue, are Graceland and the Vietnam Memorial. This notion of ritual as the encounter with sacred space and time is powerfully evoked in Sarah Pike's essay on the Burning Man festival held annually in the Nevada desert. In this three-day extravaganza of ironic art and alternative community, Pike sees a group of people making a pilgrimage to a place so removed from ordinary life that radical experimentation with self and community becomes possible. Through symbolic city making, body marking, various forms of ritualistic art, and chronologizing that defines events in relation to the festival (pre–Burning Man and post–Burning Man), festival participants act out what historian of religion Mircea Eliade identified a generation ago as a fundamental need of the religious person—to periodically reimmerse him- or herself into a time and place perceived as eternal and indestructible (*The Sacred and the Profane,* 1959). It turns out that may be a need shared by many ostensibly nonreligious Americans as well.

In a setting so different it makes the mind reel, Jennifer Rycenga finds at the Precious Moments Chapel, in Carthage, Missouri, at Christmastime, a ritualized space that fosters "total absorption in the 'holiday spirit,' centered around buying and selling." The demarcation of sacred space and time may be less evident in considerations of southern barbecue and Super Bowl spectacles, but in these, too, we can see the marks of ritualized time and space. The almost taboo aura of the barbecue pit, the power of the barbecue joint to break down powerful regional social boundaries, as Roof describes it, and the pre-game "birthing" of Super Bowl players through a long fabric tunnel described by James McBride, the socially deviant behavior that is normalized in the football stands—all of these indicate that in these settings, too, participants have stepped out of ordinary time and space into another world where different rules inhere and new possibilities emerge.

In a multiethnic and religiously diverse society like the United States (which of course includes a huge portion of purportedly nonreligious people), the sacredness of certain times and spaces is not a given, as it is, say, for the Catholic in Rome during Holy week or the Jew in Jerusalem during Yom Kippur. It is an interesting feature of the American religious landscape that while in traditional religious experience, the space and time themselves create the sense of the sacred for the participant, in the secular spaces and times considered here, participants imbue the sites with meaning through their own ritualized actions. By reference to powerful experiences or deeply held values—whether national, regional, subcultural or even purely personal—places like football stadiums (or the Barcaloungers from which they are observed), an anonymous and barren piece of the Nevada desert, and even a local restaurant can become sites of intense ritual meaning.

A second theme that surfaces repeatedly in these analyses of popular ritual is that of transformation. Set off as they are from everyday existence, these rituals, like their traditional religious counterparts, apparently create a space in which personal and sometimes collective change can occur. In his influential work on ritual, anthropologist Victor Turner focused on the transformative nature of ritual, especially rites of passage and their power to move an individual from one social status to another. While none of the events described by our authors would typically be called a rite of passage, they do share this transformative power.

According to Turner, subjects involved in ritual transformation pass through a liminal phase in which the structures of the society are temporarily suspended, even upended and mocked, and where intense experiences of *communitas*, or a sense of communion of equal individuals, occur among participants. This kind of liminality is clearly evident in Pike's description of the Burning Man festival, where every imaginable aspect of contemporary American culture (and especially its institutional religions) are lampooned. But Pike's analysis of post–Burning Man reports on Internet bulletin boards suggests that this play is actually part of a serious ritual restructuring of identity. Many festival goers describe finding their true selves and their true "homes" in this stripped down but wildly imaginative desert setting. Burning Man is also, Pike indicates, a place of potential social transformation where utopian visions of a society—defined by all of that which (in the participants' view) strait-laced, consumerist, Christian America is *not*—can be imagined and briefly experienced.

But it's not always this dramatic. To identify ritual as a site of transformation is simply to note that we are somehow *different* after partaking in the ritual from how we were when it began. American men might find some of their (mostly subconscious) anxieties about women assuaged following a Super Bowl Sunday gathering. Southerners might find that ties of family, church, and geography feel a little stronger following a shared barbecue supper.

In traditional religious ritual, the safe release of antistructural (playful, non-hierarchical, antiauthoritarian, subversive) energy is contained within the ritual action, and the rules and status systems governing the way things are normally done reemerge intact at the other end of the ritual process. Mardi Gras, the traditional reveler knew, would inevitably be followed by Ash Wednesday. In this way, the release ultimately serves to strengthen that which it ritually challenges. Whether or not the secular rituals of popular culture similarly reinforce the structures of the wider society or whether they might at least in some cases more radically alter the inherited cultural system is an interesting question raised by the studies in this section. Does Burning Man's revolutionary art yield any lasting social or personal change?

Does the blood ritual of barbecue have any real "jollifying" impact on the sober Protestantism of the South? While it is tempting to argue that ritual divorced from the doctrines and institutions of organized religion has more potential for lasting subversive impact, it is evident that many secular rituals have profoundly conservative effects. McBride's analysis of the Super Bowl, for instance, tells us that all the anxiety, exuberance, tension, and violence of the spectacle of professional football finally serve to reiterate and reaffirm the institution of American manhood. And pilgrimage to the Precious Moments chapel at Christmastime is nothing, Rycenga tells us, if not a festal reauthorization of "patriotism, patriarchy, respect for authority, and Christian exclusivism."

It is also important to note that these secular rituals are bound up with a different kind of structure, that of commercial enterprise. It may be that the commodification that attends these rituals (even, increasingly, Burning Man) works as its own kind of damper on the antistructural force of the ritual. In places like the Precious Moments chapel (ironically the only site considered here with explicit religious content) the intersection of ritual and commerce is shamelessly displayed, and antistructural forces stand no chance at all.

A third theme these essays raise is the way in which ritual of all kinds both exposes and helps resolve conflicts of various sorts. There are tensions involved in even the most carefully scripted religious rituals, as theorists have pointed out for nearly a century. The moment when an adolescent undergoes the rite of passage into adulthood, for instance, is fraught with tensions surrounding changes in sexual and social status. The threat those tensions pose, in fact, can be seen as a primary explanation for the closely controlled action of ritual. It is as if the repeated words, the predictable action, and the familiarity of the ritual acts offer a safe and comfortable route through crisis situations. One way of thinking about ritual, then, is as an organized set of behaviors that both heighten and ultimately help to resolve, or at least diffuse, the conflicts that threaten personal and collective life.

In each of the essays in this section, the authors see powerful conflicts crystallized in ritualized actions. In McBride's discussion, the conflict is individual and psychological; in his view, the Super Bowl reiterates the male's early childhood development and symbolically resolves his "ambivalence toward women who bear the legacy of the mother." Roof's treatment of southern barbecue sees it as a culinary resolution of the intracultural conflict between the "two cultures" of the American South—one folk, kin-based, and sensuous, the other official, ecclesial, and ascetic. The Burning Man festival, according to Pike, exposes and struggles with the conflicts between radically individual self-expression and the quest for a community of common ideals. Making a Christmas journey to the gift shop—encased Precious Moments Chapel, Rycenga argues, helps devotees to maneuver among some powerful conflicts indeed—Christian piety and consumerism, the efficiency of mass production and the desire for the singular, American individualism and an interdependent economic system. By "acting out" of their habitual norms in these formalized ways, partakers in these secular rituals are working out (sometimes consciously, sometimes not) significant conflicts that are engendered by, but unresolvable within, the structures of regular existence. Conflict is inherent in all religious ritual, but it offers an especially useful interpretive key to ritual in American culture, where so many conflicting worldviews and identities intersect.

A final theme suggested by these case studies of secular ritual is not only the diversity of contemporary American ritual (for instance, Burning Man is very consciously a ritual of cultural resistance and subversion, while the other three events described here are more socially conservative), but also the diversity of meanings attached to ritual activity when it operates independently of religious structures. Divorced from the specific mythic narratives that accompany much of traditional religious ritual, activities like these take on as many meanings as they have participants, for while the scholars here have all hazarded interpretations of what these activities "mean," they all also suggest how fluid and multivocal those meanings are. This may suggest that when it comes to ritual, the doing is more important than the interpreting; that is, it is possible to come together in organized, deeply meaningful activity with those for whom that meaning is significantly different. It may be that the need for communion in so large, diverse, and fragmented a society as the United States feeds the ritual impulse and draws us together into shared acts of eating, dancing, spectating, and buying, so that even if we can't agree on what we believe, we can at least feel that, for a few moments anyway, we all hold on to a slim thread of communal life.

Blood in the Barbecue?

Food and Faith in the American South

WADE CLARK ROOF

Anyone growing up in the American South, or even a visitor just traveling through the region, knows that barbecue and Dixie go together like honey and flies. No other food is so distinctively southern, as obvious in the signs seemingly everywhere for barbecue, or simply BBQ, posted on billboards, the sides of buildings, and menus of restaurants, cafes, and honkytonks scattered from Mississippi to Virginia. By barbecue, I mean mainly pork (but it can include beef and chicken) cooked slowly and basted often with carefully prepared sauces; hence the word as southerners use it refers both to the food and its style of preparation. Anything less is not barbecue; indeed, southerners bristle when outsiders casually talk of barbecuing but really mean just grilling burgers or throwing some chicken legs on a burner. To defame the word *barbecue* in this latter way is not just a sign of ignorance, but a violation of a sacred regional norm.

In this chapter, I look at barbecue as a deeply embedded symbol in southern culture. Food symbols are important in any culture; more than just an object of curiosity or taste, they are bound up with a people's way of life, their deepest values and identities. That being the case, food symbols inevitably are implicated in religious and political matters. In fact, I shall argue that barbecue — and especially barbecue pork — is of crucial symbolic significance for the South, for both its unity of experience and cultural distinctiveness as a region.

BARBECUE AS SYMBOL

Why single out pork barbecue? It could be argued that barbecue is a national food today, particularly at truck stops across the country. Yet it is also true that regional preferences remain deeply embedded when it comes to the choice of meat: pork is preferred east of the Mississippi, beef in the cattle country and in the West (Fabricant 1996). And nowhere is there as much variety in eating pork as found in the South. Southerners like pork fixed in endless ways, be it chicken-fried pork chops, cracklins or pork rinds, pickled pigs' feet and snouts, sausage, ham, or bacon, but mainly it's pork barbecued — whether chopped or pulled or sliced or made into hash—that they like the most. Indeed, hash in many southern towns has lost its generic meaning as a type of food; the term refers simply to a pork dish served on rice, alongside a bountiful supply of slaw and pickles. And then there are ribs. Mouth-watering ribs basted with a home-made sauce and dry rubbed to seal in the juices, cooked with dry, cool smoke—for this there is no substitute this side of heaven.

Like any food that becomes so much a part of the culture, pork in the South is more than just the meat of choice. It's a fundamental symbol whose meanings penetrate deep into the region's way of life. Evidence for this is apparent even in the sheer number and types of signs for pigs, in one form or another, found all over the South. Well-known observer of southern culture, sociologist John Shelton Reed of the University of North Carolina at Chapel Hill, writes:

> For years I've kept a mental log of barbecue joint signs. I've seen pigs reclining, running, and dancing; pigs with bibs, with knives and forks, with crowns and scepters. I've seen pigs as beauty contest winners, pigs in Confederate uniforms, and pigs in cowboy hats (one with a banjo). I've seen Mr. and Mrs. Pig dressed for a night on the town, and Mr. and Mrs. Pig as American Gothic. But I've never seen pigs like I saw in Memphis. Pigs in chef's hats and volunteer firemen's helmets. A pig in a Superman suit rising from the flames. A pig reclining in a skillet; another on a grill, drinking beer. Two pigs basting a little gnomish person on a spit, and (on the T-shirts of a team called the Rowdy Southern Swine) a whole trainload of partying pigs. It's a hard call, but my favorite was probably some pigs with wings and haloes, from a team called Hog Heaven. (Reed 1995, 148)

Pigs are extraordinarily versatile: they can be dressed in popular garb to fit any audience, working class, middle class, or upper class, no matter how formal or informal the occasion. The animal takes on almost totemic proportions as anyone knows who has ever heard University of Arkansas Razorback football fans chant, calling the hogs—Wooooooooooooooooooo! Pig! Suuuuuuuuuuu-eeeeeeeeeeee! And like any symbol as pervasive as this one, it serves to bring southerners together around celebrations and common activities. Few other places in the South enjoy as much joviality, sociality, and sharing as do those places where pig symbols are displayed. Like in any liminal moment or setting, old boundaries tend to lose force and a new basis of social solidarity emerges. To quote John Shelton Reed (1995, 47) again, "A good barbecue joint may be the one place you'll find Southerners of all descriptions—yuppies, hippies, and cowboys, Christians and sinners, black and white together."

Of course, Reed is speaking about barbecue in the New South where increasing numbers of southerners (both old-timers and new comers) find a pig sign more acceptable than a Dixie flag. Southerners of late have been hunting for a new regional emblem and the pig ranks high on that list. The fact that pigs and barbecue have all gone mainstream in recent times helps—Memphis has its World Championship Barbecue Cooking Contest; Hillsboro, North Carolina, its annual Hillsboro Hog Day; Climax, Georgia, its Climax Swine Time; and not to be overlooked, there's the Chitlin Strut in Salley, South Carolina. These aren't just commercial ventures to attract tourists, efforts at trading on southern tradition to hungry outsiders (though southerners aren't adverse to making a little money on it); they are symbolic markers of sorts, reminding a changing, expanding world of the continuing importance of barbecue. The fact that southern barbecue is now exported to other regions of the country reinforces the need for dramatizing its symbolic presence and significance within the homeland. If nothing more, it reminds people who live in the South and those who grew up there of a reality that borders on the timeless. Upscale magazines like *Southern Living* do their part as well to package barbecuing as a southern fine art. These magazines regularly carry recipes for suave, middle-class southerners interested in advancing the skills of making good sauces and concocting new culinary delights like "Cheesy Barbecue Popcorn." Hence barbecue—replacing grits—emerges as the symbol of a new, more prosperous and respectable South.

But these celebrations and upscale recipes notwithstanding, the real meaning of barbecue in the South lies in its more traditional setting—in the joints and shacks where most of it is still served, close to the pits where it is cooked. Largely a male enterprise, barbecuing in this context has long signaled an ordered world of social patterns and activities. Anthropologist Mary Douglas (1972, 61) writes, "If food is treated as a code, the message it encodes will be found in the pattern of social relations being expressed. The message is about different degrees of hierarchy, inclusion and exclusion, boundaries and transactions across boundaries. Food categories therefore encode social events." One could not find a better example in the South of what Douglas has in mind than with the preparation and serving of that most favorite of foods—pit-barbecued pork and the "fixins."

In a basic sort of way, eating barbecue defines a southerner. This is true not just in the sense of "you are what you eat," which of course is to some extent true, but also in the sense that groups are known by their food habits. Especially in a region with so distinct a consciousness of itself as being over against others—

in-group versus out-group—foodways function as a symbol of group identity. The practices surrounding even the homeliest and most mundane of food easily emerge as significant. Barbecue pork is just such a homely and mundane food, long serving as a visible boundary distinguishing southerners from other Americans. That boundary has not disappeared; if anything, it may have become even more visible as southern-style barbecue has spread across the country creating a space for southern culture in the most alien places—like Yankee territory. The boundary is increasingly tied less to physical space, and more to the presence of southerners wherever they live. Both within the region and outside of it, southerners continue to relish being different even to the extreme of boasting about it, as we know from bumper stickers proclaiming that "Southerners do it slower" or, as in Hank Williams's classic lyric, "If heaven ain't a lot like Dixie, I don't want anything to do with it." Moreover, the fact that such bumper stickers show up in great numbers on cars, pickups, and vans outside barbecue joints where Hank Williams's music still plays on jukeboxes underscores something of Mary Douglass's point about food categories encoding social realities.

Certainly for the major social institutions of southern life, barbecue is very much at the center of action. For example, it continues to be the favorite food at political rallies. Democrats and Republicans, and nowadays mostly Republicans, routinely hold political events featuring barbecue—often chopped pork with hash, rice, slaw, and hush puppies. That tradition reaches far back into the past. Even as far back as the election of 1832, the *Louisville Journal* reported that "swallowing a pig" was an effective technique in winning the voter's favor (Remini 1971). Then as now, eating dramatizes and enacts fundamental cultural values—it combines taste with rhetoric and conveys not just what is good to eat but what people feel about how things are going on the farm, in the town, for themselves, and for the larger world. Even more important, for southerners a political rally with barbecue bonds the group and symbolizes a world governed by law and order. It communicates something of the sacred and the profane, the two at some point juxtaposed against one another. The most profane of things, as Emile Durkheim reminds us, has the capacity to evoke the presence of the sacred; and conversely, that which is regarded as sacred mingles freely in and around the profane. In many rural areas and small towns radios still carry, often at noontime, daily reports on local stock prices interspersed with Gospel music—"hogs and hymns," as we called it in South Carolina when I was growing up. The latest prices on hogs and cattle come together with inspirational and country music, and often a political commentary, in what amounts to a mediated ritual of southern identity and celebration.

God approves of barbecue, or so it would seem considering the thousands of church cookbooks published across the region. Just about every First Presbyterian church has a cookbook and, for sure, the biggest Southern Baptist and United Methodist churches in every city have one, and all have recipes for barbecue sauces. Often the recipes are personalized, such as "Miss Maggie Clark's BBQ Sauce" with instructions about how to prepare it. It is common for such information—the "esoteric knowledge" of barbecuing—to come from someone who is widely known and respected within a church, and often it has been handed down from a master cook from a previous generation. The church supper is of course the occasion *par excellence* for eating barbecue, symbolizing a shared religious and social world and communal belonging. Both the frequency of church suppers and the attention given to food in religious gatherings for southerners point to the symbolic significance of food. The meal mediates between the individual and the community and serves as a ritual affirmation of the gathered community itself. Because both the political and religious institutions are closely identified with the same food—with barbecue pork and fried chicken, the latter being the second best-known food of the region—the two institutions themselves are closely linked symbolically. It might even be said that for many southern churchgoers food is a key ingredient in ordering and sustaining a phenomenological world bringing the religious and political together.

BARBECUE AND SACRIFICE

Links between food and religion run deep in any culture—provoking powerful religious emotions associated with food. Pigs especially seem to evoke strong religious emotions. So strong, anthropologist Marvin Harris suggests, that the world can be divided into two types of people, pig lovers and pig haters. Pig hating among Jews and Muslims is well known, but pig loving is common as well, particularly in Celtic cultures. Pig hating and pig loving differ in how they symbolize relations between people and food. Pig hate leads to carefully prescribed dietary regulations and food prohibitions. Here the pig symbolizes those boundaries with a taboo-like quality: don't eat, don't touch. Pig love arouses a more mystical, unifying experience, a bringing together of the people world and the animal world. Its power to solidify is astounding, shown by Harris to work its magic in many cultures. "Pig love," he writes (1974, 46) "is a state of total community between man and pig. While the presence of pigs threatens the human status of Moslems and Jews, in the ambience of pig love one cannot truly be human except in the company of pigs." Hence, not surprisingly, in those places around the world where you find pig love you also observe close contact of people and pigs: people often have pigs in pens adjacent to where they live, sometimes even in barns attached to human dwellings. It is not uncommon for people to talk to their pigs, to call them by names; people will feed them from the family table—"slopping" as people below the Mason and Dixon are fond of saying, meaning that they care so much for their choice swine they share with them their own leftover human food. Obviously, southerners are pig lovers.

Given this close association with pigs, we can speak, not inappropriately, of the "cult of the pig" in the South. And unlike in India in the case of cows, the veneration of the pig results in obligatory sacrifices and celebratory occasions for eating pigs. To quote Marvin Harris again:

> Because of ritual slaughter and sacred feasting, pig love provides a broader prospect for communion between man and beast than is true of the Hindu farmer and his cow. The climax of pig love is the incorporation of the pig as flesh into the flesh of the human host and of the pig as spirit into the spirit of the ancestors. (1974, 46)

Communion with pigs! Obviously there's something deeply mystical about such communion binding pig lovers and their pigs. And it doesn't take a great deal of imagination to leap from this depiction of incorporating the pig as flesh to the high and holy act of eating the body and blood of Christ as practiced by Christians. In a region where there is both so much pig love *and* Christ love, and frequent eating of the flesh of both kinds, might there be an affinity between these two sacred feasts? Might there be blood in the barbecue, so to speak?

THE SOUTH'S "TWO CULTURES"

The question is not as far-fetched as it might first seem. Among white Southerners, blood has long assumed a special status. It is *the* life force: a potent symbol of family and kin bonding, of unity among people, especially in the face of an external threat. Some might go so far as to say—indeed, people have said— that blood is an obsession among white Anglo-Saxon Protestant southerners. Certainly concern about racial purity is a defining feature of southern history. Racial purity came to be a concern particularly in the years after the Civil War when southerners, suffering from defeat, sought to defend and romanticize their way of life by means of Jim Crow segregation laws and a system of rituals and etiquette respecting their pride and identity. Defensiveness and pride resulted in a powerful psychology that unified much of the southern white world around folk symbols—including the mystique surrounding blood and ancestry. This regional psychology would perhaps reach its apex in the veneration of the southern "soldier saint" who fought valiantly and spilled his blood on behalf of a way of life. It is a psychology, too, that would produce cultural distortions in its unyielding and obsessive devotion to a cause. To quote John Shelton Reed (1982, 131), who paraphrases Irving Babbitt's comment about the Spanish, "There seems to be something southern about southerners that causes them to behave in a southern manner."

Religion is a crucial element in southern identity and culture, but it is a complex reality since, as Samuel S. Hill points out, there are "two cultures" juxtaposed in southern experience. What emerged after the Civil War and Reconstruction in the latter decades of the nineteenth century, Hill argues, were two overlapping ritual systems: one, celebrating regional and folk values, and the other, affirming historic Christian beliefs and practices. Much of southern tradition ever since is a playing out of the tensions between these two ritual systems. The fact that the love ethic of Christianity was muffled in popular religious life, forced to accommodate a prideful and racially sensitive regional culture, is a big part of what makes southern religion so distinctive; in effect, social justice took back seat to a more personal, Christ-centered piety. Added is a peculiar guilt-oriented theology paralleling regional experiences of slavery and war which brought to prominence themes of sacrifice and atonement through the blood of Christ. This theological construction would dominate much of popular religious life after the fall of the Confederacy and the era of Reconstruction—which is to say, the great majority of believers, upward of 80 percent or more in some counties of Baptists, Methodists, and other low-church, sectarian Protestants. Regional values created an operative southern theology of the "problem-solution" sort, with an emphasis upon the all-important work of salvation by Christ, whose death on the cross satisfied God's violated holiness and thereby made redemption possible for any individual if only he or she would accept what had been done for him or her. As Flannery O'Connor so rightly claimed, the South became "Christ-haunted," and to understand what that means one must grasp how themes of sacrifice and atonement play out not just in church but throughout the culture.

A "Christ-haunted" culture finds expression in the region's sacred and quasi-sacred music. Nothing quite occupies the place within southern life as those old hymns like "The Old Rugged Cross," "Nothing but the Blood," and "Blessed

Assurance," all pitched to deep mystical meanings surrounding the cross, blood, and salvation. Journalist Marshall Frady (1980, XVff.) sums up this underlying message lying at the heart of southern piety in the following way:

> Religion in the South was principally a romance about the cross—a dire melo-drama of thorns and betrayal and midnight anguish, with nothing in the life of Jesus mattering quite so much as his suffering and his death. The Southern Jesus was an almost pre-Raphaelite figure of pale languishing melancholy, with a tender, grave, bearded face much like those thin faces of young Confederate officers that stare, doomed, out of ghostly tintypes. And nowhere was this Southern Christ so passionately defined as in those old heavy-hauling hymns that most Southern-ers had sung, at least once in their youth, at some summer night's revival in a bug-swarmed tent on the ragged outskirts of town: *What can wash away my sins? Nothing but the blood of Jesus . . . Oh! precious is the flow that makes me white as snow . . . in agony and blood, He fixed his languid eyes on me . . . O Jesus, Lord! how can it be that Thou shouldst give Thy life for me, to bear the cross and agony in that dread hour on Calvary . . . Oh, how I love Jesus! Oh, how I love Jeees-SUSSS!*

But how do we get from revivals and such heavy hymns back to barbecue? The answer it would seem has to do, in one way or another, with blood, sacrifice, and mystical communion. The "two cultures" of the South, though distinct, are drawn together through symbols and rituals—those of both the official religious system and the folk culture. The greater the cultural integration, in fact, the greater the chances that what happens in one ritual system will bear upon the other. And because southern culture continues to be rather tightly bound, combining distinctive regional and religious themes, it follows that folk rituals will reinforce the dominant religious and cultural themes and, to some extent, develop analogues of myth, practice, and boundary-defining mechanisms in lived experience similar to those of the official religious establishment. It is in this latter sense that food as symbolism and barbecuing as a specific prac-tice take on deep ritual meaning and significance for southerners, even if only vaguely perceived.

FOOD, PLACE, KIN, AND CHURCH

To start with, we might look for what Durkheim would call the "elementary forms of ritual sacrifice" in the popular culture. And barbecuing as a cultural practice certainly offers opportunity to do so. Much mystery surrounds barbecuing as a "food event": pork is traditionally barbecued in pits requiring careful attention to the fire, the cooking, and the sauces. The pit itself is not unimportant. The pit qualifies as sacred space of sorts, and hence is usually covered when not in use. When in use it is a place of awe and mystery, the primordial depths from which good things come. Amid the smoldering logs and smoke streaming from the bottoms of the pit, magical forces turn the raw meat into something mouth watering and delectable. A vigil-like atmosphere prevails as the meat cooks slowly, and especially when it is cooked overnight as is frequently the case. It is a time of watching and stoking the fires, of telling and sharing stories. Even today, when backyard grills have taken over much of the barbecuing and turned it into a private and family-based activity, good old boys still come together to watch the pits overnight as they prepare meals for the Lions Club, a church, or a political rally.

The fact that those watching the fires and telling the stories—the high priests—are almost always men is itself important symbolically. Cooking in the region is commonly women's work, but not so with pit barbecuing. It is viewed as a special act, set apart from regular cooking, requiring special knowledge, and hence a man's job. This ritual reversal of cooking responsibilities signals an enduring male authority and locates the artistry and craft of turning pork into barbecue clearly within a quasi-sacred province for which only men may take charge. Barbecuing is part work, part sport, and part performance, and much lore surrounds those cooks who possess what amount to esoteric skills, knowledge of recipes, and techniques of food preparation (often handed down from older males). It is not uncommon to hear stories praising the best barbecue cooks in a community and conferring upon them great respect and status, defining them as functional equivalents to a high priest officiating a sacred feast.

But there's more involved than preparing barbecue—eating it takes on particular significance as well. No blasphemy is intended when I say that loving Jesus and loving pigs have much in common: both types of love are expressed in feasts, and even more importantly, in both the act of eating is symbolically related to the crucial flow of vital life forces. The first—shared feasts—is obvious enough, but what about this latter? Is pig love an occasion for the flow of vital life forces?

To grasp how this might possibly be, it is important to remember that in the South historically there have been strong, overlapping attachments to place, kin, and church. Southern religion is closely bound up with locality and kinship. Jean Heriot's recent ethnography of a Southern Baptist congregation in South Carolina nicely underscores the fusion of these three types of identity: "Being

Baptist (is) more than a statement of doctrinal belief," she writes, "it (is) also a statement about family, kinship ties, place, and history" (1994, 57). Polls and surveys show that attachments to local communities remain stronger in this region than anywhere else in the United States, which, in turn, reinforces kinship and religious ties. Local attachments undergird a local worldview with its own sacred canopy and drama of sin and salvation, played out in a context bounded to a considerable degree by community and kinship ties. Close links between church and family abound. In Appalachia, for example, the proliferation of churches is known to result often from kin groups breaking off and organizing their own churches (Bryant 1981). And nowhere on earth are there more family reunions, cemetery associations, and church-organized homecomings—social gatherings where family and religious identities easily fuse. Moreover, such gatherings almost invariably include dinner on the grounds, frequently at a church, and often with the same people who are at church on Sunday morning meeting to eat with extended family and kin later in the afternoon. Put differently, in the context of the South's two cultures, ties of kinship and place are organizing social principles bound up with religious identity, ties so strong they often overshadow the deeper historic, universal themes of the official religious community.

Place, family, and church are all bound by ancestry, but practically speaking, it is the food practices more than anything else that keep memory alive and visibly symbolize this underlying historical unity. Eating, and certainly eating barbecue, is the one thing—sometimes it seems like the only thing— that kin groups do when they come together. By sharing a meal together, they reaffirm the ties that bind—of one to another and of all to place. But why is barbecue so important in this respect? Part of the answer lies in the fact that traditionally, stoking the barbecue pit has been a man's job. Despite clear norms about cooking as a female activity, public and outdoors cooking with a male head is important because it reaffirms the traditional social order, the unity of all things past and present. It seems reasonable to expect, in fact, that the stronger the overlapping identities of place, family, and church, the more likely outdoor food practices will take on great symbolic significance. Even in the New South of interstate highways, shopping malls, and family webpages in cyberspace, the "food event" remains of great importance to families. Gwen Neville (1987) argues that reunions, homecomings, and other such occasions involving big spreads of food provide for southerners who have left their home communities a chance to return and to renew their ties with their primal community. Such occasions are really like pilgrimages to places of origin, opportunities to re-create meaningful ties to a sacred community encompassing kin and fellow believers. Gathered around the table, often not far removed from the barbe-cue pit, generations of people bound by family, kin, and religious ties all come together, if only briefly, in what amounts to a ritual celebration of *communitas*, of the ties that really bind and give expression to the vital life forces.

Gathering around the table and pit takes on semi-sacred significance, even replacing the church for some as the dominant arena for the celebration of *communitas* for still another reason. And this has to do with the particular style of popular southern religion. While southerners are known for their high levels of religiosity, Holy Communion, or the celebration of the Eucharist, is not a particularly prominent part of the region's tradition. Low-church, evangelical Protestantism set the style historically with its emphasis upon emotions and individuals accepting Christ in their hearts rather than upon liturgical worship and celebration, or the sacramental observance of a gathered community. In practical effect, religious food was robbed of some of its mystical power. Thus, communion services in southern churches historically were infrequent, often "quarterly" (meaning every three months) among Baptists, Methodists, and other low-church denominations. Even when Holy Communion is served, grape juice replaces wine in the popular faith traditions. It was a Methodist dentist, Dr. Thomas Welch, who saw to it many years ago that unfermented grape juice was substituted in the Lord's Supper, a practice that caught on among low-church groups in the South where drinking, or activities related to drinking, was viewed as a serious moral problem. Once again, the "two cultures" thesis sheds light upon the situation. Southerners forged a popular-based unity in an official ascetic-religious call for total abstinence from alcohol—including wine—in the interest of personal piety, but in so doing created a pale imitation of the historic Christian mass that was originally modeled after the account in First Corinthians where Jesus took a cup of wine and pronounced, "This is the new covenant in my blood. Do this in remembrance of me." Grassroots southern religion—that is, the dominant religion—is left with strong moral power over individuals but weak in its sacramental rituals and mystical celebrations.

As a consequence, much of southern religion suffers from a moral asceticism and blandness, or an inability to "enjoy Jesus" in ways that Christian traditions in other cultural settings often do. Southerners tend to celebrate Jesus emotionally within the more narrow confines of their individual lives, but far less so in a lively and shared partaking of Jesus' body and blood. Yet as one commentator, Donald Horton, has pointed out, a vital aspect of lived religion is its "social jollification," or the actual enjoyment people experience with food and drink as they celebrate the mystical bonds of faith. Food has a sensuous and rejuvenating quality in a religious context, if given ritual expression. But if this doesn't happen in the communion services within popular church life, then where else might it happen?

Casual observation suggests that communion with the pig is an occasion for social jollification. In this protoritual moment vital life forces flow, helped in no small part because barbecue is often eaten with beer, and on occasion even bourbon—and not infrequently under a Dixie flag or guns or some other symbol of regional significance. Nor is it a coincidence that the usual place for eating barbecue is called a "joint," for it is in shacks and honkytonks that eating and drinking come together in what amounts to a hearty display of enjoyment. Even the more upscale places that try to disassociate barbecue from the seamier aspects of southern life like to bill themselves as places where you can enjoy yourself casually as you eat and drink. No matter where the place, or the socioeconomic status of the clientele, eating barbecue seems to make people happy and gregarious: they seem to get excited just making simple menu selections; even coming together around this special food seems rejuvenating in a Durkheimian sense. In a very simple, yet profound sort of way, regional bonds are affirmed and the simple act of eating becomes "time out of time," a moment of celebration and mystical unity. Food and memory are always bound together, but especially so in a context where emotions are less restrained and the natural unities of people easily surface. In effect, the barbecue joint and the social occasions on which barbecue is served accomplish what the church often fails to do: create an opportunity for affirming the mundane world of family, kin, and friends in an open, jovial atmosphere.

Just because the symbolic blood in the barbecue overshadows the pale substitute of the church-based communion does not mean that what happens at church is unimportant. My point is not to downplay the role of religious institutions; indeed, the many church suppers, overt friendliness, and stress upon fellowship—often a code word for getting together to eat—help to sustain the importance of food symbolism and its meaning in southern life. Rather, the two—barbecue and church—can be, and often are, mutually enforcing and are not easily separated in the ritual performance of southern identity in a context in which place, kin, and religion are all symbolically linked. What we learn in all of this is a basic Durkheimian principle: that even in the most profane, everyday activities such as eating, the underlying vital forces of social life and of primordial human bonding find sacred expression. So the next time you hear the familiar southern chant—Wooooooooooooooooooo! Pig! Suuuuuuuuu-eeeeeeeeeeee!—remember, it is about more than just pigs.

REFERENCES

Bryant, F. Carlene. 1981. *We're All Kin: A Cultural Study of a Mountain Neighborhood.* Knoxville: University of Tennessee Press.

Bultman, Bethany. 1996. *Redneck Heaven: Portrait a Vanishing Culture.* New York: Bantom.

Douglas, Mary. 1972. "Deciphering a Meal." *Daedulus* 101, 1 (Winter): 61–81.

Fabricant, Florence. 1996. "The Geography of Taste," *New York Times Magazine,* March 10.

Frady, Marshall. 1980. *Southerners: A Journalist's Odyssey.* New York: Meridian.

Harris, Marvin. 1974. *Cows, Pigs, Women, and Witches: The Riddles of Culture.* New York: Vintage.

Heriot, M. Jean. 1994. *Blessed Assurance: Beliefs, Actions, and the Experience of Salvation in a Carolina Baptist Church.* Knoxville: University of Tennessee Press.

Hill, Samuel S., Jr. 1972. "The South's Two Cultures." In *Religion and the Solid South,* ed. Samuel S. Hill, Jr., Edgar T. Thompson, Anne Firor Scott, Charles Hudson, and Edwin S. Gaustad. Nashville: Abingdon Press.

Horton, Donald. 1943. "The Functions of Alcohol: A Cross-Cultural Study." *Quarterly Journal for the Study of Alcohol* 4: 199–320.

Neville, Gwen. 1987. *Kinfolks and Pilgrims: Rituals of Reunion in American Protestant Culture.* New York: Oxford University Press.

Reed, John Shelton. 1982. *One South: An Ethnic Approach to Regional Culture.* Baton Rouge: Louisiana State University Press.

———. 1995. *Kicking Back: Further Dispatches from the South.* Columbia: University of Missouri Press.

Remini, Robert V. 1971. "Election of 1832." In *History of American Presidential Elections 1789–1968,* ed. Arthur M. Schlesinger, Jr. New York: Chelsea House Publishers.

Symptomatic Expression of Male Neuroses

Collective Effervescence, Male Gender Performance, and the Ritual of Football

JAMES MCBRIDE

Two thousand years hence, when archeologists of the future examine the remnants of a "lost" American civilization, they undoubtedly will be fascinated by the ruins of massive steel-and-concrete structures built in its major cities. Within the crumbling facades of these remains, they will find seating for tens of thousands of witnesses who had unobstructed views of a field where obviously some cardinal ritual act occurred. Archeologists may speculate as to what exactly the viewers were witnessing: assuredly it was some sort of festival, but its particulars might prove elusive. Nonetheless, being good archeologists, they would most likely conclude that, in light of the extraordinarily high capital expenditures for these stadiums and supporting infrastructures, the festivals must have been of central importance to the American identity. Such expenditures could be explained in terms of economic activity, but the design of the facility, with seating capacity in the tens of thousands, indicated that physical production was not the aim of these massive structures. Instead, it would be far more likely that they were used to produce cultural meaning, either for the societal group to which the event was directed (according to age, class, race, or gender) or for the nation as a whole. From the traditional standpoint of their academic discipline, archeologists would be inclined to believe that these stadiums and the rituals that took place within them must have had some deeply religious significance to its spectators, whether or not they recognized it themselves.

Our excursion into the fourth millennium may render contemporary cultural practices exotic, even unrecognizable, but distance has a way of bringing to light elements of our own experience that are otherwise invisible. As a boy, I remember vividly the excitement that animated the men in our small, largely blue-collar community when football season rolled around. Most worked very hard as manual and skilled laborers, steelworkers, truckers, and members of the trade unions. But despite differences in race and ethnicity, religion and politics, everyone in this male community felt bonded together as one during the season—cheering for the same team. That professional football team was the embodiment of who we were—or at least who we thought we were—and our spirits rose and fell with each victory and defeat. It was only years later, after I had studied religious phenomena, that I began to understand just how that undertaking had shaped all of us. Gaining critical distance from my childhood, I realized that this intimate, shared experience might appear very differently to those who looked upon this phenomenon from the outside.

The archeologists' conclusion that the "game" of American football is intimately related to the expression of religious and cultural identity may seem strange to the ear, but they wouldn't be wrong. For, despite the amusement we derive from stories about the "touchdown Jesus" (Christ with arms raised) seen through a gap in Notre Dame's coliseum, or the open roof of the Dallas stadium (so that "God can watch the Cowboys play"), football doesn't have just an incidental kinship to faith. On the contrary, football is fundamentally connected to religion. It is a commonplace among historians of religion to note that the etymological root of religion—Latin, *religare*—means a "binding back." That phrase implies not only a return to cosmological origins but also a return to that which gives the individual life: the community. Hence, as the founder of European sociology Emile Durkheim claimed, "far from being due to a vague innate power of the individual" (Durkheim 1965, 470), the religious ideal is carried by, and is the product of, the collectivity.

Regardless of whether one agrees with Durkheim's assertion that the gods are conceived rather than perceived by society, the Durkheimian approach demonstrates that religion is the tie that binds a collectivity together. Or, in other words, that which binds a society together is religious. From a Durkheimian perspective, what our contemporaries might consider a wholly secular society is an impossibility. Rather, human beings in groups transform the objects and activities of everyday life into the sacred—the representation of the collectivity—which in turn forms and shapes their lives as individuals. This transformation does not occur through the mere belief of individuals; group action is essential. The sacred is therefore born out of what might be called a collective effervescence. These planned gatherings paradoxically generate spontaneous expressions of group enthusiasm, even hysteria, that bind the individual with the assembly, create the primacy of collective identification, and establish the preeminent moral authority of the group over the individual.

COLLECTIVE EFFERVESCENCE

In his classic study of aboriginal societies, *The Elementary Forms of the Religious Life*, Durkheim closely examined these *corrobbori* or ritualized gatherings.

The very fact of the concentration [of individuals] acts as an exceptionally powerful stimulant. When they are once come together, a sort of electricity is formed by their collecting which quickly transports them to an extraordinary degree of exaltation. Every sentiment expressed finds a place without resistance in all the minds, which are very open to outside impressions; each re-echoes the others, and is re-echoed by the others. The initial impulse thus proceeds, growing as it goes, as an avalanche grows in its advance. And as such passions so free from all control could not fail to burst out, on every side one sees nothing but violent gestures, cries, veritable howls, and deafening noises of every sort, which aid in intensifying still more the state of mind which they manifest. And since a collective sentiment cannot express itself collectively except on the condition of observing a certain order permitting co-operation and movements in unison, these gestures and cries naturally tend to become rhythmic and regular: hence come songs and dances. (246–47)

Many may recognize in Durkheim's description the experience of being in the stands at a football stadium. The charged atmosphere, the ubiquitous signs, the cheering and screaming, the rhythmic chanting (e.g., "we will, we will rock you"), the wave, the iconic use of favorite player numbers or symbols (e.g., "cheeseheads"), even the use of team colors in clothing or its application to the bodies of spectators are all reminiscent of the *corrobbori*.

The passions of football bear all the markings of a ritual at a religious site or temple (Latin, *fanum*). Derived from this etymological root, the name given participants in the ritual is fanatics, or in American parlance, fans. As partisans of a particular team, fans are allowed, even expected, to be carried away with enthusiasm for their side. In Durkheim's *corrobbori* "the passions released are of such an impetuosity that they can be restrained by nothing. [Participants] are so far removed from their ordinary conditions of life, and they are so thoroughly conscious of it, that they feel they must set themselves outside of and above their ordinary morals" (247). So too is the case in football. Fans may not only "boo" the opposing team, but they may even physically attack its supporters. It is not uncommon for fistfights to break out, for victorious fans to tear up the turf or tear down the goalposts, or, particularly after a league championship game or the Super Bowl, to engage in full-fledged urban riots—"celebrations" which have gotten "out of hand."

In the midst of an assembly animated by a common passion, we become susceptible of acts and sentiments of which we are incapable when reduced to our own forces; and when the assembly is dissolved and when, finding ourselves alone again, we fall back to our ordinary level, we are then able to measure the height to which we have been raised above ourselves. (Durkheim 1965, 240)

Every professional football game is accompanied by what sociologists might deem deviant behavior. Ostensibly law-abiding citizens engage in illegal acts, much of which is tolerated by law enforcement. One sportswriter in Baltimore reported that drinking and urinating in public, littering the ground with trash and beer bottles, trampling over lawns and flower beds in the surrounding neighborhood, and even driving on sidewalks are all prevalent. Police frequently look the other way. He concluded:

> Pro football has taken on a status akin to religion in this country. A bunch of guys drinking beer at a tailgate party is not going to be treated the same as a bunch of guys drinking beer on a corner. We've decided when, where, and why our laws against the public consumption of alcohol will be enforced. They will not be at pro football games. (Kane 1997)

Such behavior is tolerated by the authorities because of the nature of the game whose effects police recognize as being "larger than life." What produces such antics? What turns ostensibly normal individuals into "rabid" fans?

Durkheim suggested that the reason for such behavior in *corrobbori* lay in group identification by which individuals become a channel for the expression of collective power. The very suspension of individuality yields an infectious euphoria—what we might call, from a dispassionate perspective, "mob consciousness"—which endows the fan with a seemingly irresistible strength. By becoming a member of the collectivity, by becoming a fan, the individual is recognized as having the authority to wield that power, to become a conduit of collective triumph. To do so in the context of American football, as in aboriginal religious ritual, one need only identify oneself with the totemic representation of the clan or team. Like aboriginal identification with totemic creatures, American football teams take the names of animals (Lions, Broncos, Bears, Rams, Dolphins), birds (Falcons, Seahawks, Eagles), or heroic figures (Chiefs, Vikings, Giants, Saints, 49ers). As one sportswriter put it, "Football is very tribal in that way. You paint your face and you put on your colors and you square off against a tribe from another part of the country with different colors. And sometimes it gets a little ugly" (Nelson 1991, 93).

Although at first glance it might seem that identification with the totem is the means by which to acquire the totem's attributes, Durkheim disagreed. "It is not the intrinsic nature of the thing whose name the clan bears that marked it out to become the object of a cult" (1965, 236). Hence, even though the attributes of a "Steeler" or "Packer"—both identified with workers who have exercised limited social power in American history—may not be comparable to the mythic powers of natural creatures or legendary figures, the totem nevertheless exercises an equivalent power in the imagination of the fans, no matter what name is chosen. As Durkheim concluded, "The totem is before all a symbol, a material expression of something else." What is that "something else"? For Durkheim, the totemic principle becomes the god of the clan, the ultimate reality for members of the collectivity, but this god is not a transcendent cosmological figure. Rather, this god, transcendent to the individual, is the clan itself, "personified and represented to the imagination under the visible form of the animal or vegetable which serves as totem" (236).

By being born into the clan or "raised a fan" of a particular team, the individual is constituted by identification with the totemic symbol of the group. "Since society cannot exist except in and through individual consciousness, this force must also penetrate us and organize itself within us; it thus becomes an integrated part of our being and by that very fact this is elevated and magnified" (Durkheim 1965, 240). The collectivity therefore lives in and through its members or fans and, likewise, the individual lives in and through totemic identification. To be a "true blue" or "diehard" fan is to organize individual identity around the team. The Packers, 49ers, Saints, or Bears become the fan's lifeworld, and the fortunes of the team directly affect the fan's self-perception and attitudes. Fans immerse themselves in the totem. They wear baseball caps or Styrofoam football helmets with the team's insignia emblazoned. They paint their faces and bodies with the team colors, even baring their chests in subfreezing temperatures. They wear the team's jersey with the number of their favorite player and vicariously live his triumph or defeat.

SOCIETY OF SPECTACLE

In contemporary society, however, fan identification with the fate of their heroes on the field is not an aberration from life. Late capitalism has made spectacle the rule of human experience. Whereas premodern society was characterized by the sense of touch as the sign of humanness, today touch has been replaced by sight. What is seen is to be believed and cathartically experienced. In what Guy DeBord has called "the society of the spectacle" (1995), the activity of individuals has been displaced by its representation, whether that be "in person" or via the media. These representations are incarnate in the form of commodities. Late capitalism is the world of the commodity—a product designed for the market. The commodity serves as a screen on which human desires and attributes are projected. It is the commodity that is intelligent, sophisticated, strong, desirable, and sexy, not the person. One need only look at commercial advertising and its ubiquitous presence in newspapers and magazines, on billboards and television to know this fundamental postmodern truth. In the eyes of consumers, the presentation of the commodity is more real than everyday life. The reality of everyday is measured by how closely it resembles the "reality" of commodity images. Individuals realize "their" desires—desires created and infused by advertising itself—by consuming with their eyes the spectacle of the commodity. Although the underlying rationale for advertising lay in sales, the world of the spectacle transcends pure economics. It is a way of being in which we see and experience life as representation and representation as life itself.

The postmodern spectacle (which replaces the concrete with the image, reality with appearance) is evident in the relationship of the fan to American football. Informed and shaped by totemic identification, fans follow the "game" *as if it is their own destinies* that are played out on the gridiron. It makes no difference whether the fan is watching from the stands, the local sports bar, or the living room. The spectacle played out on the field is just as removed "in person" from the individual's actual private life as it is on television. (There is a certain absurdity in the assertion that one watches a spectacle "live.") In either case, the existence of the spectator is lived out by another, an image, with which the spectator identifies. To live life as representation is to alienate oneself from the concrete and to reify human experience. The spectacle therefore signifies the "negation of life that has *invented a visual form for itself*" (DeBord 1995, 14).

The concept of the spectacle—the hallmark of postmodern society—is no stranger to Western culture. It merely posits life's double, a transcendent realm that stands in separation from lived experience. "The spectacle," concludes DeBord, "is the material reconstruction of religious illusion" (17–18). The identification of the believer with the suffering and triumph of cosmological deities is evident in religious pilgrimage, veneration, and festival. Members of religious groups believe that religious narratives play out their own fate, for example, the passion and suffering of Jesus. In short, they define themselves according to the religious community to which they belong and the religious spectacle to which they bear witness. Ironically, it is precisely the advance of economic development in late capitalist society which provided the material preconditions for the reintroduction of religious sensibilities in an ostensibly secular culture. As in medieval Europe, this realm becomes the fountainhead for human worth and achievements. Of course, there is a distinction between premodern and postmodern religious expression. Whereas the excitement of religious ardor was experienced directly by participants in the premodern *corrobbori*, postmodern religious expression is once removed, vicariously experienced by those who observe the "religious" ritual. Spectating therefore replaces participating.

"The spectacle," as DeBord reminds us, "is capital accumulated to the point where it becomes image" (24). From television to the Sony walkman, from cinema to the World Wide Web, the material transformation of the globe has metamorphosed human actors into passive consumers. Life is lived through transcendent image, rather than in concrete reality. In postmodern America, this hyperreality signifies an authenticity that the reality of everyday life seeks to imitate. "For one to whom the real world becomes real images, mere images are transformed into real beings—tangible figments which are the efficient motor of trancelike behavior" (17). That trancelike behavior is evident in the daily consumption of imagery by Americans whose eyes are glued to their computer terminals and television screens or by fans who live and breathe the fate of their team during football season. Their lives are therefore predicated on loss—the impoverishment of their own personal experience—for "it is only inasmuch as individual reality *is not* that [the spectacle] is allowed to *appear*" (16). In short, spectators make spectacles of themselves. They are disconnected from their own emotional state, which is increasingly dependent upon and overwhelmed by their teams, their heroes, their doubles.

DeBord, however, warns that the spectacle is not merely the individual's array of images or fantasies; instead, it is a societal arrangement mediated by images. As the social form of alienation, spectacle provides a sense of solidarity or kinship among its members, even though its members know each other as little as they know themselves. Their sense of solidarity and commonality emerges from this representation of themselves as other than what they are. But, as DeBord notes, the relationship between spectacle and spectator is a one-way street. The group provides a simulated identity to its members, but its members provide no identity to the group. In the context of the spectacle, individual differences are suspended, even erased. Differences cannot even be recognized because where what is perceived is determined by the image and the image constitutes the person, individual departures from the image are inherently unrecognizable.

MALE GENDER PERFORMANCE

The spectacle of football, of course, begs the question: What simulated identity is being propagated? The answer is obvious to virtually anyone who watches. American football represents an image of American manhood. When the euphoria of collective effervescence and totemic rivalry die down, football is legitimated pedagogically. Football players are seen as role models for young men, much in the same way that the G.I. served the generations that followed World War I and World War II. As Douglas MacArthur, the American general who served as a conservative icon over the past fifty years, claimed, "For youth, as it crosses the threshold of manhood, football has become a rallying point to build courage when courage seems to die, to restore faith when there seems little cause for faith, to create hope as hope becomes forlorn" (Maikovich 1984, 74). However, just as the brutality of war is frequently hidden behind noble sentiment, so too does the ringing idealism of MacArthur's statement shield the violence of football. "Football doesn't build character," admitted Texas football coach Darrell Royal. "It eliminates the weak ones" (Maikovich 1984, 72). The savagery of the sport, its rules of territorial conquest, and its emphasis on victory and defeat suggest that football is the representation of war among men—a violent spectacle of totemic violence with which a predominantly male audience identifies.

But why do young men need to be taught what it means to be a man? Football is an example of what Judith Butler has called "*regulatory practices* of gender formation" (1990, 16). She alleges that "masculinity" is not natural but rather learned largely from cultural spectacles like movies, television, and sports. Far from there being a "biological gender," the "gender core" of an individual is a result of gendered performances, whose signs are easily recognizable to others as being part of a gender code signifying "maleness" or "femaleness," quite apart from the individual's physiological sex. Men are men and women are women insofar as they "act the way men and women are supposed to." Of course, gender performance is tautological: "the way men and women are supposed to act" is based *not* on what sex they are, but rather on how men and women traditionally "sign" or communicate their gender, that is, through gender performance. It is not surprising that given a heterosexually dominated society, the normative image of male and female is, by definition, heterosexual. Football as spectacle teaches men, both young and old, how to "act like men," and women, both young and old, what to expect from them.

Although Butler's explanation helps to illustrate the relationship between spectacle and gender formation, it does not explain why male performance is so identified with violence and territorial domination. Theorists like Lionel Tiger (1984) and Desmond Morris (1967) have argued that male aggression is rooted in sexed biological drives and a consequent natural division of labor. It is as if men cannot help themselves, even though it would seem that they construct the most elaborate cultural outlets for "natural" aggression, governed by complex sets of rules. However, too often the discussion about gender roles is split between two opposing parties: one which argues that it's simply a matter of biology while the other contends it is an arbitrary distribution of social power. Neither explanation is very satisfying. I believe that one can avoid the Scylla of nature and the Charybdis of culture by reflecting upon the dynamic of early childhood experience illuminated by Freudian and Lacanian psychoanalysis. I would suggest that the answers to American gender performance and the extraordinary spectacle that is football lie in the working out of the relationship between the male child and the mother.

A PSYCHOANALYTIC INTERLUDE

Before language, before separation and differentiation as an individual, there was the mother, the one, the undifferentiated unity, the ground of our being. The separation of the mother from child, the weaning away from the breast, is an inevitable development of the human condition; and yet, what is inevitable seems incomprehensible and blameworthy to the child. As Lacan has noted, the prerequisite for subjectivity itself is the split between mother and child—a space into which the child places the "not-mother," or what Lacan has called the "paternal metaphor" (Mitchell and Rose 1985, 39). In other words, what comes between the unity of mother and the child is the world itself—a world inhabited by the father and men in general, a world in which the mother inevitably must live. In its own eyes, the child has been betrayed by the mother, a betrayal explained by Sigmund Freud as the origin of the Oedipus complex (1974, ii: 269–76). The male child desires the touch of the mother, the mother's physical gratification of its biological and psychic needs, and sees in the image of the father (whether or not the biological father) his rival (1974, vii: 173–206).

Here a child experiences a second birth. It is not only a matter of being born into the world; it is also being born into the world of the father. The mother is identified with pleasure and the gratification of the child's physical and psychic needs; the father, on the other hand, represents a world of absence (the absence of the mother, of satisfaction) marked by language. Whereas in the world of immediate gratification—the idealized world of the mother—there is no need for language, the world of the father is based upon loss, upon what is absent. Language emerges as a means to indicate the presence of what is absent. To Lacan this world of absence, this domain of language, is intimately associated with the symbol of the father: the phallus. The child is therefore born once into the physical world and then a second time into inherently phallocentric language which re-presents what is absent, what is immediate, what is gratifying (Lacan 1977b, 285).

Language attempts to do what is seemingly impossible: it attempts to retrieve what is absent through the magic of the word. Just as Sigmund Freud's little nephew Ernst learned to manipulate the presence and absence of a spool of thread by tossing it out of and pulling it back over the side of his crib, so too do all children learn to command the presence of what is absent through speech (xviii: 14–15; see also Lacan 1988, 178). Yet the world of presence, the immediacy of the mother-child dyad, what Jacques Lacan calls the "Real" (1977a, 55), can never be recovered. It is lost forever, at best to be re-presented in the "Symbolic" (1988, 156–58)—the speech act which attempts to command the presence of what of is absent. Of course, before the split between mother and child, before the establishment of the child's subjectivity, this Real could not be distinguished. It is only noticed after the split between mother and child occurs, after the establishment of the child's subjectivity, after the Real has already been irretrievably lost. The child is assimilated into the Symbolic order, the world of the not-mother, the world of language, the world of the phallus, forever barred from the Real for which it nostalgically longs.

This—our semiotic—reality is not without its affective fallout. Language does not fit into the world without a remainder. In falling short of capturing the Real, the semiotic project inevitably frustrates desire, which echoes forth from the hollow left by the absence of the mother. Psychoanalysis postulates that there are distinctive patterns which little girls and boys enact in order to deal with their frustrated desires. Freud believed that little girls who identified with their mothers physiologically as female transfigured their longing for the mother by desiring what the mother desired: the not-mother, the phallus, the father—a desire too dangerous to actualize. Hence, these young women had to negotiate a double transition from desire for the mother to desire for the father, and from desire for the father to desire for a husband. When such affect was not discharged through what Freud considered the "normal" channels of patriarchal culture, the overflow of affect produced symptom formation, transforming the body from erotogenic to hysterogenic modes, resulting, for example, in various forms of neurasthenia. His patients included young women who had lost feeling in various parts of their bodies—physical locations associated psychologically with the father's voice, touch, or possessions.

Young boys likewise desired the touch of their mother and the sound of her voice. Yet, they soon learned to identify physiologically with their fathers. By their identification with the father, male children reinscribed their desire for the mother who was likewise the love object of the father. Yet, in light of the size of their rival, young boys found the desire for the mother too dangerous to express. As maturing young men, they had to transfer their desire from the mother—to girlfriends, wives, or mistresses. When that desire was not successfully transferred, what happened? How did men deal with unfulfilled desire? How did they expend that psychic energy? Whereas repressed desire led to hysteria among young women, what Freud called "sublimated" (rather than repressed) desire among young men led to "culture-building activities": law, government, war, sports, religion, and so on. Of course, Freud's unbalanced treatment of the repression of desire in men and women only makes obvious what he hoped to hide, perhaps even from himself: male culture-building activities are merely different forms of what may be called "male hysteria." Some may be more evident to us than others—war, for example. But even religion, law, and most assuredly sports are all vehicles for the expression of male neuroses.

All are symbolic performances that reiterate the origin of separation anxiety in the male child. Whereas women have the opportunity to overcome that anxiety through isomorphic identification with their mothers—their bodies being the same as their mothers', and indeed most have the option of becoming mothers (their object of desire) themselves—men have no such possibility. The split between the mother and child is doubly inscribed in male offspring by the gendered difference of their bodies. They feel abandoned and alone with nothing to hold on to but themselves, their phallus, their language, their games, their hysteria—and therefore patriarchal society (the world of the father) is planted thick with male rituals.

If culture-building activities such as male sports embody sublimation of repressed desire, then football necessarily is a form of male hysteria. Hysteria may be considered a sign of dysfunction and therefore a state warranting treatment; however, in a male-dominated society, forms of male hysteria like war and football are socially accepted ways of working out psychological frustrations. In games men may play over the origins of those frustrations which lie at the center of their world. If the phallus represents what is absent—the immediacy of maternal love—then it must also be the focal point of the game. In football, the ball is the phallus, replete with the meanings of masculine identity, fulfillment, and triumph. Hence, men are compelled—and if you've ever attended an NFL game or even a Super Bowl party, you'll know what I mean—to recapitulate the pre-Oedipal trauma of separation from the mother, in games in which "boys will be boys."

That trauma is marked by a certain ambivalence: on the one hand, men exhibit anger toward the woman in their mothers and toward the mothers in all women for what they unconsciously perceive as their abandonment. It is one of the reasons that many a man who adamantly refuses to "grow up" finds it difficult to remain committed to a woman—particularly one he loves. For the woman (mother) who once loved him also abandoned him, and he unconsciously feels as if he should never allow such dependence on one woman to happen again. It is through his weaning that the male child undergoes a second birth as a subject, cut off from his ground, cut off from his mother, cut off from the Real, destined to suffer phallocentric anxiety. Thus she must pay for his being born. On the other hand, the mother is the object of desire, that with which he seeks to merge, in which he seeks to bury and lose himself. His desire remains the reacquisition of the womb: to possess a mother-woman, only this time under his dominion, not hers, under the sign of the phallus. This legacy of the pre-Oedipal trauma of separation is evident in all his relationships with women who either symbolically or literally serve as the site for the reenactment of desire and anger.

Ritual performances of masculine identity are replete with the rhetoric of castration (reducing the opponent to woman), phallic penetration (the fantasized reacquisition and dominion of the womb or the Real) and destruction (revenge upon the mother-woman for abandonment of the child). Even though the opponents are male, they are rendered female through rhetorical emasculation and physical domination—not judged (as less than men) in order to be metaphorically castrated but metaphorically castrated in order to be judged. Male games like war and football are symbolic expressions of hostility toward women—expressions that sometimes spill over into the literalizations of emotional abuse, physical battering, rape, and even murder, whether that be on the battlefield or in American homes on Sunday afternoon.[1]

The fantasized crime of revenge against the mother, sublimated in ritual performances of masculine identity, is frequently complemented by the theft of maternal power, for by stealing the power of creation, the male has no need for that which abandoned him. As Phyllis Chesler has argued, "men created civ-ilization in the image of a perpetual erection: a pregnant phallus" (Easlea 1983, 10). Men give birth to alternative worlds—for example—in which women are interlopers and outsiders. They are unwelcome, except in the form of veiled presences—symbols and metaphors, tightly controlled by the men who design and rule these worlds.

FOOTBALL HYSTERIA

It shouldn't be surprising, therefore, to find the reiteration of similar fantasized crimes in an American sport that dominates the leisure time of men in con-temporary society. Football is a masculine ritual that symbolically plays out men's unresolved separation anxiety—the desire for and hostility toward the mother in every woman and the woman in every mother. Whether they are phys-ically present in the stadium or watch the game on television, men are carried away by a religious enthusiasm that turns their attention back to their origins. The game reiterates the male's early childhood development and relives the ambivalent feelings of the male child toward the mother. The basic structure of the game, pitting opposing teams against one another, mimes the binary opposition of father/mother, phallus/not-phallus. The object of the game is the control over his life, born into the world of the mother (as a fetus) and the world of the father (as a phallus). The phallus represents the Symbolic: the domain of the "Father," which is predicated on alienation from the world of maternal immediacy but nonetheless signifies the presence of what is absent (the mother) (see Lacan 1982). Whereas in early childhood development the child is under the control of the mother, here the child-grown-to-manhood has the opportunity to control the mother, the object of his desire, symbolized by the phallus. Yet, as the symbol of *his* desire, the phallus has a double signifi-cation. It not only signifies the longing for the Real; it also signifies his own self.

The crowd shares in the *agon* of their heroes on the field of battle who strug-gle over possession of the ball that in psychoanalytic terms symbolizes the phal-lus. The fan identifies with the fate of the ball that is simultaneously both his object of desire (the presence of what is absent) and himself. He is both the fetus who was once one with the mother in undifferentiated unity and the phal-lus who embodies the loss of and desire for that unity. The fetus/phallus/spec-tator is born with the "snap" of the ball, delivered between the legs of the center into the waiting hands of the quarterback. The spectator lives its/his own destiny—a destiny controlled by the quarterback, with whom the spectator also identifies. For in this game the fan vicariously has his fate in his own hands. But to what end?

As the castration rhetoric of the game attests, spectators fantasize rendering their opponents ball-less and penetrating the latter's defenses in order to go "all the way," to "score." As Dave Kopay, a professional who played on a number of NFL teams, attested,

> We were told to go out and "f**k those guys" ... to take that ball and "stick [it] up their asses" or "down their throats." The coaches would yell, "knock their dicks off," or more often than that "knock their jocks off." They'd say, "Go out there and give it all you've got, a hundred and ten percent, shoot your wad." You controlled their line and knocked them into submission.
>
> Over the years I've seen many a coach get emotionally aroused while he was diagramming a particular play into an imaginary hole on the black board. His face red, his voice rising, he would show the ball carrier how he wanted him to "stick it in the hole." (Kopay and Young 1977, 50)

Such language is not uncommon in the locker rooms, in the stands, and on the fields among football players, their coaches, and their fans. Football films and books are replete with these allusions. This usage of sexual innuendo and metaphor (and the intensity with which they are uttered) seems somewhat remarkable in a "sport." It is as if football is taken far too seriously to be just a game. But, of course, it isn't just a game.

The appearance of such vulgar speech makes sense only if spectators unconsciously sense that this male gender performance addresses a psychic need that seems otherwise unresolvable. The game plays out their ambivalence toward women who bear the legacy of the mother. By symbolically castrating their opponents, male spectators turn their opponents into women over whom they claim victory, the victory of the team, of themselves, of the phallus. They have both "scored" winning touchdowns, metaphorically fulfilling desire, and destroyed and humiliated the surrogate of the mother who rejected them. By winning, they accomplish what is impossible in everyday existence; hence, football is an experience of mythic proportions, an exercise that is "larger than life." Spectators prove themselves to be "men" ("in control") to other men and thereby allay the deep-seated anxiety that is normative in the male world. For to lose is to be less than a "man" ("in control"). To lose is devastating. As Vince

Lombardi, the most famous professional football coach, once allegedly stated, "Winning isn't everything. It's the only thing."[2] Of course, winning a football game does not solve the paradox of living. Postgame realities bring back the alienation that is normative for living in the world of the father. But football banishes those anxieties temporarily in the euphoria of the moment. That elation can be psychologically addicting to such a degree that men feel compelled to watch football every weekend during the football season and lament its passing every January, just as "football widows" mourn the loss of their husbands each fall and winter.[3]

CONCLUSION

The "game" of football has all the trappings of a religious *corrobbori*, and yet it is reframed within the context of a society of spectacle. It speaks of our origins and ends, but these are not cosmological; rather, they are personal and societal. Our archeological foray into this male ritual uncovers the origins and ends of the male psychic economy—fated to be repeated season after season, year and year, as the narrative of male being-in-the-world. In that sense, the notion of history as an index of change, so cherished in the modern age, is an illusion. For postmodern American men prefer to live in the realm of the imagination where unconscious desires and fears arise and myth holds sway.

NOTES

1. Although there is widespread anecdotal evidence among battered women that link incidence of domestic violence with football, particularly the Super Bowl, there is only limited statistical evidence to support the allegation. The problem for researchers lies in the fact that statistics on battering in this country are not uniformly gathered but are compiled by private agencies according to methods differing from state to state. Most domestic violence organizations collect data monthly; hence, showing a statistical correlation between the Super Bowl, held on a particular date, and battering is problematic (see McBride 1995).

2. The statement was actually made by Red Sanders, UCLA football coach. See Maikovich, 1984, 100.

3. Obviously, women as well as men suffer separation anxiety from the mother and are likewise born a second time into the symbolic order of language. Whereas women most frequently compensate for that loss through physical (isomorphic) identification with the mother and inculturation ("becoming female"), some women may choose to become football fans—unconsciously embracing the game in order to work out their own hostility toward their mothers and identification with their fathers.

REFERENCES

Butler, Judith. 1990. *Gender Trouble: Feminism and the Subversion of Identity*. New York: Routledge.

DeBord, Guy. 1995. *The Society of the Spectacle*, trans. Donald Nicholson-Smith. New York: Zone.

Durkheim, Emile. 1965. *The Elementary Forms of the Religious Life*, trans. Joseph Ward Swain. New York: MacMillan.

Easlea, Brian. 1983. *Fathering the Unthinkable: Masculinity, Scientists and the Nuclear Arms Race*. London: Pluto.

Freud, Sigmund. 1974. *The Standard Edition of the Complete Psychological Works of Sigmund Freud*, ed. and trans. James Strachey. London: Hogarth.

Kane, Gregory. 1997. "Football Fan's Rude, Illegal Behavior Is Intolerable." *Baltimore Sun*, October 22.

Kopay, David, and Perry Deane Young. 1977. *The David Kopay Story: An Extraordinary Self-Revelation*. New York: Arbor House.

Lacan, Jacques. 1977a. *The Four Fundamental Concepts of Psychoanalysis*. London: Hogarth.

———. 1977b. "The Signification of the Phallus." In *Ecrits: A Selection*, trans. Alan Sheridan. New York: W.W. Norton.

———. 1982. "The Phallic Phase and the Subjective Import of the Castration Complex." In *Feminine Sexuality: Jacques Lacan and the Ecole Freudienne*, ed. Juliet Mitchell and Jacqueline Rose, 99–122. New York: W. W. Norton.

———. 1988. *Seminar of Jacques Lacan: Book I: Freud's Papers on Technique, 1953–54*, ed. Jacques-Alain Miller, trans. John Forrester. New York: W.W. Norton.

Maikovich, Andrew J., ed. 1984. *Sports Quotations: Maxims, Quips and Pronouncements for Writers and Fans*. Jefferson, N.C.: McFarland.

McBride, James. 1995. *War, Battering and Other Sports: The Gulf between American Men and Women*. Atlantic Highlands, N.J.: Humanities Press.

Mitchell, Juliet, and Jacqueline Rose, eds. 1982. *Feminine Sexuality: Jacques Lacan and the Ecole Freudienne*, trans. Jacqueline Rose. New York: W. W. Norton.

Morris, Desmond. 1967. *The Naked Ape*. New York: McGraw-Hill.

Nelson, Kevin. 1991. *Football's Greatest Insults*. New York: Putnam.

Tiger, Lionel. 1984. *Men in Groups*. New York: Marion Boyers.

Dropping in for the Holidays

Christmas as Commercial Ritual
at the Precious Moments Chapel

JENNIFER RYCENGA

"Christmas is the season to visit the chapel. Even if you've been here before, you must come and see the lights." This enthusiasm poured from a reception-ist at the Precious Moments Chapel in Carthage, Missouri, describing the glo-ries of the yuletide displays. When I actually arrived in mid-December, however, the lights were not what caught my eye.

Entering the chapel grounds requires one to navigate through a phalanx of gift shops. The first such emporium I encountered, to my left, was a special seasonal store. Thematically decorated Christmas trees, rows of porcelain orna-ments, and other tinny, tiny geegaws proliferated in the small space, swallow-ing the consumer/collector in their elaborately and abundantly precious universe. The other "regular" gift stores were similarly sagging under the pres-sure of the commercial truism that the Christmas season is the financial "make-or-break" point for the entire year. Indeed, for all employed at the chapel, Christmas is the season when they pray you will visit.

The Precious Moments universe is the creation of nondenominational evan-gelical artist Sam Butcher. Coming from a background in the Child Evange-lism Fellowship, Butcher designed a series of note cards in 1975 featuring children with large heads, compressed bodies, and the iconic attribute of teardrop-shaped eyes. Picked up by the Enesco Corporation in 1978, the Pre-cious Moments children were transferred to the medium of porcelain figurines, where they met with unqualified (and still growing) success. Now the top gross-ing line of porcelain figurines (finally outstripping their illustrious European predecessor the Hummels in the mid-1990s), they are sold internationally, and a vigorous secondary market flourishes for fans and collectors. The participants in Precious Moments culture consider the chapel to be a primary pilgrimage site, both because of Butcher's ongoing creative work there, and because of the gift stores, which offer the widest selection, as well as pieces unique to the chapel grounds (Wells 1995, 160–61; Martin 1994, 20).[1]

Butcher deftly crafts his figurines to combine common cultural themes of childhood innocence, domesticity, and a simple Christian faith. His art is dependent on two salient features of Christianity: its narrative richness and its theological claim that people can be saved despite being sinful. Both of these features give Butcher leeway to depict his characters sentimentally. For example, a figurine shows the baby Jesus in a crèche, with two little children looking in on him. The girl is whispering to the boy "His Name is Jesus" (the title of the figurine; see Martin 1994, 242). Theologically, this portrays the frailty and ignorance of the human condition, but not in a condemnatory manner. We are invited to project our limited selves into the salvific situation, and imagine that we could have played a role—perhaps as cute comic relief—in the cosmic drama. Since this cosmology assumes that we are all children in the eyes of God, each of us has the potential to be similarly winsome and lovable. God's transcendence is maintained, especially given the evangelical overtones of the figurine's title, but that transcendence is ultimately no more unbridgeable than that between parent and child.

Hand-wringing over the commercialization of Christmas is as old as the holiday's prominence in America (Nissenbaum 1996, 140, 318). Christians of many denominations have decried the appropriation of Jesus' birth in the service of fattening corporate profits (Schmidt 1995, 5–6). Genuine though these concerns may be, they tend to overlook larger cosmological contexts—specifically the overarching universalism of contemporary capitalism and the ambiguous design of placing God amid these business details. The Precious Moments Chapel happily provides a site for baptized capitalism, where a religious sheen enhances the magic and greases the wheels of commerce. The chapel's ritual of Christmas shopping represents the annual rebirth of a gentle apotheosis of capitalist calculation.

Ritual commonly uses sacred objects: props such as incense, flowers, vestments, animals, food, and coins. Similarly, any commodity, in its use-value, "is, first of all, an external object, a thing which through its qualities satisfies human needs" (Marx 1977, 125). Despite the fact that both capitalism and ritual employ material objects, they disengage from that very materiality, deliberately projecting a cosmological overlay or abstract meaning onto objects. Instead of linking us to our physicality, our bodies, and our materiality, the processes of elevation in formal rites and of leveling quantification in capitalism tend to alienate participants from the material qualities of objects and from the ways in which they are made and exchanged (Marx 1977, 126–28; Grimes 1990, 14).

Of course, such alienation has not gone unnoticed, and various attempts have been made to overcome it. The more radical wings of the Protestant Reformation, for example, repudiated the inherited ritualism of the medieval church.

But such total rejection brought in its wake a strengthening of body/mind dualism, and therefore did nothing to ease the alienation from matter. A seemingly more promising route emerged when the domestication of white urban America throughout the nineteenth century entailed moving both ritual and the exchange of commodities into the charmed intimate circle of home. No moment better encapsulates this strategy than the Christmas season, and few places rival the Precious Moments Chapel as an illustration of the collapsed logics of religious sentiment and capitalism. Christmas shopping becomes an adjunct ritual, a public enactment of one's commitment to the ritual affirmation of personal domestic bliss. Sentimentality must be highlighted at every turn, either in the hopes of providing authenticity, or in the calculation and manipulation of human desires. As a ritual about buying commodities, Christmas shopping reinforces ritual and religious logic. The seasonal decoration of the grounds of the Precious Moments Chapel supports an atmosphere of total absorption in the "holiday spirit," centered on buying and selling. Contradictions emerge when one inquires how, and how much, the entire operation is commercialized, and when one views the extent to which the attempts to disguise commercialization are both (and sometimes simultaneously) sincere and disingenuous.

Christmas is, indeed, the season to see just how cute theology can get. Upon entering the Christmas store at the chapel complex, the ornaments currently in production are arrayed for purchase.[2] They include a ballerina entitled "Lord, Keep Me on My Toes"; the starchily uniformed but smiling visage of "Onward Christian Soldiers"; a girl reading the Bible in the tub, dubbed "He Cleansed My Soul"; a cheerful white policeman writing a ticket under the moniker "Trust and Obey"; and a pilot in his patched-up single-engine "Heaven-Bound" plane urging us to "Have a Heavenly Christmas." The more expensive figurines— many of them representing current issues in annual dated series—include a (most literally) fallen angel, halo askew, who looks rather startled as his bottom sinks into a cup of eggnog. In its title, this charmer assures us of yuletide cheer: our besotted angel is "Dropping In for the Holidays."

Such Christmas bibelots are tenderly described in the Precious Moments catalog:

> There is a tradition in most homes that certain ornaments on the family Christmas tree commemorate special times and special people we hold dear. Each exquisite, inspiring ornament reflects these wonderful times and loving people, and will create treasured memories for Christmases to come.... These are moments to cherish, moments to reflect, and each is very precious. (Martin 1994, 247, 225)

Precious Moments are intended to hallow domestic rituals, traditions, and gift exchanges, which are presumed to multiply around the Christmas season. Yet there is a contradiction here: the items have been designed, produced, and put up for sale prior to the events they are meant to commemorate. The mass marketing of intimate gifts, embedded in the very name of the Precious Moments, means that your most personal moments have already been cast in porcelain, ahead of your experience of them. This is openly acknowledged in the description, which states that the ornaments *"will create* treasured moments." This is not merely a question of linear time: it represents the nearly imperative (and commercially marketable) demand for sentimentalization.

Such contradictions, embedded in the calculating creation of "needs" in consumerist society, has been apparent since the beginnings of the domestic Christmas in the United States (Schmidt 1995; Nissenbaum 1996). Shunned by the Puritan authorities of early New England because of its connections to pagan seasonal celebrations and to sexual[3] and alcohol excesses, the colonial Christmas was celebrated mainly by the working class as an occasion for public revelry and carnival. The eighteenth-century Christmas often became riotous; it was decidedly *"not* centered around the family or on children or giving presents" (Nissenbaum 1996, 38 [emphasis added]). The transformation of Christmas into a domestic holiday coincided with the growth of consumer culture in nineteenth-century America. This process created a new set of holiday rituals, such as stockings, the decorating of Christmas trees, gift wrapping, holiday card exchanges, and Santa Claus.

Such innovations obviously lacked direct biblical precedents and warrants. Indeed, Christmas has always been a difficult holiday for Christianity to baptize. The pagan seasonal connections, as well as the lack of biblical evidence for dating the birth of Jesus, led to rejection of the holiday by some branches of Christianity (e.g., the Puritan authorities mentioned above and the Jehovah's Witnesses), and to an uneasy blessing from some other branches (Nissenbaum 1996, 3–9). The sometimes tenuous connection between Christian piety and Christmas celebrations suggests that in our own time, "Christmas represents a residual Christianity" (Bocock 1974, 114). It is this *residual* nature of religion in Christmas, in which the specifics of Christianity are replaced by a hazy nimbus to be invoked when convenient, that makes it a ripe target for exploitation by capitalist interests. Residual religion contributes a prestigious aura, and, in a manner similar to how secular authorities have used the "higher" mandates of religion as a justificatory device for secular policies, advertising for religious products can invoke a religious aura to insinuate that they are above the base aspects of commercialism.

In contemporary America, residual Christianity is particularly promoted by the narrative specifics and family relations present in the Nativity mythology. These include the idyllic Holy Family, the vulnerability of the baby Jesus being born in a stable, the Magi as gift givers, and the copious angelic appearances around the natal event. Schmidt refers to this constellation of narrative qualities as Christmas's "greater potential for consecration," in which the season's "dense symbols" play effectively "in the marketplace" (Schmidt 1995, 124, 126). Ironically, Christmas outpaces even Easter as a celebrated holiday in the United States, precisely because the marketplace can better appropriate the symbols and theology of the (innocent and cute) baby Jesus than it can the crucified adult. Theologically malleable, largely bereft of terror, the Christmas narrative is easily applied to placid, consumerist "family values."[4]

The culturally imposed gift-giving requirements of Christmas generate the seasonal ritual of Christmas shopping. The annual "official" beginning of the Christmas shopping season the day after Thanksgiving, the cheery newspaper announcements of the number of shopping days left, and the shared, mad rush of Christmas Eve shoppers—all these carry aspects of what scholars have termed "ritualization." While it is obvious that a coronation or a Catholic Mass are formal rites, there are many social activities that share the characteristics of ritual. Ronald Grimes has enumerated such qualities of ritual, maintaining that "when an activity becomes dense with them, it becomes increasingly proper to speak of it as ritualized" (1990, 14). Drawing from Grimes's list of characteristics, the following are applicable to Christmas shopping, and especially to the ethos of Christmas shopping at the Precious Moments Chapel:

> performed, embodied, enacted, gestural (not merely thought or said), formalized ... stylized ... (not ordinary, unadorned) ... repetitive ... collective, institutionalized ... patterned ... standardized ... ordered ... traditional ... deeply felt, sentiment-laden, meaningful ... symbolic, referential ... perfected, idealized ... ludic ... religious ... conscious, deliberate. (14)

This accretion of ritual characteristics renders holiday shopping into a prime example of ritualization, defined as "an activity that is not culturally framed as ritual but which someone, often an observer, interprets as if it were potential ritual. One might think of it as infra-, quasi-, or pre-ritualistic." (Grimes 1990, 10)

Understanding the Precious Moments worldview requires such an "infraritualistic" approach, because its roots in evangelical Protestantism and its portrayal of quotidian scenes as reflections of biblical lessons do not invite formalized, sacramental rites. But the link between the Precious Moments theology and the capitalist consumer marketplace creates a formalized, institutionalized context for ritual-like activity in the buying and selling of Precious Moments articles. This institutionalized context supports both the activity of the marketplace itself and the intended sentimental spiritual functions of the Precious Moments product line. The Precious Moments Chapel builds these elements into a holiday spectacle, where one can participate fully in consumer culture without feeling guilt about sullying the birth of Jesus with obeisance to Mammon. Billboards on the way to the chapel encourage us to "Celebrate the Spirit of the Holiday," and there's even an ornament of a tortoise, enjoining us to "Slow Down and Enjoy the Holidays" (Martin 1994, 254). This critique of the marketplace ritual of Christmas shopping is itself not immune to co-optation and incorporation into the commodities for sale at the chapel.[5]

This co-optation occurs seamlessly because the Precious Moments Chapel, for all its religious sincerity and religious trappings, is actually a business, not a church, operated from the perspective of business interests. Its religious nature is already fully intertwined with the marketplace. But this raises larger theological and cosmological questions. In an essay in the *Atlantic Monthly* in March 1999, Harvey Cox relates how he detected theological patterns on the financial pages, once he saw how "The Market" had taken on the mystery, reverence, and omnipotence of God, to become "the only true God, whose reign must now be universally accepted and who allows for no rivals" (20). This insight reveals the universality of commodity logic; but this universality does not preclude the sham individualism of "niche marketing" the need to appear to treat us all as individuals:

> The Market already knows the deepest secrets and darkest desires of our hearts — or at least would like to know them. . . . The Market wants this kind of x-ray omniscience because by probing our inmost fears and desires and then *dispensing across-the-board solutions, it can extend its reach.* (Cox 1999, 22, emphasis added)

One hundred and fifty years earlier, in the *Communist Manifesto*, Karl Marx defined this dynamic of capitalism as a reduction of human relations, in which bourgeois society has "put an end to all feudal, patriarchal, idyllic relations. . . and has left remaining no other nexus between man and man than naked self-

interest, than callous 'cash payment.'" Marx adds that this reduction has, specifically, "drowned the most heavenly ecstasies of religious fervor, of chivalrous
enthusiasm, of philistine sentimentalism, in the icy water of egotistical calculation" (1974, 70).

The subservient role of religion within capitalism, to which it contributes
valuable luster and justificatory rhetoric, is aided by the manifold parallels
between religious practices and structures of the marketplace.[6] Like much religious doctrine, the dynamics of the marketplace have a tendency to universal-
ize themselves. Religions and economic systems are human creations that lull
themselves (and others) with the brief authority of a false naturalism.[7] Maintaining the natural inevitability of a given religious or economic system entails
masking or rationalizing not only its human construction but, even more
urgently, the preventable harm it causes. Because the leveling, antihuman
effects of the market have seeped into every corner of our sacred and secular
lives, a great deal of effort must be poured into disguising this fact, in the realms
of both exchange and production. Cox and Marx are correct that the mechanisms of capitalism have leveled human relations and drowned out competing
cosmologies in a sea of coins. This ironically highlights the material ways in
which religion lends its halo to obfuscating the machinery of capitalism.[8]

The Precious Moments Chapel contains many rooms in the castle of The
Market, starting in the most literal sense of having more than half a dozen gift
stores on site. The ritualization of the Christmas shopping season, in particular,
plays on deep-seated desires for authentic human relations and friendships; but
it uses these impulses to jump-start a (profitable) buying frenzy. Commercial culture lures us with promises that it can improve our human relations, if only we
buy the right objects by the designated date. Precious Moments ratifies this by
representing our human relations as reflections of a larger Christian cosmology.

The Precious Moments figurines present a world of domestic bliss in homol-
ogous relation to the heavenly realm. The private, domestic realm played a crucial role in the development of Christmas in the United States, as the
celebrations moved indoors (Nissenbaum 1996, 132). Once inside, "little
moments of familial ritual and gift giving were at the heart of the middle-class
Christmas" (Schmidt 1995, 153). These very moments are now themselves
iconicized by Precious Moments, evident in product lines emblazoned with
"Baby's First Christmas" or "Our First Christmas Together," let alone more
detailed representations of intimate scenes, such as the eggnog drenched angel,
or the mischievous, ribbon-unfurling puppy of "Tied Up for the Holidays"
(Martin 1994, 225, 253ff).[9]

Precious Moments intends to celebrate the private and the personal. But it can only do so through the public mediation of the market. The chapel grounds does its best to hide this mediation while also keeping the cash registers jingling. One time-honored American method for achieving this is by sanctifying the stores themselves, and making them seem like a cozy home or a grand church. The Nativity scene on the front lawn, the roadside billboard "Celebrate the Spirit of the Holiday," and the Christmas shop's multiple thematic trees all point to the grounds themselves as a repository of holy holiday sentiment. When the "marketplace itself" is so "stunningly consecrated," there is "no clear line between church and mart, between the sacred and the secular" (Schmidt 1995, 159). The chapel also wants to blur the boundary between home and mart, between the domestic and the public, so that traveling to the chapel and buying Precious Moments merchandise become extensions of the domestic "family values" bliss they represent. The conscious coexistence of commercial concerns with the religious and social means of disguising them are evident (if not cynically so), in the admission of Howard L. Kratz, who designed similar displays in Philadelphia in the early decades of the twentieth century: "Christmas cathedrals were intended to present the store as "above commercialism," while at the same time winning big results for the business" (Schmidt 1995, 167).

This knowing wink, which acknowledges the simultaneity of commercial and noncommercial interests, has the further effect of masking (and iconocizing) production relations. This phenomenon is hardly limited to the Precious Moments products: the stepped-up demands of the holiday season require most workers today to labor harder and for longer hours during the holiday season than at other times, which hardly enables domestic idylls (Nissenbaum 1996, 310). Santa Claus delineates one effective means "to disguise the fact that most . . . presents . . . were commodity productions": he "mystified production and distribution" (Nissenbaum 1996, 172, 175).[10] But the elfin mythology of Santa Claus is too naïve for Precious Moments, which shows the actual production process in a series of storyboards (in the museum at the chapel), featuring pictures of the happy Thai workers who produce the figurines (Martin 1994, 35–38). Like the sanctification of the stores, this portrayal of the production process is meant to allay our fears about commercialization, but the attempt to glamorize the situation is easily doused, as it was by the icy water of *Forbes*'s analysis: "Most of the figurines and decorative plates are manufactured cheaply in the Far East. They can be sold at a low price and still command handsome margins" (Schifrin 1995, 48).

These photos of the production process return us to another contradiction: the mass production of what are meant to be personal gifts. The earliest commercial Christmas gifts were often devotional in nature; the Bible itself was a popular item for commodification, variation, and price inflation (Nissenbaum 1996, 147–48, 151–55; Schmidt 1995, 116, 128; McDannell 1995, ch. 3; Moore 1994, 34–35). By marketing commodities that are religious and sometimes devotional in their ethos (including illustrated Bibles), and maintaining a neo-Victorian moral outlook, Precious Moments returns to the earliest manifestations of the commercialized domestic Christmas. But the primary mechanism by which Precious Moments (attempts to) avoid the "aesthetic of the serial, the machinic, the mass-reproduced" is in its very name, invoking the individual moment and its fragility (Morris 1993, 318). Each figurine is supposed to be individuated by each owner's "moment." But the moments are prefigured by the presuppositions of the Precious Moments worldview.

This is where the ritualization plays its hand. The tension between American individualism and the interdependent nature of our economic system is mediated by the rhetoric of tradition. Commodity culture benefits by exploiting the balance between individuality and tradition. Consider, for example, the continual debates over traditional versus modern weddings. In the specific instance of that ritual, the need for props means that commodity capitalism can create, market, and sell an ever-proliferating panoply of goods for each discrete type of event, and for a range within them. Precious Moments is fully implicated in that logic: weddings, graduations, and birthdays are all occasions for which Sam Butcher has supplied baubles. But Christmas has a commercial density, calendric certainty, and religious patina that no other holiday can match. The presumption that "everyone" celebrates Christmas, that they will celebrate it annually, and that domestic gift-giving circles will increase through the generations fuel the holiday and fuel the commercial need to reinforce its sanctity as insurance for future profits. The ritualization of Christmas shopping sidesteps contradictions in mass-produced gifts by flooding us with ever-increasing numbers and kinds of objects for sale. The Precious Moments line of products is also increasingly insistent on its projection of an intrinsic link between its goods and "tradition." The serial nature of the Precious Moments figurines intensifies that link in creating a desire to own a complete set and to make the ornaments and figurines part of one's own family tradition.

Catherine Bell notes that "activities that are not explicitly called 'rituals' may seem ritual-like if they invoke forms of tradition" (1997, 145). Centering Christmas traditions squarely within sentimental domesticity, the Precious

Moments Chapel gift stores proselytize participation in a public ritual of buying for time-honored private rites of gift exchange. Tradition is evident in all aspects of the figurines and of the chapel grounds. The teardrop-eyed characters support all planks of traditional family values ideology, albeit without explicit political engagement. The children are shown in patched-up homespun fashion, with the girls almost always in ankle-length skirts. Grandmothers knit, mothers bake, fathers and boys fish. Marriage commemoratives abound; same-sex commitment pieces don't exist. Workers ask for divine help—"Lord, Help Me Stick to My Job" shows an overburdened secretary (Martin 1994, 188)—but they don't organize into unions.[11] The chapel's Christmas store broadcasts the message that the "traditional" Christmas is a quiet, domestic one, complete with snow, trees, gifts, and touching moments of personal connection. Tradition hallows the entire operation.

The traditions evoked here are nineteenth-century in tone and style. For instance, the ornament titled "Share in the Warmth of Christmas" features a bonneted girl, tightly bundled in a long-sleeve, high-neck top and a thick quilted skirt below (Martin 1994, 246). She strides toward us from a past time, which the artist and the corporation (with different degrees of sincerity, perhaps) want us to believe was "more 'in touch' than our own (time) with 'what really matters'" (Nissenbaum 1996, 316). But there are three problems with the projection. First, the unsullied traditional Christmas is a myth. Second, the representation of the unsullied Christmas is itself a commodity. Third, the projection of this myth of a more authentic past carries with it a desire for a cultural hegemony of religious moralism; while it is ironic that capitalism is achieving such universal hegemony instead of (and perhaps at the expense of) religion, both benefit by the projection of a closed cosmology.

Precious Moments creates a universe of sentiment, both at the chapel and in the world. An advertising display in one of the gift shops proclaimed the good news that "Precious Moments Are Your Passport to Loving, Caring and Sharing," invoking three themes of capitalism: universality, accessibility to all that you want, and commutability across differences. It may seem that the Precious Moments universe is harmless, a gentle apotheosis, as I termed it earlier. Yet this cosmology is hardly innocent of ideological underpinnings. Uncle Sam's patriotism links seamlessly with his support for the phone company as he jingle-istically reminds us to let "Let Freedom Ring" (Figure 1); ideologies of patriotism, patriarchy, respect for authority, and Christian exclusivism[12] undergird what appears to be an idealistic world of innocence. The contradiction

Figure 1. Precious Moments figurine titled "Let Freedom Ring."

between the charming children, who never appear to be doing anything that would require severe chastisement, and the existence (and representation) of soldiers, policemen, and sermons is not played out within the Precious Moments representations. It is enacted in the larger socioeconomic-political context outside of the chapel grounds. One decorates the family Christmas tree with "Trust and Obey" and "Onward Christmas Soldiers" ornaments, not because the domestic ritual of familial togetherness is threatened by unruliness. Rather, the function of the ornaments is to reinscribe familial and state authority, and chastise those who are not a part of the Precious Moments universe, those who stand outside of the warm cosmology of Christ, Christmas, and family.

This is made explicit by a Precious Moments collector, Judi Thomas, in a Fourth of July piece in *Precious Insights* magazine. She laments that

while the *majority* of Americans still hold to a belief in the Judeo-Christian values on which this nation was founded, we find ourselves in a quagmire of lurid
and disgusting art. . . . If America were a neighbor or friend, we would send "get
well" cards and flowers . . . because America is sick. If America were a toddler,
we would spank her and put her to bed for a nap . . . because she's stubbornly
pushing the limits of reasonable authority. (7, emphasis hers)

With the infantilization of the country and the use of reasonable authority to
punish it, the actual world behind the Precious Moments facade emerges.
These teardrop shaped children are standing up for innocence, against the
debasement of culture caused by actual diversity of opinion and diversity of
people.[13] At Christmas, the chapel, in coalition with capitalism, can bring it all
together—hearth and home, gift exchange and commodity exchange, tradition
and innovation—and sustain this traditionalism like a talisman against
encroaching evil. The Precious Moments universe, at least, is already purified:
it depicts how joyous the world would be if everyone capitulated to "reasonable
authority."

This, finally, explains why "domesticity and capitalism themselves, 'family
values' and accumulative, competitive ones, have been deeply interlinked from
the very beginning, even when they have appeared to represent alternative
modes of feeling (or seemed to be in conflict with each other)" (Nissenbaum
1996, 318). The family realm represents a supposed haven from sordid competition, while the marketplace promises unlimited opportunity and abundance for individuals. Both the family and the market want us to believe that
their existence is natural, their authority "reasonable." But, in strictly logical
terms, capitalism doesn't need the family (capitalism "has torn away from the
family its sentimental veil, and has reduced the family relation to a mere money
relation" [Marx 1974, 70]), and the family, if it wants to be a location of genuine human relations, would reject the alienation created by capitalism. So why
do they get along so well? Perhaps it is because they both want universal authority, but choose to mask it under the guise of love. They work hand in glove to
sustain monotheism and monoculture, whether it is called God or the Market.
As political theorist Barry Adam (1999) puts it, "a significant part of the success of the neoconservative agenda has been due to their . . . combining the neoconservative economic 'pill' with the promise of cultural hegemony for moralist
authoritarianism" (26). This cultural hegemony joins with capitalism because
they both participate in what Adorno (1998) calls mythical ever-sameness: "In
the like-for-like of every act of exchange . . . the balance of accounts is null. If

the exchange was just, then nothing should really have happened" (159). While Adorno points out that this "doctrine of like-for-like is a lie," it is a powerful one, which can be materialized in the commodified, precious frozen moments of a nostalgic family idyll.

Where is the Christian God in these details? It will not do to doubt the subjective validity of people's faith. Perhaps for some a mass-produced figurine perfectly captures their hierophanic experience. But the presence of God in the foreground details, and the faith and intention of Sam Butcher, cannot loosen the grip of the commodity fetish. In fact, they lend it the perfect justificatory cover. When the market says it is time to buy, the Christmas rush begins, basking in a hallowed glow. The chapel sets up the seasonal gift store, the light show, the Nativity, the holly and pine. The special Christmas figurines evoke tender memories: a boy in his pajamas standing by a coal-burning stove suggests "May Your Christmas Be Warm," while a girl is "Dropping In for Christmas" (Martin 1994, 226, 227), merrily skating, her old-fashioned scarf waving in the breeze above her folded hands. But the veneer of religion is thin; she is already tumbling through into the icy waters of capitalist calculation.

NOTES

1. Much of this information was gleaned from three visits to the chapel and tours of the grounds in June 1995, April 1996, and December 1998. My intent was to observe the structural workings of the mercantile and religious ideologies, and so I do not address questions concerning the subjective meaning of Precious Moments products to collectors, nor did I interview collectors for this essay. I wish to thank Kenneth Kramer, Michelle Gubbay, Elizabeth McAlister, Leonard Primiano, Kate McCarthy, and Deborah Dash Moore for their suggestions and critiques.

2. Many other pieces are "suspended," which increases their value on the secondary market. This is a deliberate strategy on the part of the parent company, Enesco, to generate interest and to trigger the desire for completeness among collectors.

3. Cotton Mather preached against sexual licentiousness at the solstice, and apparently with good reason: "There was a 'bulge' in the number of births in the months of September and October" in the early eighteenth century (Nissenbaum 1996, 22).

4. Consider, for instance, how the Slaughter of the Innocents doesn't get a great deal of commercial attention as a Christmas event. There is no Precious Moments figurine commemorating this horrifying episode from Christian mythology, despite its theological importance. Medieval representations of the slaughter were common; Giotto's work provides an exemplar of this. From one Christian era to another, the emphasis has shifted in the retelling of the

narrative. The needs of capitalism explain this change of emphasis rather efficiently.

5. Schmidt notes the phenomenon of "nested commodities": "By the 1930s, in a series of hybridized fusions, chocolate bunnies drove cars, played the accordion, or golfed; they themselves, in other words, had become model consumers. Such goods are suggestive of the nested quality of modern shopping—one commodity points to another commodity, which points to another, and so on" (1995, 224–5). What needs further development, and what I am trying to do here, is to show how religious commodities, in particular, feed on such nested structures and reinforce the fetish of the commodity form.

6. Cox notes that most religions have capitulated to market logic: "Most of them seem content to become its acolytes or to be absorbed into its pantheon, much as the old Nordic deities, after putting up a game fight, eventually settled for a diminished but secure status as Christian saints" (1999, 23).

7. As Marx says sardonically, theologians "establish two kinds of religion. Every religion which is not theirs is an invention of men, while their own is an emanation of God.... Thus there has been history, but there is no longer any" (1977, 175, fn. 35).

8. I am not opposing my analysis to Marx's, by the way. Another way of perceiving the halo provided by religion is to return to the second half of Marx's famous "religion is the opiate of the masses" quote, where he also opines that religion is "the heart of a heartless world" (Marx 1967). The world is heartless because of avoidable inequities, because of capitalism's dominance. Religion is a way of addressing the hunger for genuine human relations. But religion itself fails in this task because it, too, is so easily appropriated into the capitalist ethos and cosmos.

9. The use of puns in the names of the Precious Moments figurines reflect the public/private dynamics of the keepsake marketplace. To "get" the names, one must participate in a shared community, because the names require a knowledge of idiomatic American English. But the "precious" aspect retains the flavor of an "inside" joke.

10. The Precious Moments universe does not dwell on the mythology of Santa Claus; instead it replicates the contradictions and tensions between commerce and obfuscation. Whether Santa Claus is left out of the domestic bliss of sharing Precious Moments because of theological uneasiness with his origins on the part of the evangelical Butcher or because he represents a rival iconography, I cannot say with certainty. But it is likely a combination of the two. With almost no representations of Santa Claus in the Precious Moments world, Butcher's palette dwells on the domestic archetypes (Grandma in a rocking chair, children sneaking a look inside wrapped gifts, etc.).

11. I see this as a mollification of working-class culture, directed from above, rather than as an expression of job satisfaction or adaptability; it contrasts with the heartier attitude of country-western songs such as "Take This Job and Shove It."

12. Religious intolerance within the Precious Moments universe is muted by the laissez-faire tolerance of the marketplace. Thus there are both Catholic and King James versions of Precious Moments Bibles, and the president of Enesco, Eugene Freidman, does not hide his Jewish upbringing, gladly proclaiming the universality of emotions evoked by the Precious Moments characters. But it is

hard not to see Christian exclusivism in pieces like "I Believe in the Old Rugged Cross" and "Happy Trails Is Trusting Jesus" (sic) (Martin 1994, 250).

13. I say actual diversity of opinion and people because Butcher is a past master at repainting his works to include children of color. His representations of Native Americans are especially stereotypical, though he claims to have grown up "among the Pit River Indians in Big Bend, California" where he "formed a fondness for Indian people" (museum exhibit, Precious Moments Chapel).

REFERENCES

Adam, Barry D. 1999. "Moral Regulation and the Disintegrating Canadian State." In *The Global Emergence of Gay and Lesbian Politics: National Imprints of a Worldwide Movement*, ed. Barry D. Adam, Jan Willem Duyvendak, and André Krouwel. Philadelphia: Temple University Press.

Adorno, Theodor W. 1998. *Critical Models: Interventions and Catchwords*. Translated by Henry W. Pickford. New York: Columbia University Press.

Bell, Catherine. 1997. *Ritual: Perspectives and Dimensions*. New York: Oxford University Press.

Bocock, Robert. 1974. *Ritual in Industrial Society: A Sociological Analysis of Ritualism in Modern England*. London: George Allen & Unwin.

Cox, Harvey. 1999. "The Market as God: Living in the New Dispensation." *Atlantic Monthly*, March, 19–23.

Grimes, Ronald L. 1990. *Ritual Criticism: Case Studies in Its Practice, Essays on Its Theory*. Columbia: University of South Carolina Press.

Martin, Laura C. 1994. *Precious Moments Last Forever*. New York: Abbeville Press.

Marx, Karl. 1967. *Writings of the Young Marx on Philosophy and Society*. Translated and edited by Loyd D. Easton and Kurt H. Guddat. Garden City, N.Y.: Anchor Books.

———. 1974. *The Revolutions of 1848: Political Writings, Volume One*. Edited by David Fernbach. New York: Vintage.

———. 1977. *Capital, Volume One*. Translated by Ben Fowkes. New York: Vintage.

McDannell, Colleen. 1995. *Material Christianity: Religion and Popular Culture in America*. New Haven: Yale University Press.

Moore, R. Lawrence. 1994. *Selling God: American Religion in the Marketplace of Culture*. New York: Oxford University Press.

Morris, Meaghan. 1993. "Things to Do with Shopping Centers." In *The Cultural Studies Reader*, ed. Simon During, 295–315. New York: Routledge.

Nissenbaum, Stephen. 1996. *The Battle for Christmas*. New York: Vintage.

Schifrin, Matthew. 1995. "Okay, Big Mouth. Profile of Stanhome Chief Executive G. William Seawright." *Forbes* 156, 8 (October 9, 1995): 47–48.

Schmidt, Leigh Eric. 1995. *Consumer Rites: The Buying and Selling of American Holidays*. Princeton, N.J.: Princeton University Press.

Thomas, Judi. 1994. "Happy Birthday, America." *Precious Insights* 7, 3 (June/July 1994), 7.

Wells, Rosalie J., ed. 1995. *Official 1995 Secondary Market Price Guide for the Enesco Precious Moments® Collection*, 13th ed. Canton, Ill.: Rosie Wells Enterprises.

Desert Goddesses and Apocalyptic Art

Making Sacred Space at the Burning Man Festival

SARAH M. PIKE

A sculpture composed of mud and chicken wire and dedicated to the Vedic god Rudra burned spectacularly in the Nevada night sky on Labor Day weekend 1998. The fire sacrifice to Rudra consisted of a two-hour-long "opera," during which professional opera singers and classically trained musicians as well as dozens of costumed dancers and drummers paid homage to the god, while thousands of participants at the Burning Man festival sat watching in a circle on the prehistoric lake bed of Black Rock Desert. And this was only a warmup for the festival's main event the following night when a forty-foot-tall wooden effigy—"the Man"—also went up in flames to the drumming and cheers of ten thousand festival-goers. As I left behind the burning remains of the man and walked toward the lights of our temporary city of ten thousand, I saw artists torching sculptures that I had wandered by many times over the past several days. Then suddenly, along the distant horizon, a galloping horse (a bicycle cleverly covered with electroluminescent strips) appeared, followed by a huge dragon-fly with flashing wings.[1] A feast for the senses, Burning Man merges the enchantment and playfulness of children's worlds with adult content, and it is this mix of elements that draws participants of all ages from across the country, from New York to nearby Reno.

As many commentators note, Burning Man started in 1986 as a small gathering of friends on a San Francisco beach. When it became too large and wild to escape the attention of city police, it moved to the desert. Larry Harvey burnt a wooden effigy at the end of a relationship and the "Burning Man" soon became an important rallying point for a small community of artists, musicians, and interested onlookers. Burning Man first came to the Black Rock Desert in 1990. Every year the festival attracted more participants, and as this happened, the organizers began to describe their vision for this event and established a few rules, such as "leave no trace." By 1997 and 1998, the years I attended Burning Man, it had become a weeklong festival involving weeks of advance preparation and cleanup afterward, mostly done by volunteer crews. A "Public Works" crew creates "streets" that mark out the half-moon shaped city—"Black Rock City"—that comes to life as festival-goers arrive with camping gear, pavilions, art installations, and a range of temporary desert homes. The city borders the "playa" as a real city might develop along a lake front. Out on the playa are large sculptures, including the Man himself, and installations, but no campers. Concerts, performance art, and other events are scheduled every day and night of the festival, but most festival-goers spend their hours wandering around the temporary city looking at art and visiting "theme camps," which are a blend of campsite and interactive art installation. Both years I attended, the festival attracted around ten thousand men and women. Many, but by no means all, participants were white, middle-class, "twentysomething ravers, fiftysomething hippies and thirtysomething computer whizzes" (Lelyveld 1998).

Seeking their dispersed community on the Burning Man Internet bulletin board several days after the festival was over and they had returned home, participants mourned the end of Burning Man and discussed its impact on their lives: "It was life-changing and the most spiritual experience I've ever had," wrote Shannon (b.b., 2 September 1997).[2] And another message promised, "In the dust I found my family, In the dust I found my clan, In the dust I found hope for us all. Until we burn again I will hold my screams inside, I will keep the ashes burning until again I join my tribe" (Kaosangel, b.b., September 2, 1997). Peri agrees that Burning Man is a place of belonging: "In the Black Rock Desert, I've found a new hometown, where my imagination can sail without limits and bounds. . . where the aliens and the child-adults find common ground" (b.b., September 28, 1998). Another bulletin board participant called Burning Man "the enactment of the city of the heart" (September 2, 1997). In the *Black Rock Gazette*, Burning Man's official newspaper, artist Charlie Gadeken said, "Sometimes I feel like my real life exists for 10 days a year and the rest is a bad dream."[3] In his poetic tribute to the festival, I Shambat declares, "When life returns to the desert Humanity is rejuvenated/with dew on our lips and paint on our bodies we enter the kingdom of god" (b.b., September 11, 1998).

This charged language sharply contrasts with journalists' accounts of the festival. While participants focused on the sacred or life-changing experiences that they brought home, *U.S. News and World Report* called it "the anarchist's holiday of choice" (Marks 1997); *Life* reported it as "the largest wienie roast ever" (Dowling 1997); *Wired* editor Kevin Kelly, writing in *Time*, designated Burning Man a "meaningless but mesmerizing ritual" (Kelly 1997); *Print* called it a "pre-apocalypse party" (Kabat and Ivinski 1997); and the *San Francisco Chronicle* described it as an "eccentric six-day art festival in the Nevada desert" (Whiting 1997). News stories tended to focus on the art and elements of debauchery:

"measured in terms of artistic and sexual freedom, there is no place else like Black Rock City," Sam Whiting wrote in the *San Francisco Chronicle* article. However, what most intrigued me about the festival was that for many participants Burning Man was an event of *religious* significance, characterized by powerful ritual, myth, and symbol; experiences of transcendence or ritual ecstasy; experiences of personal transformation; a sense of shared community; relationship to deity/divine power; and, perhaps most important, sacred space.

Burning Man is open to anyone who will pay the gate price ($65 in 1998) and follow a few rules, such as "Do Not Drive Your Car in Camp" and "All Participants Are Required to Remove Their Own Trash and Garbage." It provides a locus where cultural problems, and especially problems of ultimate meaning, are expressed, analyzed, and played with. This festival is an important cultural and religious site that exemplifies the migration of religious meaning-making activities out of American temples and churches into other spaces. Scholars of American religion have judged the decline in church attendance to signal a disestablishment (see Hammond 1992), or the increasing personalization of religion (see Bellah et al. 1985; Roof 1993), while others have noted the shift from mainline churches to conservative, experiential forms of Protestantism such as Pentecostalism and independent evangelical churches (see Cox 1995). I want to first situate the festival in its historical context on the American religious scene and then explore the ways in which festival participants create the sacred space that makes transformative and intense experiences possible. Finally I will explore the ways in which Burning Man reveals crucial tensions in contemporary American life that emerge because of the unique space that the festival creates. In so doing, I want to suggest that popular religious sites like the Burning Man festival are essential to an understanding of contemporary issues and future trends in American cultural and religious life.

THE FESTIVAL AS A PLACE APART

Burning Man is hailed as the "new American holiday," "a circus of chaotic behavior," "a Disneyland in reverse," and "an arena of visionary reality."[4] It belongs to a growing trend (since the late 1960s) of large-scale cultural and religious events that offer alternatives or place themselves in critical opposition to ordinary life—neo-pagan festivals, raves, women's music festivals such as "Lilith Fair," and Rainbow gatherings, all of which offer participants sacred space and ritual.[5] Burning Man and these other events fit David Chidester's characterization of American sacred space: "sacred meaning and significance, holy awe and desire, can coalesce in any place that becomes, even if only temporarily, a site for intensive interpretation" (1995, 14). It also belongs to a tradition of collective occasions which (to borrow historian Jon Butler's phrase) first flourished in the "spiritual hothouse" of the nineteenth century. Chautauquas, outdoor revivals, camp meetings, lyceum programs, and Spiritualist conventions were all intended to transform the minds and spirits of nineteenth-century men and women (see Moore 1994).[6] I want to turn briefly to look at these earlier American religious events in order to place the Burning Man festival in a tradition of American worship that has provided alternatives to mainline churches and other established religious institutions. An understanding of how Burning Man becomes religiously meaningful to participants may also shed light on this stream of American religiosity.

Like contemporary festivals, these events of earlier eras were consciously experienced apart from the rhythms of daily life and drew boundaries between their gatherings and the rest of society. They were occasions on which a multitude of meanings and desires converged on the beaches and wooded areas where these gatherings were held. They served as vacation retreats, as opportunities for conversion experiences, and exposed their participants to new and radical ideas. Historian of American religions R. Laurence Moore notes that nineteenth-century evangelical camp meetings and revivals were "theatrical" and "carnivalesque." "Critics complained," Moore writes, "but the setting of the revival, for the space of the few hours or days, often protected practices that were elsewhere forbidden." Camp meetings were occasions for indulging the senses as well as seeking conversion (1994, 45–46; see also Schmidt 1995).[7] Likewise, Burning Man participants come looking for spiritual enlightenment, artistic pleasure, sensual indulgence, and "radical self-expression," to borrow one of founder Larry Harvey's favorite phrases. Evangelical camp meetings and festivals like Burning Man have very little in common in form and appearance with religious gatherings in mainline Protestant or Catholic churches. Historian Nathan O. Hatch says critics of camp meetings "perceived a manifest subversiveness in the form and structure of the camp meeting itself, which openly defied ecclesiastical standards of time, space, authority and liturgical form" (Hatch 1989, 50). Because their wild surroundings heightened the contrast to everyday life, controversial behavior like ecstatic dancing was exaggerated in these settings. Burning Man's site in a barren desert, like camp meetings in the hills of Kentucky, makes it strange and wild to city dwellers because it provides a sensual and aesthetic contrast to the everyday world. These nineteenth-century attractions for religious seekers prefigured celebrations like Burning Man, where embattled Silicon Valley employees escape from "the world of engineers and clocks" to spend a week in Black Rock City (Ed, b.b., September 10, 1998).

As in descriptions of their nineteenth-century forebears, accounts of Burning Man have in common the impression that festivals are *not* like the everyday world in which most of us live and work. Black Rock City comes to be a place of powerful and transformative experiences that cannot be had elsewhere. What is it about this festival that produces such powerful impressions in participants? How does Burning Man come to be imagined and experienced as such a different place from the world outside? Or, in the words of geographer Yi-Fu Tuan (1997, 6), how does a "space" which is "open and undefined" become a "secure and familiar . . . place" for festival-goers?[8] The festival is transformed into a sacred space that contrasts to the outside world in a number of ways. Festival participants create what cultural theorist Rob Shields calls "place-myths," composites of rumors, images, and experiences that make particular places fascinating. Burning Man participants tell stories designed to locate the festival in what Shields describes as "an imaginary geography vis-à-vis the place-myths of other towns and regions which form the contrast which established its reputation as a liminal destination" (Shields 1991, 112).[9] Participants work before, during, and after festivals at making an experience set apart from their lives "back home."[10]

Much of the advance planning and networking as well as postfestival discussions take place on the Internet, where contact information, festival journals, photographs, and short videos are shared. Cyberfiction writer Bruce Sterling notes in his report from Burning Man that the festival has evolved into "a physical version of the Internet" (1996, 198). An extended festival narrative of words and pictures exists through links from website to website, allowing festival participants to keep their community alive across the country. The World Wide Web, notes Janet Murray in her study *Hamlet on the Holodeck: The Future of Narrative in Cyberspace*, "is becoming a global autobiography project . . . pushing digital narrative closer to the mainstream" (1997, 252; see also Turkle 1995). Burning Man is just one of many real-world events that are extending their life through the Internet and creating new forums for narrative. At the ninth Annual Be-In in January 1997, Larry Harvey discussed the similarities and differences between Burning Man and cyberspace: "on the one hand, says Harvey, Burning Man is a compelling physical analog for cyberspace" because "it is possible to reinvent oneself and one's world aided only by a few modest props and an active imagination," but on the other, Burning Man, unlike cyberspace, is an experience which heightens awareness of the body (Burning Man website, http://www.burningman.com).

Its life on the Internet contributes to the sense that Burning Man is not like the churches and homes of ordinary life; it is a marginal site, or "heterotopia," to borrow Michel Foucault's term. There are places in every culture, says Foucault, "which are something like counter-sites, a kind of effectively enacted utopia in which . . . all the other real sites . . . are simultaneously represented, contested, and inverted" (1986, 24).[11] At Burning Man, Mark writes to the bulletin board, "I felt as if I BELONGED somewhere, a sensation that is curiously difficult to maintain in the Midwest" (September 12, 1998). Like many others, Pan-o'-Playa regrets his return to ordinary life: "I'm trying not to let the tar, nicotine and sludge of this, the Outer World, drag me down" (b.b., September 15, 1998). Festival-goers reject and vilify the outside world in order to heighten their sense of the festival as a more important reality. I noticed this when I returned from Burning Man '98 and began reading messages on the Burning Man bulletin board, many of which expressed a longing to return to Burning Man and contempt for normal life: "Buddy, this is our church, this is our respite from suffering through 358 days of christian-inspired, bore-me-to-death society with all its mind-numbing institutions, corporations, and television. This is where we pray, this is our sacred place," wrote Mark (b.b., September 2, 1997). Like Mark, many festival-goers describe their Burning Man experience in such a way as to protest the ordinary world outside festival bounds. After Burning Man '98 I Shambat described the contrast between being in the outside world and being at the festival in a long poem he wrote to the bulletin board: "Come, disaffected/suburbanites/Souls like oil-splattered rags/Minds torn up in the clock:/Come, take your mind-rags/and heart-rags/And let desert/Cleanse them/With Holy Fire" (b.b., September 11, 1998). In this view, the outside world has corrupted and oppressed the men and women who arrive at Black Rock City to be cleansed, renewed, and initiated into a different reality.

The festival is conducive to powerful experiences because it is imagined as a blank canvas, a frontier of possibilities and unrealized potential—"the vacant heart of the Wild West" as one observer put it.[12] Larry Harvey instructs festival-goers to "imagine the land and the looming lakebed of the playa as a vast blank screen, a limitless ground of being."[13] And *Piss Clear*, one of Black Rock City's two newspapers, reminds festival-goers: "All that lays before us is the wide open playa floor. It is our palette and canvas, to create the world we can't enjoy at home." The land is thought of as something passive that human imaginings can be projected upon, and at the same time as a living force that must be dealt with. In "Burning Man and the Environment," Harvey explains the relationship between Black Rock Desert and the festival: "We have discovered a new land; it is a place, a home, a living earth we can possess. And just as surely as our sweat will saturate this soil, it will possess us" (Burning Man website, http://www.burningman.com). The construction of Burning Man as a place apart is aided by its remote location in a desert about 110 miles north of Reno, near the tiny town of Gerlach. Black Rock country, a small portion of the Great Basin, is surrounded by the Granite, Calico, Black Rock, and Selenite mountain ranges. In the Nevada desert survival is an issue; scorching sun, sandstorms, and sudden rain make the environment challenging for city dwellers. Storms wreak havoc on campsites and art work at the same time that they bring together festival-goers in the common project of keeping their tents up and sheltering each other from the elements.

One of the most effective ways that Burning Man establishes itself as a "church" of sorts is through antireligious art and the subversive appropriation of familiar symbols. One example of festival-goers' playful irony is the Temple of Idle Worship at Burning Man '98. A sign at the temple instructed visitors: "You can light candles and prostrate yourself all you want, but your prayers won't be answered: the Deity is napping."[14] In the "What, Where, When of Burning Man '98," a guide to festival events and exhibits, the Temple of Idle Worship is described as a "spiritual power point on the playa," but visitors to the temple are warned that "it makes no difference in what way you recognize this power as all forms of ritual and observance are meaningless here." In "Festival: A Sociological Approach," Jean Duvignaud writes that "all observers agree that festival involves a powerful denial of the established order" (1976 19). Folklorist Beverly Stoeltje explains that "in the festival environment principles of reversal, repetition, juxtaposition, condensation, and excess flourish" (1992, 268). These principles are everywhere apparent at Burning Man and help to give participants memorable experiences through contrasts between everyday life and the festival.

Although festival-goers contrast their Burning Man experience to life in the outside world, they borrow the idioms of that world in order to criticize organized religion, consumerism, and social mores. During Burning Man '98 I came upon a confessional in the shape of a large wooden nun painted colorfully with flames coming up from the bottom of her robe and words along her head reading "Sacred Disorder of the Enigmata!?!" and "Confess Your Conformities!" In front of the nun confessional a framed sign, "the Enigmatic Psalm of Eural," was written in biblical language, but its meaning was intentionally obscured. When I walked through the confessional's curtains I was faced by a

Interactive ritual art at Burning Man 1998. Photos by Sarah M. Pike

round mirror decorated and painted with the message: "Be Your Own Messiah."
The appropriation of religious symbolism — messiah and confession — both rei-
fies and critically comments on Catholic practice. It is a playful display, yet serious in its underlying critique, an attitude mimicked in dozens of other festival
appropriations of religious symbolism. On my first day at Burning Man '97 I
noticed a two-foot statue of the Virgin Mary squirting out a stream of water for
thirsty festival-goers. In the Burning Man world all religions and traditions are
up for grabs, and authenticity, authority, and purity are not at issue. In the
eclectic world of Burning Man artists and performers also borrow from non-
Christian religions and cultures that are foreign to most Americans. An advance
notice of "performances" published on the Burning Man site two weeks before

the 1997 festival described the "daughters of Ishtar," a lavish production of opera, music, dance and ritual: "This ritual of death and resurrection is a revival of an ancient Sumerian cult, after 3,000 years of latency." Another announcement, this one for "Blue Girl," promises: "The intergalactic Fertility Goddess from the 16th Dimension will arrive to seduce you with eerie multilingual arias; her ship is fueled by drummers and such cult leaders as the Buddha, Krishna, L. Ron Hubbard and the Easter Bunny." Here futuristic thinking— "intergalactic"—is grounded in the ancient notion of a fertility goddess and juxtaposed with cultural figures as serious as the Buddha and as marketable as the Easter Bunny. Many theme camps included signs with religious references like "Buddha's Seaside Den of Iniquity," "Confess Your Sins!" and "Repent." If sin is not exactly celebrated at the festival, its meaning is called into question by festival-goers' playful irony and an atmosphere of revelry.

Religious idioms are decontextualized in order to make fun of and protest religious institutions of the outside world, but they can also be appropriated for constructive purposes and made to serve the festival community. On my first afternoon exploring the playa by bike I spotted a series of signs with sketches of churches on them that directed people to an orange tent called "The Cathedral of the Wholly Sacred." In front of the tent opening was a hand-painted sign that read, "Offer something, leave anything, anything sacred to you, your dog, our time here on the playa, the desert, Jewel, Leo Trotsky, whatever. (Sanctity is Contingent.)" I stepped inside the carpeted tent, glad for some relief from the desert heat. An altar, covered with Indian-print cloth and candles as well as a variety of objects left by visitors, served as the cathedral's centerpiece. Offerings left in front of the altar included good luck candles, incense, a basket with chili peppers, Chapstick, tobacco, a conch shell, silver sandals, a mother goddess statuette, clay figures fashioned of clay left out for visitors to use, sunglasses, and necklaces. Visitors had written messages in a small notebook left out for that purpose: "free to be you and me," "Death, abandonment, pain, sorrow — Burning Man show me happiness again," "the desert exposes us — shows our true nature and forces us to learn lessons. I pray that I am strong enough to endure even when there is despair. Love, freedom, life;" "I give thanks to the ancestors;" and other notes. Like a traditional church or shrine, the "cathedral" offered a space of contemplation in which festival-goers could share with each other their thoughts about the festival, and the altar within the shrine created a focal point for visitors' reflections.

Altar art is one of the most ubiquitous forms of expression throughout the festival and the smallest of sacred spaces. Public altars invite participation by the whole community and are specifically designed to contribute to the festival experience. One of the altars I saw in 1997 was covered with photos, a plastic skull, bottles of beer, candles for saints and other odd objects; a sign instructed people to "alter the altar." This community altar made possible a conversation between participants who might never meet each other face to face. It also gave them an opportunity to help create the meaning of Burning Man with their shared prayers and confessions. Participation is a key festival theme: "No Spectators" is one of Burning Man's slogans, and festival-goers are constantly reminded that they are responsible for the production of festival space. Altars and other sacred places are self-consciously designed to bring together individual and community. They serve diverse purposes and accumulate meanings over a short period of time by providing points of focus in the midst of the visual complexity of festivals.

Sculptures, shrines, altars, and installations become the focal points of ritual performances, usually scheduled at night. Burning Man '97 and '98 featured lavish Saturday night performances that converged on temple/sculptures which festival-goers had photographed, admired, and worked and climbed on over the past few days. These sculptures were created by Bay Area artist Pepe Ozan out of playa mud and chicken wire and filled with dry wood. Professionally trained opera singers, dancers, and musicians combined with festival volunteers to create the late-night spectacles. The 1998 Sacrifice to Rudra, the Vedic god of fire, began at around 3 a.m. and opened with an invocation to Rudra in Sanskrit. The dark expanse of desert was illuminated by a full moon and flaming batons spun through the air by fire dancers. A hundred costumed dancers split into groups representing earth, water, air, and fire. Watching from the temple sculpture a priest and priestess stood in long gowns that flowed over stilts. Other characters circled the Rudra sculpture with the dancers: drummers marched with their drums strapped over their backs, and a man with a lizard mask rode in a chariot. At the end of the performance the temple was torched by performers and thousands of spectators danced around the fire. Ritual organizers evoke powerful emotional responses from festival participants by borrowing elements of ancient cultures, but providing their own interpretations rather than trying to duplicate other cultures' ritual practices.

SACRIFICE AND TRANSFORMATION

If Burning Man art and ritual feel apocalyptic or postapocalyptic, as many observers and participants have remarked, this is because fire and sacrifice are their central idioms.[15] One news story recounted, "Nevada's sixth-largest city was torched Sunday night as the Burning Man spit sparks and fell over backward onto the desert floor" (Whiting 1997). Crosses dot the Burning Man landscape and are played with and redefined by festival-goers. The *San Francisco Chronicle* reported that before the actual burning of the man, "a man named Highway Hal stood naked on a motorized cross" (Whiting 1997). A festival-goer named Fred describes his experience this way: "The man burnt and so did my outer skin giving me space and movement to grow into another year" (b.b., September 2, 1997). Fire symbolically strips off the self at the same time that it is physically felt, furthering the purification the festival is expected to bring about. Shady Backflash explains the symbolism of the Burning Man: "It felt like the collective fears, rage and frustrations of everyone there were going up in smoke" (b.b., September 11, 1998). The Man, writes Bruce Sterling, "becomes a striking neon symbol of pretty much everything that matters." It is ironic that the sacrificed Man stands at the center of the festival, a community that celebrates its opposition to organized Christianity. The sacrificial meaning of Burning Man varies from person to person. It may aid the cause of personal renewal, cleanse self and community, or provide a means of creating a new self and world out of the ashes of the old.

Festival-goers embark on a kind of pilgrimage as they leave behind the ordinary world and travel to the desert to be transformed—"pilgrims to a new land" the 1997 web guidelines called them. Festival-goers travel toward Black Rock City with expectations built up in earlier conversations about the festival and then maintained by festival rituals and works of art that affirm that their lives will be changed by the festival experience. "As pilgrims to a new land, each of us becomes a founder," notes Larry Harvey.[16] These festival-goers' accounts of their preparations and trips to festivals are similar to the stories of other religious people described in studies of pilgrimage.[17] Burning Man, George points out on the bulletin board, is "what today's faithful experience in Mecca or Rome, only without all that burdensome dogma" (b.b., September 2, 1997). In his introduction to a collection of essays on pilgrimage, Alan Morinis explains that what is essential to pilgrimage is a quest for what is sacred, especially the valued ideas and images of communal and personal perfection (1992, 18–21). Burning Man participants set off from home hoping to experience ideal communities and to discover new selves at the festival, which then becomes for them a sacred space of unlimited possibilities.

The journey is often described by festival-goers as one of personal transformation and healing. Because identity is malleable in festival space, self-transformation comes more easily. Hanuman tells other bulletin board readers: "My old self has been torched! I am reborn!" (b.b., September 2, 1997). Participants create the festival with art, dance, and ritual, but Burning Man also acts on them in ways that open up the possibility for natural and supernatural experiences otherwise unavailable: "I can't believe the power that all of you have helped me see within myself," writes Pamela (b.b., September 2, 1997). Many reports from Burning Man mention the ways in which it is a life-changing and initiatory experience. During the festival participants mark these changes on their bodies. Sam writes to the bulletin board: "I got my head shaved while I was there . . . and emerged a new person" (b.b., 6 September 1997). Some festival-goers wish for friends and community to be renewed as well as for self-transformation. In the journal where visitors to the "Temple of the Wholly Sacred" put down their thoughts about the festival, one person wrote: "May men find their gentleness as they rise phoenix-like from this fire here. The new face of power." Self-transformation is mirrored in the hybrid art forms that abound at Burning Man, such as art cars and bicycles masquerading as giant insects or horses, or the lifelike figures that seemed to be emerging out of the playa dust (or sinking into it). "Cars morph into bugs and software programmers into painted pagans," reported Jennifer Kabat in *Print* (1997). The boundaries between human and nature as well as between human and machine are open to question and experimentation during the festival.

Festivals promote creative self-expression and sensual enjoyment, and in so doing, enable festival-goers to go beyond their usual ways of carrying themselves and acting toward others. In order to create a "superreal" festival world of meanings absent from the workplace and urban landscape, festival-goers highlight what is lacking for them outside, such as sexual freedom. Moving more slowly helps festival-goers to forget the fast pace of their everyday lives. They speak of the festival as a place of enhanced sensory perceptions or altered awareness.[18] Even time is lived differently at the festival, as Pan-o'-Playa points out in a diary-like message to the bulletin board: "I am very quickly slowing down to a Playa clock and mindset" (b.b., 23 September 1998). This slowing down, the sense that festival space and time are different from ordinary life, is experienced through the body, and it is the body as much as the mind that is changed by Burning Man. One participant, in her third year of law school, remarks on the contrast: "After spending the year in the oppressive confines of a rigorous brain-washing, soul-crushing enterprise like law school, Burning Man brings me back to myself. I remember what it feels to laugh until I cry! . . . to dance until I fall down . . . to make friends with people I have no immediate reason to distrust . . . to walk around naked and love it, never feeling ashamed of my body, but rather being fully present in it" (Julie, b.b., September 5, 1997). Layney, a first-time festival-goer, gives thanks for "the chance to be part of something that really makes sense. . . . i have it in my bones." She describes the heightened aware-ness of being in her body and moving differently from her usual ways of mov-ing that resulted from dancing around a fire late at night: "i danced myself into a new existence. . . . i ground myself into the sweet desert earth and set free to a blazing fire" (b.b., September 2, 1997). The body is simultaneously liberated and constrained. The hot and dry festival environment constantly reminds festival-goers of their embodied existence. But nudity, dancing, body paint, and costuming can liberate the body as well as insist on its presence.

BURNING MAN AS HOME AND FAMILY

Festivals are not only places of "anarchy" and unlimited self-expression; transformative experiences are possible because Burning Man is at the same time "home," "tribe," and "family." It is a place where men and women say they experience an ideal community and where they create anew familiar concepts like neighborhood and church. Annual journeys to festivals are simultaneously adventures to exotic "uncharted shores" and to familiar, homelike, memory-laden places. The world festival-goers represent as being on the fringes of "mainstream" culture becomes the center of their most meaningful activities. Soon after leaving the festival, Kaosangel calls Burning Man "the place we all call home, in the place we are alone, together under a firelit sky" (b.b., September 2, 1997). Some participants describe a sense of oneness with other festival-goers and the feeling of belonging to an extended family, while others speak of it as a tribe: "I walked alone for twenty years, I have screamed since I was born, this world had almost killed me, before I found my home. We are all one tribe" (Anonymous, b.b., September 2, 1997). For many participants, festivals are an ideal way of being with others, and for this reason they relate more intimately to each other at festivals than in other social environments. Mistress Cinnamon reminisces a month and a half after Burning Man '98: "i've felt misplaced ever since i got back, brc [Black Rock City] is my home and the citizens are my people" (b.b., October 18, 1998). Festivals become home-like places where participants can be the kind of children they want to be, can share intimate secrets and play in the ways schools, parents, and religions in the outside world deny them. "Got 'Home' Tuesday morning. How fucked up is that? BRC is my HOME dammit! . . . I believe I'll relocate to my home on the playa. . . . I'm dreading the commute to LA daily but it beats suburbia." Over e-mail, festival-goers share with each other their reluctance to return to normal life after the heightened experience and welcome sense of community at Burning Man. References to village, home, family, church, and tribe attest to festival-goers' desire for an experience of community that is lacking in daily life.

Even more than a spiritual home or substitute for church and family, Burning Man symbolizes utopian hopes: "That's what Burning Man brings back to my heart: Hope" says Migwitch, who continues: "We are the ones who create the world that we all long for, the imaginary community to which we constantly compare the one in which we live" (b.b., September 11, 1998). "Remember," writes another festival-goer to the bulletin board, "THERE IS ANOTHER

WAY" (Ranger Thumper, b.b., September 9, 1998). "Dark Angel of Black Rock" puts it this way: "The beauty of Black Rock City is powerful. It is stronger than the world we have escaped from. . . . Burning Man is no longer merely a festival. It has metamorphosed into a way of life for the new millennium" (b.b., September 15, 1998). Festival-goers believe they are the vanguard, visionaries who will usher in new ways of making art and living life.

CONCLUSIONS

In the many ways I have suggested, Burning Man participants establish — through narrative, ritual, and fantasy—a contrast between the festival world and everyday society, in which the former takes on a heightened reality and represents for participants a world made over by festival-goers' views of economics (barter system), law enforcement (tolerance and self-policing), gender, ecology, and the nature of the divine. Mike explains that for him Burning Man was "idol worship in the purest sense," rather than "a media-created god or goddess" (b.b., September 2, 1997). Anthropologist Margaret Thompson Drewel, building on the work of Victor Turner and Clifford Geertz, writes that in Yoruba culture, "rituals operate not merely as models of and for society that somehow stand timelessly alongside 'real' life. Rather they construct what reality is and how it is experienced and understood" (1992, 174). Burning Man works hard to represent itself as a new reality. Festival organizers' website statement, "Building Burning Man: The Official Journal of the Burning Man Project," begins by explaining that the festival is a critical response to corporate America and an antidote to consumerism, then asks rhetorically, "Where else, but in America, would people be invited to pack their belongings, journey into a desert wilderness, and there create the portrait of a visionary world?"[19] There is an expectation and excitement in the festival atmosphere that makes participants feel that they are contributing to a powerful social force. Festival literature and art installations underscore this aspect of the festival with their apocalyptic language of sacrifice and redemption.

The themes of sacrifice and redemption, death and rebirth, disintegration and creation suggest that for many participants the festival's impact is profound. But the symbolic significance of the Man's demise is still up for grabs: "'Meaning' is dog meat in the face of experiment and experience" is how *Village Voice* writer Erik Davis sums up festival-goers' attitudes toward interpretations of Burning Man (1995). In fact, festival-goers debate the festival's meaning before, during, and after Burning Man. The most striking characteristic of bulletin board discussions about Burning Man and Burning Man literature are the conflicts that emerge as participants and organizers create festival space, experience the festival, deconstruct their experiences after the fact, and plan for next year's festival. In a multipart message to the bulletin board called "A Newbie's Perspective-or-THIS is community?" Gomez Addams described nasty neighbors who stole tools and water, harrassed people, played over the sound level restrictions, and sabotaged other camps (b.b., September 11, 1998). Criticism as well as praise of the festival appeared on the bulletin board and fueled debates over intrusive photographers, "gawkers," neighborliness, and environmental issues. Concern for the festival's environmental impact have threatened its future at this site.[20] In the two years I attended Burning Man, the theme "leave no trace" appeared on all e-mail messages from the organizers and on all other festival literature. It continued to be an issue in the messages of horrified festival-goers who saw bags of trash dumped along the roads leading away from the festival site when they traveled home.[21] Other bulletin board readers responded by urging everyone to focus on the positive, life-affirming aspects of Burning Man, rather than its failures. By emphasizing first their separation from the outside world and, second, their unity as tribe and family, the Burning Man community tries to downplay inner differences and contradictions.

Participants expect Burning Man to embody their ideals, but the festival does not always live up to such expectations. In fact, it may perpetuate the social problems festival-goers say they want most to change, such as wastefulness and rigid organizational structures. "Like it or not, Burning Man is not about survival. At its most *extreme*, it's about projecting our God-fearing red-blooded American values of waste, greed and debauchery on an empty canvas of dust and air. And at its most innocent, it's an *escape* valve from the societal rules that bear down on us daily."[22] Thus the opposition between festival and outer worlds is often complicated by the many differences *among* festival-goers, and the realization that instead of leaving the outer world behind, they have brought its problems with them. Tripper, for instance, understands Burning Man somewhat differently than the "many airheads" who "gush on about what a utopian experience Black Rock City is, when all it really is is an amalgam of twisted reflections, magnifications, and rejections of the culture we purport to leave behind" (b.b., September 23, 1998). Controversies at Burning Man follow a pattern described in an extensive literature by folklorists and anthropologists on festivals as places where conflicts are worked on and resolved. In "Shouting

Match at the Border: The Folklore of Display Events," Roger D. Abrahams argues that public events provide opportunities for "perilous play": confrontation, negotiation, and creative responses to social tensions. Festivals and fairs, explain Abrahams, "in part dramatize and reinforce the existing social structure," but they also, as in the case of Burning Man, "insist . . . that such structure be ignored or inverted, or flatly denied" (1982b, 304).

An uneasy dynamic develops at Burning Man which reveals the tensions between individual and community that the festival is intended to harmonize. Festival-goers gather to share a common experience, but in so doing they may discover the many differences that separate them and threaten their efforts at community building. Of all the tensions and contradictions that characterize Burning Man, none is as charged as the relationship between self and community. In "The Year of Community—You Are a Founder," Larry Harvey describes his understanding of Burning Man: "Ours is a society of activists and your experience of our community will be defined by two essential elements: radical self-expression and a shared struggle to survive."[23] Burning Man participants engage in self-exploration and commune with nature at festivals, but they also establish important friendships and intimate relationships with other festival-goers. Observers of the relationship between self and community in the contemporary United States have argued that Americans tend to emphasize the needs of the self over those of the community. Robert Bellah and his colleagues point out in *Habits of the Heart* that when Americans describe their spirituality they talk most about personal empowerment and self-expression rather than the requirements of community (1985; see also Roof 1993; Anderson 1990). In contrast, Burning Man emphasizes both the needs of the self and the creation of community. Self-expression is encouraged but must be constantly tempered by consideration for one's neighbors.

If the festival is a site for life-changing experiences of self and community, for the creation of new religious and cultural visions, then, for these reasons, it is a contested site. The festival works its transformative magic on participants because of a set of contradictions that exist within it: festival-goers escape their home life when they journey to the festival, and at the same time expect festivals to be the location of "home" and "family"; they imagine the desert as a "blank canvas" as well as a "living land"; the language of "tribes" and "villages" coexists with advanced electronic technologies; festival-goers constantly negotiate between self-expression and the needs of community; in festival art and ritual they express desire for both sacrifice and salvation; and Burning Man's apocalyptic overtones are meant to both describe the disenchantment and decay of American life today and envision a future that is rejuvenative as well as destructive. It is the creative work that characterizes Burning Man—playing with symbolic meanings and creating new rituals from old—in response to these contradictions that transforms the festival into places of meaning.

NOTES

1. Photographs of some of these were on the Fruit of the Lumen website (www.scumby.com/~wes/Bman98/).
2. The hundreds of messages on the bulletin board were one of main sources for this essay. All bulletin board messages (designated as "b.b." and a date) were read at http://bbs.burningman.com/index?14@^8013@/ or available through the archives at this address. Clearly there are biases inherent in gathering information this way. Not all Burning Man participants are computer users, though I expect a majority are. I first heard about the festival in 1996 when one of my students told me about his experience there. I then attended the festival in 1997 and 1998 as a participant-observer. Other sources I used were two newsletters published during the festival: *The Black Rock Gazette*, and *Piss Clear*; informal conversations with other festival-goers during the festivals and with several of my students back in ordinary life; and the Burning Man website and other websites of participants. I also read through a variety of media accounts of the festival, both in print and online.
3. Interview by Lee Gilmore, September 5, 1998.
4. Sterling 1996, 11; Scotty, Burning Man b.b., September 11, 1998; Kelly 1997, 62 (quoting Larry Harvey); Harvey, "Radical Self-Expression," Burning Man website, 1998.
5. During two years of reading through the Burning Man bulletin board I saw mention of raves, Lilith Fair, Lollapalooza, pagan festivals, Grateful Dead shows, Rainbow gatherings, and the original Woodstock. Pike (2000) is a study of ritual and sacred space at contemporary pagan festivals across the United States. For an in-depth description of national Rainbow Family gatherings see Niman 1997. Information about raves is easily available on the Internet; for example, a rave network with many links is at http://www.hyperreal.org/raves/.
6. R. Laurence Moore discusses Chautauqua Sunday School Institutes (1994, 151). The essays in *The Celebration of Society* cover a wide variety of festivals, sporting events, masquerades, and other celebrations in the United States and elsewhere (Manning 1983).
7. Schmidt discusses "the peddling of festivity" at church festivals and hawkers waiting on the outskirts of camp meetings to sell "food, liquor, patent medicines, books, ballads, shoe polish, and daguerreotypes" (1995, 21).
8. Also see Bachelard [1958] 1964; Lefebvre [1974] 1992; Soja 1989.
9. G. Rinschede and S. M. Bhardwaj describe "place mythologies" as narratives of the virtues and sanctities of specific sites (1990, 11). But the sites they identify, like Burning Man, probably have negative associations as well. Other studies of

place mythologies that have helped me understand festivals as "places apart" include Agnew and Duncan 1989; Sears 1979; Buttimer 1993; Duncan and Ley 1993; and Hiss 1990. For some good examples of place myths see Griffith 1992; Scott and Simpson-Housley 1991.

10. Anthropologist Victor Turner contrasts flexible, egalitarian liminal events to the stratified, normal world (1974, 200–1).

11. Much of Foucault's work is taken up with issues of power and space. My understanding of festivals as "places apart" has also been helped by Gregory 1994; Stoeltje 1992; Duvignaud 1976; Falassi 1987; and MacAloon 1984.

12. Darryl Van Rhey, "The New American Holiday" in "Building Burning Man: The Official Journal of the Burning Man Project" (Winter 1998).

13. Larry Harvey, "Radical Self-Expression," Burning Man website, August 1997.

14. *Black Rock Gazette* 1997.

15. Scholars disagree on the meaning and appropriate usage of the terms *apocalypticism* and *apocalyptic.* I follow folklorist Daniel Wojcik's suggestion that *apocalypse* "refers to the catastrophic destruction of world or current society, whether attributed to supernatural forces, natural forces, or human actions" (1997).

16. "The Year of Community—You Are a Founder" (August 7, 1997).

17. For instance, see Turner and Turner 1978; Orsi 1991; Crumrine and Morinis 1991; Morinis 1992; Haberman 1994; Myerhoff 1974; and Rinschede and Bhardwaj 1990.

18. There is much discussion about drug-use and abuse at Burning Man. From festival-goers' own descriptions of their festival experiences, it would seem that drugs play a part as often as not. However, perhaps as a result of the visible police presence the two years I attended, drugs are not as common as alcohol.

19. Winter 1998.

20. In February 1999 I received an issue of "Jack Rabbit Speaks," urging festival-goers to write letters to the Bureau of Land Management (BLM) which oversees Black Rock Desert. This was the most recent request for help from festival organizers in several years of negotiating with local authorities and other groups concerned about the festival's effects on the land. The Burning Man website has links to more information about these issues.

21. A heated and contentious discussion of trash on the bulletin board lasted for months after Burning Man '98.

22. Stewart McKenzie, "Bitch Bitch Bitch about Burning Man," *Piss Clear* 1997 (the "other" Burning Man newspaper).

23. Burning Man website, 1997.

REFERENCES

Abrahams, Roger D. 1982a. "The Language of Festivals: Celebrating the Economy." In *Celebration: Studies in Festivity and Ritual,* ed. Victor Turner, 161–77. Washington, D.C.: Smithsonian Institution Press.

———. 1982b. "Shouting Match at the Border: The Folklore of Display Events." In

"And Other Neighborly Names": *Social Process and Cultural Image in Texas Folklore*, ed. Richard Bauman and Roger D. Abrahams, 303–21. Austin: University of Texas Press.

Agnew, John A., and James S. Duncan, eds. 1989. *The Power of Place: Bringing Together Geographical and Sociological Imaginations*. Boston: Unwin Hyman.

Anderson, Walter Truett. 1990. *Reality Isn't What It Used to Be: Theatrical Politics, Ready-to-Wear Religion, Global Myths, Primitive Chic, and Other Wonders of the Postmodern World*. San Francisco: Harper and Row.

Bachelard, Gaston. [1958] 1964. *The Poetics of Space*. Translated by Maria Jolas. New York: Orion Press.

Bauman, Richard, and Roger D. Abrahams, eds. 1982. *"And Other Neighborly Names"*: *Social Process and Cultural Image in Texas Folklore*. Austin: University of Texas Press.

Bellah, Robert N., Richard Madsen, William M. Sullivan, Ann Swidler, and Steven M. Tipton. 1985. *Habits of the Heart: Individualism and Commitment in American Life*. San Francisco: Harper and Row.

Buttimer, Anne. 1993. *Geography and the Human Spirit*. Baltimore: Johns Hopkins University Press.

Chidester, David. 1995. "Introduction." In *American Sacred Space*, eds. David Chidester and Edward T. Linenthal, 1–42. Bloomington: Indiana University Press.

Cox, Harvey. 1995. *Fire from Heaven: The Rise of Pentecostal Spirituality and the Reshaping of Religion in the Twenty-First Century*. Reading, Mass.: Addison-Wesley.

Crumrine, N. Ross, and Alan Morinis, eds. 1991. *Pilgrimage in Latin America*. New York: Greenwood Press.

DaMatta, Roberto. 1991. *Carnivals, Rogues, and Heroes: An Interpretation of the Brazilian Dilemma*. Notre Dame, Ill.: University of Notre Dame Press.

Davis, Erik. 1995. "Terminal Beach Party: Warming Up to the Burning Man." *Village Voice*, October 31, 31–34.

Dowling, Claudia. 1997. "*Life* Goes to the Burning Man Festival." *Life*, August, 16–18.

Drewel, Margaret Thompson. 1992. *Yoruba Ritual: Performers, Play, Agency*. Bloomington: Indiana University Press.

Duncan, James, and David Ley, eds. 1993. *Place/Culture/Representation*. New York: Routledge.

Duvignaud, Jean. 1976. "Festivals: A Sociological Approach." *Cultures* 3, 1: 13–25.

Falassi, Alessandro. 1987. *Time Out of Time: Essays on the Festival*. Albuquerque: University of New Mexico Press.

Foucault, Michel. 1986. "Of Other Spaces." *Diacritics* 16: 22–27.

Gregory, Derek. 1994. *Geographical Imaginations*. Oxford: Blackwell.

Griffith, James. 1992. *Beliefs and Holy Places: A Spiritual Geography of the Pimeria Alta*. Tucson: University of Arizona Press.

Haberman, David L. 1994. *Journey through the Twelve Forests: An Encounter with Krishna*. New York: Oxford University Press.

Hammond, Phillip E. 1992. *Religion and Personal Autonomy: The Third Disestablishment in America.* Columbia: University of South Carolina Press.

Hatch, Nathan. 1989. *The Democratization of American Christianity.* New Haven: Yale University Press.

Hiss, Tony. 1990. *The Experience of Place.* New York: Knopf.

Kabat, Jennifer, and Pamela A. Ivinski. 1997. "Operation Desert Swarm." *Print,* September/October, 4–5.

Kelly, Kevin. 1997. "Bonfire of the Techies." *Time,* August 25, 60–62.

Lawless, Elaine. 1988. *God's Peculiar People: Women's Voices and Folk Tradition in a Pentecostal Church.* Lexington: University Press of Kentucky.

Lefebvre, Henri. [1974] 1992. *The Production of Space.* Translated by Donald Nicholson-Smith. Oxford: Blackwell.

Lelyveld, Nita. "Wild Westfest." *The Philadelphia Inquirer,* September 9, 1998 (phillynews.com/inquirer/98/Sep/09/lifestyle).

MacAloon, John J., ed. 1984. *Rite, Drama, Festival, Spectacle: Rehearsals toward a Theory of Cultural Performance.* Philadelphia: Institute for the Study of Human Issues.

Manning, Frank, ed. 1983. *The Celebration of Society: Perspectives on Contemporary Cultural Performance.* Bowling Green, Ky.: Bowling Green University Press.

Marks, John. 1997. "Burning Man Meets Capitalism." *U.S. News and World Report,* July 28, 46–47.

Moore, R. Laurence. 1994. *Selling God: American Religion on the Cultural Marketplace.* New York: Oxford University Press.

Morinis, Alan, ed. 1992. *Sacred Journeys: The Anthropology of Pilgrimage.* Westport, Conn.: Greenwood Press.

Murray, Janet H. 1997. *Hamlet on the Holodeck: The Future of Narrative in Cyberspace.* New York: Free Press.

Myerhoff, Barbara G. 1974. *Peyote Hunt: The Sacred Journey of the Huichol Indians.* Ithaca, N.Y.: Cornell University Press.

———. 1982. "Rites of Passage: Process and Paradox." In *Celebration: Studies in Festivity and Ritual,* ed. Victor Turner, 109–35. Washington, D.C.: Smithsonian Institution Press.

Niman, Michael I. 1997. *People of the Rainbow.* Knoxville: The University of Tennessee Press.

Orsi, Robert A. 1991. "The Center Out There, In Here, and Everywhere Else: The Nature of Pilgrimage to the Shrine of Saint Jude 1929–1965." *Journal of Social History* 25, 2 (winter): 213–32.

Pike, Sarah M. 2000. *Earthly Bodies, Magical Selves: Contemporary Pagans and Search for Community.* Berkeley: University of California Press.

Rinschede, G., and S. M. Bhardwaj, eds. 1990. *Pilgrimage in the United States.* Berlin: Reimer Verlag.

Roof, Wade Clark. 1993. *A Generation of Seekers.* San Francisco: Harper.

Schmidt, Leigh Eric. 1995. *Consumer Rites: The Buying and Selling of American Holidays.* Princeton, N.J.: Princeton University Press.

Scott, Jamie, and Paul Simpson-Housley, eds. 1991. *Sacred Places and Profane*

Spaces: Essays in the Geographies of Judaism, Christianity and Islam. Westport, Conn.: Greenwood Press.

Sears, John. 1979. *Sacred Places: American Tourist Attractions in the Nineteenth Century.* Oxford: Oxford University Press.

Shields, Rob. 1991. *Places on the Margin: Alternative Geographies of Modernity.* New York: Routledge.

Soja, Edward W. 1989. *Postmodern Cartographies: The Reassertion of Space in Critical Social Theory.* New York: Verso.

Sterling, Bruce. 1996. "Greetings from Burning Man." *Wired* November 4, 196–207.

Stoeltje, Beverly. 1992. "Festival." In *Folklore, Cultural Performances, and Popular Entertainments: A Communications-Centered Handbook,* ed. Richard Bauman, 266–69. Oxford: Oxford University Press.

Tuan, Yi-Fu. 1977. *Space and Place: The Perspective of Experience.* Minneapolis: University of Minnesota Press.

Turkle, Sherry. 1995. *Life on the Screen: Identity in the Age of the Internet.* New York: Simon and Schuster.

Turner, Victor. 1969. *The Ritual Process: Structure and Anti-Structure.* Ithaca, N.Y.: Cornell University Press.

———. 1974. *Dramas, Fields, and Metaphors: Symbolic Action in Human Society.* Ithaca, N.Y.: Cornell University Press.

———. 1982. *From Ritual to Theatre: The Human Seriousness of Play.* New York: Performing Arts Journal Publications.

———, and Edith Turner. 1978. *Image and Pilgrimage in Christian Culture: Anthropological Perspectives.* New York: Columbia University Press.

Van Gennep, Arnold. 1960. *The Rites of Passage.* Chicago: University of Chicago Press.

Whiting, Sam. 1997. "A Blaze of Glory." *San Francisco Chronicle,* September 2, E1–E2.

Wojcik, Daniel. 1997. *The End of the World as We Know It: Faith, Fatalism, and Apocalypse in America.* New York and London: New York University Press.

part 3: popular spirituality and morality

Those of us who work in the field of religious studies have occasion to talk about religion with a wide variety of people, and conversations with colleagues suggest that we often encounter a similar sentiment. "I'm not really *religious*," we hear from students, strangers on airplanes, and long-lost relatives at family reunions, "but I consider myself a very *spiritual* person." Sometime in the past generation, it seems, a rift has developed between "religion," which appears to connote for many institutional affiliation, rigid dogma, medieval metaphysics, and a kind of mindless obedience to authority, and "spirituality," which seems to betoken an individualized, eclectic, and free-form personal engagement with the transcendent, however an individual may understand it.

We hear the word "morality" much less often in these encounters, yet the moral decision making that people do on a daily basis is inevitably bound up with (though not necessarily always in concert with) the wider spiritual (or religious) worldview within which they operate. In this section, we look at popular culture with an eye not so much toward specific behaviors and narratives that invite religious interpretation, but rather toward those places where Americans seem to be turning (or being led) for resources in the day-to-day task of building spiritual and moral life.

Margaret Miles's recent effort at defining spirituality is a good point of departure: "Spirituality is a consciously chosen set of beliefs, attitudes, values, and practices that the person selecting them anticipates will serve the purpose of *more life* by providing orientation and specifying responsibility" (*Seeing and Believing* 1999, 15). These beliefs, attitudes, values, and practices were once subsets of overarching and comprehensive religious worldviews: one prayed the rosary because one was a Catholic; one didn't eat pork because one was a Jew. In the United States today, however, secularization, the decline of institutional religious affiliation, and widespread knowledge of and interaction with diverse religious traditions have meant that spirituality now exists for many in American culture as a free-floating entity unto itself, the eclectic product of exposure to multiple religious, psychological, and other interpretative frameworks. The chapters that follow collectively argue that the popular culture products we encounter casually as daily entertainment are an increasingly important source in that mix.

One thing these sources tell us is that for all the apparent secularization of American popular culture, classic moral and spiritual themes from the Christian religious tradition are surprisingly persistent in American consciousness. Jean Graybeal's analysis of the *Cathy* comic strip, for instance, exposes the spiritual structure of the obsession with diet and exercise that makes Cathy's struggle so familiar to American women. Not dismissing the feminist critique of the culture of dieting that assaults women's physical and mental health, Graybeal nonetheless asks us to consider that the cycle of beginning, falling off of, and recommitting to weight-loss regimes might also represent a kind of spiritual discipline in which women cultivate hope, attend to the self in culturally permissible ways, and find community. What's more, she uncovers a religious substratum in our society's demonization of fat and overeating, discerning all seven deadly sins of the Christian tradition in Cathy's struggles against chocolate, her avoidance of the gym, and her despairing self-assessments in department store dressing rooms. Spiritual notions of sin and salvation still structure the apparently secular lives of many Americans, Graybeal's discussion suggests, even if the ideas and activities to which they apply them have changed dramatically.

Another strange manifestation of traditional spiritual and moral disciplines is explored in Suzanne Holland's analysis of the success of Judge Judy Scheindlin and Dr. Laura Schlessinger, voices of moral authority for millions through their television and radio programs. In a media-soaked and commercial society with no official religion and in which religious institutions have lost moral hegemony, it is perhaps not surprising that TV judges and hosts of radio call-in programs should emerge as arbiters of right and wrong. Noteworthy in these cases, though, is that the voices are female and, to say the least, somewhat acerbic (Dr. Laura calls what she does "nagging," Judge Judy's program is advertised as "justice with an attitude"). While many commentators have noted that these programs represent a backlash against moral permissiveness and reflect a deep-seated desire for moral absolutes in a time of relativism, Holland, drawing on the work of cultural theorist Michel Foucault, also sees in the popularity of these voices a resurfacing of centuries-old Western passion for ritualized confession. For many, she argues, the public (and ritualized) airing of "sins" in these venues, whether they be bad marriage decisions or irresponsible credit card use, the "penance" of public humiliation, and the "absolution" dispensed by a source of unambiguous righteousness are instrumental in the cultivation of a subjective sense of selfhood.

As much as traditional spiritual patterns are kept alive in secular sites, they are also, as Lisle Dalton, Monica Siems, and Eric Mazur demonstrate with respect to the animated television series *The Simpsons*, the stuff of incisive (and hilarious) parody. The authors show that swipes against traditional religious morality and spirituality are a mainstay of *The Simpsons*'s humor; the Evangelical Christian neighbor is an insufferable milksop, the mainstream Protestant minister a faithless mouther of liberal platitudes, the only regularly featured Jew a greedy, chain-smoking, child-loathing professional clown. The absence (at least officially) of religious hegemony in the United States means that all traditions are fair game for ridicule, though the viciousness of *The Simpsons*'s humor seems to increase proportionally with the level of power and influence wielded by the group in question. That is, Protestants come off especially badly; the Hindu convenience store operator, if a caricature, is generally handled sympathetically.

Plainly, *The Simpsons* does not represent a reemergence of forms of moral and spiritual discipline like those authors of the first two chapters see in their subjects. What this show does represent, the authors claim, is a place where the tensions of a multireligious society—in which innumerable (and universally flawed) moral meaning systems come into conflict—get humorously, and perhaps cathartically, aired. For all the irreverence of *The Simpsons*, its characters reckon with real moral dilemmas and their resolutions reflect real moral insight.

Elijah Siegler makes a similar case for the moral significance of another television genre, the ensemble police drama. In his look at *Law & Order*, *NYPD Blue*, and *Homicide*, Siegler identifies differing treatments of religion (as disruptive social fact, as personal salvation, and as theological speculation), but a common concern with a singular moral question: "How can one act morally in a fundamentally immoral world?" The police officers in all of these shows, contending with "the bureaucracy of police work and the chaotic, multiethnic pluralism of the streets," face the often conflicting claims of what is right and what is just. This is a very different moral world, he notes, from the black-and-white ones inhabited by earlier TV cops like Joe Friday and Harry Callahan.

And just as Holland hears echoes of the confessional in Dr. Laura's exchanges with callers, Siegler (also drawing on Foucault) sees it in "the box," the police interrogation room, which he contends is "the best example of sacred space on prime-time television." What makes that space sacred is the fact that in the interrogation, before the defense attorneys and prosecutors have arrived, the police have an opportunity to wrest justice from bureaucracy, the criminal has the opportunity to confess and thereby find redemption, and the audience is afforded "an opportunity to grapple with the same moral ambiguities explored during each episode, and to 'confess' its sins vicariously." In *The Simpsons* and these police dramas, the authors claim, a popular entertainment product becomes a venue for consideration of serious moral and spiritual issues. The time viewers spend with these products, even though they may be passing the time before dinner or bed, may also be valuable moments in which to reckon with the complexity and ambiguity of moral life in contemporary America.

Few would argue that *Cathy* presents a spiritual discipline equivalent to the *Exercises* of St. Ignatius Loyola, that all those who listen to Dr. Laura and watch Judge Judy are in search of a mother confessor, that Homer Simpson's Everyman is as spiritually instructive as his counterpart in medieval morality plays, or that vicarious entry into "the box" of the *Homicide* squad room is as fundamentally transformative as the ritual of confession was and remains for many Roman Catholics. And yet, these analyses insist, these are not the trivial time wasters they might initially appear to be. If indeed, in our information-soaked and overwhelmingly diverse society, moral and spiritual identities are patchworks of beliefs, attitudes, values, and practices culled from everything from traditional religions and family custom to Internet chat rooms and popular song lyrics, it makes sense to examine those places in our culture where the idiocies, ambiguities, and insights of that eclectic process are surfacing. Even those who are affiliated with traditional religious institutions, if they watch network TV or read the comics, are drinking, consciously or not, from these spiritual wells. In the end, perhaps the most interesting thing these popular culture products can tell us about spirituality in America today is how powerful and endlessly mutable religious patterns are in a multicultural society that has (so far) resisted religious homogenization. In such a world, these entertainment venues demonstrate, an apparently limitless number of worldviews can come into contact, conflict, and, in fascinating ways, confluence.

Cathy on Slenderness, Suffering, and Soul

JEAN GRAYBEAL

Many studies have documented the prevalence of a preoccupation with body size and slenderness among American women. The percentages of women dieting *permanently*, the tender age at which we begin to worry about weight, and the tremendous amounts of money, time, attention, and energy we spend on diets, appearance, and fitness—all point to an important cultural phenomenon. In what follows, I will attempt to show how this dieting fixation may also be seen as a "religious" or quasi-religious phenomenon; I will argue that part of its staying power in the face of powerful critiques derives from the fact that despite its primarily destructive nature, it seems also to fulfil certain felt needs related to suffering and the soul. As part of this attempt I will take a look at a contemporary commentator who discerns the underlying values of the cult of thinness and expresses them with wry resignation and a grain of appreciation: Cathy Guisewite, author of the popular comic strip *Cathy* and insightful theologian of the hopeless religion of body control.

For several decades, feminist theorists have been developing trenchant and convincing critiques and analyses of women's preoccupation with weight control. Kim Chernin's *The Obsession: Reflections on the Tyranny of Slenderness* was one of the first to argue convincingly for the "meaning" dimension of the phenomenon. Chernin analyzed "our culture's tendency to encourage women to retreat from strength and physical abundance into a sinister self-reduction" and showed in a complex and subtle argument that retrieval of the right to a full and natural-sized body would mean a huge step forward for women's sense of their true humanity (1981, xxii). Naomi Wolf's *The Beauty Myth* (1990) interpreted the cultural pressure to be as physically insubstantial as possible as part of a backlash against women's growing power. Susan Bordo's *Unbearable Weight: Feminism, Western Culture, and the Body* (1993) analyzed the deep philosophical biases, privileging mind over body, that are played out on the bodies of women in our society.

An abundance of powerful analysis has thus shown, very convincingly, that the whole phenomenon is a tremendous waste and has tried to talk women out of participating in it. Feminists make it extraordinarily clear that women have much better things to do with their time and money than torture themselves in quest of this particular unattainable ideal, but still women stubbornly insist on holding on to their irrational, even self-destructive, behavior. For American women approach dieting and the task of perfecting our bodies with what some might call a "religious" attitude. Driven by faith in the unseen rather than results or evidence (which never justify our actions), we spend countless hours, billions of dollars, and unimaginable psychic energy on the thankless and almost always futile goal of attaining an image of physical perfection, and then blame only ourselves when we do not attain it. Blaming ourselves, we enter another cycle of repentance, renewed commitment, and repeated failure.

Just as atheists and critics of religion such as Freud and Marx have long tried to analyze religious believers and practitioners out of their delusions, showing them the futility of their prayers, demonstrating to them the intractable nature of human behavior, and generally attempting to deprive the masses of their comforting though misguided fantasies, critics of women's devotion to their unattainable goal have tried to wean women from it. But both crusades have so far been unsuccessful; the enduring fact is that people perversely insist on holding on to all sorts of practices, whether traditionally religious or otherwise, that give them some kind of comfort, even though such forms of comfort may seem to outsiders to be illusory, masochistic, or both.

Perhaps we may see the persistence of such irrational behavior in the face of convincing and sound critique as having something to do with its fundamental nature. After all, religious thinking and behavior are notoriously circular; people become so precommitted to their comprehensive world views that it is difficult for them even to see, much less give credence to, evidence that things might actually be otherwise.

Clifford Geertz has explained this aspect of religion in his now famous, practically canonical definition of religion. He says a religion is:

(1)   a system of symbols which acts to
(2)   establish powerful, pervasive, and long-lasting moods and motivations in men [*sic*] by
(3)   formulating conceptions of a general order of existence and
(4)   clothing these conceptions with such an aura of factuality that
(5)   the moods and motivations seem uniquely realistic. (1973, 90)

Clearly the obsession with dieting is for many women a "system of symbols." Body obsession provides focus, center, direction, and motivation for the activities of many women's daily lives, as traditional religious frameworks are said to do. It has its own rituals (calorie-counting, label reading, scale cursing), its personal calendars of fat/fit cycles (day 10 as the only "good body" day of the month), and mandatory visits to auspicious places (health clubs, gyms, spas, and salons). It provides repetitious, time-consuming inspirational reading (fitness, "health," and beauty magazines and books), meetings, formal and *ad hoc* discussion groups, and a shared frame of values that can be assumed among the practitioners.

Like more traditional symbol systems, the obsession creates a clear enemy or picture of evil (fat, chocolate, sinful foods, and the evil tempters who purvey them) and provides magical devices for resisting the enemy. Refrigerators, bathroom scales, measuring tapes, aerobics classes, and bathing suits all play their symbolic roles, along with countless other totemic items. The religion establishes iconic figures of success, or "saints," whose depictions are omnipresent in pop culture—fashion models, actresses, rock stars, and advertising images. It calls for continual investment and expense, activities which in themselves create greater commitment. And, just like traditional religions, it even has its "fringe" elements, fundamentalists or fanatics who "go too far" with the practices, into the realms of illness (anorexia, bulimia) or extremism (bodybuilding, body modification, surgery addiction).

This system, reinforced by constant reminders from advertising and the media, "acts to establish powerful, pervasive and long-lasting moods and motivations," controlling both the feelings and the behaviors of everyday life.

The next component of Geertz's definition of religion speaks of "conceptions of a general order of existence." For many people, this requirement would exclude anything so petty as size-fixation from the realm of religious behavior, because they believe that the dieting practice is not as cosmic or all-encompassing as this. After all, does the dieting woman really believe that the *ultimate* point of all of life is to reach a size 6? Would she go so far as to affirm that slenderness is the most important thing in human existence? Sometimes women will indeed go this far, but I do not think that a conscious acceptance of such ideas or a willingness to profess them openly is necessary to show that one believes them. On the contrary, it is sometimes the case that the most deeply held convictions and perspectives have been inherited or formed over years of unreflective absorption and are inaccessible to conscious scrutiny and analysis. If the unhappy woman always adverts to fantasies of slimness and beauty, imagining that losing weight will make her happy; if she subordinates other activities, interests, and pleasures to the goal of losing weight; if she sees herself and others in these terms first; and if her most common response to the question of what she would choose if she could have one wish is "to lose weight," I think it is fair to say that a "conception of the general order of existence" is at work here.

Geertz notes that not all cases of fervor deserve the rubric of religiosity: "A man can indeed be said to be 'religious' about golf, but not merely if he pursues it with passion and plays it on Sundays: he must also see it as symbolic of some transcendent truths" (1973, 98). (It is interesting that golf is the example chosen by Geertz, since so many golfers have indeed written about the transcendent truths it represents to them!) I shall say more about this dimension of the dieting religion below, when we begin to examine the concrete case of Cathy Guisewite.

Section four of Geertz's definition says that the symbol system "cloth(es) these conceptions with ... an aura of factuality." Women are deeply convinced of the factuality and the eventual efficacy of their ritual religious practices, despite all evidence to the contrary. Despite readily available and widely publicized statistics regarding the long-term failure of dieting to reduce body weight and size, all women who engage in it are certain that they are among the 5 percent for whom the loss will be permanent. For this practice is not about facts; it is not about recognizing that nineteen out of twenty of us are engaged in an expensive, demoralizing, and endless enterprise; it is, rather, about an "aura of factuality," an ambient haze of counterfactual claims, promises, and images. Yet this glow of factuality is evidently more satisfying, more motivating and motivational, than the real facts can ever be.

Geertz says that finally "the moods and motivations seem uniquely realistic." While one is a devotee of this particular religion, nothing can take the place of the elation of losing two pounds, the fantasy of the beautiful party dress fitting, the sense of control and power gained by exerting control over the enemy, the appetitive body. Uniquely realistic these moods and motivations seem, because in many cases they are the most powerful symbolic system readily available to many women. Various traditionally "female" identities make women especially vulnerable to those symbols. Women are, after all, the consumers par excellence of mass media with their constant barrage of images and fantasies, the persons who still define their worth and value in terms of attractiveness to men, and the mothers who train their own daughters in the requirements of the hopeless religion.

Geertz's definition may help us to see why the phenomenon of dieting keeps its hold on its adherents. But it proposes no consolation or even hope for those of us still stuck in it. We understand that we are oppressing ourselves and that patriarchal capitalist society is oppressing us, as feminist analysis has shown, and we grasp that we are in the grip of an "aura of factuality" that in this case has no basis in reality. But here we continue to stand (or jog in place). Is there no hope for the hapless victims of the hoax, unable to free ourselves through understanding?

I would like to propose here another angle of approach to this phenomenon, one that tries to see the religious aspects of this cult with a somewhat gentler, more accepting eye, an angle that might allow some of the slightly more redemptive, positive, and "soul-making" aspects of the obsession to emerge into view. After all, can something that so many intelligent, educated, self-respecting women tacitly insist on remaining committed to, despite of all the waste and pain, be *all* bad? Are there *no* positive values that lurk beneath the admittedly wasteful and futile practices of dieting and fitness obsession? As I explore these less obvious values and teachings, I'll make use of the comic strips of Cathy Guisewite, who I believe sheds a softer light on the obsession with weight.

Guisewite, a self-professed longtime devotee of the cult, began her career as a cartoonist as a way of dealing with her unhappiness and food. She says, "I only drew the (first) picture because I was several hours into a sugar overload, and had reached that giddy stage of total despair when humor and tragedy smash into each other head-on" (1991, 215). Her comic strips deal with what she calls the "four basic guilt groups: food, love, mother, and career" (viii). Her drawings show her alter ego, Cathy, coping daily with the requirements of her religion, and strangely benefiting from the ways it which it fails her. A brief look at the titles of some of her many books is revealing: *Thin Thighs in Thirty Years* and *Wake Me Up When I'm a Size Five* are my favorites. Others are *I'll Pay $5000 for a Swimsuit that Fits Me!*, *Yes, I Love Myself Enough to Stay on This Stupid Diet*, *The Family Thigh Problem Begins with the Mouth*, and *Cathy's Recipes and Foodstyles of the Stars*. Guisewite shows us a youngish, normal, self-aware career woman whose adherence to the religion of dieting brings her not only grief but certain ambiguous yet undeniable satisfactions as well.

One of the values that the futile religion seems to offer to women is the permission, otherwise sometimes difficult to gain, to spend time and money on themselves. Puritanical ideals, which we imagine we have left so far behind, still linger in the psychology of many women; to pursue simple pleasure and self-satisfaction can still be interpreted as selfishness. But when it is devoted to the purpose of losing weight or getting fit, the narcissistic or self-centered activity becomes socially acceptable. Taking a walk for pleasure or enjoyment, or for no purpose, is more suspect for women in our goal-obsessed culture than is "power-walking" to lose weight. Spending on ourselves in a guilt-ridden way seems to justify much more expense than simple enhancement of the day ever could.

(1991, 229)

Here fat has become the part of the self on which it is acceptable to spend money. What would we do without it as justifier of luxurious expense? It is worth noticing that the money Cathy laments spending has gone to a health club, books, a robe, and a tanning session, all expenses that one might see as pleasurable or enjoyable if they were not explicitly pointed toward the great self-alteration goal that American society validates for every woman.

Besides time and money, attention to oneself becomes permitted to women when they subscribe to the physical perfection cult. They observe and monitor their own behavior and activities, keeping track of the details of their lives in ways that might be considered egocentric or excessive if the self-observation were focused on emotions, ideas, or inner experience. To be too self-aware or inwardly directed is suspect in women, whose main focus is still presumed to be the welfare of others, but if the focus is on the recalcitrant body, such close attention is deemed admirable. Cathy says: "On my new weight-loss program, I record protein, carbohydrates, and fat intake . . . keep a log of exercise activity . . . compute calorie expenditure . . . chart the figures over to goal-visualizing photographs . . . cross-reference behavior patterns with priority checklists . . ." When she is asked, "Why don't you just eat less?" she responds, "It's too complicated" (1991, 233).

I take her reply quite seriously. To eat less would require a level of simple uncomplicated permission just to live and be that is actually quite complicated for a woman to attain in our society. Much less complicated as a way to gain the freedom to pay attention to oneself is the technological, sophisticated, record-keeping mode of paying attention to the minutiae of the diet. Perhaps as women learn how to give themselves permission to spend time, money, and attention on themselves, these abilities may one day carry over into self-permission to become truly uncomplicated.

Another value that sometimes emerges from women's dieting religion is solidarity, or at least a sense of being in the same boat with others. (Of course, one must hate women thinner than oneself, so the bizarre ultimate goal must be to be the thinnest, least-liked girl on the block!) In the meantime, those who fail to become that desirable object of hate find tremendous commonality in the shared struggle toward the unattainable goal.

I work in an office with a group of other women and just a few men. The most common topic of casual conversations among the women transcends economic, racial, and age differences: it is food and weight. As we pursue our daily patterns of movement through the building, all paths cross in the kitchen, where coffee is brewed, popcorn is popped, lunches are prepared, and temptations are shared. The one topic of discourse which all have in common is food. We know that in this realm our assumptions are shared. Even people who like cold, rainy weather can agree with others that brownies are the devil; even people who hold diametrically opposed expectations of politics, of the police, of the future, know and can assert with confidence to each other which brand of nonfat yogurt is the best.

Boxes of candy and cookies are brought to the office as a way of passing on temptation to the others. Better to infect the whole group with chocolate craving than to go through it at home alone. Rounds of knowing laughter, outbursts of accusations, fits and flights of silliness all come from the kitchen and are the sounds of women acknowledging their commonality around food and their feelings about it. Women of many different backgrounds know something about each other, as we sigh collectively over the ravages effected by the holiday season with its endless parties and treats. Until one of us breaks out of the cult, either by achieving the goal (which never happens) or by giving it up (which also never happens), we are all in the boat together. If one of us were to become svelte and slim, she would lose our trust. Of course, a woman who starts out that way is forgiven; she can't help it, and we do know she only stays that way through her own devotional practices. But if one of us were to succeed, change, and *become* beautiful and slender, she would no longer be one of the seekers. Our solidarity rests in our common failure.

Failure brings on introspection, says our theologian Guisewite. She has Cathy say:

(1991, 222)

Guisewite, the analyst of guilt, tells us that to do something virtuous is not to gain self-knowledge. It is only in the context of "sin," of doing what one does not want to do, that that particular gift appears. The soul wants to speak, but it does not articulate itself in moments of success and goodness. It calls out in the moments of failure instead.

As we begin to look at the ambiguous but important values that can emerge from the experience of failure, another theorist of the religious dimension provides helpful insight. The depth psychologist James Hillman has written at length in many works about the meaning of various forms of experience for the development and deepening of the "soul" dimension.

Hillman believes that "the human adventure is a wandering through the vale of the world for the sake of making soul" (1975, ix). To define soul—a notoriously slippery term—he says:

> First, "soul" refers to the deepening of events into experiences; second, the significance soul makes possible, whether in love or in religious concern, derives from its special relation with death. And third, by "soul" I mean the imaginative possibility in our natures, the experiencing through reflective speculation, dream, image, and fantasy—that mode which recognizes all realities as primarily symbolic or metaphorical. (1975, x)

For Hillman, events are just occurrences and remain meaningless until they are deepened by soul into personal experiences. The soul lives and develops in relation to death and to death-related concerns like failure and suffering. And soul sees everything as meaningful, understanding that food, eating, the body, and everything with and through which we live in the world is symbolic.

Naturally, Hillman views "symptoms" (among which we can surely include debilitating syndromes like the dieting bug) as symbolic or metaphorical as well. Symptoms are tools that the soul uses to knock the ego off the throne it has climbed up onto. Hillman writes:

> to be afflicted like Job in spite of being godly to the best of one's ability, is a humiliating, soul-awakening experience. Symptoms humiliate; they relativize the ego. They bring it down. . . . The humiliation of symptoms is one of the ways we grow humble—the traditional mark of the soul. (1967, 55)

When Cathy fails, and "falls" into eating sinful foods, she looks inward and wonders why, and she learns about herself. She recognizes and "confesses" her anxiety, her fear of closeness. If she just eats a carrot, though, she remains "in control." Nothing new happens, no suffering or failure or lack of coherence in the self happens, so no self-knowledge can emerge—no soul-growing happens.

There is at least one other major virtue that the hopeless quest teaches women, and that is the ability to continue to *hope* in the face of failure. Daily the devotees strive for something they cannot and will not attain. For almost all people who lose a significant amount of weight soon gain it back, and we all "know" this. Unless one changes one's life completely, becoming a bicycle racer rather than a sedentary worker, the size the body wants to be takes over. Daily the faithful ones chart the ups and downs of a permanently unwinnable battle, but never let go of the goal, no matter how far into the distance it recedes.

This expertise in the ability to continue to fail seems to me to be one of the most remarkable skills learned through the practice of the losing battle. For so much in life is indeed loss; to learn to lose and fail must surely be as important as to learn to win. We do lose so much more than we win, after all, and in the end we must lose it all. The Buddha's First Noble Truth, that life is suffering, *dukkha*, imperfection, impermanence, "lack of fit," is most closely and daily exemplified in the lives of many American women by the "suffering" of being the wrong size, of literally "not fitting." In a time when so many genuine and more serious forms of suffering have nearly been eliminated from or at least delayed in our lives, could it be that we actually seek and create more venues for soul making, for the grinding, wearing sense of everything being not quite right, that sense that ultimately propels one to wonder, to look beyond, to seek detachment, to have compassion? Jose Marti said it this way: "Man needs to suffer. When he does not have real griefs he creates them. Griefs purify and prepare him." (How might this happen for men on such a daily basis? In their addiction to televised sports, with the perpetual failure and disappointment to which their teams inevitably treat them?)

Cathy tells us about living with loss and failure. Exhausted by her perpetual diet, she says:

(1991, 236)

Again, she says more than she may know. To lose weight, which is the ostensible goal of the quest, would have to be to lose hope as well, for the hoping and wishing and imagining are attached to a perfected vision of the future self. The self free of the heavy weight that makes her strive would not only be unrecognizable to herself, but would also be empty of the drive and desire that have kept her going for these many years. If she were to lose weight, what would she do with all that time, that money, that focus, that attention, that desire . . . and what would she do with all that hope?

Living with loss and failure and constantly reaffirming the lifestyle that commits one to loss and failure must surely qualify as some form of spirituality. Misguided we know it to be; masochistic, too; wasteful and sad, no doubt. But my claim here is that, in addition to being inculcated and encouraged by social pressures, somehow and for some reason, it is *chosen*, and what is chosen and continually rechosen by definition has meaning for the soul.

What is it in the soul, then, that wants to suffer? The part that knows its oneness with the body, which will suffer and die; the part that knows its solidarity with the other, whose suffering is too easily shut out; the part that knows that depth is not a characteristic of ease and youth and beauty. Soul seeks depth and *chiaroscuro*, not simply out of romanticism but out of an innate connection to the reality of things, a reality that is mixed of pleasure and pain, joy and suffering, light and dark.

The unattainability of the goal of women's obsession gives us a way to suffer, both together and alone, and a way to experience the values and virtues of devotion, persistence, and faith in an era when such values have lost their anchors in traditional religions and in traditional women's roles. The soul seeks objects for such virtues, and only objects that are permanently out of reach will do. Family and religion are traditional sites for such virtues to exercise themselves, but in their absence the goal of bodily perfection will have to do.

Once again Clifford Geertz's discussion of the functions of religion sheds light on the role of suffering. When he is unpacking the ways in which symbol systems "formulate conceptions of a general order of existence," he notes that one of the central problems that call out for such a conception is suffering. He writes:

> As a religious problem, the problem of suffering is, paradoxically, not how to avoid suffering but how to suffer, how to make of physical pain, personal loss, worldly defeat, or the helpless contemplation of others' agony something bearable, supportable—something, as we say, sufferable. (1973, 104)

Women, through their years of practice in failure to reach their dubious goal, learn "how to suffer," how to bear what they think all along is unbearable.

The historian Caroline Walker Bynum has written about food and suffering in the religious lives of medieval women. Her book, *Holy Feast and Holy Fast*, provides a picture of women of a very different era and their use of the practice of fasting in attaining their religious goals. For medieval women, she writes, "Fasting was not merely a substitution of pathological and self-defeating control of self for unattainable control of circumstance. It was part of suffering; and suffering was considered an effective activity, which redeemed both individual and cosmos" (1987, 207). Suffering's efficacy held a very specific meaning within medieval Christianity, a meaning that does not transfer directly to today's society, but the suffering of the dieting religion may have its own spiritual meaning. Bynum writes, "Our modern use of food and body as symbols of all that we seek to control seems to me a vain effort to hide from ourselves the fact that our control is not—cannot be—total.... For unless we conquer death, suffering must always be a reminder of it—a foretaste of our own death and of the loss of those we love" (301). She hopes, as I do, for another way for contemporary women to spend their lives, but also hints at the meaning implied by suffering that is chosen.

I have been discussing the patient and persistent "virtues" women may learn through the practice of futility, but the "soulful" side of the self emerges also in relation to the "vices" the dieting religion encourages its devotees to experience.

Many traditional religious definitions of sinful behavior have fallen away, but somehow the psyche continues to manufacture or redefine notions of sin and vice, as though these too were needed in order to experience life as sufficiently meaningful and dramatic. If what was once taboo becomes sanitized and desacralized, new taboos and new definitions of sin and guilt must evidently arise. Most people today do not believe that the devil is literally waiting around the corner to tempt them into evildoing, but it is perfectly apparent to most normal American women that there is indeed a powerful tempter lurking in the bakery, the ice cream shop, the candy store, and the deli section. Certain foods are particularly demonized, most notably chocolate, and naturally therefore must be ritually exchanged and devoured (destroyed) on numerous occasions. Valentine's Day is the time when men are expected to produce emblems or tokens of the tempter, and women ritually to vilify them and then ingest them.

Cathy finds herself in the grip of the chocolate demon:

Cathy © Cathy Guisewhite. Reprinted with permission of Universal Press Syndicate. All rights reserved.
(1996,119)

Eating forbidden foods puts women in touch with their desire and their ambivalence about desire. The indulgence of desire may ostensibly be condoned in today's society, but still we have created for ourselves a new venue in which to experience the traditional vice of "gluttony." Is craving all right or not? Wanting success, fame, fortune, happiness, possessions, beauty . . . the desires for all of these seem to be fine, and are socially approved and even encouraged. But encountering the desire for food, especially a "forbidden" food, is still a chance to experience the multiplicity of the self, and its capacity and perhaps craving for guilt. If we did not need this sense, why would we constantly create and re-create for ourselves new definitions of what is taboo or forbidden?

Faced with the ice cream store, Cathy agonizes: "I shouldn't. I shouldn't. I shouldn't. . . . I shouldn't but I deserve it. . . . Well, I might not deserve it, but I need it.... I don't actually *need* it, but I want it.... If I have this one tiny scoop of ice cream, I will skip dinner and do two workout tapes tonight.... I'll eat only plain green salads for three days, go to the gym every night for a month, and *forgo all temptations for the duration of the year!!*" Finally she buys her ice cream, and her mother asks, "What flavor did you get?" Cathy answers, "Guilt ripple." (1996, 122)

To enter the place of temptation and undergo this struggle with the self is to demonstrate the apparent need for a site in which to experience one's own nature, a nature full of desire, discomfort, and anxiety, convinced that self-denial is better than self-indulgence, and faced with the inevitability of sin and the fall. Why do people need these experiences of temptation, heroic resistance, failure, repentance, redemption, and then a repetition of the cycle? Is there something about the psyche that craves a sense of constant drama, a way to understand the feeling that things are not right and to project that lack of fit onto an external source? Perhaps there is something about the self that seeks definition both through identification and through abjection or dissociation. "You are what you eat," but you are also defined by what you don't eat. Vegetarians don't eat meat; health nuts don't eat junk food; good women don't eat fat. Injunctions about what to eat and what not to eat, what is kosher and what is not, are so common in religions as to form one of the most basic features they have in common. Is it any surprise that the religion of slenderness has its forbidden fudges and its holy rice cakes as well?

Another of the traditional "deadly sins" was pride. Today we are encouraged to be proud of ourselves, to love ourselves, and to take credit when it is due. But the sin of pride has a new venue in which to work, through the fantasy dimension of the dieting phenomenon. Against all evidence, the dieter's pride holds on to an image of herself that is permanently different from the reality, and supposedly superior to it:

Cathy © Cathy Guisewhite. Reprinted with permission of Universal Press Syndicate. All rights reserved.
(1996, 79)

Three more of the traditional Christian sins—covetousness, lust, and envy—are so central to the emotional constitution of the slenderness religion as to scarcely require mention. Fueled by the ubiquitous barrage of advertising images in women's magazines and other media, these dominate the inner landscape of the practitioner, and gain full expression at the gym.

Cathy © Cathy Guisewhite. Reprinted with permission of Universal Press Syndicate. All rights reserved.
(1991, 241)

Anger too has its place in the range of vices experienced in the dieting complex. Although solidarity with coreligionists is part of the story, as mentioned above, the other side is the hostility and resentment that find expression in the self-abuse of dieting and compulsive exercise.

Cathy and her aerobics classmates tell their instructor why they are seeking to lose weight:

Cathy © Cathy Guisewhite. Reprinted with permission of Universal Press Syndicate. All rights reserved.
(1996, 84)

Even the seventh deadly sin of sloth comes into play in this religion, making its adherents feel guilty and culpable for taking a day off, for lounging and doing nothing when they could be working out, for wearing sweat pants in front of the TV instead of doing glamorous things in any of the dozens of too-small outfits hanging in the closet. If we've come so far from these traditional ideas of sin and temptation, why have we re-created them in this cultural phenomenon of our own making?

It is my contention that no trivial thing is going on here. If a common complex of behaviors and attitudes is the site of extreme emotions, of a sense of compulsion or obsession, of the personification of temptation, and of a sense of multiplicity within the self, it is a meaningful complex. The fact that the meaning is not clear or univocal is no argument against its existence or importance. Like much complex human behavior, the diet cycle is overdetermined and multifaceted, but simply to condemn it and demand its demise both underestimates its meaningful character and may ultimately perpetuate its grasp. Also needed, I believe, is an approach that sees it as having something to do with soul, with depth, with the need to become acquainted with one's own capacity both for virtues and vices as somewhat autonomous factors in the self.

If one can become free of this obsession, one should, and all avenues of liberation are to be applauded. If not, though, I cannot believe that all is lost and decades of experience have been totally wasted. It is possible that in the long term these experiences of virtues and vices may lead women to another phase of soul-making life, one in which they are able to begin to understand the general goal of self-perfection in a new way. Under normal circumstances of aging, the fiction of attainable bodily perfection usually begins to pall, the images of models and mannequins grow more and more unbelievable as potential representations of reality, and women sometimes begin to find other sources of strength and power in their lives besides their youth and sexual attractiveness. As a sense of realism about the lifelong pursuit sets in, women may eventually begin to achieve a kind of resignation about the hopeless religion itself.

As they experience the loss of these religious/spiritual goals, many women go through the stages of loss described by Elisabeth Kübler-Ross in her classic work *On Death and Dying* (1969). At first the reality of the situation may be resisted; *denial* of the final unattainability of the goal functions wonderfully for a time, especially since it has been the major defensive tactic practiced over the decades of volunteer slavery. But then *anger* may emerge. "How can it be that I am growing beyond this stage of life? Who's in charge around here? How outrageous it is!" *Bargaining*, again, is a skill that's been sharpened to a fine edge. "If I give up all treats, surely I can get back to where I was; if I just get to the gym every day instead of four times a week, then I can stop this process."

But as the reality of the situation begins to set in, *depression* may arrive. Depression is truly a place of soul. To go down, to be pressed down, to be in the dark, is to encounter opportunities for letting go, for the decomposition of calcified attitudes and parts of the self, for reverie, for reorganization, so that eventually new patterns of growth and change may emerge. The soul regroups itself in depression, and when it emerges is ready not only for *acceptance* but for new creation. Hillman says it this way: "Through depression we enter depths and in depths find soul. Depression ... brings refuge, limitation, focus, gravity, weight, and humble powerlessness. It reminds of death. *The true revolution begins in the individual who can be true to his or her depression*" (1975, 98).

Perhaps the virtues and skills learned by women in the lifelong practice of the hopeless religion of body perfection are truly survival skills after all. Though it may take us decades to learn or accept that the body religion has been false and misguided, the soulful habits and mindsets we have acquired—patience, persistence, hope against all odds, self-valuing, sharing with other women—may be applied to new goals and pursuits; our experience with the sins and vices, too, has given us a richness of understanding about the devious and deviant ways of soul. We go into politics and the arts, back to school or into new lines of work, and pursue new spiritual paths, learning that new goals, though no more fully attainable than our original ones, may be just as motivating. For the painting, too, can never be perfected, nor the poem, nor the community we serve. But all can benefit from the arts learned and the wisdom gained in the soul-making practices of women's early lives, wherever they are found.

REFERENCES

Bordo, Susan. 1993. *Unbearable Weight: Feminism, Western Culture, and the Body.* Berkeley: University of California Press.

Bynum, Caroline Walker. 1987. *Holy Feast and Holy Fast.* Berkeley: University of California Press.

Chernin, Kim. 1981. *The Obsession: Reflections on the Tyranny of Slenderness.* New York: Harper and Row.

Geertz, Clifford. 1973. "Religion as a Cultural System." In *The Interpretation of Cultures.* New York: Basic Books.

Guisewite, Cathy. 1991. *Reflections: A Fifteenth Anniversary Collection.* Kansas City, Mo.: Andrews and McNeel.

———. 1996. *Cathy Twentieth Anniversary Collection.* Kansas City, Mo.: Andrews and McNeel.

Hillman, James. 1967. *Insearch: Psychology and Religion.* New York: Charles Scribner's Sons.

———. 1975. *Re-Visioning Psychology.* New York: Harper and Row.

Kübler-Ross, Elisabeth. 1969. *On Death and Dying.* New York: Macmillan.

Wolf, Naomi. 1990. *The Beauty Myth.* Toronto: Vintage Books.

God in the Box

Religion in Contemporary Television Cop Shows

ELIJAH SIEGLER

A middle-aged woman is on trial for planting a bomb that killed a young mother-to-be in an abortion clinic. Against the advice of counsel, the defendant takes the stand. She swears her oath on the Bible, then admits to planting the bomb. When the district attorney asks her if this makes her guilty of murder, she replies, "Not before God."

—*Law & Order*, aired January 8, 1991

A detective with the New York Police Department and his wife, an attorney, stand in a Greek Orthodox church. Their newborn son is undergoing the "churching" ceremony. The priest, holding the baby up to God, walks down the aisle of the church, saying a blessing at each stop. The detective, following behind, prays for God to keep his new son and his eldest son, who was recently killed while attempting to stop a robbery.

—*NYPD Blue*, aired May 21, 1996

After a cursory investigation of a double homicide inside the Baltimore jail, a detective has been told to cease his work on the case. But the detective believes that one of the witnesses, an African-American man named Elijah facing a life sentence for first-degree murder, is holding back. The detective wants to return to the jail to interview him again. Elijah is "looking for redemption," the detective says.

—*Homicide*, aired October 18, 1996[1]

January 31, 1993, saw the premier of another new hourlong ensemble drama. Helmed by big-name movie director Barry Levinson (*Rain Man, Bugsy*), it first aired in the most coveted slot of the year: following the Super Bowl. More than one hundred hours of television later, one of the first lines of that first episode ("Gone for Goode") best defined the show's central theme. As Detective Howard says to Bayliss on the first day of his new job as detective, "This is homicide. We work for God." This chapter is an effort to make sense of this kind of intrusion of religious language, symbols, and themes into the secular venue of the TV cop show.

Few would disagree with the fact that television is important. If nothing else, it's all pervasive. Ninety-two million homes in America have at least one television set (98 percent of the total population), and more homes are equipped with TV than with telephones. The average TV set in this country is on at least seven hours every day (Allen 1992, 1). By the time the average baby boomer was sixteen years old, she had watched between twelve thousand and fifteen thousand hours of television (Roof 1993, 53).

Cultural theorists have gone beyond statistics to speculate on the effects television has had on the transformation of modern consciousness. Some see television as having replaced traditional institutions of socialization such as the family and the church. In his essay, "Blurred Boundaries," Wade Clark Roof argues that the erosion of authority of leadership institutions has resulted in an increased role for media industries and greater personal autonomy in religion. He cites Stewart Hoover's theory that public communication controls the public sphere "and thereby defines the meaning-contexts in which other types of communication take place" (including communication about religion) (Roof 1996, 6). According to this view, religion becomes flattened and reinterpreted in the light of mass media.

If television shapes our values, then surely it's important to ask what's on TV. But all too often, the content of television is overlooked. Scholars write about television as if all programming were the same, instead of acknowledging that different producers create different programming for different (and increasingly fragmented) audiences. For example, one of the questions Diana Crane asks in *The Production of Culture* (1992)—What values does television inculcate?—is certainly important but does not acknowledge the difference between an hour of PBS, an hour of the Christian Broadcasting Network, and an hour of the Playboy Channel.

Even worse, many otherwise intelligent cultural critics seem to be in the thrall of the "television as wasteland" motif. Here my own discipline, religious studies, is particularly guilty. However scholars of religion frame the central problem of contemporary society—as a decline in civil religion or public morals, as a fragmentation of community, as a fragmentation of the self, or as just a precipitous decline in our national attention span—television is seen as a big part of that problem. In *Producing the Sacred*, Robert Wuthnow makes a throwaway reference to television. Decrying the use of spectacle in public religious ritual, Wuthnow writes, "speech alone is seldom powerful enough to constitute an engaging public ritual. Television again is one of the reasons why" (1994, 140). Challenging the "wasteland" view, I argue that television can be and is a locus of real thought about serious religious issues. Cop shows are my case study.

THREE SQUAD-ROOM DRAMAS

Too much analysis of the place of religion on television has been a matter of counting the shows that are explicitly religious (*Touched by an Angel*, *Soul Man*), and the references to God, priest, or the church on nonreligious shows (Skill et al. 1994).[2] While useful in a limited way, this approach fails to consider an important aspect of television narrative. A television series is not a collection of discrete moments. Television drama is an open narrative; the audience gains pleasure from viewing regular characters operating in predictable ways. The more knowledge the viewer has of the characters, the more pleasure, knowledge, and understanding is available. For example, if a character on a TV series is shown to have a certain religious outlook on life in episode three, regular viewers can read that character's actions in future episodes informed by that outlook, even if that outlook is never explicitly acknowledged. Then if, say, in episode twenty-five the same character has a crisis of faith, the audience can "read" back to the previous episodes that led up to it. All this is of course beyond the ken of the religious media watchdogs who rate programs by counting key words and images and evaluating whether their religious views are portrayed in a positive or negative light.

With that in mind, I examine three television series in a genre not usually considered religious—the police drama, where, in fact, religion shows up everywhere. The three programs are *Homicide: Life on the Streets* (NBC), *Law & Order* (NBC), and *NYPD Blue* (ABC). *Law & Order* has been on the air since 1990; the other two since 1993. *Homicide* was canceled in 1999; the other two are still on the air. All three are rerun daily on cable networks.

These series are all hourlong crime dramas. Richard Sparks has identified the crime drama as able to meet the viewer's weekly expectations by conforming to one of two traditional narrative structures: the finished and the soap operatic (1992, 128–29). The first draws the story line to a satisfactory conclusion at the end of the hour. The second features several continuing story lines. *Law & Order* is the perfect "finished" show; it follows a single criminal case, from investigation by New York City police (the "order") to prosecution by the district attorney (the "law"). Even though one episode takes place over several month's time (indicated by titles announcing the date and location of each scene), each episode invariably begins with the police being called to the scene of a crime, usually a murder, continues through the investigation and prosecution, and ends with the verdict.

NYPD Blue, also set in New York, follows a format invented by Steven Bochco for his 1980s cop show *Hill Street Blues*, also used in his early creation *LA Law*, which combines finished and soap operatic elements. The "Bochco" format involves an ensemble cast of characters in a well-defined location with many intertwining story lines that combine the personal and professional, the serious and the comic, some ending after one episode, some lasting a few episodes, some ongoing for the year.

Homicide, set in Baltimore, takes the most formal risks of the three programs. Some episodes follow a standard Bochco format; some are focused on a single story line. Several shows take extreme narrative risks—entire episodes are set in one room or are told from perspectives other than those of police protagonists, for instance, that of a stalker or of the families of murder victims. The series is based on a book by journalist David Simon, who spent a year with the Baltimore police.

Certainly these three shows are of high quality in a time that is often seen as a golden age of TV, second only to the 1950s. All three appear regularly on TV critics' lists of top ten shows. *NYPD Blue* and *Law & Order* have both won Emmys for outstanding TV drama, while *Homicide*, the sleeper of the three, made the *TV Guide* cover with the headline "The Case for *Homicide*: The Best Show You're Not Watching" (December 28, 1996). Besides superior acting, directing, and writing, these programs are worth following because they have something to say. These are not just shows about catching the bad guys; in many ways, religious issues—questions of ultimate concern—are at their heart. All three programs deal consistently, seriously, and self-consciously with religious and moral concerns.

One need only look at the titles of individual episodes to notice how frequently and deliberately religion is the theme of these shows. *NYPD Blue* gives us "Torah! Torah! Torah!" and "Guns n' Rosaries." *Homicide*'s episode titles include "Nearer My God to Thee," "Extreme Unction," and "Kaddish." *Law & Order*'s pithy titles have religious connotations most often: "Forgiveness," "Blood Libel," "Confession," "Sanctuary," "Angel," and "Heaven" are just a few. Note, too, that these titles are used only by the production staff as reminders and are not usually known by the viewing public. But more than just the titles suggest that the writers and producers are conscious of the religious subtext of these shows. Tom Fontana, the producer of *Homicide* and winner of an award from the Catholics in Media Association (CIMA), has publicly stated that all the characters on his show are on some kind of faith journey (Sariego 1998).

So even if the audience is not invited to foreground the religious, the critic cannot be accused of overreading the producers' intentions.

But each series treats religion differently. *Law & Order* is concerned mostly with the social aspects of religion. There, religion is a marker of identity, much like race, economic status, or gender. Religion is one more way violence may erupt in the social order, one more way the precarious urban peace can be toppled. *NYPD Blue* occasionally uses religion for local color or comic relief, but principally explores the personal, private aspect of religion. The detectives, recovering from grief, addiction, and otherwise damaged lives, seek redemption, forgiveness, second chances. Sometimes they find salvation. *Homicide* asks the toughest religious questions. What are the root cause(s) and consequences of evil? What is the nature and meaning of death? Detectives test their faith, while criminals must look for confession and absolution. *Homicide* is thus the most self-consciously theological of the series.

LAW & ORDER: RELIGION AS SOCIAL FACT

Law & Order uses religion and morality in three different ways. First, religion helps locate the characters. The first episode of the 1995–96 season saw the introduction of a new regular, Detective Ray Curtis. In his first scene Curtis crosses himself in front of a corpse. That gesture, combined with his dark complexion, and his later reference to his three beloved daughters, let the audience know he is a good Hispanic Catholic. In guest roles, too, religion serves as a shorthand for character: a witness wears a Jewish skullcap, a suspect talks of going to church.

Second, the show presents a kind of moral reasoning evocative of religious analysis of ethical issues. In the second half of each show, lawyers must untangle ethical knots and engage in what John Leonard calls "moral math" (1997, 159). *Law & Order* provides a weekly object lesson in casuistry. The recent attempt by Richard Miller, professor of ethics at Indiana University, to resurrect casuistry as modern morality might have benefitted from including television in its analysis. He writes that, "Like jurists, casuists are interpretive and practical: They seek to reflect about the merits of our conduct in one situation or another, help us perceive the morally salient features of human experience, and render judgments that are fair."

But he also understands its downside as "something vaguely medieval, suggesting a kind of scholastic sophistry in the service of moral mediocrity ... a form of chicanery" (Miller 1996, 1). Both of these definitions work well for the series' two assistant district attorneys: Ben Stone (1990–94) and his replacement, Jack McCoy (1994–).

The third and most important way *Law & Order* uses religion is as a destructive force that would confirm the worst fears of the average viewer. "Religious fanatics" bomb an abortion clinic in one episode ("Life Choices," aired January 8, 1991) and murder an abortionist in another ("Progenitor," aired January 25, 1995). Parents belonging to a fictitious religious community, clearly modeled on Christian Science, let their daughter die rather than seek medical help ("God Bless the Child," aired October 22, 1991). A charismatic cult leader is charged with murder, and after his conviction his followers commit ritual suicide ("Apocrypha," aired November 3, 1993). An observant Catholic woman cremates her baby; she wanted her daughter to be with God in heaven, she explains on the witness stand ("Angel," aired November 29, 1995). In all of these cases, the religious impulse is a negative one; to be religious is to be abnormal.

Here is a more detailed example of how religious convictions are presented negatively, from the episode "Trophy," which originally aired on January 31, 1996: Two African-American youths are found murdered. Police suspect a copycat killer because the crimes closely resemble a series of slayings of African-American youths a few years before for which a man, a known racist, was convicted and is now in prison.

Detectives Briscoe and Curtis investigate. Curtis has an idea: "Maybe there's a religious angle—Justin played for a church basketball team; Shawn's wearing a crucifix." This reminds Curtis of a witness they had interviewed earlier, whose apartment had a big wooden crucifix in the front hall.

They return to question Simon, an African-American security guard, who was working in the vicinities where each of the boys was abducted. The cops think they have their man, but they can't prove it. So Curtis engages in what can only be called religious badgering:

CURTIS: I see you keep a Bible here.

SIMON: Yes.

CURTIS: Swear on the Bible you didn't kill those boys.

SIMON: You don't know what you're asking me to do.

CURTIS: Swear to God and we'll leave. Go ahead, swear.

This gambit is possible only because the detective doing it is, we know from previous episodes, a good Catholic, so he has a "right" to force someone to swear on a Bible to extract a confession. If the detective were a Jew or an atheist the audience would likely find him too unsympathetic.

The next scene is in the precinct, Simon having confessed to the murders. Simon says one boy deserved to die because he "looked at dirty magazines." "Justin was a martyr to our Lord" and "God put 'em in my path," Simon declares. Presumably, his constant references to God show how crazy and guilty he is.

In *Law & Order*'s defense against the charge of an antireligious bias, one might say that because the program is so focused on crime, all professions or institutions are portrayed in a negative light. Doctors molest their patients, come to work drunk, or impregnate women with their own sperm. Exclusive prep schools are havens for privileged boys who assault or murder or for teachers who sleep with their students. In this series, which plays to the viewers' distrust and institutional suspicions, religion gets off no worse than the worlds of finance, medicine, or education.

Alone among police dramas on the air, *Law & Order* deals with religion exclusively as a social fact. The realities of Jewishness and anti-Semitism, for example, have played large and small parts in episodes throughout *Law & Order*'s nine seasons (see, for example, "Sanctuary," aired April 13, 1994, or "Blood Libel," aired January 3, 1996). *Law & Order* is therefore the only show treated here that admits no essence, no substance to religion. Religion is one among many of the motivating factors in human behavior, and therefore can be as productive for the protagonists (manifested as zeal for justice or as compassion) as it is destructive for the perpetrators (manifested as homicidal mania or as insanity).

NYPD BLUE: RELIGION AS PERSONAL SALVATION

Religion does not play a large role in most episodes of *NYPD Blue*, but it can be said to be at the heart of the series. In *NYPD Blue*, explicit depictions of religion provide local color or "atmosphere." In "Hollie and the Blowfish" (aired March 26, 1996), Father Ramos alerts Detective Martinez to a crime involving Santeria. This subplot of warring *brujos* is mere comic relief to the "real" story about a police informant, a junkie with AIDS, who helps out with a drug bust, but is then betrayed by the careless words of a DEA agent. And in "Torah! Torah! Torah!" (aired October 31, 1995), Lubavitcher Jews report the theft of an ancient Torah scroll. Detective Medavoy, the stammering cop, handles this subplot. He and Sipowicz go undercover and dress as rabbis to meet the thief, as synthesized klezmer music (an eastern European Jewish fold music) plays in the background.

More substantial is the religion that remains unsaid for most of the season.

The season finales of *NYPD Blues*'s first three seasons (the big finish/cliffhanger that ends a season and keeps a viewer eagerly awaiting the fall season) have directly concerned religion. At the end of the first season, a "beat" cop confesses to a priest that she murdered a gangster who was blackmailing her. The second season ends with Detective Andy Sipowicz, the brutal, alcoholic, racist anti-hero, marrying Greek-American Assistant District Attorney Sylvia Kostas in an Orthodox ceremony. The third season ends with the same priest who married Andy and Sylvia "churching" their newborn son. Priests have pivotal roles only at the end of the arc of a season: at the end of the day, when a cop's work is done, he or she must reckon with God.

The religious themes of fall and redemption come to the forefront of *NYPD Blue* in the episode titled "The Bookie and the Kookie Cookie" (aired May 9, 1995). Andy and Sylvia are planning to get married. They go for marriage counseling and fill out a questionnaire at the Orthodox church, decorated with Greek flags, and get advice from Father Kanakerides, the Greek Orthodox priest Sylvia has known from childhood.

PRIEST: Do you believe in God?
SIPOWICZ: I'd just as soon not get into that.
PRIEST: Have you lost your faith?
SIPOWICZ: Yeah. . . .
PRIEST: Don't give up on God. He may not be through with you yet.

Prophetic words indeed. In the four seasons since the priest told Andy that God may not be through with him, Andy's eldest son was killed trying to thwart a robbery, his longtime partner died of heart failure, and his wife was shot dead in a courthouse. While the death of Andy Jr. provoked the most explicit use of religious imagery so far in *NYPD Blue* (Jesus, in truck driver garb, appearing to Andy in two dreams), his wife's death provoked the most profound: Andy praying alone at the bedside of his young son, Theo (which happens to mean "God" in Greek), in the sixth season finale "Safe Home" (aired May 25, 1999).

If it took years of personal tragedy for Andy to slowly regain his faith, what made him lose it to begin with? At the end of the "Bookie" episode, Andy gives Sylvia one answer: a few years back he was investigating a kidnapping of a four-teen-month-old boy, but found out that the father killed his son when he got angry with him, and then fed the child to their dog. Sipowicz had to kill "the poor dog" to retrieve the pieces of the baby. "I got faith in you," he tells Sylvia, and we fade to black. The horror of the crime implies the existence of true, unredeemed evil and justifies the erosion of Sipowicz's faith in God.

HOMICIDE: RELIGION AS THEOLOGICAL SPECULATION

Witnessing evil has had the opposite effect on Detective Frank Pembleton, the moral and dramatic center of *Homicide*. For this brilliant African-American detective, evil proves the existence of God, as he tells us in an exchange from "Nearer My God to Thee" (aired October 14, 1994):

BAYLISS: Do you believe in God, Frank?

PEMBLETON: Look at the evidence—this murder is proof that evil exists. If evil exists, then surely God must exist.

Homicide asks the existential question of what kind of person would be a homicide cop. The program provides us with as many answers as there are detectives. For Detective Megan Russert, the memory of her dead husband keeps her going. Detective John Munch has a cynical fascination with the macabre. Beau Felton used his job as a ticket out of the rough neighborhood in which he grew up. Tim Bayliss, whom we meet in the first episode as a rookie, is still searching for his answer, though it is clear it has to do with his identification with dead (unloved) children, and by the fifth season ("Betrayal," aired January 10, 1997) we know why.

Bayliss's partner is Frank Pembleton, who knows exactly why he is a homicide cop: "to speak for those who cannot." He is a speaker for the dead. His motives are explicitly religious. In more than one episode, Pembleton's passion for justice and skill at interviewing murder suspects in the interrogation room are attributed to his Jesuit schooling.

When questioning Gordon Pratt, a wiseacre white supremacist gun freak suspected of shooting three detectives, Pembleton discovers that the suspect's copy of Plato's *Republic* is in the original Greek, and asks Pratt to read an excerpt. Pratt confabulates something about how the little guy gets trampled on. "Let me show you what the Jesuits taught me," says Pembleton, snatching up the book and giving an impromptu translation. Pembleton is angered not by Pratt's racism, but by his stupidity and lack of responsibility ("End Game," aired February 10, 1995).

Connection to Jesuit training is made in *Law & Order* as well. The two district attorneys (Stone, and later, McCoy) also have clear minds and a talent for extracting information from witnesses, and these qualities have also been attributed to Jesuit training (although more in passing than in Pembleton's case). This connection is intriguing, particularly given the double image Jesuits have in segments of the public imagination; they are at once a "force of indubitable moral integrity in the face of the vast corruptions that had invaded church and society" (Wogaman 1993, 136), but they also seem guilty of spiritual and intellectual arrogance and moral sophistry.

The religious and moral issues that consume Pembleton and the series as a whole are best expressed in the three-part episode that opens *Homicide's* third season. A serial killer is murdering young women—conspicuous do-gooders all—stripping them naked, putting white gloves on them, and dumping the bodies near Catholic churches. A nun who had worked with one of the victims in a women's shelter is called in to identify the body. "It wasn't her," she says to Bayliss and Pembleton as she exits the morgue.

BAYLISS: It wasn't? Are you sure?
PEMBLETON: The light is gone, her soul. The body is just an empty vessel.
NUN: You were trained by the Jesuits, I bet.
PEMBLETON: "Give me a boy until he is seven, and I will give you the man."

In an exchange of words lasting less than ten seconds, the engaged viewer will discover Pembleton's religious upbringing, how it shapes his work as a homicide detective, and his ambivalence about his Jesuit training as expressed in the gently ironic tone of the last line.

Bayliss, Pembleton's partner, is the audience stand-in—eager, naïve, and one step behind Pembleton's detective work. Bayliss's "religion á là carte" is a foil for Pembleton's rigorous religious training and moral insight, and is also representative of the average viewer. Driving to a church later in the same episode ("Nearer My God to Thee"), the conversation once again turns to religion:

PEMBLETON: What religion were you raised?
BAYLISS: You know, I was a mutt. My father, he believed in the Colts.[3] I was baptized by the Presbyterians, confirmed by the Episcopalians, and my girlfriend in college—she was a knockout—a Unitarian, so I joined. How about you, Frank? Still a Catholic?
PEMBLETON: You know the Jews have Orthodox, Conservative, and Reform? There are two kinds of Catholic: devout and fallen. I fell.
BAYLISS: What's up with the three-hour Mass? I was at a wedding and I got up to receive the host. I had to ask for two, I was so hungry.
PEMBLETON: You're not Catholic and you took communion?
BAYLISS: Is that wrong?
PEMBLETON: If my God wins, you're screwed.

Pembleton, the premodern—however facetiously—sees religion as divine warfare. Bayliss, the modern, sees religion as a convenience to be changed or discarded as needed. Indeed in *Homicide*'s final season, Bayliss, after a near-fatal shooting attempt, is "reborn," as it were, as a Zen Buddhist. His newfound serenity is mocked by fellow detectives and is severely tested when he investigates the meaningless killing of an American Buddhist monk ("Zen and the Art of Murder," aired April 2, 1999).

In the conclusion, the "white glove" killer—or rather, someone occupying the same body as the killer—walks in to the squad room. When Pembleton realizes that Pamela Wilgus, a young Catholic woman, committed the murders and that she has multiple personality disorder, he tries to play one personality off the other by badgering, cajoling, and seducing to obtain a confession.

But it's too late. One of Wilgus's personalities had previously called a lawyer, who shows up and takes her away. Before Wilgus can be arrested, she makes a tearful confession on live television. She plays the victim and claims she was raped as a child. She pleads insanity. And in a subsequent episode, Wilgus sues Pembleton for having violated her civil rights in the interrogation room.

This is the triumph of modernity over Pembleton's world of traditional moral responsibility. Philosophers who lament modernity would recognize all too well its symptoms in the "white glove" murder case. Here is the triumph of the therapeutic (Wilgus is sick, insane; it's not her fault because she was abused; she does not take responsibility for herself), the mediated (she relives her experience on a live broadcast and becomes a media celebrity), and the litigious (even a serial killer has a right to sue).

AN ETHICAL BASIS FOR ACTION

Do these three shows deal with any of the same religious issues? Of course, all three shows deal with ethics—they all attempt to answer the question: Is there an ethical basis for police action? Answers might involve negotiating a path between upholding the law and combating evil. But the question can be put another way: How can one act morally in a fundamentally immoral world? This is not a new question in American popular "crime" culture; one thinks of Raymond Chandler's 1930s private eye, Philip Marlowe. Chandler answered with a streetwise code of chivalry. His Marlowe was a lone knight upholding a personal code of honor, which is all but spit upon in the corrupt matrix of Los Angeles. The answer given by 1990s cop shows owes something to Chandler, especially the first season of *NYPD Blue*, where David Caruso (playing Detective John Kelly), with his pale skin and flaming red hair, stands out in the muted gray squad room like a saint in hell. But Marlowe worked alone in a more or less white Los Angeles. Kelly must contend with the bureaucracy of police work and the chaotic, multiethnic pluralism of the streets.

There is a thin line between what's right (represented by the police) and what's just (represented by the law). In *Law & Order*, for example, in the first half of a show, Detectives Briscoe and Green might search a suspect's home and uncover a murder weapon which leads to the arrest of the guilty party (apparently the right thing); in the second half, a judge might rule that the search was illegal and exclude the weapon from the prosecution's case (apparently the just thing). In *NYPD Blue*, Detectives Sipowicz and Sorenson are always "reaching out" to suspects to confess their involvement in the crime and lead them to the real killer. The detectives bamboozle the suspect by impersonating a district attorney or another suspect, for instance. They do this to get to the bottom of a crime before the lawyers step in and take matters out of police control. In *Homicide*, Pembleton uses his Jesuit-trained mind to obtain a confession from a suspect. He may know a suspect is guilty of murder, but since he has no evidence, he must use logic, finesse, and casuistry to make something out of nothing.

Both the investigation of a murder and its prosecution are hampered by rules, laws handed down from above that favor the criminal's civil rights. In effect, the concept of justice is shown as being incommensurate with the concept of civil rights. The investigation might involve gathering evidence without a search warrant, canvassing neighbors who "didn't see anything," or examining unreliable witnesses. Then the cops find the man or woman who is guilty. Eventually, that suspect will be handed over to the district attorney or ask for a lawyer—"lawyer up," in *NYPD Blue*-speak. Quite often, improprieties in the investigation come back to haunt the police officer protagonists. If evidence or testimony was improperly gathered (without enough regard for the rights of the criminal), the case is dismissed. If a witness recants, if the district attorney cuts a deal or is incompetent, if the defense is clever, if the accused is well-connected or comes across as sympathetic, or if the jury is tired of being cooped up in the jury room (as was the case in one episode of *Homicide* ["Justice, Part 2," aired February 16, 1996]), the defendant will be set free. The law on these television shows is not pure but mired in a miasma of mitigating circumstances and conflicting interests.

So between an investigation weighed down by procedure and a trial crippled by the criminals' rights and the lawyers' slipperiness, how can the good be accomplished? How can the cops—our heroes—do the right thing? For the earliest cop shows, this was not a question that needed answering. Sergeant Joe Friday of *Dragnet*, and his ilk, lived in a world of absolutes; they always did the right thing. Later, the answer was found in vigilantism, in cops "taking the law into their own hands," as with Clint Eastwood's "Dirty" Harry Callahan or Charles Bronson in *Death Wish*. This violent solution worked best in the 1970s, the "me" decade, and in the movies, not on TV. Theorists have convincingly argued that these genre films represent an ideologically conservative backlash to a perceived liberal criminal justice system (Ryan and Kellner 1988, 42–46). But in today's cop show, "moral certainty is replaced by moral epistemology" (Sumser 1996, 156). It is not enough to apprehend the guilty party. A confession must be obtained, within a certain amount of time, using the proper methods.

THE BOX

And so the answer to the question of moral action at which these three shows arrive is found in the police interrogation room. Between the investigation and the prosecution, there is one moment, limited in both time and space, where an act both good and lawful, both fair and just, can take place. This moment occurs in the interrogation room—known on *Homicide* as "the box." From a structural (narrative) point of view, this moment is important because if a skilled interrogator can obtain a written confession from the suspect before the law dictates that the suspect must be released (usually twenty-four hours after making an arrest), the cop does not have to "waste time" gathering evidence to prove the suspect is guilty; a trial is not even necessary if the defendant pleads guilty. From a dramatic point of view, the interrogation is the turning point of the story, not to mention a showcase for "award-winning" acting. From our religious perspective, this is a moment where communion between the police and the criminal is possible, where the former can find the truth and the latter can seek absolution, and where the audience can find meaning.

Each program situates "the box" differently. In *NYPD Blue*, the gray, grimy interrogation room is the stage for a personal confrontation between criminal and cop. The detective will "reach out" and help the "perp" (perpetrator) by "putting in a good word" with the district attorney if the perp is merely stupid or unlucky, and not evil. But if he is clearly and maliciously guilty, the detective must use his own inner resources—psychological pressure ("finesse") or physical violence ("lay hands on," an intriguing play on words from the religious context)—to obtain a confession.

The same dynamic occurs in *Homicide*'s pale yellow brick interrogation room, but is taken to a more abstract, existential level. In the first episode ("Gone for Goode," aired January 31, 1993), Lieutenant Giardello ("Gee") shows the rookie Bayliss around the squad room. The box, Gee says ironically, is "where we match wits against the city's finest criminals." Certainly the dialogue in *Homicide*'s box is wittier and more pyrotechnic than the strained, hesitating phrasings of *NYPD Blue* (perhaps making the latter more realistic). But more to the point, the detectives in the box in *Homicide* confront the nature of evil, the "why" of murder, not merely the "who" and the "how." But the "why" does not come easily. After arson detective Mike Kellerman tricks a confession out of an arrogant arsonist/murderer ("Fire [2]," aired October 27, 1995), he tells Lieutenant Giardello that he does not understand why the arsonist, a chemistry teacher, would murder one of his own students. Giardello tells him to content himself with the who, what, where, and when of murder, and to leave why alone. But of course Kellerman cannot, and when he is subsequently invited to join the homicide unit permanently, his desire for an answer to why leads him to accept the assignment. Admittedly, it would be quite an interpretive stretch to impart religious significance to *Law & Order*'s box, usually host to very brief interrogation scenes that serve mainly to advance the plot and typically end when the suspect's lawyer arrives in a huff.

The box admits only one or two cops and the suspect. But often a third party may be present, standing on the other side of the two-way mirror—the silent watcher or listener. The box turns into a display, what French philosopher Michel Foucault calls the panopticon (1977, especially 195–228), that permits those watching to exert a form of power over those being watched. Therein, the police work becomes a performance; the detective knows he is being observed, the suspect may or may not (depending on how many times he has been in the situation before). Who watches? Usually people in authority. The commanding officer watches to make sure the detective does not beat or abuse the suspect ("crossing the line"). The district attorney watches to see if there is enough to warrant an arrest. Other detectives watch to see "how it's done."

Or, in a plot device used by all three shows, a suspect is made to watch the questioning of his partner in crime from behind the mirror. The observed suspect readily pins the blame on the other to cut a better deal for himself. In one example from *NYPD Blue* (aired December 10, 1996), a drug dealer mother who used her sixteen-year-old son as a "mule" (a delivery boy for heroin) tries to pin the blame on him. The camera pans (a move common to all three shows) to show the audience that the son has been watching exactly what they have. The son later agrees to "give up" (testify against in court) his mother and the drug runners for whom she works. The dramatic stakes are raised because the boy was once under the foster care of Lieutenant Fancy, the squad commander.

The box, then, is a place where the normal rules are suspended. With no clocks and no windows, the box has no time. The box is the site of the enacted ritual of confession. The police usually prevail because they are clever and good, of course, but also because the suspects *want* to confess. "Giving it up" produces a sense of relief for the criminal, the cop, and audience alike. In fact, the box (often used as a slang term for the television itself) provides the most meaningful moments of revelation and experience for the viewers, who are themselves watching the interrogations, as well as watching those watching the interrogations. This voyeurism transcends simple audience-actor relationships, but in fact provides the viewer with an opportunity to grapple with the same moral ambiguities explored during each episode and to "confess" its sins vicariously.

Foucault locates our desire for confession in power relations:

> The obligation to confess is now relayed through so many different points, is so deeply ingrained in us, that we no longer perceive it as the effect of a power that constrains us; on the contrary, it seems to us that truth, lodged in our most secret nature, "demands" only to surface. (1980, 60)

Indeed, Foucault historicizes the beginning of the confessional mode in the West, dating it from the Lateran Council's codification of the sacrament of penance in 1215. This, he argues, eventually led to changing procedures in criminal justice that "helped to give the confession a central role in the order of civil and religious powers" (58).

The box on *NYPD Blue, Homicide,* and *Law & Order* is a confessional located at the intersection of several different discursive fields: the prosecutorial and investigative, the public and private, the civil and religious, and the audience and actors. It turns the loosely moral and ethical issues of the crime drama into larger religious dramas. In that sense, the box is the best example of sacred space on prime-time television.

CONCLUSIONS

As any cultural product "of quality" should, these three series express social concerns and anxieties. But the argument is not just that *Law & Order, Homicide,* and *NYPD Blue* are examples of "quality" television. The argument here is that today, television best expressed religious and moral concerns through police dramas, and that the interrogations in the box magnify the experience and the communication of meaning between the actors of the program and the viewing audience.

Of course, this meaning is not univocal and is more often than not ambiguous. This not only sets these programs apart from the television cop dramas of yesteryear, but also permits them to reverberate more directly with the experiences and emotions of the audience. We don't necessarily aspire to be Joe Friday or Harry Callahan anymore. Instead, we recognize the dilemmas of the programs, and in some ways sympathize with the very human reactions of the characters we have come to know over time. Each new season provides new variations to the themes presented above, while remaining consistent to its overall vision of the role of religion. *Law & Order* stays its course with its depiction of religious mania. A recent episode in which religion played a major part concerned a defrocked nun who tried to exorcise the demons inside a misbehaving boy by pressing on his rib cage until he died ("Disciple," aired February 24, 1999).

NYPD Blue's view of religion as personal salvation was depicted at its most graphic in Bobby Simone's ninety-minute death scene (in "Hearts and Souls," aired November 24, 1998), which seemed to combine popular narratives of near-death experience (reliving his life) with notions of Christian salvation (Bobby meeting St. Peter).

The canceled *Homicide* ended its low-rated run with an episode that focused not on murder, detection, or even the problem of evil, but on forgiveness. Scenes of series regulars coming to terms with each other for past wrongs were underscored by a subplot: a nun forgives her brother-in-law for murdering her sister ("Forgive Us Our Trespasses," aired May 21, 1999) Religion began and ended that unusual series.

Sometimes funny, sometimes tragic, sometimes simply confounding, the elements of everyday life are brought to the fore on the modern television cop drama, and the audience is brought in as a partner to the men and women who have to face these issues. Their problems are familiar, personal, deeply religious, and recognizable as our own. And in the box (either the television set, or the interrogation room it presents), salvation and deliverance are (at least temporarily) possible for them, the criminals, and, ultimately, the audience.

NOTES

1. Air dates and episode titles have been obtained from websites dedicated to each program: http://www.epguides.com/HomicideLifeontheStreet/ (*Homicide*); http://www.epguides.com/LawandOrder/ (*Law & Order*); http://www.epguides.com/NYPDBlue/ (*NYPD Blue*).

2. See also the Media Research Council's website: http://www.mediaresearch. org/mrc/ specialreports/relcov.html.
3. The Baltimore NFL franchise, now playing in Indianapolis.

REFERENCES

Allen, Robert C., ed. 1992. *Channels of Discourse, Reassembled.* Chapel Hill: University of North Carolina Press.

Anderson, Randy, former producer of *Homicide.* 1996. Personal interview, March 22.

Crane, Diana. 1992. *The Production of Culture.* Newbury Park, Calif.: Sage Publications.

Foucault, Michel. 1980. *Discipline and Punish: The Birth of the Prison.* Translated by Alan Sheridan. New York: Pantheon Books.

——. 1980. *The History of Sexuality, Volume I: An Introduction.* New York: Vintage Books.

Leonard, John. 1997. *Smoke and Mirrors: Television, Violence and Other American Cultures.* New York: Basic Books.

MacIntyre, Alasdair. 1984. *After Virtue.* Notre Dame, Ind.: University of Notre Dame Press.

Miller, Richard B. 1996. *Casuistry and Modern Ethics.* Chicago: University of Chicago Press.

Roof, Wade Clark. 1993. *A Generation of Seekers: The Spiritual Journeys of the Baby Boom Generation.* San Francisco: Harper San Francisco.

——. 1996. "Blurred Boundaries: Religion and Prime-Time Television," unpublished paper.

Ryan, Michael, and Douglas Kellner. 1988. *Camera Politica: The Politics and Ideology of Contemporary Hollywood Film.* Bloomington: Indiana University Press.

Sariego, Ralph, President of Catholics in Media Association (CIMA). 1998. Personal interview, May 22.

Skill, Thomas, James D. Robinson, John S. Lyons, and David Larson. 1994. "The Portrayal of Religion and Spirituality on Fictional Network Television." *Review of Religious Research* 35 (March): 251–67.

Sparks, Richard. 1992. *Television and the Drama of Crime.* Buckingham, England: Open University Press.

Sumser, John. 1996. *Morality and Social Order in Television Crime Drama.* Jefferson, N.C.: McFarland.

Weston, Anthony. 1997. *A Practical Companion to Ethics.* New York: Oxford University Press.

Wogaman, J. Philip. 1993. *Christian Ethics.* Louisville, Ky: Westminster/John Knox Press.

Wuthnow, Robert. 1994. *Producing the Sacred: An Essay in Public Religion.* Chicago: University of Illinois Press.

Our Ladies of the Airwaves

Judge Judy, Dr. Laura, and the New Public Confessional

SUZANNE HOLLAND

I grew up Catholic in the 1960s in the house of my mother, who made no bones about our being "good Catholics." That meant that my siblings and I attended Catholic schools and went to Mass on Sundays (and sometimes during the week), and it definitely meant going to confession whenever "they" said you were supposed to. My mother's philosophy was, "While you live in my house, you will obey my rules—and that means going to church!" She was, as Judge Judy puts it every day, "the boss, applesauce."

This part of my history constitutes the backdrop for the exploration of this chapter. Confession is a ritual that was part of my not-so-distant past, and it both does and does not resemble the kind of confessional ritual that millions of us tune in to each day in the television court room of Judge Judy Sheindlin and on the radio call-in show of Dr. Laura Schlessinger.

Who are these women, and what compels millions of Americans to tune in to women who seem to specialize in berating the very people who come to them for advice and judgment? Why do people feel compelled to "confess" their "sins" to these two *femmes fatales* only to find themselves in an airwaves equivalent of a dominatrix's dungeon? Are Judge Judy and Dr. Laura wearing stiletto heals under the robe and behind the microphone?

When we Catholics went to confession, we would slink into a dark booth (called a "confessional") and wait, terrified, to hear the sound of the screen sliding open; this signaled the presence of the priest waiting to hear the catalog of your childhood or adolescent or adult atrocities. The confessional booths were located on the side walls of churches, and though everyone else waiting in line knew you had "gone to confession," the act itself was something done in private. Only "Father," you, and God knew what had been confessed, what had been forgiven, and what penance you were assigned as contrition for your sins.

That did not keep the curious among us (nearly all of us) from trying to guess what someone had confessed. A sure sign of the gravity of your sins was the length of time you were in the confessional, and the length of time you had to spend praying afterward. The less pious ones of us waiting our turns in line occupied ourselves with this game—until it was our turn. I suppose there's some human nature in this, for it seems to me that even though the practice of confession as a high liturgical art has nearly disappeared in this country, we are still like Catholic schoolchildren lining up for confession, taking vicarious comfort in the sin and stupidity of others, who, braver than we, submit themselves for judgment and absolution—no longer in a church, but on the airwaves.

THE MORALIZING VOICES

"Hi, I'm Dr. Laura Schlessinger. My number is 1–800–D–R–L–A–(pause)–U–R–A, and we try to determine right from wrong on *this* program. . . .".

"I have a moral health show . . . and it's not that *I'm* right, it's that *God* is right. I'm just reiterating the Ten Commandments. . . ." (McClendon 1999, 24, 73).[1]

The *Dr. Laura* show—with twenty million Americans listening each week— is no ordinary radio call-in-for-advice show; nor is it a therapy hour. You might say Dr. Laura is the antishrink, whose newfound religious conversion has taken on a kind of evangelical fervor as she assumes the role of mother-confessor each weekday on the radio. These transcripts speak for themselves:

DR. LAURA: Hello M___, welcome to the program.

CALLER: Hello? How are you doing?

DR. LAURA: Hi, what can I do for ya?

CALLER: Well, I have a problem. I have this really great girl but uh . . . for the past six months I've been cheating on her . . . and I kinda want to tell her . . .

DR. LAURA: Uh huh.

CALLER: . . . and I think the biggest problem is that I've been cheating with her sister.

DR. LAURA: Uh-hmmm.

CALLER: And . . . I mean I . . . I really like her, but I don't know if I'm just . . . if I'm just a pig or if I can't help myself or . . .

DR. LAURA: You're a pig.

CALLER: . . . or well—

DR. LAURA: You're a pig! You can help yourself. You and her sister are *both* pigs!

CALLER: OK . . . so . . . I mean, what . . . what should I do from this point on?

DR. LAURA: Not see either one of them anymore . . . and get some spiritual assistance.

CALLER: You see, but the . . . the problem is that, you know I—
DR. LAURA: No, there is no problem other than you should see neither one of
            them anymore because that would destroy their family—*and* you
            should get some spiritual assistance! (McClendon, 36–37)

As this case plays out on the air, the caller keeps trying to explain himself, including that he has actually talked to a priest. Dr. Laura commends him for this but says that it obviously didn't work, that the caller did not act on whatever the priest told him, that he has character flaws and needs to stop being a self-absorbed pig and accept some responsibility for his actions. Here it is easy to see the movement from a failed consultation with a priest to a new and public confession before radio's mother-confessor, a hint of a ritual I will further elaborate in these pages.

CALLER: I have a sex addiction problem.
DR. LAURA: No, you have a character problem. I don't want you to go to one
            of those therapists who'll pat you on the head and tell you that you
            have a disease.
CALLER: But I was abused as a child . . .
DR. LAURA: So what? You're still responsible for your actions now.
            (Schrof 1997)

Radio dialogues like these are what prompts a critic to damn with faint praise: "Laura Schlessinger has the soul of a hall monitor, the manner of a drill sergeant, and a moral message that draws 20 million listeners" (Schrof 1997). She is the scolding, finger-wagging "mommy" who receives between fifty thousand and seventy-five thousand phone calls (depending on who's counting) in each three-hour block of radio time. Why do people jam the airwaves for a turn with the self-described "equal-opportunity basher?" Because, speculates one writer, "with fewer nuns around and Mom off at work, to whom can we turn for a good lambasting when we need it? To Dr. Laura" (Manning 1997). Sounds like a Catholic school education all over again to me. And that's ironic since Dr. Laura Schlessinger, 53, is an observant Jew (a relatively new convert from atheism).

There's further irony in the fact that the other crisply moral voice on the airwaves is also Jewish and female—Judge Judy Sheindlin. Sheindlin, 56, is the queen of television with her courtroom show, the prototype for the new brand of judge shows crowding television programming—including Judge Mills Lane,

Judge Joe Brown, and Sheindlin's husband, Jerry, who has replaced former New York mayor Ed Koch on *The People's Court*. But it's Judge Judy who rules! Only *Wheel of Fortune* and *Jeopardy* can boast larger viewing audiences among syndicated television shows today.

Perhaps part of Judge Judy's popularity has its roots in childhood fantasies, reenacted voyeuristically and vicariously for television viewers.[2] As *Time* magazine reminds us, "There are fewer pleasures greater than watching somebody get yelled at. You loved it when your mom stuck it to your brother, and you love it now, rubbernecking to see a cop pull a car over. One of the best spots for catching good, stern lectures in our authority-free culture is the bench of lower-court judges. These guys can lay into punks and deadbeats like *Father Knows Best* on a caffeine jag. And that may explain the success of Judy Sheindlin, a former New York City family-court judge and the resident scourge on *Judge Judy* . . ." (Stein et al. 1998).

Notice that this is the same kind of rationale given for Dr. Laura's radio popularity. In fact, one writer compares the two directly: "the no-nonsense Judge Sheindlin's popularity—she's kind of television's equivalent of radio's reigning lord of discipline, Dr. Laura Schlessinger . . ." (Paeth 1998). No nonsense. Discipline. Crack the whip. Americans seem to want a moralizing mother figure to whom they can "confess," and who will cut to the chase with a kick in the pants, offering repentant children light abuse, provisional solutions, penance, and absolutions: "Now go take on the day!" (or, more recently, "Now go do the right thing"). As one British writer commented, Americans seem either to be masochistic, or characterized by a "burgeoning public mania for confession and contrition" (Powell 1999, 13)—or both?

In the snippet that follows, we get a sense of what fascinates Americans about the *Judge Judy* show:

> In a typical episode, Sheindlin chides one plaintiff—a mother on welfare, for being a burden to taxpayers—then blasts a defendant for not bringing in evidence. To a woman whose case involves a crushed hat, Sheindlin offers the advice, "You better get a life, madam." Sick of waiting for a straight answer, she'll tap on her forehead and ask, "Does it say stupid here?" Or she'll bark, "Baloney! Baloney! Baloney!" Sheindlin's justice is both extreme—Cheri Oteri parodies her on *Saturday Night Live*—and extremely entertaining." (Gliatto and Young 1998).

Is it entertainment or morality people want? Ritualized abuse or vicarious absolution of guilt? Why has *Judge Judy* become a $75 million-a-year business with "more viewers than *Oprah*, *The Today Show*, and everything on the fledgling WB" (Gunther 1999)? "She's the mom who won't put up with your whining. The jurist who scolds litigants with such statements as . . . 'You have no moral upbringing—maybe that accounts for the ridiculous look on your face'" (Hall 1998). Then again, maybe it's just a case of what the British observe about us: "Once the inner child made it into the national psyche it was only a matter of time until an outer mother came along to smack its ungrateful backside" (Powell 1999, 13).

As different as Sheindlin and Schlessinger are (perhaps the obvious difference is that one is a jurist, the other a therapist), it is interesting to note that they share a common public perception, among both fans and critics alike, that they are "mother-figures." Schlessinger credits the columnist Clarence Paige with coining the moniker that appears on her own website: the "national mommy" or "America's mommy" (Schlessinger 1998). Not the earth mother bending tenderly over nature's children; no, the scolding, nagging, stiff-upper-lip, razor-tongued mother of American mythology who's hard to please, whose chief task seems to be to induce enough guilt in her inadequate children about the things *she* values that these children will be able to function as she would like them to when she isn't there to scold them into it.

Admittedly, it is Schlessinger who sees herself as imbued with a mission to "preach, teach and nag" to millions about morality and the truth of the Ten Commandments. "When asked if she sees herself as a kind of rabbi, she remarks, 'I'm more of a Jewish mother. I nag"(Brawarsky 1998). Yet, her conversion to Judaism precipitated a revelation about her life's purpose that, she says, brought her running to her husband, yelling, "Lew, I'm a priest and my mission is to help God perfect the world!" (Schrof 1998). Then there's the evangelical Christian minister, Ray McClendon, who compares Dr. Laura to the Biblical judge and prophetess Deborah, as well as to Jesus. Heady stuff.

And as for Judge Judy? While her show carries a moral message (stop being a victim and use your brains!), it does not carry overtly religious overtones; nor does Scheidlin ever compare herself to a religious leader or prophet. In fact, aside from the fact of Scheidlin's being Jewish (and acting the part of a "Jewish mother" on the bench), we know very little about her own religious practices or beliefs. Perhaps this variance between our two ladies of the airwaves can be attributed solely to the difference in their occupations. Judge Judy is schooled in the American juridical system, which is usually at pains to maintain a clear separation of church and state.

And what about the listening/viewing audiences? It's interesting that the audiences for these two shows, though they are distinct, are also marked by one striking resemblance—both audiences are dominated by middle-aged people, male and female.[3] Is there some kind of "mommy complex" going on here? If there is, it's about "Mommy dearest," not Harriet Nelson. Psychologist Helene Goldberg, writing about Dr. Laura, offers the observation that what Schlessinger seems to do is to attract people who are in need of help, and then twist a psychological knife even further into their already victimized psyches. Goldberg writes:

> People call Laura because they are in pain and need help, but they also believe that they don't deserve to be helped. Thus when Laura twists the knife a little deeper into a suffering caller, blaming the victim, she absolves the rest of us for a moment from our own guilt. She also confirms our belief that we don't really deserve help. She constantly reminds us that "God helps those who help themselves." But what about the helpless? The price of her absolution is that we too turn our backs on those in need, and, at the same time, deny our own inner cries for help. . . . Her anti-psychological rapier slashes through our Gordian tangle of guilt but leaves us scarred in the process. (Goldberg 1998)

Of course, for Dr. Laura there are no real victims; it's all a matter of getting over the effects of pop psychobabble, of picking up our moral failures and getting on with our lives. No excuses tolerated. "'Guilt is good,' she declares. She banishes the term self-esteem and laments the 'Age of the Victim' where 'nothing is anybody's fault.' In her version of morality, willpower is paramount" (Schrof 1997).

Can we have dilemmas in life that may not be *moral* ones? Dr. Laura does not think so, as the following dialogue with a young bulimic girl shows:

CALLER: I'm sixteen and I'm bulimic or anorexic, whatever, both of them. . . .

DR. LAURA: OK . . . so you do need medical intervention. What you're doing to yourself could kill you. . . .

CALLER: Yeah, but I don't really care that it might kill me.

DR. LAURA: Yes, but the "not caring" is temporary. . . . Aren't there some days you care a lot? Now be honest. Don't play dramatic on me. There are days you care a lot. You have good days in which you're blessed in your mind that you're alive.

CALLER: Yes.

DR. LAURA: Right. And you have days you don't care.

CALLER: A lot of days I don't care.

DR. LAURA: Right. I understand that. But part of why you don't care is how you choose to live your life. . . . What is it that you do that is strictly for somebody else's benefit?

[Caller doesn't understand, and Dr. Laura suggests her problem is egocentrism and that she would feel better by doing something for other people because she's only "picking out the negative."]

DR. LAURA: Do you think—tell me the truth now, I want to see your vision about life—do you think it is strictly just a complete biological accident that you're here?

CALLER: No. . . .

DR. LAURA: And what is everybody's purpose?

CALLER: I don't know.

DR. LAURA: Try. Try!

CALLER: [after floundering] To be happy.

DR. LAURA: No. And that's why you're miserable. . . .

(McClendon 1999, 66–68).

Although Dr. Laura does suggest at the outset of this dialogue that the caller needs medical help, she turns the call—a plea for help from a young woman with a serious emotional condition—into a lecture on morality. The caller is told that her problems stem from egocentrism (one of Dr. Laura's constant "nagging" themes). Then Schlessinger almost adds insult to injury in an already fragile young woman by telling her that her life has a purpose, but it is *not* to find happiness, which explains why she is miserable. Here we see the suggestions of a divine master plan to which the caller should conform herself, thereby taking responsibility for the moral failure (egocentrism) causing her eating disorder. In Dr. Laura's black-and-white world, there are no victims, and no persons whose lives couldn't be improved by making different moral choices—not even young girls suffering from eating disorders.

In a related but quite *distinct* vein, Judge Judy dedicates her latest book, *Beauty Fades, Dumb Is Forever*, to helping women understand that they do not have to be victims. This, she says, is what motivates her actions in her television courtroom.

Day after day in my courtroom, I saw what happened to women who didn't use their heads. Somewhere along the line, these women had decided, maybe subconsciously, to hide their light under the proverbial bushel in order to be more attractive to men. And the fallout of their stupid decision was the daily parade of misery that marched through family court. In most jurisdictions, ignorance of the law is no excuse, and for these women, ignorance of life was no excuse in my courtroom—and it still isn't. (Sheindlin 1999, 4)

Her remedy? Start thinking enough of yourself to recognize and use the brains God gave you. Hence, the title of the book—and her own father's maxim for her: "beauty fades . . . but dumb? Dumb is forever" (1999, 5).

While Schlessinger seems to trace all psychological problems to moral laxity and lack of moral willpower to do the right thing (at times, literally blaming actual victims), Sheindlin—whose bark may seem just as acerbic—has a bit more nuanced bite. Schlessinger's take-no-prisoners approach to emotional trauma and self-esteem ("Get over it!") is actually countered by Scheindlin's recognition that lack of self-esteem is what causes women to get into the situations that lead them to her courtroom. Instead of refusing to consider reasons why one gets into a troubling situation, Judge Judy displays a note of empathy usually lacking in Dr. Laura. Of women in a state of crisis, she writes, "There was one common denominator—a lack of self-worth. Nobody had ever told these women, in a way they could believe, that they were important in their own right" (Sheindlin 1999, 9).

While dozens of commentators have speculated about the attraction Americans have to these two moral mothers, to fully understand this phenomenon, I think we have to step outside this country and borrow the observations of the French philospher Michel Foucault.

THE RITUAL OF CONFESSION

When he wrote *History of Sexuality* more than twenty years ago, Michel Foucault included the ritual of confession as central to his geneology of the science of sex in Western society. It was Foucault's observation that ever since the Middle Ages, society has relied upon the ritual of confession for the production of truth, as it was his thesis that truth was (and is) imbued with relations of power-knowledge. Confession, then, became a means of regulating, observing, and fixing the production of power in society. Moreover, Foucault claimed, it is in the confession that truth and sex are linked together, for one was obliged to reveal in the confession that which one had a duty to conceal in public (Foucault 1978, 61). No doubt, there is much to pursue here about power, sex, confession, and our ladies of the airwaves. For the moment, however, I want to use Foucault only to describe the importance of the ritual of confession to Western culture.

The practice of confession in the history of Christianity has a long and varied history. In relation to our topic, it is interesting to note that the academic discipline of moral theology has its roots in the actual practice of auricular confession (Mahoney 1987, 26–27). With the codification of penance as a sacrament in the church (The Lateran Council in 1215), the confession gradually assumed "a central role in the order of civil and religious powers" in society. Quite simply, confession "became one of the West's most highly valued techniques for producing truth" (Foucault 1978, 58–59).

Foucault makes this crystal clear in the following passage:

> We have become a singularly confessing society. The confession has spread its effects far and wide. It plays a part in justice, medicine, education, family relationships, and love relations, in the most ordinary affairs of everyday life, and in the most solemn rites; one confesses one's crimes, one's sins, one's thoughts and desires, one's illnesses and troubles; one goes about telling, with the greatest precision, whatever is most difficult to tell. One confesses in public and in private, to one's parents, one's educators, one's doctor, to those one loves; one admits to oneself, in pleasure and in pain, things it would be impossible to tell to anyone else, the things people write books about. One confesses—or is forced to confess. . . . Western man has become a confessing animal (1978, 59).

This so clearly describes our current state of affairs and the mania behind confessional television and radio that it's tempting to think Foucault had a prescient sense, though nothing like confessional TV or radio was on the horizon at the time of his writing this text, nor even when he died in the early 1980s. More likely, however, the national popularity of Judge Judy and Dr. Laura simply attests to the strength of his theory. If television and radio ratings are any measurement at all, then Western "man" has indeed become a confessing animal.

It is a natural movement to extend Foucault's commentary on "the singularly confessing society" from the discourse of the confessional to the discourse of confessing television and radio in general (e.g., White 1992), and to the *Judge Judy* and *Dr. Laura* shows, in particular. From these highly public rituals of confession, each penitent seeks (and according to Foucault's theory, experiences) some generation of subjectivity. One becomes authenticated, so to speak, by the discourses of truth that one pronounces about oneself. Of course, this authentication of subjectivity cannot happen alone; it requires the presence of an interlocutor, whose role is to listen, to wrest the truth from the penitent, and, finally, "to judge, punish, forgive, console and reconcile." It is the presence of the interlocutor in the ritual of confession that allows the penitent to experience exoneration, purification, and redemption. And this is precisely where the "agency of domination" resides—not in the confessing subject, but in "the one who listens ... the one who questions and is not supposed to know" (Foucault 1978, 61–62).

In Christian tradition, this figure was the priest or minister; in the psychoanalytic tradition, it becomes the analyst or therapist; in the judicial tradition, it is magistrate; in the postmodern, market-driven tradition of mass media, it is the moral mother figures of Judge Judy Scheindlin and Dr. Laura Schlessinger. If Foucault is right that "the obligation to confess is now relayed through so many different points, is so deeply ingrained in us, that we no longer perceive it as the effect of a power that constrains us," but rather as a truth that appears to free us (Foucault 1978, 60), should it come as any surprise that millions of us are drawn to these two high priestesses of the airwaves?

CONFESSION ON THE AIRWAVES: THE FORMULA

Perhaps the uninitiated might be curious as to what the confessional ritual of the airwaves looks and sounds like, as it is transferred from the church to the airwaves. While Dr. Laura and Judge Judy may be taken together as representing mother-confessors, the ritual of confession varies within each one's particular domain. This difference is largely the result of two factors—the medium, television versus radio, and the venue, a courtroom show versus a call-in "moral health" show. Here I have chosen to use the *Dr. Laura* show as paradigmatic of this liturgy of public confession; I do so because the format of the show (caller/penitent and Dr. Laura/confessor) lends itself to a clearer analysis than does the plaintiff-defendant-judge format of public confession. Moreover, despite Schlessinger's protestations to the contrary, I agree with Mead's assessment that she is "a direct beneficiary of a cultural climate in which ordinary folk are accustomed to talking about their psychological problems.... Schlessinger may despise the pop-psych industry ... but without it, where would she be? That same industry has made the public confessional not only commonplace but commendable" (Mead 1997). For these reasons, it is Dr. Laura's confessional booth that we will now enter.

Every day, for three hours, callers jam the phone lines at Premier Radio Network in Los Angeles. Before approaching Dr. Laura's confessional booth every penitent must first be screened by an assistant confessor. As Dr. Laura herself explains, "My producer, Carolyn Holt, screens the calls, and she asks, 'What moral or ethical dilemma are you struggling with?' And if their problem doesn't fit into that format, they don't get on the air" (Schlessinger 1998). What Dr. Laura means is that if the caller doesn't understand his or her problem as a *moral* dilemma (a lot to ask of a person in pain), then the individual is automatically punished—she or he is deprived of the opportunity to enter the confessional.

The lucky (or sufficiently articulate) ones, however, are granted admission to the ritual, and it proceeds as follows. I have placed commentary in italicized brackets throughout to facilitate comparing the traditional Christian ritual of confession á là Foucault with the public confessional of Mother Laura.

PENITENT/CALLER: Dr. Laura, I made a conscious choice to make a stupid decision. [*Bless me Father, for I have sinned.*] It's been about four years since I've been in a relationship. [*It's been four years since my last confession.*] I've dated, but I went only so far after dating so many times, and then I moved on. If the relationship wasn't productive or healthy or just went other directions ... anyway, [*confession of sin*] I met a man and immediately felt too comfortable with him—extremely recently—and made the decision immediately to, in the afternoon, instead of continuing to watch the football game, not to watch the football game, and I ...

CONFESSOR/DR. LAURA: Decided to score in a different way?

PENITENT/CALLER: I slept with him, and ... I am disappointed in myself, and I am not ... I'm not proud of what I did. [*confesses again*] And yet, he is someone that I wish I could still get to know. However, if you show a certain character up front, you can't go back and say, "That's not who I am." [*sense of subjectivity emerging from confession*]

CONFESSOR/DR. LAURA: Wait, wait, wait, wow, wow, wow. Wow, wow, wow, wow. You are feeling uncomfortable and saying, "I did this and you know, this doesn't fit well with me; this is not how I am wanting to be. Therefore, I am backing off from that behavior." *That is* what character is about. [*subjectivity validated by confessor*] It's about assessing our actions and acknowledging sometimes that we're off our own track. That's what guilt is all about; it's about a message from inside that we are off our own track. So when you get off your own track, you get back on it. That is character! [*production of power as truth*]

PENITENT/CALLER: Can you get back on it and continue to see if the other person also feels the same?

CONFESSOR/DR. LAURA: I don't know . . . if he just wants to put-it-to-you-baby; then, no.

PENITENT/CALLER: I don't feel that way, no. . . . I guess I almost want to "cut and run" because I'm embarrassed.

CONFESSOR/DR. LAURA: I . . . well . . . see now, that's not character.

PENITENT/CALLER: Right. [*subjectivity understood*]

CONFESSOR/DR. LAURA: Then you would be disappointed and not proud of yourself again. And I don't know why, but I have this feeling that you do cut and run a lot. [*confessor mediating divine knowledge*]

PENITENT/CALLER: I have before, in the past. [*another sin confessed*]

CONFESSOR/DR. LAURA: Yes, well, let's change that. Let's face it. Let's just tell him, "I got way off-track for what's right for me. . . . But this kind of behavior was inappropriate for me." [*suggested penance*]

PENITENT/CALLER: Saying that then would make me very proud of myself, regardless of the outcome.

CONFESSOR/DR. LAURA: Yes! That's the whole point. That is character! An experiment that didn't work is not a lack of character unless it is continuous. [*begins to offer absolution*]

. . . PENITENT/CALLER: OK. I think to follow through with what you just said is much more important to me than the outcome of this one [relationship].

. . . CONFESSOR/DR. LAURA: What you just said is a very spiritual understanding. That the point to your life is not his acceptance, but it is the quality of your behavior. [*further absolution, emphasizing its religious dimension*]

. . . PENITENT/CALLER: Thank you for being there; you've helped me. Thank you for being there for all of us. It means a lot to listen to you on a regular basis, because you've helped me tremendously [*Thank you, Father. I will do better, with the grace of God.*]

CONFESSOR/DR. LAURA: Thank you. Take care. [*Go in peace and sin no more*] (Transcript from McClendon 1999, 46–48).

This was only one example among dozens I have heard or read. Each ritual of confession varies slightly, but the basic features remain constant: a posture of atonement; acknowledgment of sin and acceptance of responsibility; penance to atone for one's sin, accompanied by a morality talk; absolution and assurance of redemption.

CONCLUSION

Every liturgy has actors, participants, and ritual. Through a detailed description of the public liturgy of confession presided over by "our ladies of the airwaves," I have attempted to identify and to clarify some of these elements: a wave of national interest in the disciplinary mother; a public urge to confess and to seek judgment among the callers and the litigants; a corresponding desire for anonymity and vicarious "bashing" among the ever-growing viewing and listening audiences; and two credentialed women who fill the role of mother-confessor-judges.

Perverse though it may seem to some, the mania over the Judge Judy/Dr. Laura phenomenon and public confession is evidence that popular religion, if it is not well, is at least alive and kicking in the public square. Certainly it must be conceded that in our time — hovering between postmodern relativism and neo-Enlightenment absolutism — rituals of moral instruction are to be found in the most unlikely of places. Maybe the airwaves have become that place where we former Catholic schoolchildren can again rehearse our once-familiar rituals; still conjure the smell of incense, the curiosity about who did what and how bad it was; still experience that butterflies-in-the-stomach feeling that comes from knowing you simply can't escape the inevitability of confession: your turn is next!

NOTES

1. Transcripts of the Dr. Laura show are not readily available to general audiences. The transcripts included throughout this paper are taken from Ray McClendon, Dr. Laura: A Mother in America (Colorado Springs, Colo.: Chariot Victor Publishing, 1999). Because, as his introduction indicates, Dr. Laura asked Pastor McClendon to write the book, I suggest these transcripts can be read as an authorized anthology of the Dr. Laura show. Dr. Laura now also hosts a television program; this analysis is limited to her radio broadcasts.
2. The same claim is being made here for radio listeners of the Dr. Laura Show.
3. According to the latest market research available at the time of this writing (summer 1999) Schlessinger's audience is, for example, only slightly more popular among women than men, although in January 1998, Schlessinger indicated that she had more male than female listeners (see Schlessinger 1998). Sheindlin, on the other hand, has significantly more female viewers (61% : 39%). (Sources: Interep Research and paul.barnett@tbwachiat.com).

REFERENCES

Brawarsky, Sandee. 1998. "Laura Schlessinger; Interview." *Publisher's Weekly* 245, 21 (May 25): s16.

Foucault, Michel. 1978. *The History of Sexuality: An Introduction*, vol. 1. New York: Vintage Books.

Gliatto, Tom, and Stanley Young. 1998. "Bench Warmer: All Rise—Along with Ratings—for TV's Sassy, No-Nonsense Judge Judy." *People*, July 27: 107.

Goldberg, Helene. 1998. "Analyzing Dr. Laura." *Tikkun* 13, 6 (November 1): 25ff.

Gunther, Marc. 1999. "The Little Judge Who Kicked Oprah's Butt." *Fortune*, 10, 32.

Hall, Steve. 1998. "Judge Judy Dishes Tough Justice." *Indianapolis Star*, September 3, E2.

Mahoney, John, S. J. 1987. *The Making of Moral Theology: A Study of the Roman Catholic Tradition*. Oxford: Clarendon Press.

Manning, Anita. 1997. "Dr. Laura Dispenses Morality over the Radio." *USA Today*, September 25. Quoted in Ray McClendon, *Dr. Laura: A Mother in America* (Colorado Springs, Colo.: Chariot Victor Publishing, 1999): 33.

McClendon, Ray. 1999. *Dr. Laura: A Mother in America*. Colorado Springs, Colo.: Chariot Victor Publishing.

Mead, Rebecca. 1997. "The Angriest Woman on the Radio and Why We Keep Listening." *Redbook* 189, 1, May, 114ff.

Paeth, Greg. 1998. "TV Judges Rule Ratings Bench." *Washington Times*, December 3, C13.

Powell, Alison. 1999. "The Toughest Love." *Guardian (London)*, May 14, 13.

Schlessinger, Laura. 1998. Interview. "Dr. Laura Wants You to Stop Whining," *Psychology Today* 31, 1, January 11, 28ff.

Schrof, Joannie M. 1997. "No Whining!" *U.S. News & World Report*, July 14, 48.

Sheindlin, Judy. 1999. *Beauty Fades, Dumb Is Forever: The Making of a Happy Woman*. New York: Cliff Street Books.

Stein, Joel, Dan Cray, and William Tynan. 1998. "Here Come the Judges," *Time*, August 24, 70.

White, Mimi. 1992. *Tele-Advising: Therapeutic Discourse in American Television*. Chapel Hill: University of North Carolina Press.

Homer the Heretic and Charlie Church

Parody, Piety, and Pluralism in *The Simpsons*

LISLE DALTON, ERIC MICHAEL MAZUR, AND MONICA SIEMS

Most of the family shows are namby-pamby sentimentality or smarmy innuendo. We stay away from that.

—Matt Groening

The story goes like this: Marge and Homer take some time for themselves and leave Bart, Lisa, and Maggie with Grandpa. Agents from child welfare discover the children running amok and place them into foster care with the neighbors. The new foster father, Ned Flanders, faints upon hearing that the children have never been baptized, so he packs up the children and his own family and heads for the Springfield River. Homer, missing the point, panics because "in the eyes of God they'll be Flanderseses." At the river Homer pushes Bart out of "harm's way," and the baptismal water falls on his own head. When Bart asks him how he feels, Homer responds, in an uncharacteristically pious voice, "Oh, Bartholomew, I feel like St. Augustine of Hippo after his conversion by Ambrose of Milan." When Ned Flanders gasps, "Homer, what did you just say?" Homer replies nonchalantly, "I said shut your ugly face, Flanders!" The moment of spiritual inspiration has passed, and the children are back with their parents, unbaptized and safe ("Home Sweet Home-Diddily-Dum-Doodily").[1]

The prominent role of religion and the attitude toward it are not unique to this episode. Once a week for nearly the past decade (and more in syndication) *The Simpsons* has proved itself unafraid to lampoon Evangelicals, Hindus, Jews, and religion generally. The frequency of religious plots and subthemes would itself be enough to distinguish this show from other prime-time fare. Not since the Lutheran program *Davey and Goliath* has a cartoon addressed religion so forthrightly. But while that Sunday morning program carried moral lessons of faith, this Sunday evening program ridicules the pious, lampoons the religious, and questions traditional morality. Instead of sermonizing at the audience, this program speaks with them, and possibly for them as well.

This half-hour series emerged as one of the most popular shows of the 1990s, and it regularly addresses issues involving institutional religion—including representations of religious traditions, discussions of moral and religious themes, and portrayals of mythological figures—as well as that which is often labeled "spirituality." Regular characters include a Hindu convenience store manager, a Jewish entertainer, an Evangelical neighbor, and a Protestant minister. Evil, morality, sin, the soul, and other religious themes are openly discussed. In terms of the genres associated with the show—the situation comedy and the animated cartoon—*The Simpsons* represents quite a departure from traditional fare in which religion is rarely if ever addressed. The writers' treatment of religion might even be construed as a heresy of sorts. Yet it is often an insightful heresy, for although the program thrives on satire, caricature, and irony, it does so with a keen understanding of current trends in American religion. *The Simpsons* implicitly affirms an America in which institutional religion has lost its position of authority and where personal expressions of spirituality have come to dominate popular religious culture.

"DON'T HAVE A COW, MAN!": REACTIONS TO *THE SIMPSONS*

The Simpsons were the brainchild of Matt Groening, who developed the characters in short cartoons on the *Tracey Ullman Show* in the late 1980s. When *The Simpsons* aired in January 1990, it was the first animated prime-time series on American television in more than two decades. An immediate success, within a year it was the highest rated show on its network and was often among the top ten shows on television. It occasionally outperformed *The Cosby Show*, a family-oriented situation comedy that dominated the ratings in the late 1980s. Over time its weekly ratings have declined, but the program still consistently ranks as one of the network's top shows. Its success has continued in syndication, ranking first among reruns during the 1994–95 season (Freeman 1995, 14).[2] The program has become so popular that it is able to attract popular cultural icons (including actors, comedians, musicians, athletes, and talk show hosts) as guest "voices."[3]

The Simpsons has also been a merchandiser's dream. During its first season, more than a billion dollars' worth of licensed Simpsons merchandise was sold in the United States. In 1991, licensed manufacturers shipped up to a million T-shirts per week. In an example of a show's cultural impact, some school principals banned a shirt featuring Bart and the slogan "Underachiever and Proud of It" (Riddle 1994, A5), and unlicensed merchandise (including one with Bart depicted as an African American) is commonplace despite millions spent to enforce copyright (Lefton 1992, 16).

This popularity also brought in intense scrutiny from critics. Emerging amid the family values debates of early 1990s, *The Simpsons* has undergone close examination for its portrayal of family life. One famous jibe came from President George Bush in a 1992 speech before the National Religious Broadcasters Association, in which he called for "a nation closer to *The Waltons* than *The Simpsons*."[4] Other critics have damned *The Simpsons* as a symptomatic expression of the contempt for traditional values that permeates American culture. In his critique of the entertainment industry, Michael Medved catalogs instances of religious characters portrayed as duplicitous, hypocritical, insincere, and even criminal (1992). He cites one scene from *The Simpsons* in which Bart utters an irreverent prayer ("Two Cars in Every Garage, Three Eyes on Every Fish") as proof of the industry's pattern of religious insensitivity. Another media critic, Josh Ozersky, places *The Simpsons* in a wider critique of "anti-families" that includes *Roseanne* and *Married . . . With Children*, noting that while "the playful suppression of unhappiness has always been one of TV's great strengths," this new breed of sitcom also deflects public concern away from social disintegration related to the decline of the family. As such, the irony and sarcastic humor of these shows—though he admits *The Simpsons* often tends toward "witty and valid social criticism"—serve to extend television's unhealthy influence over the American public's self-image. "TV," he laments, "has absorbed the American family's increasing sense of defeat and estrangement and presented it as an ironic in-joke." And while this mocking might temporarily placate the dysfunctional tendencies of our times, it does not "lift the spirits." Ozersky argues that the deployment of irony in the face of domestic discontents is an "assault on the family and on all human relationships" since it acts as the "antithesis of deep feeling," "discourages alarm at the decline of the family," and disparages the "earnest, often abject bonds of kin" that lie at the heart of family life. He urges readers to reject "the soullessness of TV's 'hip, bold,' anti-life world" (1991, 11–12, 14, 93).

Despite such condemnations, reactions to *The Simpsons* have not been entirely negative. Many writers (in secular and religious periodicals) praise the show's clever writing and, oddly enough—considering this is a cartoon—its realism. Danny Collum praises *The Simpsons* for "grasping the complexity and ambiguity of human life." He credits it for its insightful, even realistic portrayal of an American family that is frequently abrasive, argumentative, and beset by financial problems. Collum notes that the Simpsons are among the few TV families that go to church or consult a minister. And while he recognizes their religiosity tends toward "pretty lame K-mart evangelicalism," it merits consideration because it shows characters striving for a "moral anchor" and a "larger sense of meaning" in the midst of otherwise chaotic and aimless lives (1991, 38–39). Chiding religious groups and educators who have denounced the series as promoting bad behavior, Victoria Rebeck praises it as sharp satire that shows how parents are often ill equipped to cope with their children's (and their own) problems. For her, this comes as a welcome departure from the "pretentious misrepresentation of family life that one finds in the 'model family' shows"(1990, 622). Similarly, Frank McConnell notes that The Simpsons "deconstructs the myth of the happy family" and "leaves what is real and valuable about the myth unscathed. . . . They are caricatures not just of us, but of us in our national delusion that the life of the sitcom family is the way things are 'supposed' to be" (1990, 389). He praises the show's humanism and rapid-fire humor, which he considers "profoundly sane."

"GABBIN' ABOUT GOD": SCHOLARLY VIEWING OF RELIGION AND TELEVISION

That The Simpsons generates such divergent reactions from critics suggests that it has struck a sensitive nerve that lies close to the heart of the public debate over the portrayal of religious values in the media. In an ambitious 1994 study of religion on television, researchers conducted a five-week analysis of religious behaviors on prime-time shows. After cataloging the activities of 1,462 characters in one hundred episodes, the study found that religion was "a rather invisible institution" in prime time; fewer than 6 percent of the characters had an identifiable religious affiliation, and religiosity was rarely central to the plots or the characters. The report concluded that "television has fictionally 'delegitimized' religious institutions and traditions by symbolically eliminating them from our most pervasive form of popular culture" (Skill et al. 1994, 251–67, especially 265). The study may have been biased; other explanations for the "symbolic elimination" of religion in prime-time television range from skittishness about offending religious adherents to alleged irreligiosity within the entertainment industry.[5] Nonetheless, as Medved claims, the result is programming that often seems an "affront [to] the religious sensibilities of ordinary Americans" (1992, 50).

On the other hand, other scholars argue that it is better to analyze television using broader conceptions of religion. For them, the very act of watching television serves as a religious event—a domestic ritual of devotion to stories that would function like religious narratives in other cultures and eras. Gregor

Goethals, borrowing from sociologists Peter Berger and Thomas Luckmann, asserts that television provides a symbolic universe that serves as an overarching framework for ordering and interpreting experience (1981, 125; see also Greeley 1987). Hal Himmelstein analyzes television programming in terms of various persistent "myths," including "the sanctity of the ordinary American family," "the triumph of personal initiative over bureaucratic control," and "the celebration of celebrity." He further argues that these myths sustain the political and economic needs of various social institutions (1994, 3, 10).

These debates over religion on *The Simpsons* reflect what anthropologist Clifford Geertz called the "intrinsic double aspect" of cultural products that are both models *of* and models *for* reality. Does *The Simpsons* reflect our attitudes—particularly toward religion—or does it shape them? Does television act as mirror to show us ourselves as we really are, or as we ought to be? As the reactions to *The Simpsons* suggest, it is an important debate. Geertz argues that such cultural patterns "give meaning . . . to social and psychological reality both by shaping themselves to it and by shaping it to themselves" (1973, 93). The reaction to *The Simpsons*, mirroring broader debates about America's values and morality, suggests that the show serves as a model of contemporary belief and behavior in American life; the show is a microcosm of what Americans currently do and do not hold sacred. This picture of America delights some, and appalls others. And although *The Simpsons* targets many social institutions, myths, and presumptions, religion inspires some of the show's sharpest satire, and correspondingly some of its best insights into contemporary America.

"HOME SWEET HOME-DIDDILY-DUM-DOODILY": WELCOME TO SPRINGFIELD

It is the world of the Simpson family that feeds the recriminations and fears of those who despise it, while offering humor, irony, succor, and a subtle morality play for those who adore it. Through the television lens (or more appropriately, its mirror), viewers see the mundane lives of the Simpsons, and themselves in the reflection—an odd but often uncannily accurate portrait of Americana. The cast represents a cross section of ages, genders, races, and religions; it includes police officers, teachers, entertainers, clergy, bartenders, and janitors. The Simpson family includes Homer (a dim employee at a nuclear power plant), his wife Marge (a devoted but overworked housewife), and their children: Bart (a good-natured but mischievous boy), Lisa (a precocious, sensitive girl), and infant Maggie.

The fact that the characters are cartoons presents an interesting dynamic, separating the "reality" of our lives from the "pretend" world of the Simpsons. Even so, the family presents noble truths, painful realities, and ironic depths in a very "real" way, enabling viewers to identify with the sentiments and to be altered by them. This two-way relationship invites viewers to enter the Everytown of Springfield,[6] to visit the Simpsons' world and perhaps comprehend how it informs their own. While they rarely "mug" for the camera, the self-reflexive actions of the characters help by constantly acknowledging their television status. From the show's opening sequence that depicts the characters racing home to watch their own opening credits to the frequent subreferences to other television shows, networks, and personalities, viewers are reminded of television's importance in the lives of the Simpson family and—since we are watching them watch—our own. Indeed, as if to mock our own viewership, the Simpsons' television is often alluded to as the sixth (and most appreciated) member of the family. The Simpsons watch television and are conscious of its influence over their lives, while we watch them and ponder, fret, and complain about how they are reflecting and shaping our thoughts and attitudes.

In Springfield, representatives of religious communities are rendered as stereotypes, easily identifiable to viewers and easily objectionable to adherents. The only regularly appearing Jewish character, Herschel Schmuykl "Krusty the Klown" Krustofsky, is the star of Bart and Lisa's favorite television program. He is anything but devout. A gross caricature of a stereotypically secularized Jew corrupted by wealth and fame, Krusty is addicted to cigarettes, gambling, and pornography. He dislikes children, finances his lavish debt-ridden lifestyle by over-marketing his own image unabashedly, and fakes his own death to avoid paying taxes. In an episode that parodies *The Jazz Singer*, Krusty recites a Hebrew prayer while visiting the Simpsons and later admits that as a youth he disappointed his father by abandoning rabbinical studies to become a clown. The rest of the episode involves the attempts by Bart and Lisa to reconcile the estranged father and son. Using advice from various Jewish sources, they eventually succeed ("Like Father, Like Clown").[7]

Another character, Apu Nehasapeemapetalan, is manager of the local "Kwik-E-Mart" and one of the few identifiable Hindus on network television. Apu practices vegetarianism, maintains an in-store shrine to the elephant-headed deity Ganesha (quite plausible insofar as Ganesha's connection to prosperity appeals to the ambitions of the Hindu diaspora), and marries according to Hindu ritual. In Springfield, however, Apu must endure the slights of his incredulous customers; Homer belittles Apu's diet, throws peanuts at the shrine, and suggests that Apu "must have been out taking a whiz when they were giving out gods" ("Homer the Heretic"). More problematic is the inference that South Asians manage all convenience stores; Homer joins Apu on a Himalayan pilgrimage to visit the high "guru" of Kwik-E-Marts, and during a visit to a seaside town, the Simpson family stops at a local convenience mart managed by another South Asian ("Homer and Apu"; "Summer of 4 ft. 2").

The subjects of the most mockery, however, are the Simpsons' evangelical Christian neighbors, the Flanders family. Exceedingly cheerful, Ned, his wife Maude, and their "goody-goody" children Rod and Todd provide the perfect foil to the Simpson family. They are polite, well-liked, righteous, generous, peaceful, and neighborly—all qualities the Simpsons seem to lack. They are also extraordinarily pious: spotting escaped zoo animals running through town, Ned exclaims that he has seen the elephants of the apocalypse. Maude reminds him that the Bible describes four horsemen, not elephants. "Gettin' closer," he replies ("Bart Gets an Elephant"). Bart uses a special microphone to fool Rod and Todd into thinking that God is communicating with them over the radio. On another occasion they bounce on a trampoline and exclaim, "Each bounce takes us closer to God," and "Catch me Lord, catch me," before crashing into each other ("Radio Bart"; "Homer Alone").

Stereotyping is not the only way institutional religion is lampooned; religious leadership is the butt of much of the program's humor. Though other religious figures appear on the program (most notably in an ecumenical radio program entitled "Gabbin' about God" with a minister, Krusty's father the rabbi, and a Catholic priest ["Like Father, Like Clown"]), there is no doubt that the Reverend Timothy Lovejoy represents all clergy—to their general misfortune. When ever-righteous Ned Flanders telephones Lovejoy upon learning that the Simpson children were never baptized, Lovejoy—clearly annoyed by Flanders's intrusion—suggests that Ned consider another religious tradition: "They're basically all the same," he notes before hanging up. When Marge asks if a particular activity is a sin, Lovejoy picks up the Bible and exclaims, "Have you read this thing lately, Marge? Everything's a sin" ("Home Sweet Home-Diddily-Dum-Doodily"). He encourages Marge to seek a divorce during a weekend retreat she and Homer attend to fix their marriage ("War of the Simpsons"). And when a comet threatens to destroy Springfield—and immediately after Homer laments not being religious—Lovejoy is seen running down the street yelling, "It's all over, people, we don't have a prayer" ("Bart's Comet").[8]

Lovejoy's anemic approach condemns all religious leadership and is part of a larger critique of religious traditions consistent with the other stereotypes and the actions of the regular characters. After eating potentially poisonous sushi, Homer prepares for death by spending his last moments listening to the Bible on tape. Unfortunately, the "begats" put him to sleep, causing him to miss the sunrise he had hoped to die watching ("One Fish, Two Fish, Blowfish, Blue Fish"). (He survives.) Bart responds to a request for grace with a somewhat irreverent prayer: "Dear God: We paid for all the stuff ourselves, so thanks for nothing" ("Two Cars").[9]

The program also uses familiar supernatural religious figures for comic effects. Both Satan and God have appeared on the program, and their portrayals mix the sublime and demonic with the ridiculous, presenting them as much human as they are supernatural. Satan is a familiar visitor to Springfield; in various episodes he offers Homer a doughnut in exchange for his soul; holds appointments with Montgomery Burns, the devious owner of the local nuclear plant; and uses a personal computer to keeps tabs on lost souls. Satan manifests in different forms, and typical of the program's use of irony, he is portrayed in one episode by Ned Flanders ("Treehouse of Horror IV"). In contrast, God is a cross between Mel Brooks's "Two-thousand-year old man" character and Charlton Heston's aged Moses—a familiar stereotype with a humorous and not-too-blasphemous sting. As might be expected of an anthropomorphic God, however, certain divine attributes (omniscience, omnipresence) seem lacking; in a meeting with Homer, God inquires whether St. Louis still has a football team (at the time, it did not) and later excuses himself to appear on a tortilla in Mexico ("Homer the Heretic").

The depictions of God and Satan reinforce the morality play qualities of the Simpson characters. Homer, as Everyman, is a poorly educated working man. He is simple, well meaning, loving, and committed to his family, regardless of how much they annoy him. Marge, as Charity, is always doing for others, particularly her family, while neglecting herself. In the few cases where she is self-indulgent, she ends up plagued by guilt, and though tempted by vices, she always returns to care for her loved ones. The eldest child, Bart, as Temptation, is the animated Tom Sawyer. He is an irascible boy who never studies, serves detention, plays pranks, yet loves his sister, obeys his mother, and occasionally respects his father. The eldest daughter, Lisa, as Wisdom, is the smart student and teacher's pet, the child who dreams of Nobel prizes and presidential elections and who relies on her saxophone and the Blues to release her from her torment. The youngest child, Maggie, represents Hope, the embodiment of innocence and vulnerability.

Juxtaposed with the dubious portrayals of institutional religion are nuanced and intricate examples of admirable and noble behavior. Krusty, Apu, and Ned are volunteer fire fighters who help put out the burning Simpson home after Homer falls asleep on the couch smoking a cigar (and skipping church) ("Homer the Heretic"). Ned, despite Homer's frequent ribbing and abuse, adheres closely to the Christian ideals of turning the other cheek and practicing charity. He invites the Simpsons to his barbecues, shares football tickets with Homer, offers to donate organs (without solicitation), lets the town come into his family's bomb shelter to avoid a comet's destruction, and agrees to leave it and face near certain doom when it becomes too crowded ("Homer Loves Flanders"; "When Flanders Failed"; "Homer's Triple Bypass"; "Bart's Comet") Even the Simpsons, "America's favorite dysfunctional family" (Rebeck 1990, 622) often overcome their John Bunyanesque characterizations. Marge and Homer reject opportunities to be unfaithful, attend a retreat to save their marriage, and drag the family to a seminar to improve their communication skills. Homer attempts to improve his relationship with his father, hunts down his half-brother, and tolerates his annoying sisters-in-law. Though constant rivals, Bart and Lisa share genuine affection and occasionally work together; when Lisa becomes the star goalie of Bart's rival ice hockey team, the two put down their sticks and exit the rink arm-in-arm rather than compete for their parents' love. Bart even solicits the assistance of a Michael Jackson sound-alike to help write Lisa a birthday song ("Life on the Fast Lane"; "The Last Temptation of Homer"; "Colonel Homer"; "War of the Simpsons"; "Bart's Inner Child"; "One Fish, Two Fish"; "Grandpa vs. Sexual Inadequacy"; "Oh Brother, Where Art Thou?"; "Lisa on Ice"; "Stark Raving Dad").

The diverse attitudes toward religion come together in the episode titled "Homer the Heretic." Refusing to attend church, Homer embarks on a journey of personal spirituality, encounters Apu's Hinduism and Krusty's Judaism, and ultimately comes face to face with God. During a dream God grants Homer permission to miss church, and when he awakens he is a changed man: calm, peaceful, and able to commune directly with nature. The following week, while asleep on the couch, Homer sets the house alight, and the volunteer fire department (Krusty, Ned, and Apu, or as Reverend Lovejoy puts it, "the Jew, the Christian, and the miscellaneous") rushes to put it out. Homer questions the value of attending church, since the Flanderses' house is also on fire. "He's a regular Charlie Church," Homer notes, suggesting that religious faith did not protect the Flanderses' home. But just as Homer utters these words, a providential cloud forms over the Flanderses' home and rain extinguishes the blaze— but leaves the fire burning the Simpson home. Asked by Marge if he has learned anything, Homer notes that God is angry and vengeful. The Reverend Lovejoy replies that it is the charity of the pluralistic volunteer fire department and not God's anger that is the lesson to be learned. The house is saved, and so is Homer's faith—in humanity, if not in God.

And so, perhaps, is the viewers', if the focus shifts from the show's content to its context, to what is happening on *this* side of the glass. Reverend Lovejoy's sentiment—that "God was working in the hearts of your friends and neighbors when they came to your aid"—represents the sort of generic Christianity prevalent in today's mainline Protestant churches and in most television portrayals of religion. Against the backdrop of declining religious authority, increasing personal choice, and "flattening" of doctrines into more palatable themes, television presents revamped morality plays such as this in which personal piety, religious pluralism, and sincere goodness rate higher than denominational adherence and church attendance. The show's coda reinforces this point: having promised to be "front row center" in church the next Sunday, there is Homer, snoring through Lovejoy's sermon, dreaming of another tête-à-tête with God (in which God informs Homer not to be upset, since "nine out of ten religions fail in their first year").

"SEND IN THE CLOWNS": ANALYZING THE SIMPSONS

It is helpful to take a step back and remember that this is (after all) a cartoon, written by comedy writers and drawn by comic artists. Several episodes feature gestures that highlight the characters' traditionally animated hands: three fingers and a thumb. Indeed, whatever "reality" is posited in the program is of the viewers' making. By working both sides of the reality mirror, the show engenders feelings of both identity and difference—the characters are both "us" and "not us." They are "us" in the sense that they are not ideal, but "not us" in the sense that—their cartoonishness aside—they fall far shorter of the mark than we think we do. The television mirror here is a funhouse one, which provides an exaggerated, distorted, yet still recognizable image of ourselves. Ozersky notes this and criticizes the show not only for failing to provide a positive model but for rewarding an attitude of superiority and ironic smugness in its viewers. Closer to the mark, however, might be Rebeck's observation that such critics "have missed the point. *The Simpsons* is satire," and as such its characters "are not telling people how to act" (1990, 622).

Interestingly, Rebeck illustrates her point with a religious-themed episode; she compares *The Simpsons*' detractors to a minor but recurring character in the show, the Sunday school teacher. Beleaguered by the children's questions about whether their pets will go to heaven—particularly Bart's inquiries about an amputee's leg and a robot with a human brain—she finally blurts out, "All these questions! Is a little blind faith too much to ask for?" ("The Telltale Head"). At best, some critics want proactive television that encourages viewers to maintain a level of "blind faith" in certain cherished ideals and values. At worst, they lambast *The Simpsons* because it fails to reinforce our society's "dominant ideology" with its cherished myths of eternal progress and traditional authority structures.

But exposing a myth to ridicule and debunking it are two different things. Recall that McConnell's highest praise for *The Simpsons* was that "it deconstructs the myth of the happy family wisely and miraculously leaves what is real and valuable about the myth unscathed" (1990, 390). Rebeck notes that the Simpsons are not characters to be emulated, but "if anything, they are giving people an outlet so they won't have to act out" (1990, 622). Herein lies another paradox; it is precisely *because* the program fails to offer us any sustained ideals of its own—least of all desirable ideals that challenge the majority—that it serves as a negative model for mainstream ideals of family and religion, if only by default, and offers instead a catharsis generated by a good laugh.

If many of television's early sitcoms were little more than thinly veiled presentations of the "American dream," *The Simpsons* and shows like it come much closer to actually representing "comedy" than most of its predecessors. Himmelstein notes that, to those having difficulty handling "the chaos of daily life," comedy represents "the logical order of the ideal" by revealing the "ludicrous and ridiculous aspects of our existence." It is most powerful, he concludes, "when it is possible for both the artist and the spectator to note the contradictions and value conflicts of society." Comedy shades into satire when it deals with what he calls "traditional and ever-present irritations which people know as evils but which they also find themselves powerless to eradicate" (1994, 77).

On *The Simpsons*, the disjunction between the way things are and the way they ought to be persists, and any bridge across that gap proves temporary and largely unrecognized by the supposedly victorious Simpsons themselves. At the end of an episode, the family often debates the "lesson" they've learned, with none of them seeming to get the point. Thus, if the inclusion of humor at the expense of institutional structures marks *The Simpsons* as satire, this recurring failure to offer true resolutions distinguishes it as irony. Defined by literary critic Alan Wilde, irony in our era is "a mode of consciousness, a perceptual response to a world without unity or cohesion" which nonetheless bears "the potential for affirmation" of both the world's absurdity and its "unfinished" nature (1981, 2, 6). Here it seems that the models "of" and "for" society coalesce. Rebeck notes, "The Simpsons show us . . . what it was about our upbringing that made us brats as kids and neurotic as adults" (1990, 622). They do not show us how to remedy those conditions, implying that they don't need fixing. In an imperfect world one fares best by behaving imperfectly.

Ozersky sees *The Simpsons* functioning this way, with profoundly negative implications for society. He argues that the show makes viewers "less inclined to object to the continuing presence of unsafe workplaces, vast corporations, the therapy racket, and all the other deserving targets of *The Simpsons'* harmless barbs" (1991, 92). But Ozersky fails to see another side to the "irony" coin. For segments of society who *cannot* object to those failings, *The Simpsons* reminds them that they are not *completely* powerless as long as they can laugh at the forces that oppress them. James Chesebro identifies irony as the "communication strategy" of the disenfranchised that reassures an audience because it presents characters who are "intellectually inferior and less able to control circumstances than is the audience" (Chesebro 1979; quoted in Himmelstein 1994, 79). In other words, the character's life is more absurd than the viewers'— a funhouse mirror. This is especially true in cases of what Chesebro calls "unknowing irony" in which the character's "ignorance and social powerlessness" are not feigned. Archie Bunker, the somewhat pitiable and perennially unredeemed bigot of *All in the Family*, is a perfect example of "unknowing irony" from the pre-*Simpsons* television era. In order for ironic programming to serve as a model "for" society, he had to remain unredeemed. Otherwise the show would have been something substantially different from what it was. As Himmelstein notes, self-knowledge and self-criticism in Archie would "sacrifice" the show's "unknowing irony" and turn it from "a biting artistic revelation of bigotry in a contemporary social milieu" to a "a popularized group-therapy session thrown in the audience's face" (1994, 125). And while *The Simpsons* contains far fewer "serious" moments than *All in the Family* did—Homer is clearly more absurd and less pitiable than Archie ever was—the two proceed in a decidedly "live and don't learn" manner.

No surprisingly, Homer's lack of intellectual and moral progress is expressed most powerfully in the religious-themed episodes. The accidental baptism in the Springfield River mentioned earlier elicits in him only temporary piety. He becomes a messianic leader for the "Stonecutters" (a men's organization modeled on Freemasonry), but his attempts to get the members to dedicate themselves to charitable acts causes the group to disband ("Homer the Great"). In the "Homer the Heretic" episode, not even a face-to-face encounter with the Almighty can change Homer's character. At every turn the opportunity for redemption passes, and Homer is back where he started: marginal, powerless, and unenlightened. In all these episodes, it is not unbelief that is counseled, but rather belief in basic values (for example, charity, camaraderie, and support) in a different way—within the family rather than outside it. In the end, Homer realizes the folly of striving too hard to "belong," and instead ends most episodes proud and confident of who he is, warts and all. As Richard Corliss notes, "Homer isn't bright, but he loves his brood." He is also a faithful husband and father who "will do anything—go skateboarding off a cliff, defy his boss, buy Lisa a pony—if the tots scream loud enough and if Marge gives him a lecture" (1994, 77). In other words, Homer's progress (or lack thereof) in each episode reveals a character who can be counted on to do the right thing, if accidentally or begrudgingly. This conveys a sense of an underlying human goodness, however many layers of ineptitude one might have to penetrate to find it.

"ALL THE WORLD LOVES A CLOWN":
THE SIMPSONS AS RELIGIOUS ARCHETYPES

And thus we return to the notion of the Simpsons—especially Homer—as "us" and "not us." He has the same values and desires, but expresses them in a buffoonish style. This is the key to discerning the significance of *The Simpsons* not only as satire of religious phenomena, but also as a religious phenomenon in itself. The history of religions has many examples of clowns who convey messages to the faithful. Historian Don Handelman describes the linguistic connections between "buffoon" and "fool" and notes the "affinities" between the fool in medieval drama and the clown as religious performer. According to Handelman, "Clowns are ambiguous and ambivalent figures. . . . The clown in ritual is at once a character of solemnity and fun, of gravity and hilarity, of danger and absurdity, of wisdom and idiocy, and of the sacred and the profane" (1987). A character such as Homer Simpson oscillates between knowing and not knowing, between knowing that he knows and not knowing that he knows. He approaches the divine but simultaneously defames it, and thus embodies the irony of a character who knows no real resolution.

In some religions, the identity and difference between clowns and their audiences is an immensely significant dialectic—that paradox of "us" but "not us." In the Hopi tradition, ritual clowns perform actions backward, upside down, or in an otherwise ridiculous fashion—for example, entering a plaza by climbing head-first down a ladder. They may engage in exaggerated simulated intercourse and perform other activities that violate Hopi social norms. Interpretations have stressed two aspects: entertainment value and the pedagogic value of illustrating the foolishness of misbehaving. In this sense, Hopi clowns foster a sense of superiority among the audience members who know more and are more sophisticated than the clowns. However, as Emory Sekaquaptewa notes, clowns, while parodies of the society, must be recognizable in order to have an effect. It may be a funhouse mirror, but it's still a mirror, and clowns show that the way *not* to behave is precisely the way we often behave in an imperfect world. As Sekaquaptewa explains, clowns show that people "have only their worldly ambition and aspirations by which to gain a spiritual world of eternity.... We cannot be perfect in this world after all and if we are reminded that we are clowns, maybe we can have, from time to time, introspection as a guide to lead us right" (1989, 151).

Thus sacred clowns, through their mockery of norms, serve to reinforce a tradition's values. They "contradict the laws of society to remind people of distinctions between the sacred and profane. They cross ordinary boundaries in order to define them" (Bastien 1987). *The Simpsons* represents both a model of and a model for contemporary American society, not only because it reveals contemporary attitudes about religious institutions, morality, and spirituality, but also because it functions in the time-honored way of religious satirists. As Joseph Bastien notes, "Traditionally, religions have employed humor and satire to bring people together and dissolve their differences. Clownish antics ... [are] not intended to desecrate the sacred but to dispel some of the rigidity and pomposity of the church-goers" (1987). The targets of *The Simpsons'* ridicule are hardly malevolent forces but rather exponents of what Victoria Rebeck calls a "sincere but useless" form of religion, teaching us that the most ridiculous thing a person can do is take anything in life too seriously (1990, 622). "The laughter of fools," Bastien says, is "praise to a God who disdain[s] pride among his people" (1987). But surely such a God would permit us to be proud of ourselves for getting the joke.

CONCLUSION: "A NOBLE SPIRIT EMBIGGENS THE SMALLEST MAN"

In a cartoon universe that thrives on irony, satire, and endless subversion there can be no heresy save an unreasonable dedication to convention. In Homer's world, and perhaps in our own, there is no longer a well-defined orthodoxy against which a meaningful heresy might be mounted. This does not diminish the fact that the Simpsons fulfill the important function of the sacred clowns — sustaining what is important by poking fun at religious conventions. What is important to believe and do, however, defies description. In keeping with the show's insight into the contemporary religious scene there is a persistent message of a loss of institutional authority (although institutional practice and loyalty linger) coupled with diverse forms of personal and noninstitutional religiosity. In this light the would-be "heretic" Homer fulfills the role of the American spiritual wanderer; though linked culturally (if unsteadily and unenthusiastically) to biblical tradition, he regularly engages a mosaic of other traditions, mythologies, and moral codes. In the face of these ever-shifting layers of meaning, he stumbles along, making the most of his limited understanding of their complexities. His comic antics remind us that the making of meaning (religious or otherwise) is ever an unfinished business and that humor and irony go a long way toward sweetening and sustaining the endeavor.

NOTES

1. Title names are taken from Richmond and Coffman 1997 and are rarely used on the air.
2. In February 1997, the program passed *The Flintstones* to become the longest running prime-time animated series.
3. See Richmond and Coffman 1997.
4. See Rosenthal 1992, A17. Writers for *The Simpsons* responded. In one episode Bart quips, "We're just like the Waltons. We're praying for the Depression to end, too." In another incident, Bush administration "drug czar" William Bennett noted he would "sit down with the little spikehead [Bart]" and "straighten this thing out." The show's producers replied: "If our drug czar thinks he can sit down and talk this out with a cartoon character, he must be on something" (Olive 1992, 61).
5. The American Family Association commissioned this study, often highlighting opinions compatible with its criticism of television programming. However, the article eventually appeared in a refereed journal. The study took place during the first year *The Simpsons* aired, and probably included several episodes in its sample. None of the explicitly religious episodes discussed here aired until 1991. There is little quantified research to challenge its basic findings (see "Primetime Religion" 1992, 60).
6. Every device is used to obscure Springfield's location. The fact that *Father Knows Best* was located in a "Springfield" seems only to reinforce *The Simpsons'* contrasting image of traditional American television families.
7. Jackie Mason, who trained for the rabbinate before entering show business, provides the father's voice.
8. The comet disintegrates in the thick layer of smog permanently settled over the town, making Lovejoy's rantings that much more ridiculous. However, Ned's

personal religiosity is redeemed; he selflessly offers his family's fallout shelter to the unprepared townspeople and leaves it when it fills beyond capacity. The shelter collapses just as everyone—moved by Ned's generosity and singing "Que sera, sera"—exits to face down the comet with him. Flanders has, in effect, saved the town twice: once by generosity and once by selfless example, both motivated by his religious interpretations.

9. This scene inspired Michael Medved's criticism noted above.

REFERENCES

Bastien, Joseph. 1987. "Humor and Satire." In *Encyclopedia of Religion*, ed. Mircea Eliade. New York: Macmillan.

Chesebro, James. 1979. "Communication, Values, and Popular Television Series—A Four-Year Assessment." In *Television: The Critical View*, 2d ed., ed. Horace Newcomb, 16–54. New York: Oxford University Press.

Collum, Danny Duncan. 1991. ". . . Because He Made So Many of Them." *Sojourners* 20 (November): 38–39.

Corliss, Richard. 1994. "Simpsons Forever!" *Time* 143, 18, May 2, 77.

Freeman, Michael. 1995. "The Official End (1994–95 Syndication Season Led by *The Simpsons*)." *Mediaweek* 5, September, 18, 14.

Geertz, Clifford. 1973. "Religion as a Cultural System." In *The Interpretation of Cultures*, 87–125. San Francisco, Calif.: Basic Books.

Goethals, Gregor. 1981. *The TV Ritual*. Boston: Beacon Press.

Greeley, Andrew. 1987. "Today's Morality Play: The Sitcom." *New York Times*, May 17, 1, 40 (Arts and Leisure).

Handelman, Don. 1987. "Clowns." In *Encyclopedia of Religion*, ed. Mircea Eliade. New York: Macmillan.

Himmelstein, Hal. 1994. *Television Myth and the American Mind*, 2d ed. Westport, Conn.: Praeger.

Lefton, Terry. 1992. "Don't Tell Mom: Fox Looks to a Degenerate Clown and a Violent Cat-and-Mouse Duo to Revitalize 'The Simpsons' Merchandise Sales." *Brandweek* 33 (10 August 10): 16–17.

McConnell, Frank. 1990. "'Real' Cartoon Characters: The Simpsons." *Commonweal* 117 (June 15): 389–90.

Medved, Michael. 1992. *Hollywood vs. America: Popular Culture and the War on Traditional Values*. New York: HarperCollins.

Olive, David. 1992. *Political Babble: The 1,000 Dumbest Things Ever Said by Politicians*. New York: John Wiley and Sons.

Ozersky, Josh. 1991. "TV's Anti-Families: Married . . . with Malaise." *Tikkun* 6 (January/February): 11–14, 92–93.

"Prime-time Religion." 1992. *Christianity Today* 36 (March 9): 60.

Rebeck, Victoria A. 1990. "Recognizing Ourselves in *The Simpsons*." *Christian Century* 107 (June 27): 622.

Richmond, Ray, and Antonia Coffman, eds. 1997. *The Simpsons: A Complete Guide to Our Favorite Family*. New York: HarperCollins.

Riddle, Lyn. 1994. "A Rascal Cartoon Character Sets Off a Controversy in South Carolina." *Los Angeles Times*, March 1, A5.

Rosenthal, Andrew. 1992. "In a Speech, President Returns to Religious Themes." *New York Times*, January 28, A17.

Sekaquaptewa, Emory. 1989. "One More Smile for a Hopi Clown." In *I Become Part of It: Sacred Dimensions in Native American Life*, ed. D.M. Dooling and Paul Jordan-Smith. San Francisco: Harper San Francisco.

Skill, Thomas, et al. 1994. "The Portrayal of Religion and Spirituality on Fictional Network Television." *Review of Religious Research* 35 (March): 251–67.

Wilde, Alan. 1981. *Horizons of Assent: Modernism, Postmodernism, and the Ironic Imagination.* Baltimore: Johns Hopkins University Press.

Polls show that most Americans consider themselves either religious or spiritual (and occasionally both), but more and more are likely to mix and match religious ideas and practices, while fewer are likely to spend their entire lives within one religious tradition. This phenomenon has its roots in a variety of factors, including the level of freedom with which Americans may select among religions with minimal social repercussions (see Hammond, *With Liberty for All*, 1997; Roger Finke and Rodney Stark, *The Churching of America, 1776–1990*, 1992). But also instrumental has been the breakdown of the monopoly enjoyed by religious institutions in contemporary culture. Wade Clark Roof (*A Generation of Seekers*, 1993) argues that more and more people—particularly those born since the beginning of the "baby boom" generation—prefer experimenting with religion/spirituality, and as a result are often seen as less loyal to the religious communities of their birth.

This freedom to move among religions according to one's conscience has produced a culture in which people are increasingly mobile between religious traditions, but also increasingly happy meeting their religious/spiritual needs by nontraditional means. Tom Beaudoin (*Virtual Faith*, 1998) argues that, because of increased suspicions toward institutions, Americans—particularly those in "Generation X"—are increasingly likely to satisfy their religious/spiritual needs in seemingly anti-institutional, seemingly nonreligious ways. Because of the lessons they learned from observing their parents' generation, they no longer feel a need to go to church to get whatever it was that they might have gotten there. And because of a variety of cultural events in their collective memories, they don't trust institutions—religious or otherwise—to serve them anyway.

This does not mean that religious institutions are useless, but that they apparently have lost their monopoly in the construction and maintenance of meaning and community in contemporary America. Feeling a need to congregate but a suspicion toward institutions, many Americans reconstitute their own popular "churches" that provide those elements once monopolized by the church. Whether it is in a message from Jimmy Buffett or a hip-hop artist, in a virtual community or a celluloid one, many people have relocated their religious impulses and congregate in seemingly nonreligious settings that serve them in a seemingly religious capacity.

The essays in this section share this theme of distancing from traditional religious institutions. In some cases, it may take the form of suspicion of— or disdain for—familiar cultural institutions that no longer reflect the community. Robin Sylvan, exploring the spiritual implications of rap and hip-hop, notes the difficult economic and social conditions from which many of the artists emerged. He argues that the music runs "directly counter to the religious worldview of the mainstream culture it has come to permeate" and that it "refuses to take refuge in the hope of otherworldly salvation." Painfully direct and grounded in the lives of its performers, hip-hop communicates ancient styles and symbols in a new, often anti-institutional venue. Representing an entirely different world, Julie Ingersoll's essay examines "parrotheads" and identifies an anti-religious people who are quasi-institutional in their desire for community, ritual, mythology, and meaning found at Jimmy Buffett concerts. Ingersoll concludes that they are "irreverent toward institutional religion and yet often draw analogies between the way Buffett philosophy shapes their views of the world and 'spirituality.'"

In other cases, distance can be created symbolically rather than by suspicion and can result in parallel institutions that unintentionally replace institutions like the church. For example, Rubina Ramji enters cyberspace with her investigation of multiuser domains (MUDs) and discovers a world that, though disembodied and electronic, constitutes a "virtual" religious environment in its propagation of rules, rituals, morality, and community. She argues that MUDs "bolster the norms and values of traditional religion . . . that are usually considered exclusive to traditional ecclesiastical institutions." Eric Mazur and Tara Koda argue that the Walt Disney Company, with its product line of symbols and its mass marketing of meaning, is unintentionally competing with traditional religious institutions. Rather than labeling Disney a religion, Mazur and Koda argue that, because of the shifting role of religious institutions in America, "Disney's products . . . fill many of the roles often filled by religion." In a culture where religious/spiritual needs can be met outside of religious institutions, cyberspace and Disney seem acceptable providers for the religious/spiritual needs of their consumers.

The possibility that institutions can earn a profit in the religious world illustrates another powerful—and seemingly inevitable—element of the popular "churches": commercialism. All of the following essays describe experiences based on a commercial exchange, whether in the production and distribution of music, attendance at a concert, the use of electronic equipment, or admission to a theme park or theater. And although salvation always has a price—your soul, your heart, or your wallet—popular "churches" distinguish customers from bystanders (in what Mazur and Koda call the "religification" of a commodity). All are welcome at a Buffett concert, on cyberspace, or at Walt Disney World, as long as they can pay for admission. Even in the world of rap and hip-hop, the commercial conditions that produced the experience—economic hardship—still provide an important backdrop against which the art form has developed. Without money to record and distribute the message, or to buy and play the CD, one cannot participate fully.

With the price of salvation measured in dollars rather than piety, class often plays a part in the popular "churches." As Ingersoll notes, parrotheads are "predominantly middle and upper middle class" and "invariably white"; Mazur and Koda point out that Disney is not much better. However, participation in either Jimmy Buffett's world or Walt Disney World is not explicitly restricted to those groups, and the attraction of rap and hip-hop to the larger non–African-American population has made it one of the most powerful movements in contemporary music. And as anyone knows who has ventured online, in cyberspace no one needs to know what you look like. Anyone who pays to play, and plays by the rules, can participate.

These commercial and seemingly egalitarian qualities of the popular "churches" mask the fact that more than economics is at the heart of these alternative institutions. Though the ideology is grounded in consumerism, it can still provide meaning in a commercialized world. These popular "churches" combine elements of ritual, myth, morality, and spirituality and provide instruction that is transforming, prescriptive, and elevating for participants. The worldview that they provide often appears this-worldly, narcissistic, and manipulated for the financial benefit of the corporation. But as Mazur and Koda point out, it is pervasive, in tune with the times, and even satisfying to those who accept it, even if it isn't necessarily consistent with traditional religious ideology.

In the end we are left with the impression that these popular "churches" are not altogether different from traditional "churches." The themes these essays share—distancing from traditional religious institutions, commercialism, class, race, and ideology—are common in religious history. The significance here is not that the popular "churches" are unlike anything ever seen, but rather that they are consistent with social patterns for relocating the religious impulse. As we noted earlier, everything connected with the search for meaning is ripe for comparison with those elements usually reserved for institutional religion. This includes the act of institutionalization, and as the following essays show, John Calvin's notion—that the "visible church" is different from the "invisible church" of the saved—has not been abandoned, but instead has been reapplied by those searching in new places for their own salvationary community.

The Thin Line between
Saturday Night and Sunday Morning
Meaning and Community among Jimmy Buffett's Parrotheads

JULIE J. INGERSOLL

The sea of people dressed in brightly colored clothes surrounds me as I walk the rows between the thousands of cars. Lyrics from different Jimmy Buffett songs blend together as I move out of range of one stereo system and into another. Everyone I pass is singing one song or another. But the parking lot partiers wearing beach clothes and tropical attire are not as surprising as the makeshift beaches, portable resorts, and volcanic islands they have brought with them. More than one group of cars has parked in such a way as to leave room for the sand they brought with them in pickup trucks. On the mounds of sand they have set up beach chairs and blankets, beach balls and other inflatable toys. There is even a volleyball net.

One group of parrotheads[1] has rented a flatbed to transport a generator that provides energy for the jacuzzi that bubbles and steams beneath the group's papier-maché palm trees. Another parrothead club has set up an island-themed bar complete with a pencil-thin mustached bartender (in a Ricky Ricardo jacket) and blenders for the frozen margaritas that members share with passersby. And finally—my favorite—an enormous volcano has been erected in the center of the parking lot; the attached parrotheads in Hawaiian shirts and grass skirts sing, "I don't know, I don't know, I don't know where I'm gonna go when the volcano blows ..."

The party was held at Irvine Meadows Amphitheater in the fall of 1995. The annual Irvine Buffett Shows run for two nights each year, and (at least according to parrothead lore) this is one of the biggest parking lot parties at any of the shows. It starts about noon on Friday and runs until the wee hours of Sunday morning when the last of the long line of cars drives out of the lot.[2]

While one might be surprised at the level of creativity here, on the surface, at least, this is pretty much what one would probably expect of fans of Jimmy Buffett, whose two best-known songs are "[Wasted Away Again in] Margaritaville," and "Cheeseburger in Paradise." There's no seriousness here; and if there is anything resembling religion it is just pure unadulterated hedonism, right?

The rationale for a religious analysis of parrothead life[3] is unlike the typical rationale for scholarly undertaking; interest in the topic cannot be attributed to its uniqueness. On the contrary, this topic is academically interesting because it clearly illustrates an underrecognized influence of "religion" in our everyday world. Two basic questions frame this inquiry. First, in this apparently irreligious phenomenon, how many parallels to aspects of traditional religions can we find? And second, can our positing this seemingly irreligious phenomenon as "religion" give us theoretical insight into questions about the nature of religion and its role in modern "secular" society?

THE PARROTHEADS

According to the 60 Minutes interview that aired on May 11, 1997, Buffett had thirty concert dates scheduled for the season—all of which sold out—with more than one million people attending his shows annually. Buffett himself has called the parrotheads "cult-like" (in an affectionate sort of way).[4] Many parrotheads know the words to all his songs—and since play lists are readily available on the World Wide Web well before the shows, pretty much everyone in the audience knows the lyrics to each of the songs played at any given show. It is not unusual for the fans to drown out the band in their "hymn" singing.

A typical parrothead at a pre-concert party in Nashville, February 1999. Photo by Wanda Stewart.

Perhaps most surprising, though, is the broad age span of fans. Parrotheads range in age from children of seven or eight years old to retired folks. I sat next to a couple in their sixties (in lawn seats, no less) at their first show in San Francisco two years ago. I have played guess-the-song lyrics with a nine-year-old (and nearly lost) and I have had a critical mass of self-described parrotheads in several of the undergraduate courses I have taught. While parrotheads include people of all levels of education and economic status (I know at least three religious studies Ph.D.s who consider themselves part of the phlock[5]), they are predominantly middle and upper middle class. The sociological characteristic that seems most constant among them is race: they are invariably white.

THE ANTIRELIGIOUS STANCE OF BUFFETT, HIS MUSIC, AND HIS FANS

By all accounts Jimmy Buffett has led a life that flouts traditional religious sensibilities.[6] He glorifies sex and drugs, he seemingly advocates irresponsibility in the name of freedom, and he openly derides traditional religion. In one of many possible examples, on a recent album this former Catholic altar boy sings: "Religion, religion. Oh there's a thin line between Saturday night and Sunday morning." Poking fun at both Catholics and Protestants, the same song from the *Fruitcakes* album goes on to include the "Mea Culpa" and then to lampoon the simplemindedness of televangelists. As Buffett puts it, "Religion's in the hands of some crazy ass people" (Buffett 1994).[7]

On another recent album he parodies the "Seven Deadly Sins" (Buffett 1995) while an older album includes a song titled "My Head Hurts, My Feet Stink, and I Don't Love Jesus" (Buffett 1976a). In another example, this self-proclaimed Calypso poet tells us more than we may want to know when he sings: "I don't wear underwear, I don't go to church, and I don't cut my hair" (Buffett 1976b).

Parrotheads are equally irreverent toward institutional religion and yet often draw analogies between the way Buffett philosophy shapes their views of the world and "spirituality."

PARALLELS BETWEEN PARROTHEADISM AND TRADITIONAL RELIGION

Despite its irreverent tone and occasional hostility toward religion, there are many ways in which parrotheadism functions in the lives of Buffett fans that parallel aspects of traditional religion.[8]

The first parallel, which helps make sense of many of the others, is the parrotheads' notions of utopian paradise. Parrotheads are considered citizens of Margaritaville. (Before performing the hit song "[Wasted Away Again in] Margaritaville," Buffett often begins: "Please rise for the national anthem.") A website titled "Bubba [a nickname for Jimmy] for Beginners" includes a "Survival Guide for New Parrotheads /or/ Where is Margaritaville Anyway?"

> So, where IS Margaritaville, anyway?! Well, that's a tough one to answer. For some it's a paradise island in the Caribbean; for others it's a powder white beach along the Yucatan; and for some, sleeping along a gentle river as their rod bends at a biting fish. It's as much a state of mind as anything.[9]

Margaritaville is the community of parrotheads that is not geographically bound. It exists across space and time in the hearts and minds of Buffett followers. These parrotheads measure the here and now against their conception of mythic sacred space: a tropical island and a sailboat; a world characterized by freedom, good friends, and time to play (i.e., fishing and flying especially). This is not escapism. On the contrary, parrotheads strive to make this paradise part of their everyday lives and look upon those who put off the enjoyment of life in favor of drive and ambition with derision as, at best, hopelessly misguided or, at worst, lacking in real humanity. Many Buffett songs celebrate this orientation toward life, but one that lays it out most clearly is Buffett's 1978 "Cowboy in the Jungle." It talks about out-of-place tourists who "try to cram lost years into five or six days" because it "seems that blind ambition erased their intuition" (Buffett 1978).

Forget suburban homes. Even trailers are a bit too pedestrian in Buffett ideals. In 1974 he sang

> Mobile home's are smotherin' my Keys [a reference to the Florida Keys]
> I hate those bastards so much
> I wish a summer squall would blow them all
> The way up to fantasy land
> Yeah they're ugly and square and they don't belong here
> They looked a lot better as beer cans. (Buffett 1974)

For parrotheads, the limits to our ability to live in this mythic paradise (i.e., sin) are our materialism and lack of appreciation for the simple things in life. "Life Is Just a Tire Swing," Buffett sings in one song, while in another he longs for the days before he put "quarters in his [penny] loafers." And he confesses:

"Now times are rough and I've got too much stuff—I can't explain the likes of me" and critiques a world overrun by self-storage units and lacking in poets.

But sacred space does exist in real time and not just as mythic imaginings of Buffett and his flock of parrots. New Orleans, Louisiana, and Key West, Florida, are two places that have had a great impact on Buffett and his music, and these places loom large in the minds of parrotheads; many have visited the sacred sites and many more long to do so. When devotees pull out a photo album of their travels to Buffett shows, the albums often also include pictures from trips to either of these pilgrimage sites.

Recreational use of alcohol and drugs is celebrated and elevated to the point of ritual that transports parrotheads from their everyday existence. Other ritual aspects include an annual pilgrimage to shows and participation in the pre-concert gatherings. The Head Parrot himself has pointed to the ritual aspect of the events: "It's a tribal celebration—a rite of summer passage no different than the kinds of parties thrown by our primitive relatives in the cave days."[10] Sacred time is marked off from profane time as parrotheads participate in the madness surrounding a show. According to Buffett's interpretation, "They transform into Parrotheads . . . they come to the show with their own personal Mardi Gras attached to them." They have "their feeding frenzy [a song reference] and return to normal life."

Just as Mardi Gras precedes Lent, the preshow party prepares devotees for the transcendent experience to come. There is a revival-like atmosphere inside the concert venue in which concertgoers sing lyrics to songs, many of which they consider profoundly poetic and meaningful. When Buffett sings about a friend of his who, upon reaching the age of forty, reflects on somber realizations of midlife in "A Pirate Looks at Forty" (which he performs at every show now), it is not at all uncommon to see middle-aged men, eyes closed, sitting and quietly singing along. I have even seen them join hands and sway together in what seems clearly to be a shared experience of something transcendent.

On a website that asked parrotheads to write on the topic "Why I Love Jimmy Buffett Music," fans posted comments that sounded decidedly like descriptions of mystical experiences. One said that "Jimmy's music is a drug; the best kind of drug." Another wrote, "His music is medicine for my mind. It clears out all the stress and anxiety. He takes us to our own Margaritaville. . . . He gives me my only peace of mind. . . . My world revolves around his music. I've left the planet for a minute."

At least two contributors to this site actually made the comparison between Buffett and the transcendent. One noted that he loved Buffett's music because "he [Buffett] makes life seem not so threatening . . . he's like a god because he creates parrotheads wherever he goes." Another wrote, "Jimmy knows how to spell life out in simple terms. What he writes about is [sic] those issues that we all have to deal with on a daily basis. If I thought god had a brother it would be Jimmy for sure. He speaks the Truth!"[11]

But most parrotheads would see Buffett as more of a prophet than a savior, a religious leader rather than a god. Buffett espouses a philosophy of life and a value system[12] that parrotheads are drawn to, but the community of parrotheads has taken on a life of its own. The clearest way to illustrate this is to point to the concert/preconcert party experience. While the concert is the ostensible reason for gathering, in many ways the real event is the preconcert party. I have been to shows where the venue officials squelched the preconcert party by opening the parking lot only a couple of hours before the show and by prohibiting (and enforcing the prohibition of) barbecue grills and alcoholic beverages in the parking lot. The atmosphere at such shows is decidedly different.

Irvine Meadows, on the other hand, seems to encourage the parrothead gathering. According to parrotheads, a key official at that venue is a member of the phlock—and indeed, I have seen a parking lot security cart (resembling a golf cart) decorated with crepe paper and parrots, cruising the aisles of cars and parking lot partiers. Parrotheads who don't manage to get tickets to the Irvine show sometimes come to the parking lot party anyway. They often do manage to buy tickets from someone once they are there but I have heard people say that if they didn't get into the show, the party itself was worth coming for. In some ways the show itself is just the icing on the cake. Parrotheads gather to renew old friendships; to sing and dance; to drink margaritas, rum drinks, and Coronas; and to renew their Caribbean souls. Then they go to the show.

And while Buffett lampoons traditional religion, the fact that he sees the mythic element to his work is made clear with his dedication of the album *Off to See the Lizard* to Joseph Campbell. A song line specifically refers to a comment made by Campbell to Bill Moyers. Campbell told Moyers that he pitied people with "no invisible means of support," a phrase that became a line in a Buffett song.[13]

But there are more parallels between parrotheadism and traditional religion than these philosophical, mystical, and ritual comparisons. There is also a sociological similarity in terms of the way membership as a parrothead contributes to both an individual sense of identity and a sense of community. As explained earlier, a group of parrotheads is referred to as a flock (phlock) and while the intended reference is clearly to a flock of birds, in the case of the argument at hand it is notable that the term "flock" also commonly refers to the members of a church congregation. One has to wonder if the multiple meanings might not be intentional. Parrotheads make friends at concerts and meet up again with the same people year after year, but they also connect with each other in a nationwide network of parrothead clubs and a multitude of websites and chat rooms on the Internet.

Parrotheads in Paradise is the officially recognized club network, which in 1995 boasted fifteen thousand members in eighty-one clubs. The network's annual convention, called "The Meeting of the Minds," drew 750 participants in that same year. Clubs typically meet on a monthly basis for "fellowship" (their term) and to work on the ongoing community service and environmental projects they undertake. According to *Coconut Telegraph*, the national club newsletter, "Civic minded parrotheads in cities across the country have voluntarily gathered under the Buffett banner to promote peace, justice and the American way." Clubs have provided volunteers for the Red Cross, Unicef, and the Children's Wish Foundation. They have organized to help flood victims, participated in "adopt-a-highway" programs, and joined environmental cleanup efforts. According to local club newsletters, a parrothead club in Massachusetts organized a Special Olympics and the Left Coast Parrotheads in Southern California work for Habitat for Humanity and the area's Ronald McDonald House.[14]

Parrothead club members not only meet regularly during the year but also have special events including concert trips, camping trips, and fishing trips. One northern California couple invited parrothead friends from around the country to their parrot-themed wedding.

But Buffett fans also connect with one another over the Internet. There are innumerable websites, but one in particular seems most suited for discussion in this paper. The Church of Buffett, Orthodox, invites visitors with this greeting: "All ye faithful believers enter our hallowed halls. Those who believe in Jimmy Buffett the musician, not Jimmy Buffett the entertainer. . . . Please, kick the dust off your sandals and enter these holy pages by clicking on the menu."[15]

While most parrotheads consider their sacred text to be the entire canon of Buffett lyrics, the Church of Buffett, Orthodox, argues that the "revered chief poet" has succumbed to the influence of commercialism and that his music has suffered. They mark *Changes in Latitudes Changes in Attitudes* as the turning point with some including it in the "holy writ" (their term) and others not. In particular they label "Margaritaville" as "apostasy."

COUNTERCULTURE OR MAINSTREAM?

The Church of Buffett, Orthodox, is the prophetic voice in Margaritaville calling the parrotheads (and the Head Parrot) to be faithful to the anti-materialism of Buffett philosophy, calling them to be mindful of what they trade for their material success. But the larger segment of parrotheads looks a lot like the rest of the American middle class. They are lawyers, corporate employees, entrepreneurs, nurses, and teachers.

A quick look around the parking lot party confirms this social and economic status of the parrotheads. There are few BMWs and Mercedes (even at a southern California concert) but there are also very few older cars. Parrotheads drive Hondas and Toyotas; they drive late-model small pickups and sport utility vehicles. Many own expensive motor homes in which they travel to Buffett shows (which is not easily done without some financial means). Also, the annual trek many parrotheads make to the Meeting of the Minds in New Orleans, as well as the trips to the Caribbean and Key West, also indicates a certain degree of financial stability.

Parrotheads' position in the middle class is nowhere more clear than in the social service/reform efforts of the parrothead clubs. Members who have logged sufficient participation in these activities get first crack at concert tickets (which can often be hard to get as the shows sometimes sell out in the first few hours of ticket sales).

Voluntary societies that work to help victims of tragedy, bring joy to terminally ill children, and build houses for the poor (and most recently to preserve the environment) are quintessential of the American middle class. Voluntarism, as we know it, developed concurrently with the middle class in the nineteenth century. The willingness to organize to "better the lot of the less fortunate" was a badge of social status that came with material success sufficient to allow time for such activities (Roof and McKinney 1987, 40–71; Albanese 1992, 402–24).

Yet parrotheads revere those who would make themselves free by throwing away the trappings of materialism and wealth. They recognize that out-of-control consumption in our society diminishes freedom, but, by all appearances, they join enthusiastically in America's acquisitiveness. Buffett himself is a case in point. A man of tremendous wealth, Buffett owns boats, planes, and real estate; he does not live the vagabond lifestyle about which he sings. While in many ways parrotheads put forth an incisive critique of the values embraced by the American middle class, in other ways they embrace those values.

So what can we make of this paradox? Are the parrotheads merely idealizing one value system and living an opposing one? Are they insincere? Are they hypocrites? Or is there something more going on here? Our positing parrot-headism as a religion raises parrothead activities to the level of ritual and points us to Victor Turner's work on ritual to explain how we might be able to take seriously both sides of this paradox.

In his seminal work *The Ritual Process* ([1969] 1995, especially "Liminality and Communitas," 94ff), Turner explores various dimensions and character-istics of ritual. Turner writes, specifically, about liminality and communitas as they function—and are created—in rites of passage, but his observations also fit well the parrothead ritual attached to the annual pilgrimage to a Buffett show and help to explain how parrothead values make sense in the context of the realities of parrothead lives.

With concert ritual, parrotheads detach from their everyday lives. They enter what Turner calls a liminal stage. And finally they are reincorporated into the structure of their old lives but exist in that structure in a new way.

The detachment consists of shedding the order and reserve of their every-day lives (what Turner calls "structure"): making preparations including buy-ing tickets, planning costumes, decorating the car, and making the trip. Such detachment is the precursor to the liminal phase, in which the transformation of character takes place. Turner points to the ways in which the liminal phase creates an "intense comradeship and egalitarianism" where "distinctions of rank and status disappear or are homogenized" (95). (It is hard to tell a doctor from an electrician when both are barefoot on a portable "beach" wearing straw hats and Hawaiian shirts and drinking shots of tequila.)

It is in the egalitarian moment, according to Turner, that communitas emerges: "communitas emerges where social structure is not" (126). Turner even points to the paradox of communitas and structure existing side by side:

> It is as though there are here two major "models" for human interrelatedness, juxtaposed and alternating. The first is of society as a structured, differentiated, and often hierarchical system of politico-legal-economic positions with many types of evaluation, separating men in terms of "more" or "less." The second, which emerges recognizably in the liminal period, is of society as an unstructured or rudimentarily structured and relatively undifferentiated *comitatus*, community, or even communion of equal individuals. (96)

Turner then goes on the apply the label "communitas" to this second type of community. He explains that the egalitarian values espoused as part of the ritual process are carried back into the structure to maintain a tension between hierarchy and egalitarianism in the larger society: There is a dialectic here, for the immediacy of communitas gives way to the mediacy of structure.... Men are released from structure into communitas only to return to structure revitalized by their experience of communitas" (129).

Turner's focus is on the value of this dialectic for society as a whole; he goes so far as to argue that no society can function adequately without it (129). But what does this process mean for the individual? How are parrotheads transformed when they make their pilgrimage from their middle-class lives, through the "carnival" that is a Buffett concert, and back again? Instead of one competing value system undermining the other (middle-class consumption versus antimaterialist freedom), the ritual process actually allows the competing value systems to exist in creative tension with each other. Parrotheads may dream of giving it all up to live on a sailboat in the islands, but parrothead ritual gives them just enough time in that "one particular harbor" to allow them to keep it all together in the structure of the real world. They can keep the vision of Margaritaville alive in their hearts and minds while living their lives in Los Angeles, New York, or Cincinnati. And the nongeographical utopia has an added advantage over the geographical one: it can more readily survive the forces of history.

A RETURN TO OUR INITIAL THEORETICAL QUESTIONS

Granted, many of the analogies to religion, drawn by Buffett and the parrotheads themselves, are made as tongue-in-cheek remarks; they are drawn with irony and a sense of humor. But I contend that they make sense, and indeed are funny, only because there is more to them than the irony alone. So how does our playing with categories of religion and applying them to a seemingly irreligious phenomenon aid us in the study of religion?

First, this examination shows us something important about an issue that has occupied sociologists of religion in recent years. Proponents of secularization theories have posited the "decline of religion," coinciding with the rise of modernity. According to secularizationists, in an older society where a single religious tradition dominated, the plausibility of that tradition was maintained by the fact that most everyone in the society subscribed to it. With modernity has come increasing exposure to a plurality of world views that has, in turn, undermined the plausibility structures of these once-dominant religions.

Critics of this theory point to several apparent flaws. First, they note the vitality of religion in North America where a significant degree of pluralism and religious competition has been the norm. Second, they call attention to the worldwide increase in conservative religiopolitical movements (often called fundamentalisms). Third, they argue that new religious movements are flourishing. Fourth, and probably greatest in significance, they point to the rise of what people prefer to call "spirituality" (personalized, individualized religion).

They argue that religion hasn't declined; it has been reshaped and may no longer be recognizable to those who define "religion" in terms of churches and other institutions. Most recently they have focused on whether this increased individualism is a thing to be mourned or celebrated. "Sheila," a research subject who appeared in *Habits of the Heart* (Bellah et al. 1985), has become the classic example of individualism run rampant as she coined her own term for her individual personal religion: "Sheilaism." Bellah and his colleagues expressed their concern over our society's loss of a sense of community (plausibility structure). Wade Clark Roof, on the other hand, has celebrated the diversity and creativity he found in the often individualistic "spirituality" of his research subjects in *A Generation of Seekers* (1993). He concludes that the renewed emphasis on "spirituality" in the 1990s is actually a more "mature expression" of "the quest for a spiritual style" that took hold of baby boomers nearly three decades ago (242). Roof sees this new spirituality as being sophisticated in its grappling with questions of meaning and its embracing of the multilayeredness of belief and practice. He is hopeful about the ways in which he sees this new spirituality embracing authentic pluralism, calling people to live as transformed individuals while at the same time committed to a new sense of community.

Secularizationists have rejoined the debate, asserting that their theory had been mischaracterized and that what was meant in the phrase *decline of religion* was a decline of the cultural authority of religious institutions; that the decline predicted by secularization theory in no way refers to the elimination of religious sensibilities altogether (Yamane 1997). If these latest contributions to the debate by secularizationists are correct, then what we have is merely a disagreement of the definition of secularization with both sides agreeing that religion (outside of institutions) may still be thriving.

The case of Jimmy Buffett's parrotheads adds to the discussion of the role of religion in contemporary American life because, as we have seen, parrotheadism is not merely an individual phenomenon; it has a profoundly communal character. It is precisely the transcendent sense parrotheads have of being connected to something bigger than themselves that gives meaning to this experience. There are probably many people who buy Jimmy Buffett CDs—and even attend a concert or two—who never make the move to identifying themselves with the collectivity.[16] Being a parrothead is, by definition, seeking to align yourself with others who connect with Buffett's music and philosophy in a similar way. We may not have to choose, theoretically, between seeing religion as institutionally focused and seeing it as individually focused. It seems there may be a third form of religion and religious experience that is nontraditional, noninstitutional, but at the same time shared and communal.[17]

The second theoretical consideration that is illuminated by this examination engages an older debate in religious studies over the very nature of religion. Often scholars have focused on religion and asked if there was something about the religious experience that drew people to it. The question has made religion seem to be a "thing" out there that automatically attracted adherents. I would propose that an examination of the relgiosity of a particular group of music fans such as this one shows us that this traditional framing of the question misses the mark. What we have, it seems, is not necessarily something essentially religious that draws people in, but something essentially human that makes them seek it, whatever its form.

Essential human needs for meaning, purpose, ritual, community, and "transcendent" experience (in which I include any experience that satisfies our need to feel a part of something bigger than ourselves, whether it is an Eastern mystical oneness with the universe or Christian communion), have been met in different ways in different societies. Most recently in the West those needs have been met by institutional religion. For this reason, institutional religion has functioned as our benchmark. However, these needs are so essentially human that human beings will always find ways to fulfill them. Parrotheads, who live in a secular world in which institutional religion has lost its cultural clout and is imbued with skeptical cynicism about institutions generally, will create a sense of community where they find the necessary tools to do so.

Let me close with a parrothead benediction:

Let those winds of time
Blow over my head
I'd rather die while I'm livin'
Than live while I'm dead.

NOTES

1. The label "parrotheads" refers to fans of musician Jimmy Buffet. As with most aspects of these folk, there is no uniformity in the appellation; it is written as Parrot Head, Parrothead, parrot head, or parrothead. I have opted, for the most part, to use the latter, but when citing someone else's use of the term (or the name of a club, for instance) I have retained the form used.

2. The data for the above description and the material which follows were gathered over the course of many years of participant observation. Having been a parrothead myself for nearly twenty- five years, I have attended eleven shows in six venues, visited Margaritaville in New Orleans, Louisiana, several times, and am a member of the Left Coast Parrot Heads. I wish to thank Jon Reese of Santa Barbara, California, for his assistance with song lyrics and citations, and Rasa Lemmond, a religious studies major at Millsaps College in Jackson, Mississippi, for her help with research and analysis.

3. While Buffett himself, as "Head Parrot," and the lyrics of his songs are discussed insofar as they are relevant, the focus of the paper is, specifically, on the culture of the parrotheads.

4. "Parrot Head Phenomenon," http://pilot.msu.edu/user/gibbensr/jimmy.phenom. htm (9/8/97).

5. Birds commonly travel in flocks, and parrotheads often exchange an "f" at the beginning of a word with a "ph" (*parrothead*). Thus, a group of parrotheads is referred to as a phlock.

6. Born Christmas Day in 1946 (Pascagoula, Mississippi), Buffett was raised as a Catholic—a tradition he resoundingly rejected. His first album, *Down to Earth*, (1970) included three songs highly critical of religion and religious people whom he saw as hypocritical ("The Christian," "the Missionary," and "Truck Stop Salvation").

7. Copyright restrictions forbid lengthier use of lyrics.

8. http://www.homecom.com/mhall/cobo/abouttxt.html (9/11/97). I first saw the term "parrotheadism" on the webpage for the Church of Buffett, Orthodox, which will be discussed later in the chapter.

9. http://galenalink.com/~parrothd/buffett/Bubba.htm (9/12/97).

10. "Feeding Frenzy," interview with Buffett. http://pilot.msu.edu/user/gibbensr/jimmy/feeding.htm (9/8/97).

11. http://www.suresite.com/cgi-bin/WebX.cgi?13@210@.ee6bc0f (7/16/97).

12. This philosophy of life and value system are perhaps most clearly spelled out in Buffett's recent autobiographical bestseller, written as he reached his fiftieth birthday, *Jimmy Buffett: A Pirate Looks at Fifty*. (The book title is a reference to his much loved song, "A Pirate Looks at Forty.") It is also readily apparent in song lyrics too numerous to reproduce here.

13. Taken from a list of literary references found in Buffett's work on a parrothead's web page: http://homecom.com/cobo/FAQ/litrefs.html#1 (9/11/97).

14. In the nineteenth century, the rise of the middle class was marked by an increase in social "do-gooder" societies. Catherine Albanese has argued that the "moralism" which gave rise to the volunteerism was (and is) a central component to American civil religion (Albanese 1992).

15. http://www.homecom.com/mhall/cobo/ (9/11/97).
16. Actually, articles in magazine such as *High Times* and *Rolling Stone* belie this point and argue that Buffett's following is relatively small but so loyal that it will snap up any record he makes (or novel he writes). This is interesting and, if true, would bolster my argument, but I do not have the resources to evaluate its accuracy.
17. I am not claiming that this is a finding which is opposite that of Bellah or Roof. It is merely a refocusing on a different aspect of the various forms of religion uncovered by these and other researchers.

REFERENCES

Albanese, Catherine L. 1992. *America: Religions and Religion*, 2d ed. Belmont, Calif.: Wadsworth.

Bellah, Robert N., Richard Madsen, William M. Sullivan, Ann Swidler, and Steven M. Tipton. 1985. *Habits of the Heart: Individualism and Commitment in American Life*. Berkeley: University of California Press.

Buffett, Jimmy. 1974. "Migration." *A1A*. MCA Records.

——. 1976a. "My Head Hurts, My Feet Stink, and I Don't Love Jesus." *Havana Daydreamin'*. MCA Records.

——. 1976b. "Pencil Thin Mustache." *Livin' and Dying' in 3/4 Time*. MCA Records.

——. 1978. "Cowboy in the Jungle." *Son of a Son of a Sailor*. MCA Records.

——. 1994. "Fruitcakes." *Fruitcakes*. MCA Records.

——. 1995. "Bank of Bad Habits." *Barometer Soup*. Margaritaville Records.

——. 1998. *Jimmy Buffett: A Pirate Looks at Fifty*. New York: Random House.

Roof, Wade Clark. 1993. *A Generation of Seekers: The Spiritual Journeys of the Baby Boom Generation*. San Francisco: HarperCollins.

Roof, Wade Clark, and William McKinney. 1987. *American Mainline Religion*. New Brunswick, N.J.: Rutgers University Press.

Turner, Victor W. [1969] 1995. *The Ritual Process*. Hawthorne, N.Y.: Walter de Gruyter.

Yamane, David. 1997. "Secularization on Trial." *Journal for the Scientific Study of Religion* 36, 1 (March): 109–22.

Building Community Word by Word

Religion in the Virtual World

RUBINA RAMJI

I first logged onto the Internet in 1986 and have never stopped. The Internet allowed me a means of communicating that dissolved social boundaries constrained by space and time. As Marshall McLuhan pointed out, the telegraph, telephone, radio, and television have turned every time into here and now; computer-mediated communications take this immediacy one step further by dissolving the boundaries of identity as well. I was first introduced to multiuser domains (MUDs) while I was in graduate school by long-distance friends: it was a real-time text based virtual site where we could "meet." In order to get on to this particular MUD (LegendMUD), I had to create an identity or character by naming it (I chose Jael), describing it, giving it various skills and attributes that would affect the character's ability to deal with situations later on. Once I designed my character, I entered LegendMUD in the Arabian Nights era and immediately was presented with this narrative:

> You stand before the counter. Rows and rows of keys line the wall behind the desk and a small door leads to the back where the tenants stay. A small sign is posted on the wall. A door leads out and onto the porch.
> [Exits: s]
> A mailbox sits in the corner.
> The welcome board is standing in the corner here.
> A lamp lies dropped here.
> Asabi stands here in front of a board with many room keys hanging on it.
> Jael enters the game.

When I entered LegendMUD in 1992 there were no maps available, and so I began exploring and learning (of course, the first direction was south). My character had minimal equipment, a few coins to buy food with, basic clothing, and a basic weapon. As I became familiar with the area, I encountered other players and watched what they were doing. This is how I learned to participate in daily life on the MUD, how to do battle, and how to get ahead in this virtual world. Each time I logged on, I learned something new and met someone new, until I had accumulated my own special skills and became part of a clan, a gorup of other players who promised to assist each other at all times. By creating my cyber-identity, I built my cyber-community.

Each character who enters a multiuser domain (also known as a multiuser dungeon, dimension, or dialogue) begins as I did, by knowing nothing, having to learn to negotiate the rules of the MUD (each being slightly different) and its particular landscape. It is essential for players to read the information boards and commands provided at the outset to understand the rules of the MUD culture. Some MUDs provide maps to navigate by; others leave the player to learn the sense of space that has been written into the MUD. Players learn that their characters become hungry and must be fed or they will die; that it becomes dark at night and that a light must be lit to "see"; that when their characters are tired they must sleep or die; that experience points must be accumulated, by killing MUD creatures and characters and performing certain rituals, to move on to the next level; and that dying leads to loss of property, experience, and status. Accumulation of money and equipment allows a character to kill and perform rituals, and so leads to the experience necessary for a character to advance levels and gain status. The MUD is at once spontaneous in that the player is free to create his or her own character, but there is also a system and code that must be followed in order to gain access to the secrets of the MUD social structure.

MUDs maintain the following characteristics:

1. The player creates a representation within the data space which can then engage in such activities as moving, examining objects, smiling, fighting, eating, dying, and progressively gaining additional abilities.
2. The MUD program is multiuser, which enables many users and non-user characters to interact simultaneously.
3. The program is network based, so that many users at widely remote sites can interact together in "real time."
4. The primary interface between the user and other objects or users is text based rather than graphics based, so everything is experienced through language. (Helgert and Nesterenko 1993)

It has been argued that a MUD does not constitute a true virtual reality because it is not graphic, but rather a data structure designed to mimic an external environment. This structure can be referred to as "cyberspace" or "artificial reality." But because of its expansion onto the external environment through players, I would argue that MUDs are indeed true virtual realities.

Being text based means that words and sentences must be used to perform actions (e.g., buy a lantern, sleep, eat bread, read mail, kill a scruffy dog); it is highly visual in that characters, places, and objects continually interact (see tables 1 and 2).

MUDs are typically viewed as mere games, unrelated to "real" culture or the forces that shape it, one major force being religion. Although MUDs may be seen this way, and as part of a "culture that implicitly discourages respect for authority or hierarchical controls" (Kinney 1995, 764), I contend that MUDs, rather than being secular in nature or antireligious, are in fact cultural platforms that have been formed on the hierarchies of traditional religious institutions.

Table 1. Text-based MUD Interactions

In a Guesthouse
Rich wooden walls and smoky oil lamps greet you in this room, an inn of some quality. The chairs are tooled leather done in familiar Inca designs, but you think that the painting on the wall, beside the crucifix, is actually by a Spanish artist. The ornate windows are decorated in intricate patterns of stained glass, and of course there is a place by the door to leave your sword.

[Exits: e]

A directory board holding both news and 'welcome' information stands here.
A mailbox sits in the corner here.
A gaunt fellow stands here, eyeing everyone who comes in.

(HP:100% MV:100% MA:100%) > **list** *(<– typed command by player to see inventory)*

[Price]	Item	[Price]	Item
[24]	A small brass lantern	[24]	A little jug of fish oil
[2]	A cloth bandage	[6]	A small piece of paper
[6]	A cup of mate		

(HP:100% MV:100% MA:100%) > **buy lantern** *(<– typed command by player to purchase)*

You don't have enough money *(<– MUD response)*

(HP:100% MV:100% MA:100%) > **e** *(<– typed command by player to move east)*

Miraflores
A bustling crowd fills the streets here, and the streets are narrow. The clip-clop of horses' hooves fills the air at all hours, as carriages force their way through the press of people. To the west of you there appears to be an inn of some repute—at least its sign is ornately carved and the clientele entering seems to be moderately well-heeled.

[Exits: n w]

A woman with a fan covering her face smiles coquettishly at you.
A horse is here, straining to pull a wagon out of the mud in the street.

(HP:100% MV:100% MA:100%) > **pet horse** *(<– typed command by player to act)*

You pet him lovingly. *(<– MUD response)*

I suggest that MUDs do in fact reinforce traditional conceptions of God, including assumptions of the existence of angels and other spiritual beings, and bolster the norms and values of traditional religion through processes of ritual and concepts of the sacred that are usually considered exclusive to traditional ecclesiastical institutions.

The word "culture," when used anthropologically, refers to "the total way of life of a discrete society, its traditions, habits, beliefs, and art—the systematic body of learned behavior which is transmitted from parents to children" (Clausen 1996, 380). Cultures transform over time but have certain constant features, including a language, that differentiate them from other cultures in other times and places. A culture comes to be defined by differences and exclusions in comparison to other distinct cultures.

MUDs, as text-based cultures, can be viewed as mirrors of "real" culture or, as Michel Foucault would describe them, as "heterotopias," because they are utopias but also exist in reality (Foucault 1986). They have their own unique text-based language (e.g., IMHO: "in my humble opinion," BRB: "be right back," CUL8R: "see you later," FOFL: "fall on floor laughing," and emoticons

---

Table 2. Player Actions

ACTIONS (HELP SOCIALS)
ack/applaud/beam/bearhug/beg/blush/bark/bounce/bow/burp/cackle/cheer/choke/chortle/clap/comfort/congratulate/cough/cover/cringe/cry/cuddle/curse/curtsey/dance/defend/desire/drool/duck/eek/embrace/enthuse/eyeroll/faint/fidget/flex/flip/flirt/flourish/fondle/french/frown/fume/gasp/giggle/glare/grimace/grin/groan/grope/grovel/growl/grumble/gulp/hello/hiccup/hiss/honk/hug/ignore/jump/kiss/lag/laugh/leap/lick/lurk/meow/moan/model/nibble/nod/nudge/nuzzle/pat/peer/pet/pillow/point/poke/polish/ponder/pout/puke/purr/puzzle/question/quiver/quote/reassure/ruffle/salute/scream/scuffle/seduce/shake/sharpen/shiver/shrug/shudder/sigh/sing/slap/slurp/smile/smirk/smooch/snap/snarl/sneeze/snicker/sniff/snore/snort/snuggle/spank/spit/splash/squeeze/squirm/stagger/stare/startle/stomp/stretch/stroke/strut/sulk/swoon/tackle/tap/taunt/thank/threaten/tickle/tongue/tug/twiddle/umbrella/wait/wave/whap/whimper/whine/whistle/wiggle/wince/wink/wobble/worship/wrinkle/yawn/zone

MOVEMENT
north/east/south/west/up/down/go/enter

COMMUNICATIONS
auction/chat/info/pray/tell/emote/talk/yell/conference/reply/say/ask/whisper/send/mail/receive/mark/read/write/erase/append

COMBAT
kill/flee/kick/dodge/shoot/backstab/wary/agg/headbutt

OBJECT MANIPULATION
close/open/consign/get/take/drop/put/give/hold/wield/remove/wear/accept/bid/eat/drink/carve/fill/empty/list/value/buy/sell/cancel/reload/recite/quaff/use/junk/reclaim

MISCELLANEOUS
exits/look/examine/bug/idea/typo/sit/stand/sleep/order/wake/rest/quit/rent/offer/save/news/wizlist/consider/follow/group/split

such as smiley faces), based on time and place. Even actions and emotions become language as they need to be typed to be performed.

To those MUDding, other human beings and the "real" world do not exist. MUDs keep memory and create shared beliefs, symbols, and mutual agreements with those who participate. Everything that exists in the MUD is all that is needed and accepted to make up the existence of that culture at that time. Certain attitudes need to be maintained, and certain behaviors are demanded. If these rules of existence are not followed, the insider is punished or marginalized (see table 3).

It is sometimes argued that the computer is making culture subjective and that the "major constituents of real cultures—family, religion, ethics, manners, impersonal criteria for distinguishing between truth and falsehood—have shrunk almost to the vanishing point as authorities over individual behavior" (Clausen 1996, 387). Having viewed various role-playing MUDs (here I refer to diku-MUDs, which are database MUDs, not lpMUDs, which are programmed in a C++ variant) and participated on them, I think that the opposite is, in fact, occurring. The dikuMUD on which I spent the majority of my time is LegendMUD (mud.sig.net 9999), and therefore is the basis for MUD descriptions offered in this paper. The players on dikuMUDs engage in role playing, working alone or in groups to kill MUD creatures and characters, solve puzzles, follow MUD rules, and gain experience in the quest to become a wizard/implementer/administrator (Smith 1996). In many respects, dikuMUDs are constructed to have authority over individual behavior. There are many fixed norms in these MUDs. Diku-MUDs work on the premise that there are immortals who have created this MUD universe and its culture, and therefore are in a position of power through which they enforce rules as to how they wish to have this culture sustain itself. In order to belong to LegendMUD, and remain in it, one has to explicitly follow the rules set out or face punishment. Punishment for improper behavior begins with a warning, then a loss of assets, and finally banishment from that culture. The gods, or owners of the MUD, have complete control over the players and the environment.

Many of the moral values of mainstream religion can be found within the rules of LegendMUD. There can be no harassing of players, no unwanted sexually explicit language or action, no stealing, and no false accusations.

There are also very strict regulations regarding the killing of other players. Even though MUDs are game environments, where one of the goals is to accumulate experience and abilities, there are limits placed on how a character can

Table 3. LegendMUD Rules

LegendMUD has a few rules, but the following activities are unwelcome here. Players caught in engaging in these activities will be dealt with on a individual basis, but the basic violations listed below all potentially call for character deletion. Punitive actions can also include any and all of the following: removal of equipment or gold, alteration of stats, denied access to mud commands (e.g. being muzzled or glued), denied access to a character, forced clanning, demotion of level status, or banning of a site if repeated violations occur.

All players are held responsible for understanding and following the rules set forth below, and violations will not be less severely punished because a player claims to have not known he or she was breaking a rule. For additional information, see individual help files or immorts with the 'Admin' flag.

1. Multiplaying (logging in more than one character at a time) and trading equipment among your characters (or using one of your characters to benefit another of your characters in any way) are prohibited; additionally, only one player may play a particular character.

2. Harassing other players is prohibited.

3. Sexually explicit language, cursing, and slurs are not permitted over public channels or in public fora like illusions or character names/titles.

4. Non-clanned players may not interfere in the general activities of clans or player-kill. 'Interference' may involve, but is not limited to, using skills, spells, or in-game functions to assist a pkiller or impede his or her opponent, either directly or indirectly.

5. Non-clanned players may never loot the corpse of a clanned or non-clanned character, except anyone may remove items from the corpse of a character at that character's request to assist in corpse recovery.

6. Asking or getting immorts to reveal or change your stats is not permitted, nor is getting or asking them to load items or mobs for you or to confer other unfair advantage.

7. If you find a bug, you must report it by using BUG command or mudmail to an immortal. Taking advantage of a bug or using it to crash the mud is not permitted.

8. Intentionally placing a character over rent by loading him or her with excessive equipment is not permitted.

9. Experience may not be 'given' away by clanned characters permitting others to pkill them; repeated deaths will attract the attention of immorts.

10. In-game information may not be placed on public channels or board.

11. Making false accusations under these rules is itself a punishable offense.

go about accomplishing these tasks. A sense of fair play is always assumed, and indeed required, for a player's survival. These social and ethical codes are willingly followed by players who gather together as congregations do and engage in these communal activities.

Just as each religion has its own code of moral behavior and expression to which its believers must subscribe, the same is true for MUDs. Rooted in textuality, both maintain the continuity, uniformity, sacred space, and sacred time of its culture. Both offer a sense of belonging through shared beliefs and symbols, both involve sacred time through moments of ecstasy and revelation, and both are structured as communities with the believers on the inside, with the knowledge, surrounded by "atheists," or those without knowledge or gnosis (Chidester 1996).

Within religious institutions, members look to the hierarchical superiors for leadership and guidance. We look to imams, ministers, sheikhs, rabbis, gurus, and priests for authority within religious structures. In MUDs, these immortals are the basis for order so that players, by looking to the designated authorities for assistance and guidance, are in this virtual culture functioning in a way that is similar to real-world convention. The representation of deity becomes transformed within the social structure of MUDs, but the symbolism remains the same.

The creators of the MUD universe, the implementors, the coders, the gods and goddesses are now the new functional equivalents of traditional religious gods. These contemporary incarnations have ultimate power in this technological realm. Rusalka, head of player relations on LegendMUD, was always in demand for her knowledge and magical spells. She saved my "life" more than once.

They are a special class of players, serving to both maintain and interepret the rules of order (see table 4). These gods have special powers that allow them to maintain the MUD's cultural integrity, and these powers control the actions of players. The players choose to "live" in the universe these Gods have created, live by their rules, and spend much of their time trying to build on skills and abilities to reach greater achievements, so that they too can attain godlike

---

Table 4. The LegendMUD Cast of Immortals

IMPLEMENTOR OF ORDER	: Kaige
IMPLEMENTOR OF CHAOS	: Ptah
HEAD OF CODING	: Ea!
CODERS	: Rufus
ASSISTANT CODERS	: Tad, Snapper, Govan, Chocorua
HEAD OF ADMINISTRATION	: Sandra
ADMINISTRATION	: Bart, Zandy, Chocorua, Govan, Leila, Baca
ASSISTANT ADMIN	: Wraith, Flagg, ParticleMan, Solomon, Aermid
HEAD OF BUILDING	:
BUILDERS	: Rufus, Flagg, Wraith, Kheldar, Deanna
ASSISTANT BUILDERS	: Bart, Alhazred, LadyAce, Leila
HEAD OF PLAYER RELATIONS	: Rusalka
PLAYER RELATIONS LIAISONS	: Flagg, Spencer, Croaker, Leila, ParticleMan
PR LIASONS	: Petal
ASSISTANT PR LIAISONS	: Bart, Satsu
INACTIVE IMMORTS	: Breton, Clutch, Dominic, Gail,
	: Ganelon, Greyscot, Hunter_Rose, Joule,
	: Lirra, Matrix, Sabella
EMERITUS IMPLEMENTORS	: Sadist & Charity
	(Without these two, LegendMUD wouldn't be what it is today.)

These people are the administrators of this Mud, followed by a very simple explanation of their duties. Any questions you have may be directed toward the appropriate immort. You can type HELP IMMORT after lvl 45 for info on how to get on this wizlist.

stature, nirvana, oneness with the Creator(s). One can be transformed into a god only by other gods. The divine plan can be compared to a computer program. The gods are the equivalent of system administrators. Cyberspace itself is equated with heaven, and the soul's nourishment is equated with information (O'Leary 1996).

MUDs can be seen as an abstracted form of religion by analyzing the concept of virtual ritual. "Liturgical ritual or prayer usually consists of a group of people performing a series of actions and/or speaking, chanting, or singing the same sentences simultaneously" (Kinney 1995, 773). Although MUDders are not physically located in one place, they are together virtually as a community. Individuals telnet from their own machines into the same address and join these communities of believers that exist only through their computers. These are social virtual realities, the sharing of one space simultaneously (Turkle 1996). Just like Foucault's "heterotopias," MUDs are capable of "juxtaposing in a single real place several spaces, several sites that are in themselves incom-

---

Table 5. Building a New Character

[1] Connect to a character
[2] Establish a new character
[3] Connect as a guest
[0] Exit

[4] Request introductory docs
[5] List immortals online who can help
[6] Read about LegendMUD

Enter your choice or the name of your character: 2
Enter the name of your character: Jael
You will be known as Jael. Is this correct? Y
Please enter password for Jael:
Please verify your password: ****
Is your character male of female? F
The possible hometowns and their eras are:

[1] Arabian Nights
[3] Viceroyal Lima, Peru
[5] Port of London, 1841

[2] Celtic Ireland
[4] Medieval Germany, 1150 A.D.

[?] How hometown choice affects your character's career
[H] Help menu for individual hometowns

Where did you spend the formative years of your life? 1

The physical and mental attributes inherent to characters are:

1. Strength
2. Mind

3. Dexterity
4. Constitution

5. Perception
6. Spirit

Place your attributes in order of importance from highest to lowest—they must all be on one line with no spaces between, as 123456 or 132465. (Note! Those would probably both make terrible characters!)

Enter ? followed by number (for example enter ?2) to get information on how that stat affects your character's development.

patible" (Foucault 1986, 25). The MUD brings a whole series of places and people into one space. MUDs do become true communities, where participants share a consensus about a common and usually esoteric language, time, space, and appropriate standards of behavior.

In MUDland, all new MUDders are known as "newbies," or as Victor Turner would define them, neophytes, because they are liminal entities (Turner 1995). On LegendMUD, newbies begin by creating the virtual character (see table 5), giving it a name, specifying the gender of the character, the hometown era of the character, what attributes they wish the character to have (e.g., strength, mind, dexterity, constitution, perception, spirit). They construct their characters socially and linguistically. Through the sharing of real-time space, they build their identities.

As neophytes, they start with no power or stutus, no kinship systems or property. A neophyte or newbie is a "blank slate, on which is inscribed the knowledge and wisdom of the group, in those respects that pertain to the new status" (Turner 1995, 103). In order to grow in this world, each individual must learn skills, build a memory, encounter liminal situations, and perform certain "rituals" of entry in order to move forward in power. As a newbie, a player is at level one and is considered "clueless." As players acquire knowledge, they gain experience and levels up to fifty (after many hours invested into my character and the MUD community, I was able to reach level 41 out of 50). Then they are capable of joining those players with special powers or becoming immortalized. In MUDs, knowledge *is* power.

LegendMUD is made up of various historical eras, such as the Arabian Nights era (see table 6), Celtic Ireland, and Medieval Germany. In order to move from one historical era to the next, the liminal player must learn the secrets built into the MUD by wise predecessors, and perform the proper ritual or "rites of passage" in order to gain access. To get to ancient Arabia from Sherwood Forest, the player must find the rabbit, find a carrot so that it will follow, and at a particular place kill the rabbit as an offering. Then the player must sit and "ponder" before being transported, mirroring the act of self-reflection, similar to the liminal period of the "rites of passage" described by Turner in which the passengers, under ritual exigency, are free to contemplate the mysteries and difficulties of their own society (Turner 1995). The liminal situation is attributed with magico-religious properties, because it is dangerous to the newbie who has not been ritually incorporated into the liminal context of the MUD. If newbies do not follow the prohibitions and conditions set out, their personas

Table 6. LegendMUD Arabian Nights Era Description
The Agrabah Camela Inn
You stand before the counter. Rows and rows of keys line the wall behind the desk and a small door leads to the back where the tenants stay. A small sign is posted on the wall. A door leads out and onto the porch.
[Exits: s]
A well used map is lying here.
A mailbox sits in the corner.
The welcome board is standing in the corner here.
A lamp lies dropped here.
Asabi stands here in front of a board with many room keys hanging on it.
Jael enters the game.
On the Porch of the Agrabah Camela Inn
You are on the stoop of a reputable looking inn, despite the name. All of the locals have recommended it to you. The windows look wide and airy, and you hear they don't charge outrageous fees. The main square in town is to the southeast with a large fountain at its center. A sign hangs above the door of the inn. Steps lead down to the street level.
[Exits: n e s d]
A clean-cut youth minds his own business here.
Mikulu is LINK-DEAD is standing here.
A camel is here looking quite bored and ready for a nap.
A youthful child has arrived from the north.
The Palace Walk
You can see a good bit of the palace, although it still is partially obscured by the buildings that line the street.
[Exits: e w u]
A smudged unkempt woman looks at you pleadingly.
A scruffy mutt is here scratching for fleas.

are likely to be killed, and they lose all their property, equipment, and status, thereby remaining a liminal entity: neither here nor there. In order to locate a position in the cultural space of the MUD, the player must pass the rites set out to be inducted into this society.

Although these rituals are thoroughly and completely textual, the creation of these performative rituals through keyboards, screens, and modems *includes* traditional meanings of ritual in terms of situated action, as a dogma involving chant, gestures, and props. They are textual simulations, but their existence is necessary for the ritual to occur. In MUDs, the body is the mind, and the command is not just a word that describes an existing state of things, but rather creates a new relationship, social arrangement, or entitlement. These are instances where speech (through screens) *is* doing (O'Leary 1996). The MUD itself becomes a transformative experience that "goes to the root of each person's being and finds in that root something profoundly communal and shared" (Turner 1995, 138).

Without knowledge of this ritual, a player remains trapped in the one era and is denied access to the rest of the MUDland. Without accomplishing the "rites of passage," players cannot change their social position and therefore remain outside of the MUD social structure, or on its margins, and cannot rise from its lowest rungs. These rituals can be considered sacred moments in time for the player, moments of revelation and inspiration outside of the temporal flow. They liberate the devotee from time's constraints. Without these "rites of passage," there cannot be a cultural manifestation of community. In order to maintain the structure of the MUD, players must follow the prescriptions, prohibitions, and conditions of this community, which has been built through its own language, law, and custom (Turner 1995). Such rituals bond the players together because all have acquired knowledge that will assist them in their path to higher attainment, through shared beliefs, symbols, and mutual agreements. Within the MUD, some players band together and share the experience of these rituals, thereby assisting each other in gaining power. Many maintain virtual relationships, and even hold marriage and death ceremonies in this virtual universe. MUD community can be seen as the Durkheimian notion of "solidarity," the force of which depends upon an in-group/out-group contrast.

Such rituals can be readily found within real-world cultures. For instance, in the Catholic tradition, the concept of confession is highly ritualized. One must be within that culture to be able to partake in that ritual, must know the proper wordings and actions (e.g., "Forgive me father for I have sinned"), and must accept and follow the judgment of the priest in order to be spiritually elevated. As Victor Turner states, "Both normative and ideological *communitas* are already within the domain of structure and it is the fate of all spontaneous *communitas* in history to undergo what most people see as the 'decline and fall' into structure and law" (Turner 1995, 132). This makes the MUD culture as real a place as can be found in the physical world.

Some even compare the workings of the computer to the principle of the magic word. The commands typed into a computer are considered a kind of "sacred" speech that doesn't communicate but rather makes things happen, directly. They can be viewed as incantations, and anyone within the movement who has the knowledge then has the ability to perform this magic. The logic of the incantation can be seen permeating the fabric of society (Dibbell 1997). Just as the sacred words "This is my body" authorized and commanded by Christ become literally true for the Catholic believer, the act of "utterance" on the MUD effects what it describes, therefore creating a manifestation of the word. The word, in MUD culture, causes something to happen, thereby cre-

ating a new relationship. The word functions as a bridge between visible textual objects and spiritual reality. The passage from lower to higher status occurs
through magic rituals, and therefore a sacred component is acquired by the
"incumbents of positions during the *rites of passage* through which they changed
positions" (Turner 1995, 95). Just as religion has highly spiritual rituals, MUDs
replicate status in the same way. This knowledge is kept within the culture and
not shared with nonbelievers. Both, in their own ways, remain closed societies.
Only through adherence and belief in each can one learn the canons of the
culture, and thereby acquire knowledge, which leads to power.

For those who invest time in these virtual systems, the MUD is not a space
of anonymity and inconsequentiality, but rather is a marked and different social
location. There is an image of this "place" and a sensory perception of time in
the user's mind (one day on the MUD is twenty minutes, and there is the "sensation" of day and night), and although it is outside of *all* places, the player can
locate it in reality (Foucault 1986). Radcliffe-Brown would deem the player a
"persona," therefore only a role-mask and not the unique individual (Turner
1974). But the virtual persona in the MUD becomes more than role play: "it
becomes an extension of select aspects of the self, the uninhibited, the altruis-
tic, the superhuman, an identity considered more authentic because of liberation from the flesh" (Leeson 1996, 80). It becomes a concrete individual
within the social structure of the MUD.

Although the anonymous nature of the Internet and its secularity would
seem to allow traditional ideals to be challenged or removed, this cultural plat-
form in fact continues to support traditional norms and values of religion.
MUDs, like religions, have their own "orthodoxy and heresies, canonical myths,
professions of faith, and rites of communion and excommunication" (Chidester
1996, 748). Investment in a network identity gives members incentive for communal behavior and beliefs. Through these beliefs, they can acquire knowledge
and power.

Although secular culture tends to ignore the claims of religious (e.g., Christian) dogma, the old traditions are not easily discarded. "They survive in the
communicative cultures to which they gave birth, which may still fairly be
labeled as 'Catholic' and 'Protestant' with regard to their aesthetic conventions
and conceptions of language if not to the substantive content of their beliefs"
(O'Leary 1996, 792).

Social behavior on MUDs can be seen as direct reflections of behaviors in
real life, using mechanisms drawn nearly unchanged from real life (Curtis
1996). As religious beliefs and symbols translate into contemporary expressions

(such as cyberspace), their meaning is profoundly altered along with the medium. These symbols have found new functional equivalents in the idioms of technological culture (O'Leary 1996). MUDs may be regarded as forms of nontraditional religions, as well as a continuity of tradition which has been adapted and mutated to survive in this new communicative environment. It is a place where people experience community, through the re-creation of familiar places and social structures.

In fact, it has been said that cyberspace is the place alluded to by the mystical teachings of every religion because it is unlimited by the rules of linear time and physical reality. The development of the "datasphere can be translated as the hardwiring of the global brain." Cyberia can be imagined as the final stage of development of "oneness," but only for those who are faithful believers in the institution (Rushkoff 1994, 5).

Although this technological culture is a new invention, it is possible to see the transformation of old systems incorporated into this new form of discourse. The mores of tradition continue through the collective gatherings, symbols, rituals, and conceptions of the general order of existence in the MUD culture. Communication now has no limitations of time or space, of personality or body. As cyberspace alters the context in which we relate to the world, it should lead us to wonder what role our world plays when we relate to cyberspace.

REFERENCES

Chidester, David. 1996. "The Church of Baseball, the Fetish of Coca-Cola, and the Potlatch of Rock 'n' Roll: Theoretical Models for the Study of Religion in American Popular Culture." *Journal of American Academy of Religion* 54, 4: 743–66.

Clausen, Christopher. 1996. "Welcome to Post-Culturalism." *The American Scholar* 65, 3: 379–89.

Dibbell, Julian. 1997. "A Rape in Cyberspace: How an Evil Clown, a Haitian Trickster Spirit, Two Wizards, and a Cast of Dozens Turned a Database into a Society." In *Internet Dreams: Archetypes, Myths and Metaphors*, ed. Mark Stefik. Cambridge: MIT Press.

Foucault, Michel. 1986. "Of Other Spaces." *Diacritics* 16: 22–26.

Helgert, Joseph, and Alexander Nesterenko. 1993. *The Future of Text-based Virtual Reality*.

FTP: Seraphim@umcc.umich.edu: Grand Valley State University.

Kinney, Jay. 1995. "Net Worth: Religion, Cyberspace and the Future." *Futures* 27, 7: 763–76.

Leeson, Lynn Hershman. 1996. "Joicho and Mizuko Ito Interview." In *Clicking In: Hot Links to a Digital Culture*, ed. Lynn Hershman Leeson. Seattle: Bay Press.

O'Leary, Stephen D. 1996. "Cyberspace as Sacred Space: Communicating Religion on Computer Networks." *Journal of the American Academy of Religion* 54, 4: 781–808.

Rushkoff, Douglas. 1994. *Cyberia: Life in the Trenches of Hyperspace*. San Francisco: Harper San Francisco.

Smith, Jennifer. 1996. *Frequently Asked Questions: Basic Information about MUDs and MUDding*. Http://www.cis.ohio-state.edu/hyptertext/faq/usenet/games/mud-faq/part1/faq.html: Ohio State University.

Turkle, Sherry. 1996. "Rethinking Identity through Virtual Community." In *Clicking In: Hot Links to a Digital Culture*, ed. Lynn Hershman Leeson. Seattle: Bay Press.

Turner, Victor. 1974. *Dramas, Fields, and Metaphors: Symbolic Action in Human Society*. Ithaca, N.Y.: Cornell University Press.

———. 1995. *The Ritual Process: Structure and Anti-Structure*. New York: Aldine de Gruyter.

Rap Music, Hip-Hop Culture, and "The Future Religion of the World"

ROBIN SYLVAN

Since rap music and hip-hop culture first emerged from the South Bronx in the late 1970s, critics have dismissed them as a superficial fad that would quickly fade and be relegated to the dustbin of history. Over the course of the last two decades, however, this kind of perjorative assessment has been proved wrong time and time again, as rap has consistently dominated the music industry and hip-hop sensibility has become part and parcel of mainstream American popular culture. The most recent case in point is the enormous success of female rapper Lauryn Hill's album *The Miseducation of Lauryn Hill* (1998), which topped the charts at number one for weeks, sold several million copies, and won numerous Grammies. Or perhaps one might channel surf the television to find rap music and hip-hop styles in commercials for everything from McDonald's hamburgers to Pringles potato chips to Mervyn's department store. This is an extraordinary trajectory for an African-American musical subculture that began in what is arguably the most economically and culturally marginalized neighborhood of the country.

What is even more remarkable about the success of rap and hip-hop is that it still contains a powerful and distinctive African-American religious worldview that runs directly counter to the religious worldview of the mainstream culture it has come to permeate. Faced with the oppressive historical circumstances of African Americans' marginalized status, this religious worldview refuses to take refuge in the hope of otherworldly salvation but, rather, tells the truth about the harsh reality of this oppression and transforms the impulse toward anger and violence into empowerment, creative expression, spirituality, and positive change. Here I will look at the contradictory dynamics of hip-hop's rise to mainstream success—its historical and cultural development, its West African and African-American roots, and its spiritual dimensions—and explore the important implications for the larger landscape of religion in American popular culture.

"OLD SCHOOL": CULTURAL AND MUSICAL HISTORY

Rap music emerged as one component of hip-hop, a new street culture that included graffiti and break dancing as important forms of expression. The music for rap was put together by DJs mixing stripped-down, bass-heavy, polyrhythmic beats from turntables and samplers, drawing heavily on roots in soul, funk, and disco. This new style of sonic collage quickly became the soundtrack for street parties and "ghetto blasters" (portable tape players) throughout the Bronx. But the term "rap" actually refers to the rhyming poetry that the lead vocalist would improvise on the microphone in rhythm to the beats. Raps were spoken as well as sung, and they featured the rapper's prowess in turning a phrase. This prowess could take the form of innovative rhyming, rhythmic dexterity, boasting, humor, narrative storytelling, or even preaching. The subjects of the raps reflected the grim reality of young African Americans' life in the ghetto: racism, poverty, broken families, substandard housing, unemployment, violence, drugs, gangs, police brutality, arrests, incarceration, and short life expectancy.

Innovative DJs like Kool Herc and Afrika Bambaataa used their turntable mixing skills to create the first beat-driven sonic collages that form the foundation of rap music. These were originally dance mixes for neighborhood parties in houses, parks, and community centers. These pioneering hip-hop DJs not only drew heavily on soul and funk recordings, but also used the new technologies of the cross-fade mixer, the sampler, and the drum machine. Songs were segued seamlessly into each other for a continuous dance mix. At the same time, the breaks in each song and between songs—those places where the instrumentation would pull back to highlight the rhythm section—were emphasized and extended in a collage of peak dance beats. These became known as "break beats" or "b-beats," and DJ Kool Herc was their acknowledged master. The wild athletic dancing that accompanied these break beats became known as "break dancing," and the male break dancers became known as "break boys" or "b-boys" for short. Hip-hop DJs also developed new skills on the turntables which strongly contributed to the distinctive rap sound. Foremost among these was "scratching," a technique in which the DJ used his hand to quickly spin the record back and forth under the needle, thus producing a quirky staccato rhythm. Another technique was "backspinning," in which the DJ isolated a short verbal or musical phrase on a record, and repeated it by quickly spinning back to the beginning. One of the early creators and masters of both the scratch and the backspin was Grandmaster Flash. Both of these techniques produced cross-rhythms on one turntable while the other supplied the main groove, a clearly polyrhythmic approach to musical composition. Samplers also allowed DJs to bring a wide assortment of sound sources into their eclectic pastiches.

Kool Herc and Afrika Bambaataa each had his own group of neighborhood friends, known as their "crew" or "posse," who hung out with them and accompanied them to all their jams. Thus, rap music grew out of specific neighborhoods and local communities, each developing their own distinctive styles. Often, there were competitions between DJs and their crews for territory, both physical and sonic, in which DJs would exhibit their mixing prowess and b-boys would display their dance moves. These competitions closely paralleled the territoriality of street gangs but with one notable difference—there was no violence. Instead, the crews channeled their competitive energies into artistic expression, choosing a creative outlet rather than a destructive one. Afrika Bambaataa was a pioneer in making explicit the connection between these hip-hop crews and a sense of African identity and spiritual pride. Bambaataa, whose name means "affectionate leader" in Zulu, called his crew "Zulu Nation," and created an extended family unified not only by hip-hop expression but also by a positive vision of African-American community.

The raps themselves began with the DJs calling out on microphones over the music to exhort the audience to dance harder, repeating phrases like "rock the house," "get down," or "you don't stop." Because DJ mixing is a demanding task requiring full concentration, however, soon they brought in friends to work the microphone full time. Here again, DJ Kool Herc was an innovator in being among the first to use an MC (microphone controller or master of ceremonies). The MCs not only gave the parties more of a live feel, but they also fulfilled the important task of crowd control, maintaining a positive feeling, and keeping potential violence at bay. Very quickly, the MCs developed their own creative styles, using the latest slang and hippest rhymes to supplant the DJ as the focal point of the music. The competitive aspect shifted over to the rappers as well, as MCs dueled on the microphone trying to show who was the best rhymer.

In these early days of rap, roughly 1974 to 1978, it was still primarily an underground party phenomenon. This changed with the successful release of three seminal rap records—the Sugar Hill Gang's "Rapper's Delight" in 1979, Grandmaster Flash and the Furious Five's "The Message" in 1982, and Afrika Bambaataa's "Planet Rock" in 1983—which quickly established the commercial viability of rap. In 1986, Run-DMC completed Rap's crossover to mainstream popularity when their single "Walk This Way" hit number one on the charts. Articles on rap began to appear in bastions of mainstream journalism like the *New York Times* and *Time* magazine. Run-DMC's crossover paved the way for the commercial success of other rap artists like LL Cool J, Eric B. and

Rahim, Public Enemy, and Salt 'n Pepa, one of the few prominent women rap groups. At the same time, vibrant local rap subcultures emerged in other urban centers around the country, including Miami, Boston, Houston, Oakland, and Los Angeles, each with its own distinctive sound and style.

Artists like Public Enemy and KRS-One made a strong push toward a more hard-core musical sound and a more militant political message. In combining an unflinching critique of contemporary black oppression with a visionary call to resistance and liberation, Public Enemy and KRS-One have continued and updated a long-standing African-American musico-religious tradition of truth telling, an approach hip-hop scholar Angela Spence Nelson has called "combative spirituality" (Nelson 1991, 59).

The hard-core sound was to attain its greatest success, however, with the ascendancy of the Los Angeles area "gangsta" rap subculture in the late 1980s and early 1990s. The word "gangsta" is a reference to the centrality of gang activities among African-American and Hispanic youth in Los Angeles, which includes some of the worst crime and violence in the country and an underground economy largely based on crack cocaine. In areas like South Central Los Angeles, gang violence is commonplace, and the panicked response of white authorities has resulted in the creation of a virtual police state with its own violent excesses. The brutal beating of Rodney King by Los Angeles police, the acquittal of the responsible officers, and the subsequent riots on the streets gave an indication of the high level of hatred and tension in the area. It was out of this tableau of economic despair, gang violence, the crack epidemic, and police repression that gangsta rap emerged. The seminal gangsta group was N.W.A. (Niggaz With Attitude), whose 1988 album *Straight Outta Compton*, with its in-your-face attitude, funky West Coast sound, and gritty tales of violent gang life, sold more than two million copies. N.W.A.'s stylistic and commercial breakthrough opened the door for a number of other Los Angeles–area gangsta rap artists to attain success, including Ice-T, Snoop Doggy Dogg, and original N.W.A. members Ice Cube and Dr. Dre as solo artists.

The post–gangsta rap era has seen a new generation of rap artists break through to mainstream success as the market share of rap music has more than doubled in the last decade. In the last few years, in addition to Lauryn Hill, artists like Puff Daddy, Wu-Tang Clan, DMX, Master P, Jay-Z, Mase, and Eminem, to mention just a few, have all had their run at the top of the charts. Far from being a passing fad, rap music has proved its staying power over the course of the last two decades and has steadily grown in influence to become a permanent fixture in the mainstream world of popular culture. The fact that hip-hop is a primarily African-American subculture with strong roots in West African practices and sensibilities makes its penetration of mainstream popular culture an even more significant development from a religious perspective.

POETRY, POLYRHYTHMS, POSSESSION, AND PROPHETIC TRADITION: WEST AFRICAN AND AFRICAN-AMERICAN ROOTS

> We've been rapping forever. You know, there's nothing new under the sun. The griots were doing the same, the storytellers, oral tradition people.... And the drum's also the center of it. You can't have it without the drum. And now hip-hop is experimenting, trying new things, but really the beat is what's always. It's the drums, just like drums in any form. That's definitely African. (Malcolm 1997)

In the course of doing research in the San Francisco Bay area in 1997, I had the opportunity to spend some time in the East Bay hip-hop community known as the Oakland Underground, attending musical events and conducting interviews with aficionados. Time and again in these interviews, I was struck by the explicit recognition and conscious acknowledgment of the African roots of rap and hip-hop. These roots can be traced back more specifically to two West African geographical and cultural zones: the coastal forest belt cultures like the Ga, Ewe, Fon, and Yoruba of modern Ghana, Togo, Benin, and Nigeria; and the Sahelian cultures of the Manding, Wolof, and Peul of modern Senegal, Gambia, Guinea, Mali, and Burkina Faso.

One of the primary religious complexes in the coastal forest belt is that of possession dances, sacred ceremonies in which drum ensembles and singers supply beat-driven polyrhythmic music and the initiates dance themselves into ecstatic trance states in which the gods take possession of their bodies, becoming physically present among the community for the purposes of counseling, healing, divination, and so forth. Many of the distinctive elements of this complex made their way to the Americas through the slave trade and became important components of African-American music and religion, albeit in significantly changed forms. Rap displays strong continuities with a number of these elements. Musically, one finds the centrality of rhythm as an organizing principle, with the elements of harmony and melody stripped down almost completely. The groove is generated from interlocking polyrhythms, and even though the constituent parts are sampled or prerecorded, they operate in the same way as live drumming. As one rapper said: "That is what, to me, makes hip-hop. It's got the rhythmic conversation of the drum and the rhythmic conversation of the bass" (King 1997). Another musician put it this way: "I'm pretty much focusing on the groove. . . . If it's a great groove, then . . . that really is the bottom line" (Williams 1997). And this polyrhythmic groove provides a connection to the ancestors, expressed thus: "Our ancestors are still calling. And the break beats we used in the beginning are still from God, still ally [sic] your soul" (Guerrero 1997).

The interconnection between music and dance is also central, as is evident in the importance of break dancing in the early hip-hop subculture. Many of the hip-hop aficionados I interviewed said that break dancing was their initial entry point into the music: "I was taking the energy of the beat and then just amplifying it through my movement. Like making the music almost seem like it was coming more intensely by seeing what I'm doing, or by me feeling what I'm doing, it seemed like the music became more intense" (Gaines 1997). Some of these intensified states contain strong echoes of the possession experience:

> What I felt as a kid was strictly vibration, rhythm, and that music has a rhythm that just called my soul. It would make my soul jump out of my body, literally, and I'd have to move to it. . . . It really calls me, it really does. . . . Sometimes my body does things I can't even control and it's like I'm not even here. . . . It's just a link. Something touches you one day, just sparks your whole consciousness, and shows your body you can. Time and space is all about the rhythm in your body. . . . It's the ancients. It's definitely the ancients. (Guerrero 1997)

Interestingly, the circular form of break dancing, and even some of its dance moves, shows a striking similarity to African-American musico-religious dances like the ring shout, the Afro-Brazilian martial art capoeira, and traditional West African dances. The movements can also take the form of call and response, another classic element of African music, with the rapper's calls to "put your hands in the air" evoking an audience response of enthusiastic hand waving. These interactions demonstrate the participatory nature of the medium as well, another important principle of African music.

What is especially distinctive about rap music's continuities with West African and African-American musical principles, however, is the rap itself and its prominent foregrounding of an oral mode of expression, the roots of which are more closely associated with the Sahelian cultures of West Africa. These cultures have a long and distinguished lineage of men's societies of court poets and musicians called *jalis*, known as griots in the West, who maintained complex oral traditions of praise, lineage, and celebration. Many of the *jalis's* pieces were extremely long and had to be memorized; others were improvised on the spot for the specific occasion. In either case, a high level of oral skill was required. In these West African cultures, the spoken word was seen as potent and sacred, having the power to evoke that which was being spoken. This supernatural power of the spoken word was called *nommo*. This ancient power is something that hip-hop aficionados are able to recognize in today's raps: "Some people I hear, and it sounds like a long time ago. . . . These are words of power, like certain words, like positive suggestions of just certain frequencies of sounds" (Gaines 1997).

This emphasis on the potency of the spoken word and the oral tradition was to continue after the slave trade brought many of these West Africans to the Americas. During slave times, in the context of plantations especially, the oral tradition manifested itself in more secular forms such as the work song and the plantation tale (e.g., Brer Rabbit or Stagger Lee), as well as in rhyming jokes and singing games. Yet, these secular forms preserved elements of the sacred traditions in a way that allowed them to continue in a transformed way. The Christian church, as the only officially legitimized context for religious expression allowed to the slaves, was also an important repository for the oral tradition. This was particularly evident in the preaching style of African American ministers, who relied heavily on rhythm, rhyme, and the skillful use of other rhetorical techniques to raise energy and to give the message greater potency.

The oral tradition continued to evolve in the postemancipation era, becoming a significant component in both the major forms of African-American secular music—blues and jazz—not so much in the music itself as in the lingo of the subcultures. As African Americans moved from rural southern areas to northern cities, oral expression took the form of urban street talk, which had a more boastful, aggressive quality. Thus, practices like sounding, woofing, jiving, signifying, rapping, and telling toasts were raised to high levels of prowess on the city streets in a friendly but competitive atmosphere. Some highwater marks of this oral artistry include the Harlem Renaissance and the poet Langston Hughes, black radio DJs in the 1940s and 1950s, and the game of ritual insult called "the dozens." The Reverend Martin Luther King Jr. captivated the nation in the 1960s with the visionary fervor of his preaching style. Malcolm X also had a powerful oral style which strongly affected the African-American community in the 1960s. And the flamboyant and controversial boxing champion Muhammad Ali, widely idolized among African Americans, exposed the whole world to his boastful, humorous rhyming.

But perhaps the most important trailblazers for contemporary rap were the poet Gil Scott-Heron and the ensemble the Last Poets. Active during the late 1960s and early 1970s, the Last Poets were a group of black militant storytellers and poets who used the rhythms of conga drums to accompany their spoken political raps. Scott-Heron's brilliant work, including famous pieces like *The Revolution Will Not Be Televised* and *This Is Madness*, was innovative and influential, not only for its marriage of spoken raps with rhythmic grooves, but also for its unabashedly hard-hitting political message. Scott-Heron and the Last Poets were a source of inspiration for many key figures in the first generation of rappers, so much so that some consider them to be "the godfathers of message rap" (Perkins 1991, 42).

There is one more vitally important African-American influence on rap that must be noted, that of the blues, arguably the most quintessential of African-American musics. While there are certainly *musical* continuities among African traditions, the blues, and rap, the continuity of concern here is that of worldview or theology, particularly with respect to the oppressive historical circumstances of Africans in the New World. The Christian theology adopted by many African-American churches sought to escape the hardships of suffering in this world by placing their faith in deliverance in the next. In contrast, the blues refused to look away from the suffering experienced as former slaves in the African diaspora, and sought a measure of whatever this worldly redemption could be achieved through embodied sexuality and solidarity within the African-American community. As theologian James Cone eloquently writes:

> The blues are a lived experience, an encounter with the contradictions of American society, but a refusal to be conquered by it. They are despair only in the sense that there is no attempt to cover up reality. The blues recognize that black people have been hurt and scarred by the brutalities of white society. But there is also hope in what Richard Wright calls the "endemic capacity to live." This hope provided the strength to survive, and also an openness to the intensity of life's pains without being destroyed by them. ... That black people could sing the blues, describing their joys and sorrows, meant that they were able to affirm an authentic hope in the essential worth of black humanity. (1992, 96–97)

There is such a strong similarity between this blues theology and that of hip-hop that this quote could well be a description of the worldview of today's rappers, a continuity that has been noted by hip-hop scholars:

Contemporary rappers, like early bluespeople, are responding to the "burden of freedom," in part by relaying portrayals of reality to their audiences through their personal experiences. They also relay positive portrayals of themselves as a means of affirming their personhood (and vicariously the personhood of their people) in a world that is constantly telling them they are nobodies. (Nelson 1991, 56)

Rap music can be a profound extension of the prophetic or blues tradition and the legacy of heroism within the African-American experience. (Craddock-Willis 1989, 37)

In addition to theology, there is a strong continuity in the priestly role of the bluesman and the rapper as well, one which also has important religious implications. Ethnomusicologist Charles Keil writes:

In spite of the fact that blues singing is ostensibly a secular, even profane, form of expression, the role is intimately related to sacred roles in the Negro community. . . . As professions, blues singing and preaching seem to be closely linked in both the rural or small-town setting and in the urban ghettos. We have already noted some of the stylistic common denominators that underlie the performance of both roles, and it is clear that the experiences which prepare one for adequately fulfilling either role overlap extensively. (1966)

As I will show in the next section, this priestly function is consciously recognized by rappers and traced back through its African-American articulation to its West African roots. This conscious recognition of the African-American and West African roots of rap and hip-hop is a feature of their considerable religious quality, which demonstrates an extraordinary tenacity and adaptability in not just surviving five centuries of oppressive history but emerging strong in a vibrant new formulation of these traditions.

HIP-HOP SPIRITUALITY

Hip-hop has been represented in mainstream media primarily by the gangsta rap image of dangerous black youth—angry, violent, and destructive. Yet, in my interviews with members of the Oakland Underground, they consistently claimed that hip-hop was exactly the opposite for them—peaceful, loving, inclusive, spiritual, and a force for positive change. This seeming contradiction has been a part of hip-hop culture since its South Bronx origins in the late 1970s, and understanding the dynamics of the dialectical relationship between these two polarities is central to understanding hip-hop's essential nature. To begin with, the situation of young African Americans and Latinos in inner-city ghettos is, as noted at the outset, one of racism, poverty, broken families, substandard housing, unemployment, violence, drugs, gangs, police brutality, arrests, incarceration, and short life expectancy. So, for any form of expression to have credibility, it must address that situation head-on, much as the blues did. In this regard, as Chuck D of Public Enemy has said, rap is black urban youth's CNN, providing information about what's going on in their world. This was a function confirmed in my interviews:

> Hip-hop music is always speaking to me, the lyrics. Especially in the late eighties, there were some real conscious things in hip-hop, and that was what was offsetting high school education, mainstream society, with all the information I was getting from KRS One and Public Enemy and X-Clan, all those groups. So, I just needed it at the time. We all needed it. They were speaking to me and educating me. I know they were. And I felt it. I needed it. It came at the right time. (Malcolm 1997)

In addition to providing information and educating, the raps also serve a crucial function of truth-telling: "It's very important to speak about how you really feel about something. . . . This is one of the first times in music where you can really say what's going on. . . . It's very honest. There's a lot of references to whatever's happening right now" (King 1997). There is a deeper spiritual aspect of this truth telling beyond simply educating and informing:

> One thing about rapping is always that you've got to come with your heart, who you are. And whatever that be, whether it be L.A. gangster music or New York "righteous" music or anti-government music, whatever. It's all about coming from your heart, saying what you believe in. Whether it was Ice Cube or Chuck D, it was just the spirit there. That's what was attractive, beyond the word itself, because you knew it was coming from the heart, for real. (Malcolm 1997)

In coming from the heart and speaking their truth, rappers are also speaking for their larger community. As one aficionado put it: "There is a culture of people who feel the voices of [rappers] represent them" (King 1997). *Represent* is a word widely used by rappers to describe their function. Some take the implications of this even further and explicitly make the connection to the role of the priest and the griot:

> MCs are like the priests or the pastors of the people right now because a lot of children don't listen to their parents anymore. A lot of kids don't go to church anymore. So, MCs have been elevated to this recognizable status that's easily accessible. It's our duty as MCs to try to bring morals to the community, just like the griots in Africa brought morals and they try to pass down things that were basic... and that's like the role of MCs today. (Gaines 1997)

It is important to remember that the first South Bronx hip-hop crews of innovators like DJ Kool Herc and Afrika Bambaataa arose as an alternative to gang violence and drugs, channeling the destructive impulse into artistic expression. Awareness of this tradition continues today: "Hip-hop—originally, the dancers, the breaking groups—were this alternative similar to the fighting groups. They were just redirecting that energy. That's what they're still doing right now. You know, the energy's there. It's going to happen, it's going to get out one way or another. Hip-hop culture, to me, is one of the best alternatives that I've seen" (Malcolm 1997). This, then, is the source of hip-hop culture's seemingly paradoxical valuing of morality and spirituality at the same time it expresses anger and violent impulses—it alleviates the anger by providing a positive alternative direction to channel that energy:

> What it does for me is it calms my soul and all the struggle. I have a lot of anger in me from my ancestors and expressing it through music really gives me a venue. It's like God gave me a gift and He said, "I know that if I don't give you this gift, you're going to do a lot of crazy stuff." So I accept this gift, and I'm still struggling with it because there's a lot of bad things I want to do still, you know. But the music keeps me centered on what I'm here for. (Guerrero 1997)

And what is it that they are here for? Not anger and violence and destructiveness, but peace and love and spirituality. "One of the basic premises [of hip-hop culture] being based in peace and love for everyone, that also appealed to me. I just got absorbed into it. So, that's one of the messages that you got from hanging out in the scene" (Mena 1997).

> Hip-hop's always been a spiritual culture. To me, it's just the mainstream doesn't let that show.... I went to something called the B-Boy Summit in San

Diego... and that was just one of the most spiritual things I've ever been to as far as all young people, all different colors, connected by this culture, hip-hop. All peace and love, you know. I mean, the exact oppposite of what they'd have you think. ... To me, that's what hip-hop is all about. It always has been, that kind of thread, that spiritual thread running through the culture. (Malcolm 1997)

This peace and love spirituality is not simply superficial sloganeering, but something that must be put into practice amid the difficulties of daily life. As one rapper put it: "It's in my day-to-day everyday.... It's not different from my life. It's what I do. It's just what's in life.... It's just onbeat every day" (Guerrero 1997). In this regard, another rapper was strongly affected by an experience he had listening to the advice of KRS-One:

He said: "These are the practices we need to do. Act like the god that you know. Whatever god you know, act like him. If your god is loving and merciful, be loving and merciful. The things that you want to happen in your life, visualize them in your mind before you go to sleep." And he said something that was profound to me, because after all that attack, he came back with love, saying, "Here's something you can do for yourself regardless of what I'm saying or what you said." I talked to other people afterwards, and they were saying they do something like that every day of their life, and it works. (Gaines 1997)

This theme of hip-hop as spiritual practice emerged time and again in the interviews: "The people that I know, they're really trying to learn some things about themselves and tap into the rest of the spring that we don't use and these spiritual powers.... I've always taken the spiritual power seriously" (Malcolm 1997). "I have to be true to, not just the music and the musics that I'm bringing in, but now there's this religious thing.... I'm trying to reach another level of enlightenment" (Mena 1997).

What it means to me to be a rapper is like, I look around at everything, and everything I absorb is God and I can express that, literally.... So it's really an expression. It's like praying. It's like being with God, literally, like being with God. Hip-hop culture is a spirituality. And it's everything that I can think of. Anything I am that I can do, that happens in this world, it's like that music, it's the culture.... It just gives you a purpose. It shows you why you're here.... It knows that I know God every day.... All those values have become part of the music and now it's in me every day. (Guerrero 1997)

As this last quote shows, one aspect of hip-hop spirituality that allows aficionados to achieve this type of integration into everyday life is the fact that it
is part of a larger hip-hop culture. "Hip-hop is not the music; hip-hop is the
culture. The music is rap music.... And those fuller aspects of hip-hop are
grafitti, break dancing, MC-ing, and DJ-ing" (King 1997). "On a spiritual level,
I think what now I know as hip-hop culture and respect as such [consists of]
the grafitti, the dress, the language, the art, the people, the mindset that's the
commonality of thought" (Mena 1997). So, immersing oneself in hip-hop culture creates connections and links to many different vital aspects of one's life:
"It's just been my link to everything—my own spirituality, my self-knowledge,
and music also.... Everywhere I go, everywhere I grow, starts with hip-hop"
(Malcolm 1997). "It linked me to everything—my future, my past, my family"
(Guerrero 1997). It also creates links among different races, classes, and eth-
nicities, as one rapper observed earlier how "people" of "all different colors"
are "connected by this culture, hip-hop" (Malcolm 1997). This inclusivity of
hip-hop culture is expressed beautifully in this description of one rapper's experience at a concert:

> Everybody in the place was going back and forth at the same time. I remember
> looking back and seeing a whole moving wave of people. And it occurred to me
> how music brings people together. White people, Asian, Latino, black, different
> ages. And there wasn't any difference being noticed. Everybody was one. The
> music was pulling everyone together. (Gaines 1997)

This inclusivity, when combined with hip-hop's power to be a source of political and spiritual awakening in people's lives, leads to a sense that it can be a
vehicle for change in the larger world:

> I see it being one of the major forces in the world bringing about change.... Hip-
> hop culture is worldwide now. It's big in Japan. I know in Germany. And I hear
> from people all the time in places I would never expect—South Africa. Being
> one of the major forces bringing about change, new ways, new types of lifestyles,
> because the old ones, we just can't use them anymore. For young people, that'll
> be our political party.... it's the closest thing we have to that. It includes politics.
> It includes spirituality. It includes music. It includes having a good time. It's
> inclusive of so much.... So, the hope is there in the spirit again, people are
> putting their hope in spirit, you know, God. Not God as an abstract form, but
> God in here and in there, you know. That's what we can use to get out of this

mess. Hip-hop is just one of the manifestations. That's what we call it in the physical world.... To me, music is the future religion of the world. (Malcolm 1997)

This is an extraordinary statement, not only because it describes a significant new hybrid "manifestation" of nontraditional religiosity emerging within popular culture, but also because its hopeful idealism is firmly grounded in the harsh conditions and contradictions of the real world. In concluding this chapter, I will explore the implications for the larger landscape of religion in America.

FUTURE RELIGION OF THE WORLD:
HIGH-TECH UNIVERSALIST POSTMODERN BRICOLAGE
IN POPULAR CULTURE

The means of musical production has always been central not only to the music itself, but to the symbolism of the musical culture. For example, the drum can be seen as the instrument that symbolizes African music, the saxophone as the symbolic instrument for jazz, and the electric guitar as the symbolic instrument for rock. But, when it comes to rap music, the symbol is not an instrument at all, but the DJ's deck of two turntables and a cross-fade mixer. This simple contrast underlines an important point—that the means of musical production in rap has shifted away from traditional instruments to a new generation of electronic technologies. Moreover, this shift in musical technology has effected a corresponding shift in compositional principles. This innovative transformation in both musical technology and compositional form is a distinctive feature of rap that allows it to retain its African-American orientation at the same time that it points the way toward an emerging high-tech postmodern universalism in contemporary popular culture.

Many critics of rap music argue that the DJ is not actually creating new compositions, but simply taking already existing compositions via samplers and turntables and combining them through the mixer. However, it is precisely this ability to take music and sound from a variety of sources and combine them into an integrated whole that constitutes the craft and the musicality of the DJ, what one aficionado has called "the art of collage" (King 1997). According to one DJ, this art "is all about recombinant potential.... Each and every source sample is fragmented and bereft of prior meaning ... [and] given meaning only when re-presented in the assemblage of the mix.... A mix, for me, is a way of providing a rare and intimate glimpse into the process of cultural production in the late 20th Century" (Miller 1996). Thus, the DJ mix is a truly postmodern act of creativity, in which the traditional structures have broken down and new forms have been stitched together from the deconstructed bits and pieces in a high-tech bricolage. This postmodern cut-and-paste bricolage illustrates the universalist inclusivity of hip-hop at a musical level: "Every music made in our last millennium... leads up to hip-hop because it uses every aspect of every music completely.... It's a universal way of connecting all these different styles of music into one thing.... Mixing is like the universal language" (Guerrero 1997). The technology used in the creation of the music—drum machines, cross-fade mixers, samplers, sequencers, computers—reflects this postmodern sensibility as well. Originating in the elite, white, corporate world, these technologies were taken by low-income African Americans, used in entirely different ways, and transformed into a new mode of expression.

These new forms of musical technology and composition serve as analogical templates for a distinctively African-American approach to life in postmodern America that can be a useful model for mainstream culture as well. In her insightful musicological analysis of rap music, Tricia Rose identifies three crucial elements in its sonic architecture: flow, layering, and rupture. She goes on to spell out how these musical structures reflect a hip-hop worldview, philosophy, and code for living:

> These effects at the level of style and aesthetics suggest affirmative ways in which profound social dislocation and rupture can be managed and perhaps contested in the social arena. Let us imagine these hip-hop principles as a blueprint for social resistance and affirmation: create sustaining narratives, accumulate them, layer, embellish, and transform them. However, be also prepared for rupture, find pleasure in it, in fact, *plan on* social rupture. When these ruptures occur, use them in creative ways that will prepare you for a future in which survival will demand a sudden shift in ground tactics. (1994, 39)

As we reach the end of the twentieth century, "profound social dislocation and rupture" appears to be an accurate description not only of the situation facing African Americans, but the situation facing all of us. Global communication and political economics have put an overwhelming array of diverse cultures, technologies, and information at our fingertips at the same time it is destroying long-standing traditions and paradigms. In this regard, hip-hop culture's ability to combine broken pieces into a new integrated whole can indeed serve as a blueprint for everyone in the new millennium.

Observers of culture and scholars of religion have said many things about the slow decline of institutional religion and the death of God in Western civilization. Yet, for the members of the Oakland Underground I interviewed, and hip-hop culture in general, religion and God are not dead, but very much alive and well and dancing to a hip-hop beat. The religious impulse has simply migrated to another sector of the culture, that of popular music, a sector in which religious sensibilities have flourished and made an enormous impression on a significant number of people. It is clear that hip-hop culture is a powerful religious phenomenon and just one example of many musical subcultures that function as religions in the lives of their adherents. Moreover, as the other chapters of this book show, popular music is just one example of many different arenas of popular culture that also function as religions in the lives of their adherents. From the micro to the macro—the Oakland Underground, rap and hip-hop in general, popular music, and popular culture—these new religious forms have already irrevocably changed the lives of millions of people, not only in terms of the texture of day-to-day living, but also in the way they see the world and the social forms that have sprung from those epistemologies. They signal the emergence of a significant alternative religious choice that bypasses the narrow opposition between traditional religious institutions and secular humanism. These are important changes with large implications that should not be underestimated. Moreover, the dynamic and innovative creativity of these new forms of expression indicates that one can expect them to be a source of religious vitality and evolution for generations into the future. To repeat the words of a DJ: "To me, music is the future religion of the world. . . . Hip-hop is just one of the manifestations."

REFERENCES

Cone, James. 1992. "Blues: A Secular Spiritual." *Black Sacred Music: A Journal of Theomusicology* 6, 1 (Spring): 68–97.

Craddock-Willis, Andre. 1989. "Rap Music and the Black Musical Tradition: A Critical Assessment." *Radical America* 23, 4 (October/December): 29–37.

Gaines, Steve. 1997. Interview by author, July 20, Berkeley. Tape recording.

Guerrero, Jorge. 1997. Interview by author, August 6, Berkeley. Tape recording.

Keil, Charles. 1966. *Urban Blues*. Chicago: University of Chicago Press.

King, Paris. 1997. Interview by author, July 3, Oakland. Tape recording.

Malcolm (no last name given). 1997. Interview by author, July 12, Oakland. Tape recording.

Mena, Carlos. 1997. Interview by author, July 17, San Jose. Tape recording.

Miller, Paul D. (a.k.a. DJ Spooky). 1996. Brochure notes from *Songs of a Dead Dreamer*. Asphodel 1961. Compact Disc.

Nelson, Angela Spence. 1991. "Theology in the Hip-Hop of Public Enemy and Kool Moe Dee." *Black Sacred Music: A Journal of Theomusicology* 5, 1 (spring): 51–59.

Perkins, William Eric. 1991. "Nation of Islam Ideology in the Rap of Public Enemy." *Black Sacred Music: A Journal of Theomusicology* 5, 1 (spring): 41–50.

Rose, Tricia. 1994. *Black Noise: Rap Music and Black Culture in Contemporary America*. Middletown, Conn.: Wesleyan University Press.

Stephens, Ronald Jemal. 1991. The Three Waves of Contemporary Rap Music. *Black Sacred Music: A Journal of Theomusicology* 5, 1 (spring): 25–40.

Williams, Keith. 1997. Interview by author, July 4, San Jose. Tape recording.

The Happiest Place on Earth

Disney's America and the Commodification of Religion

ERIC MICHAEL MAZUR AND TARA K. KODA

> Our personnel sincerely sell happiness. Hell! That's what we all want, isn't it?
>
> —Walt Disney

IT REALLY *IS* A SMALL WORLD, AFTER ALL

In a classic commercial, sports celebrities caught after a contest hear a list of their accomplishments and a question: "Now what are you going to do?" Invariably they respond in what seems to be the only way possible in contemporary, commercial America: "I'm going to Disney World!" (see Fjellman 1992, 160).

Indeed, how many millions have neither experienced nor dreamed of participating in "the middle-class hajj, the compulsory visit to the sunbaked holy city," Walt Disney World (Ritzer 1996, 4)? It is just one facet of a global corporation that produces movies and television programs, owns part or all of several other theme parks, television studios and networks, sports teams, housing developments, cruise ships, retail outlets, seminar centers, and training facilities that earned more than $20 billion in 1997 (Miles 1999, 15).[1] One million people visited the California park, Disneyland, in its first seven weeks, and more than four million visited there in 1955–56, its first year of operation (Weinstein 1992, 152). In Florida, ten million visitors in 1971–72 (its first year) placed Walt Disney World ahead of the United Kingdom, Austria, and the former West Germany as a vacation destination, and more popular than the Great Smoky Mountains National Park (seven million visitors), Gettysburg (five million), and Yellowstone National Park (two million). By the beginning of the 1980s, more people visited Walt Disney World than the Eiffel Tower, the Taj Mahal, the Tower of London, or the Pyramids (Fjellman 1992, 136–39). In 1984 alone, the Florida and California parks drew nearly twenty million customers (Lawrence 1986, 65). "Since the number of visitors to both parks together exceeds the number going to Washington, D.C., the official capital," notes Margaret King, the parks could be considered "the popular culture capitals of America" (1981, 117). Appropriately, the Walt Disney World logo depicts the globe as one of three spheres used to silhouette Mickey Mouse's face; it's a small world, after all, and Disney covers it completely. The American who can avoid contact with Disney must live in a cave; to reject Disney is to defy a major global force, and challenges much that is synonymous with contemporary American culture.

But what has this to do with religion?

In contemporary America, many consider all elements of life, even intangibles, as things that can be bought, and religious leaders now find themselves financially burdened competing for congregants' attention. On television or in the pulpit, they offer salvation along with twelve-step programs and child care. They have developed sophisticated attitudes toward money and fundraising, and some have adopted businesslike attitudes toward their congregants. As George Ritzer notes, "religion has been streamlined through such things as drive-in churches and televised religious programs" (1996, 48). Not surprisingly, many people treat salvation like a product, pursue it for selfish reasons, and often purchase it in seemingly nonreligious forms for seemingly religious reasons. Americans can be found pursuing diverse activities—working out, exploring nature, or watching television—and believing that they have obtained the same benefits that they could receive from traditional religious activities. The distinction between religious and commercial activities has blurred, and as one scholar notes, such developments have made "a member of the Jehovah's Witnesses who peddled religion door-to-door on a Sunday afternoon much the same as a vacuum cleaner salesman" (R. L. Moore 1994, 256). In other words, whether it is through eternal bliss or clean carpets, salvation for many Americans is a readily available commodity.

An odd situation to be sure. But even odder when commercial ventures, operating for profit rather than piety, create competion for traditional religion. They are not simply providing paraphernalia for religious devotion—votives, Bibles, or "Pope-on-a-Rope" soap—but are *competing* (if unintentionally) with religious communities by offering similar goods: mythologies, symbols, rituals, and notions of community by which consumers organize their lives. These corporations offer (at a price) salvation from the modern world of twentieth-century American capitalism. And while, as Michael Budde argues, such a situation presents "new and imposing barriers . . . to the formation of deep religious convictions," he also recognizes that "[m]ore than any other set of social institutions, these industries collectively influence how people relate to the processes and products of economic activity." They are the "vectors and initiators for ideas regarding the valued, the innovative, the normal, the erotic, and the repulsive" (1997, 14–15, 32). In other words, these companies create the environment in which even religious ideas are communicated.

The Walt Disney Company is one such business marketing religious symbolism and meaning and providing strong—if indirect—competition to traditional religion in the United States. There are others who are also exploring this market, other purveyors of religious symbols and meaning. However, because of its market penetration, its integrated marketing, and its access to many levels of culture through its corporate network, Disney is uniquely suited for the "religification" of its commodity. And as Margaret King suggests, because a coincidence of factors unique to post–World War II America makes possible, "even obligatory—for Americans, adults as well as children, at least one pilgrimage to Disney Land [sic] or World as a popular culture 'mecca' of nearly religious importance" (1981, 117), this corporation is able to capitalize on its commodity in a way that is distinctly suited for this time and place.

THE MARKETPLACE AND COMPETITION IN CONTEMPORARY AMERICAN RELIGION

Once firmly committed to the idea that religion would fade from society as that society became more sophisticated, sociologists have come to use an economic model to explain the continued religiosity of the American citizenry (see Warner 1993). This model argues that religious communities—free of government intrusion or control—benefit from a "free market," and in competition with other religious communities ("producers") offer to religious adherents ("consumers") "products" they can compare and select rationally. These "products" (comfort, identity, community, but usually some form of salvation) are like items in a supermarket and compared in terms of their desirability, "market share," and general consumer appeal.

Though this model has its critics, it seems to explain in a more satisfying manner the continued vitality of religion in contemporary America. However, it means nothing if the "consumers" in the model—religious participants— aren't free to pick from religious options; market economies depend on consumers who are free to choose. Thus, over the past decade, scholars have examined the freedom individuals have enjoyed to "go shopping" for religion, and the loss of loyalty to specific religious communities that has resulted. Phillip Hammond argues that restrictions on religious identity have virtually disappeared, and "the social revolution of the 1960s and '70s wrought a major change: a near absolute free choice in the religious marketplace" (1992, 168). Similarly,

Wade Clark Roof notes that among members of the "baby boom" generation, "religion was whatever one chose as one's own" (1993, 244, emphasis omitted). The loss of a cultural monopoly by any one religious tradition, matched with the growing role of the individual (rather than the community) as the locus of identity, has made Americans freer to pick from among the various religious options, and to mix and match as they please.

At its logical extreme, this suggests market forces so diverse, and competition between religious "producers" so fierce, that consumers may not only choose more varied and less traditional forms of religious participation (as seems to be the case currently), but might also turn to nonreligious "producers" for the same (or similar) "products." In such a climate Disney, as much as any other for-profit venture, might be understood as creating, maintaining, and even being depended upon for the images, ideas, and emotions that were once reserved for traditional religious communities. In other words, in a religious marketplace truly free of limits, competition to provide religionlike commodities might include organizations not traditionally understood as religions, and any institution with the wherewithal can compete equally with traditional religions, regardless of its financial or religious goal.

There is a great temptation to equate everything with religion, including Disney. Even a discussion of its founder, Walter Elias Disney, suggests Christlike comparisons: a man with a vision, lifelong innocence, a message to be shared with the world, and a special affinity for children, envisions a new kingdom of heaven on earth and leaves his vision with his disciples, who build cathedrals in his honor while he awaits resurrection. The myth of his cryogenic preservation and postmortem corporate participation suggest a continued presence and guidance from beyond (see Fjellman 1992, 418, n.33; Ritzer 1996, 174–75). One author describes meetings with "the spirit" of Disney in attendance; anticipating his company's future, Walt had himself filmed for screening at meetings after his death, asking questions of participants and commenting on the status of scheduled events (Fjellman 1992, 117).

However, it would be fruitless to suggest that Disney is the same as a traditional religion, or that it is consciously designing its business for religious competition. The first claim would be foolish to make, the second impossible to prove.[2] Instead, Disney's products (tangible and intangible) fill many of the roles often filled by religion. They have entered the market at a time when many people are not only searching for alternatives to traditional religion, but are also flexible with what they find. They have also entered the market at a time when religious institutions are in competition with "global culture industries" (Budde 1997) over the construction and maintenance of meaning at the end of the twentieth century.

DISNEY AS "RELIGIOUS"? THE RELIGION OF TIME AND SPACE

Religion scholar Mircea Eliade separates the world into two types of people: nonreligious and religious. While nonreligious people go through life without distinguishing varieties of time or space, religious people observe and maintain sharp distinctions between the sacred and the profane. The sacred (the different, the powerful) is the wholly other that gives meaning and orientation to believers' lives. Writes Eliade, "Something that does not belong to this world has manifested itself apodictically and in so doing has indicated an orientation or determined a course of conduct" (1959, 27). This place of manifestation is the center of the universe, the heart of the cosmos and the place where the realms of existence interact. For example, in Judaism, Israel represents the space promised by God to the early Hebrews. Jerusalem remains the center of the Jewish cosmos, and synagogues are built so that worshipers face Jerusalem as they pray. Eliade suggests that "the sacred is equivalent to a power, and, in the last analysis, to reality. The sacred is saturated with being" (12; emphasis omitted). For religious people, sacred time and space are bounded by thresholds of power and orientation and provide a sense of the "really real," the order of the cosmos, and the unity of creation. "The threshold is the limit," Eliade writes, "the boundary, the frontier that distinguishes and opposes two worlds — and at the same time the paradoxical place where those worlds communicate, where passage from the profane to the sacred world becomes possible" (25). This boundary is well marked to differentiate between space that is common and meaningless from space that is sacred because of the power it represents.

Eliade argues that, for religious people, sacred space exists in a specific relation to sacred time, a return to the time when deities exerted their greatest creative powers, "when the world was young." Eliade notes that sacred time has virtually no relationship to time as experienced by the nonreligious. Instead, the religious person "experiences intervals of time that are 'sacred,' that have no part in the temporal duration that precedes and follows them, that have a wholly different structure and origin, for they are of a primordial time, sanctified by the gods and capable of being made present by the festival" (71). Eliade notes that "sacred time is reversible in the sense that, properly speaking, it is a primordial mythical time made present" (68; emphasis omitted). He suggests that it is "made present" by the reenactments by the believers in sacred space. Contemporary participants in the Jewish holiday of Passover ritually return to the time of their enslavement in Egypt: "It is because of that which the Lord did for me when I came forth from Egypt" (Exodus 13:8). "Me," not someone else, but the person at the ritual meal. During the Catholic Mass, the Eucharistic wafer and the wine don't represent Jesus, they actually become him ritually. Eliade's religious people long to return to the sacred time because that is the best way to fully experience sacred space, and therefore be in close contact with the deity. "In short," Eliade writes, "this religious nostalgia expresses the desire to live in a pure and holy cosmos, as it was in the beginning, when it came fresh from the Creator's hands" (65; emphasis omitted).

Both sacred time and space are re-created through the use of myth and ritual. According to Eliade, these elements provide religious people with access to sacred space and time by recalibrating life toward the divine. Myths re-insert sacred time into believers' lives. They are, writes Eliade, "the recital of what the gods or the semidivine beings did at the beginning of time. To tell a myth is to proclaim what happened *ab origine*" (95). Rituals permit the community to reenact the myths that reinsert the sacred time into their lives. Myths and rituals permit religious people to demarcate time and space, to orient the world in terms of the deity (or deities), and (according to Eliade) to avoid the meaninglessness of the nonreligious world. He notes that the religious person "lives in two kinds of time, of which the more important, sacred time, appears under the paradoxical aspect of a circular time, reversible and recoverable, a sort of eternal mythical present that is periodically reintegrated by means of rites. This attitude," he continues, "in regard to time suffices to distinguish religious from nonreligious man; the former refuses to live solely in what, in modern terms, is called the historical present; he attempts to regain a sacred time that, from one point of view, can be homologized to eternity" (70). Religious people, by operating in sacred space and time, never lose their connection to the deity, and live in a world that is reborn through ritual and myth, constantly young and full of power, wonder, and awe.

"DEEP IN THE HUNDRED-ACRE WOOD":
WALT DISNEY WORLD AS SACRED SPACE AND TIME

As an example of Eliadean sacred space, Walt Disney World (and, to a lesser extent, Disneyland) is bordered, demarcated space in which something out of the ordinary occurs. As part of the agreement over its development, one of Disney's subsidiaries was granted power that, in effect, makes the land surrounding the park an independent governmental entity (Johnson 1981, 158). This entity, which spans twenty-seven thousand acres, now produces its own money (the so-called "Disney Dollars," which are legal tender at Disney parks, resorts, and Disney retail outlets), generates its own power, manages its own trash, provides for its own fire and safety needs, and regulates its own local sales taxes on a "semi-autonomous basis approaching a city-state like Vatican City" (King 1981, 121).

As one enters the park, clues reinforce the notion that it is a different, separate space, and therefore significant.[3] Man-made mountains and ordered space carved from the waters remind the "guest" (never "customer") that Walt Disney World, a well-manicured piece of sacred space, is an oasis in the vastness of profane space. The mountains—reminiscent of Eliade's notions of the "center of the universe" and the place "where the realms of existence interact"—are the second and third highest "mountains" in Florida: Space Mountain and the Big Thunder Mountain ride (Fjellman 1992, 75). Disney's empire, like the creation account in Genesis, was created by draining swampland and channeling the water into lakes, literally letting "the waters under the heavens be gathered together into one place" (Genesis 1: 9). It is fitting that crossing into the park thus reenacts defiance against the forces of profanity. As Eliade writes, "The threshold has its guardians—gods and spirits who forbid entrance both to human enemies and to demons and the powers of pestilence" (1959, 25). Crossing the lake that separates the mundane (parking lot) from the sacred (park) on a boat that is, according to Fjellman, part of the fifth largest "navy" in the world, visitors symbolically move into a world that is spatially and temporally removed from that in which they ordinarily operate.

In the park, the visitor is presented with a choice: to visit the Magic Kingdom, EPCOT, Disney-MGM Studios, the recently opened Animal Kingdom, or all four. The decision will determine not only how one spends the day, but also the type of space with which one interacts. The Magic Kingdom, the oldest and mythically richest portion of the park, begins with a journey down Main Street USA and moves to other spaces embodying American mythic time: Frontierland, Adventureland, and so on. EPCOT (Experimental Prototype Community of Tomorrow) is a celebration of American commercialism and technology combined with a multicultural collection of international representatives encircling a man-made lake. Disney-MGM Studios provides a glimpse "behind the scenes" of Disney movies and television, and the Animal Kingdom provides an opportunity to mingle with live and animatronic beasts. Everywhere one goes there are wonderful, colorful, clean, and seemingly educational sights, tempting foods, and picturesque vistas (usually identified for photographing), "a symbolic American Utopia" (King 1981, 123). The park is truly a space unlike anything with which most people are familiar.

Ironically, just like the sacred spaces of any religious community, this space is as powerful for what isn't seen as for what is. Nowhere is there any hint of disorder, nowhere is there any sight of the mundane. Beneath the park (the Disney netherworld?), the veil of sacrality is protected as workers transport products, food, equipment, and maintain waste removal, all out of sight of the guests. David Johnson notes, "This sequestering makes it easy to forget that work is actually going on, so that the park's operation often seems far more effortless than it really is; visitors can thus enjoy their leisure without being reminded of the everyday world of work" (1981, 159). People are free to walk around and forget the crime-, hate-, and poverty-filled world from which they came. As Walt Disney noted, "I don't want the public to see the real world they live in while they're in the park. . . . I want them to feel they are in another world" (quoted in King 1981, 121).

This total experience of space is a perfect example of what Fredric Jameson calls "hyperspace," which George Ritzer defines as "an area where modern conceptions of space are useless in helping people orient themselves" (1996, 159). Like a shopping mall or a casino, Walt Disney World deprives its visitors of any reference to the outside world by making everything cross-referential. All of the signs, all of the narratives, all of the merchandise relates back to the central theme of the space, the Disney version of Eliade's "really real." Time itself is expressed spatially throughout the parks. Not surprisingly, there is no significant representation of the present, and while some of the areas represent the future (Tomorrowland, EPCOT), the greatest emphasis is on the past. Much of the space within the park is designed to conjure for the visitor a sense of times gone by — sacred times to the traditional religionist. These times are of two sorts: the romanticized (or actual) youth of the visitor and a mythic time of national innocence (King 1981, 131). Disney thus successfully exploits its relationship with adults who grew up in the 1950s and 1960s as much as children who grew up in the last few years. Writes Paul Croce: "Adults, who make up four out of five of the visitors [to the parks], are ushered back to childhood, with playful rides, mouse ears, and buildings designed on a small scale" (1991, 97). On the other hand, there are signs of a gloried American past everywhere the visitor goes. The Hall of Presidents, the references to the American frontier, the requirement to stroll down an 1890s-style street (Main Street USA is the only way into or out of the Magic Kingdom), all recall an America in its glory, when there was no Watergate, when there were no drugs, when every citizen was strong, and when every leader was honest and wise. In Eliade's words, "when the world was young." Historian Mike Wallace writes of Walt Disney, "he transported visitors back in time" (1985, 34).

However, Eliade's vision of the sacred is far too simplistic—religious people live in the real world just like the nonreligious person—and the peaceful image offered in such an analysis is often misleading. It is not surprising, then, that the version of American history provided at Walt Disney World is problematic at best, and fundamentally flawed at worst. The park designers have taken easily recognizable, pivotal images in American history and given them new (and often different) meanings. Notes David Johnson, "the Disney creators have taken the raw material from history, fantasy and other sources and packaged it into units, each with a discrete beginning, middle and end." He suggests that "they have in effect added conventional plots to inherently plotless materials" (1981, 162; emphasis deleted). By doing so, Walt Disney World staffers have re-created an American history that is not only sanitized, but also reflective of a particularly Disney version of American history—"Distory"—for millions of Americans and non-Americans who pass through the gates each year (see Francaviglia 1981). This repackaged history changes the perceptions of the visitors, and like all myths, establishes itself as the "really real" over that which is taught in textbooks. "For visitors, and especially the young visitors," continues Johnson, "Disney's version becomes the original version, which is actually more powerful than history since its form is concrete, containing 'real' people and 'lifelike' people with plenty of action and drama by both. By comparison, the history books are static, they require a more studied effort to make the history come alive; the Disney version is more interesting as well as more easily assimilated and remembered for our 'post-literate' generations" (164; emphasis deleted).

Criticizing Disney for such rewriting might be holding it to an unfair standard—does it really purport to teach people American history, or is it a place where people can encounter American history as they want it (consciously or not) to have been? As one Disney "imagineer" notes, "What we create is a 'Disney Realism,' sort of Utopian in nature, where we carefully program out all the negative, unwanted elements and program in the positive elements" (quoted in Wallace 1985, 35). It truly is utopian, almost Edenic. "Cast members" (never "employees") are always "in character"; many of the animals (even at Animal Kingdom) are animatronic and harmless (see Danyliw 1998); many of the actors are animatronic and therefore always happy, on cue, and never on strike; the park is always clean; and the visitors are free to live (or relive) their youths (or the youth of the nation) in comfort and leisure from the moment the park opens until the last tram has carried them out. It truly is the happiest place on earth, even if it seems to represent something real that never actually existed.

"YO, HO. YO, HO. A PIRATE'S LIFE FOR ME": DISNEY CO. ENCOUNTERS RELIGION, INC.

Though exploring Walt Disney World through the lens of sacred space and time provides an interesting analysis of the religious experience of that place, it is Disney's ability to market its product beyond the parks' boundaries that makes more powerful the original contention that the Walt Disney Company is marketing religionlike symbolism and competing with traditional American religion. The company encourages people to visit Disney parks when they see Disney films, purchase Disney items when they visit Disney parks or outlets, see Disney movies when they buy Disney products, and so on. By cross-referencing to its other products, Disney creates a consumer world of its own; no matter what you buy, it relates to something else from Disney. Behind the integrated marketing strategy—or accompanying it—are the myths and symbols also found at the parks. Notes Michael Real, "the Disney universe teaches values while it entertains" (1977, 70), and the stories told in the products and the movies reinforce those found at the parks, translating them into a "reality" that, though not always consistent, is pervasive, directive (directing people to the parks and directing their behaviors outside them), and accessible to all who accept it.

Because the animated features are completely constructed Disney products, they are the most powerful conveyors of the symbols and meaning systems outside the parks. They also are a staple of Disney marketing and the centerpiece of its economic revival. Though phased out by the end of the 1960s, animated films are once again being made under the Disney name, and since the beginning of the Michael Eisner era (1984), the company has released ten full-length animated feature films, as well as mixed- or alternative media features.[4] These films are the "text" underpinning a world view discernible in Disney stores, theme parks, and other venues. Like the activities at the parks, the movies (which are supported by a diverse pool of popular actors and musicians) take common or familiar stories, sanitize them, and reconfigure them to reflect myths central to the Disney worldview; compare Disney's *The Little Mermaid* (1989) to Hans Christian Andersen's original.

On the surface, these films reveal nothing surprising: an optimistic (even moralistic) American vision of the world in which freedom and independence are appreciated, where difference, though initially distressing, is ultimately affirmed, where outsiders, though initially ridiculed, are ultimately integrated into the group and those who ridiculed them ostracized, where selfless sacrifice is rewarded and selfishness is equated with villainy and destroyed, and where superficial, outward characteristics are overlooked, and all are appreciated. Notes Aladdin in the film that bears his name, "it is not what is outside but what is inside that counts." On the other hand, there is no subtlety about evil; villains are clearly differentiated behaviorally as well as physically, are often drawn or colored differently, and exhibit unmistakable hubris. The animated films also suggest ethical positions to their viewers; good and evil are defined in every Disney movie, and while the villains are offered salvation, many are destroyed—often by fire, hellishly confirming their villainy—because of their continued arrogance and evil. Heroes, though flawed, learn from their mistakes, and are willing to forgive the villains. While some need more help than others on the path toward righteousness, they ultimately do the right thing.

And yet, these seemingly innocent characterizations and ethical positions are not without controversy, and they only hint at larger conflicts over symbols used by Disney and various religious communities. In order to discern the "right thing," characters often seek help from other realms. Scholars and ethnic community representatives have protested some characterizations used by Disney in movies and at their parks as too simplistic, ridiculing a particular group, or misrepresenting them.[5] Some conservative Christians have protested Disney's presentation of morality altogether. During the summer of 1997, the Southern Baptist Convention (SBC)—the largest Protestant denomination in the United States—announced it was organizing a Disneywide boycott, an enormous task given the company's diversification. Leaders of the organization complained about Disney policies they considered "antifamily," including health benefits for same-sex partners of Disney employees, toleration toward "Gay Days" (an event at the Florida and California parks organized by gay and lesbian representatives), and acceptance of the open lesbianism of Ellen Degeneres and her character on Disney-owned ABC. They identified Disney as morally corrupt, implying it was not only unsafe but traitorous. On another front, some members of the American Catholic community decried the release of *Priest* by Miramax (one of Disney's subsidiaries), while others organized a media campaign against *Nothing Sacred*, also broadcast by ABC (Dart, 1997a; 1997b). The Miramax film *Priest* and the television show *Ellen* both addressed issues of homosexuality, while *Priest* and *Nothing Sacred* portrayed Catholic clergy as liberal, nonorthodox interpreters of Catholic doctrine.

The use of Disney products in debates over morality and religion is profound not simply for what it says about the Southern Baptist Convention's nostalgia for an American society that no longer exists (if it ever did), but also for what it says about Disney's place in American culture. Disney is not the first corporation targeted by religious organizations for economic boycott. It is a business like any other—"emblematic of capitalism itself," notes Margaret Miles (1999, 15)—and disgruntled members of religious communities may express their displeasure economically, either through boycotts or by establishing competing theme parks (such as Heritage USA). While Southern Baptists are free to own Disney stock, Disney is not a Baptist corporation (Walt was raised as a Congregationalist), and is therefore not betraying anything other than a particular denomination's conception of cultural propriety. Interestingly, while the boycott has elicited little public response from Disney, an objection from the Arab-American community over the depiction of Arab peoples in Disney's *Aladdin* resulted in changes for the video release (Fox 1993). This does not mean that the Arab-American concerns are more significant than those of Southern Baptists. As Michael Budde implies, international corporations like Disney have become "symbolic predators," taking and using familiar religious symbols for commercial purposes. As he writes, "many of the classic narratives of Judaism and Christianity (e.g., Exodus, miracles, resurrection) act effectively as deep structures in commercial messages" (1997, 91, 92). Inevitably, some Christians will be offended (to the point of boycott) at the way Disney portrays important symbols, just as it is inevitable that Disney cannot change such portrayals. Disney uses Christian religious imagery and symbols as the vehicles of the narrative. However, with the portrayal of a particular community type (such as Arabs, Africans, etc.), the image is not woven into the narrative in the same way, and changing images by eliminating cultural stereotypes is possible even when changing the premises of a story are not. Disney refines a virtually religious message, but cannot help but risk offending the religious community that sees its own story woven into the narrative. In so doing, it competes for the attention of largest segment of the consumer market, whomever that might be. And while this is good business sense, the fact that Disney appears to be trading in religious symbols and the categories of space, time, and morality means that the competition may be drawn from the religious as well as the business world.

REAL MARKET FORCES AT WORK

In *The McDonaldization of Society* (1996), George Ritzer uses Max Weber's sociological model of bureaucratization to compare McDonald's assembly-line mentality to all of American culture. He suggests that America has become McDonaldized—operating on the same assumptions that have made the fast-food chain a global phenomenon—because of a slavish devotion to "efficiency, calculability, predictability, and control" (9). But like Weber, Ritzer sees the inevitable hazard: the "iron cage," in which activities are robbed of any meaning. "By 'iron cage,'" Ritzer concludes, "I mean that as McDonaldization comes to dominate even more sectors of society, it will become ever less possible to 'escape' from it" (143).

Not surprisingly, Disney is one of Ritzer's examples. It is efficient (trash cleanup, people moving, product delivery, etc.), predictable (guests rely on this, since many are return customers), and free of disorder or mess. Like McDonald's, Disney "has succeeded because it offers ... efficiency, calculability, predictability, and control." By cross-referencing its products, it also controls its consumers, robbing them of any ability to "escape" Disney's control once they enter the Disney world. "McDonaldized systems," notes Ritzer, citing Walt Disney World, "generally lack a sense of history. People find themselves in settings that either defy attempts to be pinpointed historically or present a pastiche of many historical epochs" (158). By limiting guests' experiences to its own sense of past and future epochs, and by reinforcing those experiences outside the parks through films and other products, Disney has created a world that seems to lack any meaning beyond its own boundaries.

However, Disney *does* provide meaning to its customers, a key to Weber's "iron cage" of meaninglessness that McDonald's and other "McDonaldizers" do not.[6] Disney provides a system of meaning that orients the consumer—albeit mythically, commercially, and with a very American product—to the larger world of consumer capitalism in which they live, whether or not they are Americans. The proof of the reach of Disney's mythology is in how it has been received in different places. Ritzer reports that a French politician noted that Euro-Disney would "'bombard France with uprooted creations that are to culture what fast food is to gastronomy'" (14). In contrast, in its first ten years, Tokyo Disneyland has entertained the equivalent of Japan's population (Miles 1999, 15), encouraging Disney to explore possibilities for a park in Hong Kong (see Reckard and Tempest 1999). This difference in the reception of two non-

American cultures to Disney seems best explained by how the French and Japanese cultures integrate different myths. While French and Japanese cultures have experienced periods of xenophobia, the current Japanese attitude toward capitalism makes that culture a much more responsive audience to the idiom in which Disney operates (see Yoshimoto 1984).

Ironically, this same idiom has led to seemingly nonreligious controversy in the United States. A Virginia community rejected a Disney proposal to build an American history theme park near a Civil War battlefield, in part out of fear of increased traffic, but also because of the potential misrepresentation that might result from the park's exhibits (Hofmeister 1994). The "Distory" that is so popular in the Florida and California parks, in films, on television, and in stores across the country, and is being exported successfully around the globe, could not overcome a different sacred mythology surrounding an event that, by definition, was not clean, happy, or utopian.

CONCLUSION

In late-twentieth-century America, the lines between business and religion are often blurry at best, and organizations identified with one may venture into the world of the other—intentionally or not—making for a distinction without a difference. The religion of Disney, if there can be said to be such a thing, is the same as it is for much of late-twentieth-century America—commercialization—and Disney opponents may also be opponents of that aspect of American culture. What makes Disney unique is that its products do not simply feed the commercial needs of its consumers, but—through accessible and pervasive symbols that have been traditionally reserved for faith communities but are now incorporated into the marketplace—their souls as well. Disney's parks and films exploit the desire to live in a world of peace and beauty, to hope for a better time, and to leave troubles (either personal or societal) behind. Its movies, its television programs, and especially its parks provide a utopian time and space that allows people, if only for a moment, to re-create time and space as they could be, and as they might have been in some mythic (personal or national) past. As Eliade writes, "It is by virtue of the temple that the world is resanctified in every part" (1959, 59; emphasis omitted). Disney provides that symbolic and metaphoric temple that resanctifies the world of American consumer capitalism.[7] Through the production and maintenance of meaning and symbol systems, Disney plays the same role of orientation that traditional religion once did exclusively. And because contemporary trends in American religion have created a situation in which nonreligious entities and activities are often used for personal religious (or "spiritual") ends, Americans (and others) can find in Disney many of the elements they once found exclusively in traditional religion. Hey, America—you've conquered the global economy and provided one of the highest standards of living for your citizens. Now what are you going to do? "We're going to Disney World!"

NOTES

1. A commission of the Southern Baptist Convention lists more than 200 subsidiaries connected to Disney. (Thanks to Shawn Rapp for locating "The Disney Family Tree" at http://www.ERLC.COM/Culture/Disney/1997/famtree. htm.) Michael Budde notes that, according to Disney, "on an August weekend in 1990, 30 percent of all movie theaters in the United States and Canada were screening a feature produced by one of Disney's production companies" (1997, 30).

2. For quasi-religious analyses of Disney, see Brockway 1989; King 1981; Knight 1999; Moore 1980. We are thankful to the "Religion and Popular Culture" panel and audience at the Popular Culture Association meeting (Orlando, March 1998) who heard an earlier version of this chapter. We are particularly grateful to one participant who exclaimed that, though she lived near the park and visited often, she did not consider it religious. We are reminded that many residents of Jerusalem—the focus of major religious traditions for centuries— consider it simply another city, but we are grateful for the reminder that sometimes the sacred becomes mundane and needs re-clarification.

3. Likewise at Disneyland, where entering guests are reminded that "Here you leave today and enter the world of yesterday, tomorrow, and fantasy" (Real 1977, 50).

4. In order of release: *The Little Mermaid* (1989), *The Rescuers Down Under* (1990), *Beauty and the Beast* (1991), *Aladdin* (1992), *The Lion King* (1994), *Pocahontas* (1995), *The Hunchback of Notre Dame* (1996), *Hercules* (1997), *Mulan* (1998), and *Tarzan* (1999). Because of the timing of its release, *Tarzan* has not been included in this analysis.

5. Representatives from Native American organizations voiced their displeasure at the depiction of traditional customs in *Pocohantas*, while representatives from African-American organizations have regularly objected to the depiction of African and African-American characters in animated and live action films and at the parks. Margaret Miles notes that African-American employees refer to Walt Disney World as "the plantation" (1999, 18, n. 2).

6. Even McDonald's mythic world (including Ronald McDonald, Mayor McCheese, etc.) has been overshadowed by characters designed as tie-ins to Disney productions.

7. Margaret Miles reports that Walt Disney World is "presently the #1 honeymoon destination in the country and may soon become the #1 wedding site" (1999, 13).

REFERENCES

Brockway, Robert. 1989. "The Masks of Mickey Mouse: Symbol of a Generation." *Journal of Popular Culture* 22, 4 (spring): 25–34.

Budde, Michael. 1997. *The (Magic) Kingdom of God: Christianity and Global Culture Industries*. Boulder, Colo.: Westview Press.

Croce, Paul Jerome. 1991. "A Clean and Separate Space: Walt Disney in Person and Production." *Journal of Popular Culture* 25, 3 (winter): 91–103.

Danyliw, Norie Quintos. 1998. "The Kingdom Comes: Fake Animals Outshine the Real Ones in Disney's Newest Park." *U.S. News & World Report*, April 6, 64.

Dart, John. 1997a. "ABC Opts to Extend 'Nothing Sacred.'" *Los Angeles Times*, November 29: B1.

———. 1997b. "Southern Baptist Delegates OK Disney Boycott." *Los Angeles Times*, June 19: A1.

Eliade, Mircea. 1959. *The Sacred and the Profane: The Nature of Religion*. San Diego: Harcourt Brace Jovanovich.

Fjellman, Stephen M. 1992. *Vinyl Leaves: Walt Disney World and America*. Boulder, Colo.: Westview Press.

Fox, David J. 1993. "Disney Will Alter Song in *Aladdin*." *Los Angeles Times*, July 10: F1.

Francaviglia, Richard V. 1981. "Mainstreet USA: A Comparison/Contrast of Streetscapes in Disneyland and Walt Disney World." *Journal of Popular Culture* 15, 1 (summer): 141–56.

Hammond, Phillip E. 1992. *Religion and Personal Autonomy: The Third Disestablishment in America*. Columbia: University of South Carolina Press.

Hofmeister, Sallie. 1994. "Disney Vows to Seek Another Park Site." *New York Times*, September 30, A12.

Johnson, David M. 1981. "Disney World as Structure and Symbol: Re-Creation of the American Experience." *Journal of Popular Culture* 15, 1 (summer): 157–65.

King, Margaret. 1981. "Disneyland and Walt Disney World: Traditional Values in Futuristic Form." *Journal of Popular Culture* 15, 1 (summer): 116–40.

Knight, Cher Krause. 1999. "Mickey, Minnie, and Mecca: Destination Disney World, Pilgrimage in the Twentieth Century." In *Reclaiming the Spiritual in Art: Contemporary Cross-Cultural Perspectives*, ed. Dawn Perlmutter and Debra Koppman. Albany: State University of New York Press.

Lawrence, Elizabeth A. 1986. "In the Mick of Time: Reflections on Disney's Ageless Mouse." *Journal of Popular Culture* 20, 2 (fall): 65–72.

Miles, Margaret R. 1999. "Disney Spirituality: An Oxymoron?" *Christian Spirituality Bulletin* (spring): 13–18.

Moore, Alexander. 1980. "Walt Disney World: Bounded Ritual Space and the Playful Pilgrimage Center." *Anthropological Quarterly* 53, 4 (October): 207–18.

Moore, R. Laurence. 1994. *Selling God: American Religion in the Marketplace of Culture*. New York: Oxford University Press.

Real, Michael R. 1977. "The Disney Universe: Morality Play." In *Mass-Mediated Culture*, 44–89. Englewood Cliffs, N.J.: Prentice Hall.

Reckard, E. Scott, and Rone Tempest. 1999. "Disney May Expand Its Small World into Hong Kong." *Los Angeles Times*, March3, C1.

Ritzer, George. 1996. *The McDonaldization of Society*, revised edition. Thousand Oaks, Calif.: Pine Forge Press.

Roof, Wade Clark. 1993. *A Generation of Seekers: The Spiritual Journeys of the Baby Boom Generation*. San Francisco: Harper Collins.

Wallace, Mike. 1985. "Mickey Mouse History: Portraying the Past at Disney World." *Radical History Review* 32: 33–57.

Warner, R. Stephen. 1993. "Work in Progress toward a New Paradigm for the Sociological Study of Religion in the United States," *American Journal of Sociology* 98, 5 (March): 1044–93.

Weinstein, Raymond M. 1992. "Disneyland and Coney Island: Reflections on the Evolution of the Modern Amusement Park." *Journal of Popular Culture* 26, 1 (summer): 131–64.

Yoshimoto, Mitsuhiro. 1994. "Images of Empire: Tokyo Disneyland and Japanese Cultural Imperialism." In *Disney Discourse: Producing the Magic Kingdom*, ed. Eric Smoodin, 181–99. New York: Routledge.

CONTRIBUTORS

Karen Anijar (Arizona State University) teaches in the areas of curriculum and cultural studies. She is the author of *Teaching toward the 24th Century: Star Trek as Social Curriculum* (2000), and has published articles in *Taboo, The Journal for a Just and Caring Education, Multicultural Education,* and others.

Lisle Dalton (Hartwick College, Oneonta, N.Y.) teaches in the area of American religious history and religion and the natural sciences. In 1996 he won a national fellowship from the John Templeton Foundation for developing a course on religion and science. His publications include an essay on Alexis de Tocqueville and numerous encyclopedia entries.

Jean Graybeal (Gallatin School of Individualized Study, New York University) conducts research and teaching in the areas of philosophy of religion, psychology of religion, and women and religion. She is the author of *Language and "the Feminine" in Nietzsche and Heidegger* (1990), and is currently working on a book on religion and the body.

Suzanne Holland (University of Puget Sound, Tacoma, Wash.) teaches in the area of religious and social ethics and women's studies, and has published on topics ranging from the human genome project to the ethics of cyberspace. She is currently working on an edited book, *Beyond Cloning* (2000).

Julie J. Ingersoll (Southwest Missouri State University, Springfield, Mo.) teaches courses on the sociology of religion and religion and culture, and her work has appeared in the *Journal for the Scientific Study of Religion* and *Contention: The Journal for Religion, Culture and Science.* Julie is also the author of "Reel Life," a syndicated weekly fly-fishing column.

Tara K. Koda (University of California, Santa Barbara) is a graduate student whose interests include Asian and Asian-American religions and cultures (particularly Japanese). She is writing her dissertation on changes among Buddhists as they migrated to the United States. She has also taught at the University of California, Santa Barbara.

Eric Michael Mazur (Bucknell University, Lewisburg, Penn.) teaches courses in American religions, religion and popular culture, and religion, law, and politics. He is the author of *The Americanization of Religious Minorities: Confronting the Constitutional Order* (1999) and articles that have appeared in the *Journal of Church and State, Social Justice Research*, and anthologies on Native American issues and the sociology of religion.

James McBride (Fordham University, New York) is the author of *War, Battering and Other Sports* (1995) and co-editor of *Cults, Culture and the Law* (1983). He has written on religion and critical theory, law, feminist theory, feminist theology, and popular culture in numerous journals and law reviews, as well as the *Encyclopedia of Women and World Religion*.

Kate McCarthy (California State University, Chico) teaches in the areas of contemporary Christian thought and women and religion. She has published articles on interreligious dialogue and liberation theology and recently had a chapter published in *Explorations in Global Ethics: Studies in a Collaborative Effort* (1998). She is currently at work on a larger project on religion and American rock music.

Sarah M. Pike (California State University, Chico) teaches courses on American religions, religion and ethnicity, and new religious movements. She is the author of *Earthly Bodies, Contemporary Pagans and Magical Selves: The Search for Community* (2000) and two chapters in *Magical Religion and Modern Witchcraft* (1996). She is currently at work on a project on teens and alternative religions.

Leonard Norman Primiano (Cabrini College, Radnor, Penn.) is the author of a book on "Dignity," an American Catholic gay and lesbian religious group (forthcoming), and a documentary *I Know You Are God: The Marriage of Father and Mother Divine*, which examines Father Divine's International Peace Mission Movement (in production). He was a consultant on folk and popular religion for the touring exhibition "Angels from the Vatican: The Invisible Made Visible."

Rubina Ramji (University of Ottawa) researches the portrayal of religion, and especially Muslim women, in mass media. She is co-chair of the Religion, Film and Visual Culture Group for the American Academy of Religion. She is the author of articles included in *Identity Politics in the Women's Movement* (1999) and *Islam in America*.

Wade Clark Roof (University of California, Santa Barbara) is the Chair of the Department of Religious Studies. He has taught at the University of Massachusetts, Amherst, and the Ecole des Hautes Etudes en Sciences Sociales, Paris. He is a past president of the Society for the Scientific Study of Religion and is the author of *American Mainline Religion* (with William McKinney, 1987), *A Generation of Seekers* (1993), and *Spiritual Marketplace* (1999).

Jennifer Rycenga (San Jose State University, California) conducts research on religion and culture, especially in relation to music, sexuality, feminism, and capitalism. She has articles in *Queering the Pitch: The New Gay and Lesbian Musicology* (1994) and *Keeping Score: Music, Disciplinarity, Culture* (1997). She is co-editor (with Marguerite Waller) of *Frontline Feminisms: Women, War, and Resistance* (Garland, 2000).

Elijah Siegler (University of California, Santa Barbara) is writing his dissertation on American Taoism. He hopes to write for television someday. He was the editor of the 1993 edition of the travel guide *Let's Go: Greece and Turkey*.

Monica Siems (University of California, Santa Barbara) is writing her dissertation on the use of the Dakota (Sioux) language by missionaries and Dakota converts in nineteenth-century Minnesota. Trained in the area of American religious history and American religious thought, she has taught courses on Christianity, world religions, and Native American religious traditions at Northern Arizona University.

Jon R. Stone (University of California, Berkeley) is the author of *A Guide to the End of the World* (1993), the award-winning *Latin for the Illiterati* (1996), *Prime-Time Religion* (with J. Gordon Melton and Phillip Lucas, 1997), and *On the Boundaries of American Evangelicalism* (1997), and editor of *The Craft of Religious Studies* (1998) and *Expecting Armageddon* (2000).

Robin Sylvan (College of Wooster, Ohio) teaches in the area of religion and the arts, with a particular interest in popular music and popular culture. He is currently at work on a book titled *Traces of the Spirit: The Religious Dimensions of Popular Music*.